Beiträge zur
Dialogforschung   Band 27

Herausgegeben von Franz Hundsnurscher und Edda Weigand

Dialogue Analysis VIII: Understanding and Misunderstanding in Dialogue

Selected Papers from the 8th IADA Conference
Göteborg 2001

Edited by Karin Aijmer

Max Niemeyer Verlag
Tübingen 2004

Bibliografische Information der Deutschen Bibliothek

Die Deutsche Bibliothek verzeichnet diese Publikation in der Deutschen Nationalbibliografie;
detaillierte bibliografische Daten sind im Internet über *http://dnb.ddb.de* abrufbar.

ISBN 3-484-75027-8   ISSN 0940-5992

© Max Niemeyer Verlag GmbH, Tübingen 2004
http://www.niemeyer.de
Das Werk einschließlich aller seiner Teile ist urheberrechtlich geschützt. Jede Verwertung außerhalb
der engen Grenzen des Urheberrechtsgesetzes ist ohne Zustimmung des Verlages unzulässig und
strafbar. Das gilt insbesondere für Vervielfältigungen, Übersetzungen, Mikroverfilmungen und die
Einspeicherung und Verarbeitung in elektronischen Systemen.
Printed in Germany.
Gedruckt auf alterungsbeständigem Papier.
Druck und Einband: Digital PS Druck AG, Birkach

Table of Contents

Introduction 1

Chapter 1: Dialogical Grammar and Spoken Interaction

Per Linell, Linköping University
    On Some Principles of a Dialogical Grammar 7
Amy B. M. Tsui, University of Hong Kong
    What do Linguistic Descriptions have to say about Discourse? 25

Chapter 2: Misunderstanding as a Dialogical Phenomenon

Sorin Stati, University of Bologna
    Misunderstanding – A Dialogic Problem 49
Anita Fetzer, Universität Stuttgart
    Infelicitous Communication or Degrees of Misunderstanding? 57
Ernest W. B. Hess-Lüttich, Universität Bern
    Understanding Misunderstanding: Kafka's *The Trial* 69
Silvia Bruti, University of Florence
    Modal Competence and Misunderstandings in *The Merry Wives of Windsor* 87
Monika Dannerer, Universität Salzburg
    Misunderstandings at Work 103
Chiara M. Monzoni, University of York
    Do Italians 'Prefer' Disagreeing? Some Interactional Features of
    Disputational Talk in Italian Multi-Party Family Interaction 119
Sara Cigada, Catholic University of Milan
    The Logical Structure of Dialogue and the Representation of Emotions:
    An Example from Hitchcock's *Notorious* 131
Andreas H. Jucker & Sara W. Smith,
    Universität Zürich, California State University, Long Beach
    "He hired who?": Problems in Reference Assignments in Conversations 149

Chapter 3: Signposting in the Dialogue

Simone Müller, Justus Liebig Universität, Giessen
 The Discourse Marker *so* in Native and Non-native Discourse 169
Jesús Romero Trillo, Universidad Autónoma de Madrid
 Subjective and Objective Grounding in Discourse Markers:
 A Cross-linguistic Corpus-driven Approach 185

Chapter 4: Exploring Dialogue in Academic Discourse

Anna Mauranen, University of Tampere
 Talking Academic: A Corpus Approach to Academic Speech 201
Luisa Granato & Anamaría Harvey,
 University of La Plata, Catholic University of Santiago
 Topic Progression in Science Interviews 219
Franca Poppi, University of Modena
 Pragmatic Implications of the Use of *we* as a Receiver-including and
 Receiver-excluding Pronoun 229

Chapter 5: Dialogue and Multilingual or Multicultural Schools

Robert Maier, University of Utrecht
 Dialogues and Exclusion in Multicultural Schools 245
Silvia Gilardoni, Universitá Cattolica del Sacro Cuore of Milan
 Content and Language Integrated Learning: Interactions in Bilingual Classrooms 255

Chapter 6: Focus Group Discussions

Viveka Adelswärd, Linköping University
 Virtual Participants as Communicative Resources in Discussions on Gene
 Technology 275
Victoria Wibeck, Linköping University
 Exploring Focus Groups: Analysing Focus Group Data about Genetically
 Modified Food 287

Chapter 7: Dialogue Analysis and Corpora

Edda Weigand, Universität Münster
 Possibilities and Limitations of Corpus Linguistics 301

Introduction

The present collection of articles contains a selection of the papers presented at the 8th Biennial Congress for the International Association for Dialogue Analysis (IADA) which took place in Göteborg 19th to 21st April, 2001. A dialogical approach is necessary in order to.understand human communication and cognition not only conversation, but speech and writing in institutional and non-institutional settings, speech representation in fiction and film dialogue

Although there is now much interest in a dialogical approach and dialogical theory as a general framework for understanding and explicating human communication and cognition there is not a single approach to studying dialogue but several related approaches.

Per Linell discusses a set of 'dialogical principles' which are generally agreed on, such as sequentiality, co-construction and act-activity interdependence. In a 'dialogical grammar' which is needed to analyse spoken language there are no clear boundaries between lexicon and grammar. Constructions play an important role in dialogue as configurations of form and prosody associated with a communicative, semantic-functional potential. It is characteristic of constructions that they are organised into fields and can be coupled with activity contexts.

The focus in **Amy Tsui's** paper is on comparing critical discourse analysis (CDA) and CA (Conversation Analysis). In CDA, the object of research is the social phenomenon itself, such as power relationship, gender dominance, racism in which discourse is only a part. In CA, on the other hand, language is given primacy because of the linguistic methodology used. It is argued that the two approaches are complementary and that we need both to apply linguistic criteria and take into consideration the social and cultural dimensions shaping the discourse.

A theme which interested many of the participants at the conference was misunderstanding. As pointed out by Sorin Stati in his plenary lecture misunderstanding is a typically interdisciplinary phenomenon which can be placed at a crossroads where philosophy meets psychology, linguistics meets pragmatics and literary criticism.

Sorin Stati argues that misunderstanding is a practical phenomenon which can be a serious obstacle to successful communication. Dialogue has been forgotten as a source of misunderstanding. Misunderstanding concerns utterances and not sentences and should be accounted for on the 'parole' level. It is best understood if code theories of meaning are replaced by inferential theories inspired by Grice such as relevance theory.

Anita Fetzer's contribution has the goal to investigate the concepts of understanding and misunderstanding in the framework of the dialogue act of a plus/minus validity claim proposed by Habermas. Validity claims refer either to the objective, social or the subjective world and require validation. It is argued that degrees of understanding and misunderstanding can occur in the process of calculating the communicative meaning of a validity claim.

Literary works are a fruitful source for finding examples of misunderstanding. **Ernest Hess-Lüttich** takes a closer look at the structure of dialogue in Kafka's *The Trial* and shows that communication fails in the novel because of the systematic violation of the rules of conversation. The importance of dialogue analysis for understanding the rhetoric of misunderstanding in Kafka's novel is also shown from the macrostructural analysis of phases of conversation in the novel.

Silvia Bruti analyses some scenes of *The Merry Wives of Windsor*. It is shown that developments in the plot are intertwined with changes in the characters' modal competence. The modal competence of the characters can be defined by modal predicates such as 'can', 'must' and 'know' which can be combined in different ways to give rise to manipulation. Misunderstanding is not only unintentional in the play but it can also be linked to the characters' manipulative design.

Monika Dannerer looks at misunderstandings in multi-party conversations at the work-place. Special attention is given to how misunderstandings arise, how they are identified and dealt with or cleared up. Power relations as well as underlying conflict or different conceptions of the work task are factors explaining how misunderstanding comes about.

The analysis of disagreements and disputes has often been related to the form agreements take and to the preference organization. In this framework disagreements display a complex and marked format. **Chiara Monzoni** shows that in Italian multi-party family interactions disagreements are normally unmitigated and unmarked. The preference organization therefore seems to be an unsatisfactory model for disputational talk, at least in multi-party interaction.

Sara Cigada analyses the structure of dialogue and the representation of emotions in Hitchcock's *Notorious*. A sequence from the film is analysed by means of Rigotti's Congruity theory. Each utterance is assigned a Connective Predicate (CP) representing the communicative function of that part of the text and highlighting the logical structure of the dialogue.

Reference assignment is important for utterance understanding. **Andreas Jucker** and **Sara Smith** show that in contrast to traditional accounts of reference assignment, conversationalists often use referring expressions calling up vague and fuzzy images. It is argued that more precision is not needed or desirable because it would treat unwarranted processing effort. The authors analyse cases of reference assignment which were problematic and the means employed for repair.

Discourse markers have an important signposting function in dialogue facilitating understanding and avoiding misunderstanding. **Simone Müller** investigates the use of the discourse marker *so* by German speakers of English as compared with American native speakers. The research question is why native speakers use the discourse marker *so* more than twice as often as the non-native speakers. It is shown that learners underused *so* as a marker of result while there were no differences with the American speakers when *so* occurred at 'transition-relevant' places, e.g. at the beginning of an exchange structure.

Jesús Romero Trillo's contribution deals with the grounding effect of discourse markers in the speech of native and non-native (Spanish) speakers of English. The investigation suggests that English and Spanish differ in their organization of subjective and objective grounding. Both languages favour the use of subjective vs. objective markers but the different frequencies of these elements which make this a difficult area for learners of English.

Anna Mauranen argues that it is in dialogic situations that academic speech differs most clearly from written academic genres. The focus in her paper is on conflictual discourse in academic speech and the possibility of using corpora to uncover its characteristic expressions. It is suggested that metadiscourse is an important type of conflictual indicator which is involved in the framing of specific criticism. Other types of conflictual indicators tend to be indirect and implicit.

Luisa Granato and **Anamaría Harvey** make a case study of written interviews from a corpus of science interviews collected from Argentine and Chilean newspapers and the tape recordings of the oral interviews held with the scientists. The results of the analysis show some similarities and also important differences in the topic progression between the oral and the written interviews.

Two papers deal with dialogue in schools in a multilingual or a multicultural setting. **Robert Maier** analyses a passage from a discussion among teachers about a student in a multicultural school in the Netherlands. The aim was to identify specific types and characteristics of interaction that are connected with the success or failure of immigrant children at school.

The topic of **Silvia Gilardoni's** paper is the analysis of classroom interaction in the context of 'Content and Language Integrated Learning' (CLIL). The research is based on a corpus of teacher-pupil and pupil-pupil interaction at the Swiss School in Milan where the language of teaching was above all German. One of the results was that language alternation could be used as a discourse strategy by the teacher for various pedagogical functions.

Focus group discussion constitutes a method for collecting data that has recently increased in popularity among social scientists. **Viveka Adelswärd** investigates how non-present or virtual participants are brought into these discussions. It is shown that virtual participants were brought in primarily to show the complexities and contradictions in the opinions expressed and to express the ongoing often chaotic discussion.

Victoria Wibeck outlines a few approaches that have proved to be fruitful to analyse discourse about genetically modified food in Sweden. The analysis advocated is labelled 'dialogical content analysis' and implies that the dialogue of the participants is considered as well as the dialogicity of arguments and ideas.

A corpus approach has been advocated in many of the contributions to the volume. **Edda Weigand's** contribution takes up the question what the corpus is and what we can do with it and demonstrates both possibilities and limitations of corpus linguistics. A plea is made for not only considering language as contained in the corpus but as an integrated part of a complex human ability which can best be studied in dialogic interaction.

Thanks go to Professor Jens Allwood who was co-organiser of the conference and who helped in the reviewing process of the submitted papers.

Göteborg April 10th, 2004

Karin Aijmer

Chapter 1
Dialogical Grammar and Spoken Interaction

Per Linell

On Some Principles of a Dialogical Grammar

1. Introduction: Dialogical principles

Human communication has its primary habitat in interpersonal interaction.[1] A dialogical approach to grammar will therefore be primarily concerned with spoken language, in particular the spoken language of conversation or better: *talk-in-interaction*. This, however, must not obscure the fact that a dialogical approach is also possible, and often necessary, when it comes to the analysis of intrapersonal activities, such as writing and reading practices, the use of technical artefacts, monological speech, or solitary thinking. Indeed, dialogism can be taken as a general framework for understanding and explicating human communication and cognition.

Dialogical theory, or if you prefer: dialogism, is by no means a unitary school; rather, it is, in my understanding, a bundle of partly related approaches. These traditions and some of their partly shared understandings of language, communication and cognition have been discussed in *Approaching dialogue* (Linell 1998). Dialogical theory has roots in traditions such as phenomenology (Husserl, Schütz), pragmatism (Peirce, W. James), symbolic interactionism (Mead), sociocultural theory (Vygotsky), Bakhtin's dialogism, and language game theory (Wittgenstein). Among present-day empirical traditions, one must mention Conversation Analysis (Sacks, Schegloff), context-based discourse analysis and ethnomethodology (Garfinkel, Cicourel), ethnography of speaking and interactional sociolinguistics (Gumperz), symbolic interactionism (Goffman), interactionist psychology of language (Clark) and discursive psychology (Shotter, Billig, Potter), functional-linguistic approaches to discourse (Halliday, Fairclough), activity theory (Wertsch, Engeström), activity language analysis (Allwood) and interdisciplinary dialogue analysis (Marková, Rommetveit).

For a start, I will, very briefly, mention a couple of general, dialogistic points. A person who is indulging in communication or cognition, is "in dialogue with" two sets of contexts

---

[1] This paper was read at the IADA Conference in Göteborg, April 18–21, 2001. Basically, it is a highly condensed version of a long paper in Swedish (Linell 2002). The research is part of a comprehensive project on "The Grammar of Conversational Swedish" (Nordberg et al. 2000), funded by the Bank of Sweden Tercentenary Foundation.

simultaneously, the *immediate situation* and the interlocutors there, and the various *abstract contexts*, including his/her accumulated knowledge and assumptions about the sociocultural practices and activity types involved, as well as linguistic and other symbolic resources, which are put to use and made relevant in the specific communicative and/or cognitive activities. That is, what somebody is doing in a particular situation, there-and-then, is part of a continuity of practices, which have been accumulating over time and led to a sedimentation of knowledge that now guides the expectations of what will happen in new communication situations. Hence, there is always a 'double dialogicality' in the specific communicative activity; it involves *situated interaction* and, in and through this situated interaction, also participation in (and interaction with) situation-transgressing *sociocultural traditions and practices*. Some scholarly traditions have focused on mainly one of these aspects of the double dialogicality, either the situation or the tradition. For me, it is the combination of the situational-interactional perspective and the sociocultural-systemic one which is constitutive of a dialogical approach.

Some scholars have identified a limited set of so-called 'dialogical principles', presented under different terminological disguises. I propose to talk about three principles. First, there is the principle of *sequentiality*: utterances (turns, turn-constructional units) are characterised by responsive and initiatory (including projective) properties; these interrelational, or interactional, features point to adjacent (usually the other's) turns in the sequence. That is, (parts of) the meaning and form of utterances are dependent on their *sequential positioning*; utterances respond to prior utterance(s) and project possible next utterances.

Secondly, the principle of *co-authoring* (or co-construction) is related to notions of addressivity or other-orientation: the individual speaker's utterance is built upon understandings and reactions to the other's utterance, and the speaker sometimes borrows words (and, of course, meanings) from the other. Communicative actions are necessarily part of dialogical, joint projects; they are not monological speech acts.

Thirdly, the principle of *act-activity interdependence* assigns a crucial importance to activity types and "situated activity systems" (e.g. Goffman 1961; cf. also his "focused interaction") as meso-level concepts (between language at a macro-level and local utterance production and actions at the micro-level). Utterances and their *embedding activities* are interdependent, they implicate each other ("co-implication of activity and utterances"; Schegloff et al. 1996: 25). Utterances are understood from within an activity, genre, and/or culture.

Space does not allow me to go more deeply into these principles here and discuss concrete applications (but see Linell 1998). Instead, I will proceed to my main topic, the dialogical life of grammatical constructions.

2. Grammatical constructions

A grammatical construction is, roughly, a configuration of formal components and dimensions, morpho-syntactic as well as prosodic (and paralinguistic) ones, associated with some kind of communicative, semantic-functional potential.

As a first example, consider the cleft construction (Trask 1993: 46, Jespersen 1969: 73), or, more exactly, the it-cleft (Hedberg 2000), as exemplified in:

(1)   it was Chris who had written it (((i.e. the letter))

or in the Swedish original piece of discourse (from a private telephone conversation):

(1a)   de va Krister som hade skrivi re

The structure of this construction consists of a cleft pronoun (usually, as in this case, "it") plus a copula plus a noun phrase (NP) with focal stress (sometimes called the clefted constituent) plus a relative clause (called the cleft clause). In generative grammar (and earlier, in Otto Jespersen's work for example), various syntactic analyses of clefts have been proposed (Hedberg 2000). What interests us here is some of their semantic and pragmatic properties. Thus, most analyses (e.g. Hedberg) note that the content of the cleft clause, i.e. the relative clause, is typically presupposed when the cleft sentence is produced; this matter (in our example: someone had written a specific letter) is already in the focus of attention (and is now activated, i.e. high up in the so-called givenness hierarchy of Gundel et al. 1993). What is at stake when the cleft is occasioned is the identity of the referent of which the cleft clause is predicated, and this is in the identificational focus of the clefted constituent (here: the referent identified as "Chris").

For a dialogical account, it would be of central interest to find out and describe how presuppositions and other semantic-pragmatic properties emerge in and through dialogue. Let us look at the local context of (1), as shown in (2):

(2)   (A. Lindström: MOL1:A:4: BVC: 647ff; excerpt from a telephone conversation between Gerda and Viveka: they talk about a letter received by Gerda's family from another couple, Annika and Krister)[2]

```
1.  G:  (...) incidentally I met Annika an' she greeted me
2.      quite cheerfully, you heard that they had written a
3.      letter to us, didn't [you¿
4.  V:                       [no: I didn't¿
5.  G:  I see, well, they did, you see [.h
```

---

[2] Here, and later, I give a rough English translation, followed by the Swedish original. Transcription conventions are a (simplified) version of those now generally adopted in Conversation Analysis.

```
 6. V:                         [an'apologised [or?
 7. G:                                        [yes
 8.    (0.2)
 9. V:  but that was good, wasn't it¿
10. G:  that was mighty good.
11. V:  was it eh Chris who had writt[en it?
12. G:                               [Chris had written it.
13. V:  .yeah understood that, hehe.h
14. G:  yes Annika still didn't think there was anything odd
15.     about it. so I understand that but but it was Chris
16.     who had written it.
17.V:   yes exactly.

 1. G:  (...) ja träffa ju Annika förresten å hon hälsade så
 2.     glatt på mej, du hörde de att dom hade skrivit brev
 3.     till oss [va¿
 4. V:           [ne:ä: de hörde ja'nte¿
 5. G:  hja: jo de gjorde dom sörrö, [.h
 6. V:                               [å ba om u:rsäkt ell[er?
 7. G:                                                   [ja:
 8.    (0.2)
 9. V:  men de va ju bra¿
10. G:  de va ju jättebra,
11. V:  va de eh Krister som hade skriv[i (de)?
12. G:                                 [Krister hade skrivi re.
13. V:  .hha förstog de(h), hehe.h
14. G:  ja Annika tyckte ju fortfarande inte att de va nåt som
15.     va märklit. så de: förstår ja men men: de va Krister
16.     som hade skrivi re,
17. V:  ja just de.
```

The cleft construction occurs twice (i.e. lines 11 and 15–16) in this conversational episode between Gerda (G) and Viveka (V). The talk is about a situation in which a couple, Gerda and her husband, have received an apologetic letter from another couple, Annika and Krister. The first cleft (line 11: "va de Krister som hade skrivi de") occurs as a response to this situation in which there are two alternative referents who could have been involved in the writing of the letter. Thus, a local communicative project is occasioned in the interaction between Gerda and Viveka in which the goal is to make it mutually known *who* did it. Viveka chooses one candidate person ("Krister") in her question of line 11. (The other alternative is evidently "Annika", cf. line 1, where she is mentioned, and the confirmation on line 14.) Since Gerda seems to feel that her specification on line 12 calls for, or projects, an explanation or an account, perhaps because Viveka has received her information with laughter (line 13), such an explanation is given in lines 14–15, before Gerda once again states the identity of the author, now using the cleft another time.

As examples such as (2) show, presuppositions and other pragmatic properties do not emerge out of nowhere. On the contrary, the context space is dialogically generated; interlocutors talk themselves into a micro-situation in which the it-cleft can be appropriately used. At the point in the interaction when the use of the it-cleft is due, the premisses for its use have been dialogically assembled over a sequence. The use of the construction is a response to an immediately prior micro-situation in the dialogue; it is a solution to a communicative problem that has appeared there[3].

Notice how this contrasts with traditional accounts, in which sentences are analysed syntactically as autonomous (decontextualised) units. Often, these are given complex analyses in and through generative derivations. Some early generative analyses of clefts basically portrayed an it-cleft as a transform of a simplex sentence ("Chris had written it") (cf. Hedberg: "extraposition analysis"), while other (mostly later generative) analyses assume a structure closer to the (surface) cleft structure ("expletive analysis"), although all generative analyses tend to contain many abstract features (trees with many branches, empty categories, etc.). Other properties are explained, at least by functionally-minded analysts (like Hedberg), in terms of semantic-pragmatic relations, such as presuppositions, givenness hierachies for referents (identifiability and activation properties; Michaelis & Lambrecht 1996: 219), information structure, etc. But such presuppositions and givenness statuses are *taken as given*, as felicity conditions, when the expression in question is being analysed. By default, they are also assumed to be taken as given by the participants in the interaction. We ask instead: how are these properties given? where do they come from? One answer might be that they are given in the language system, in the language user's linguistic competence, as conditions tied to (the use of) the grammatical items and rules in question. But this only moves the need for an explanation to another place. Where, in turn, do these system constraints come from?

A dialogical account would start from interactional and processual observations. It would treat utterances, their presuppositions and the givenness statuses of utterance parts, not as felicity conditions which are simply taken for granted, but as phenomena emerging from situated and sequentially organised talk-in-interaction. Thus, the use of the it-cleft is the solution to a communicative problem that has evolved over a sequence of utterances (or turns).

Furthermore, grammatical constructions, such as the it-cleft, tend to exploit surface-syntactic patterns that are already available in the surroundings of conversational language at large. Thus, in developing new constructions, a language "borrows" from what is already available.[4] The it-cleft is a combination of a common introducer (a neutral pro-form

---

[3] It should be noted, however, that experiences of numerous such communicative events, in each of which the premises of use are assembled in the course of an interaction, will of course allow a user, under special circumstances, to deploy the it-cleft *without* such a preceding sequence. In other words, a speaker can start a communicative episode by an utterance like, say, "It was Chris who did it", thereby co-communicating (Fillmore 1985) the contextual assumption that it is obvious (to the speaker) that somebody "did it" and the issue, the *quaestio*, (for him or for the addressee) is *who* did it.

[4] One may think of this, in dialogical terms, as co-authoring on the socio-cultural level, or in terms of an "inheritance network" as in Construction Grammar (e.g. Michaelis & Lambrecht 1996).

plus copula, e.g. "it is..."), which belongs to a restricted set of very frequent clause beginnings[5] (or "frame", Anward 1999) plus a focused (and focally stressed) element (Anward: filler in the frame). This frame plus filler has a wide range of uses, and the cleft joins this pattern, adding a relative clause (which is also a widely used construction type).[6]

3. Reactive constructions

A dialogical grammar must stress the context-sensitivity of grammatical constructions. As a contrast to the it-cleft, let me now consider a much more specialised and less frequent construction, namely the incredulity response construction (IRC; the term is Lambrecht's 1990), as in (3):

(3)   (Lambrecht 1990)

1.A: and he's going to wear a tuxedo
2.B: what? him wear a tuxedo? sure.

The gist of the IRC is the non-finite nexus construction (in Jespersen's terms), i.e. the combination of a nominal (here a pronoun in oblique form: "him") and a main verb (plus complements) in the infinitive ("wear a tuxedo"). But this core is dependent on a local cotext. First, it is responsive; it presupposes certain preceding grammatical structures, as well as other, semantic and contextual conditions. It belongs to an important and large subcategory of responsive constructions which I will call *reactive constructions*. A reactive construction is a responsive construction that is parasitic on, and is elicited by, reacts to, prior utterances and their linguistic formulation, which it partly repeats and "quotes". Thus, the reactive utterance constitutes a "counter-utterance", and reactive constructions are specifically designed to do the "job" of reactive utterances. IRC is an example. In (3), it is the words "he" and "wear a tuxedo" which are taken up and reaccentuated (and appropriately modified morphologically) in a new infinitival construction.

The other side of the context-sensitivity in the case of the IRC construction is that it projects an obligatory, or almost obligatory, continuation; it strongly prefers or invites a follow-up turn-constructional unit with certain grammatical and/or semantic properties, i.e. an utterance (the ironic "sure" of line 2 of (3)) that hints at the absurdity of the prior

---

[5] Cf. Allwood (2000).
[6] Note that the relative clause can be omitted, which results in an elliptic variant called 'truncated cleft' by Hedberg (2000: 898–899).

speaker's proposal in line 1. This might have been followed by an explicit reason for doubting, challenging or rejecting the proposition expressed by the other; for example, B might have continued with something like "he hates the formal dress code".

Many grammatical constructions have, like the IRC, responsive and projective relations pointing to prior and following segments, respectively. These segments form a kind of 'outer syntax', which is a term that has been proposed in Construction Grammar (e.g. Fillmore et al. 1988; Lambrecht 1990). In order to further illustrate this, and other aspects of a dialogical grammar, I will introduce another Swedish specimen. I will refer to a fairly simple construction from modern conversational Swedish, which I will call *x-och-x* (or in English: x-and-x). It is much more frequent than IRC, but likewise marginalised in most traditional grammars.[7] *x-och-x* is a reactive construction, just like IRC. It occurs in line 6 of (4):

(4)   (Tema K: P20:1; P(olice officer) interviewing a young S(suspect) accused of attempted theft)

```
1.P:  who was it who wa- you were together with?
2.    (2.0)
3.S:  well
4.    (7.0)
5.S:  am I forced to say that?
6.P:  forced an' forced, I cannot force you to say neither
7.    one thing nor the other but it isn't (.) particularly
8.    good if you don't tell who it is cause we have two
9.    witnesses who have seen two people there

1.P:  vem va de som va- du va tillsammans med?
2.    (2.0)
3.S:  nja
4.    (7.0)
5.S:  e ja tvungen å säja de där?
6.P:  tvungen å tvungen, ja kan inte tvinga dej å säja vare
7.    sej de ena eller de andra men de e ju inte (.) särskilt
8.    bra om du inte berättar vem de e eftersom vi har två
9.    vittnen som har sett två personer där
```

x-och-x as a construction type in Swedish has been described by Jan Lindström (1996, 1999, 2001a,b).[8] Its meaning cannot be directly rendered in English by a literal translation

---

[7] SAG (1999) does treat *x-och-x*, but only in passing and at different places (IV: 813, 841, 902).
[8] Constructions similar to *x-och-x* occur in other languages too, including Danish, Norwegian and Finnish.

("x and x"). Usually, its meaning can be approximated as "not exactly X" or "it depends on what you mean by x" (Lindström 2001a). It is a reactive construction, occurring in the pre-front field of the utterance, i.e. a section which typically hosts responsive elements (see Lindström 2001b, for other kinds of examples).

As a retroactive condition, *x-och-x* presupposes a prior utterance which contains the expression X. This expression is usually, but not always, produced by another speaker. *x-och-x* reacts against the use of X in the actual situation; it expresses the speaker's difficulties in accepting X as an adequate characterisation of the things talked about. Thus, *x-och-x* is response to a particular type of situation; the speaker intervenes in the micro-situation and problematises the use of X.

But *x-och-x* is more than a reactive construction; like IRC, it exhibits both responsive and projective properties. The projective part of *x-och-x* consists in the fact that it projects a continuation (by the same speaker) in which (s)he explains, or at least suggests, in which way X is not "le mot juste". Indeed, *x-och-x* typically occurs as a syntactically non-integrated (and prosodically exposed) pre-front field of a longer utterance, the main part of which contains that explanation.

To be a bit more concrete, consider the cognitive and interactional "job" that *x-och-x* does in (4). The suspect is put in a situation in which he can either reveal the name of an accomplice, or not. After a very long pause, he formulates a question about the (degree of) coercion, force or obligation that he is confronted with. The police officer takes up the term used (i.e. *tvungen*, meaning "forced" or "compelled"). In deploying the *x-och-x* construction he tries to modify or mitigate the situation and the degree of coercion involved. He partly denies that the suspect is "forced" to give the name of his companion. But only partly; the *x-och-x* component projects a continuation where the speaker compromises his stance. In this case, it is not a question of "forcing" the suspect, but the message is nonetheless that there are quite strong reasons for the police officer's request.

4. Responsive constructions

I will now broaden the discussion to encompass also other types of responsive constructions. First, however, it is important to underscore the difference between concrete utterances (contributions to dialogue, turns at talk) and grammatical constructions. Grammatical constructions are more abstract than particular, situated utterances. While all utterances are responsive, i.e. they presuppose and respond to a prior (not necessarily linguistic) context (since responsivity is a universal property of communication), only some utterances are *responsive* in a narrower sense, i.e. they exploit grammatical constructions whose *grammatical form* exhibits their dependence on prior utterances (or more generally: prior contexts). Or in other words, only some utterances have built reflections of responsive functions into their form. (The same applies, *mutatis mutandis*, to elicitative constructions, see section 5.)

Two subclasses of responsive utterances are *elliptical* and *reactive* utterances; elliptical utterances do not repeat certain specific components of prior utterances, reactive utterances do quite the reverse, i.e. they select and repeat specific components of prior utterances.[9]

"Elliptical" utterances are usually (non-clausal) phrases, whose situated interpretation is dependent on prior utterances:

(5) (Tema K: SB1:1) (from the beginning of a telephone conversation in which a mother wants to have her child signed up for municipal child care, cf. Cedersund 1992)

```
1.B:  Katarina Falk. ((self-identifying))
2.M:  yes hi, I'd get a place in the queue for this kind of
3.    a municipal childminder or day-care centre
4.B:  mm. can I have the child's social security number?
5.M:  eighty-five eleven ten.
6.B:  and the four last ones?
7.M:  eighteen fifty-six.
8.B:  then let's see. your social security number?
9.M:  sixty-six zero five twenty-three.
10.B: and the four last ones?
11.M: sixteen ninety-three.
12.B: and telephone to your place?
13.M: seventy-five forty-one eighty-nine.(etc.) ((each relevant piece of
information is entered by B into a computer sheet))
```

```
1.B:  Katarina Falk.
2.M:  ja hejsan, ja skulle ställa mej i kö för sån här
3.    kommunal dagmamma eller dagis.
4.B:  mm. kan ja få barnets personnummer?
5.M:  och de fyra sista?
7.M:  arton femtisex.
8.B:  då ska vi se. ditt personnummer?
9.M:  sextisex noll-fem tjutre.
```

---

[9] Responsive utterances (in a narrow sense) may correspond fairly well to what Sacks (1992:322, 372, *et passim*) talks about in terms of "tying". In and through tying, "someone formulates himself as 'a second speaker'" (p. 372). In a case of tying, a "piece of conversation" is tied to another piece in the "first speaker's" utterance.

```
10.B: och dom fyra sista?
11.M: sexton nittitre.
12.B: och telefon till bostaden?
13.M: sjuttifem förtiett åttinio.. ((etc)) ((efter varje relevant svar
från M för B in uppgifterna på dator))
```

Excerpt (5) contains a number of "elliptical" utterances. The most well-known "elliptical" utterances are answers to prior interrogative utterances, on which they are structurally parasitic. For example, line 6 is parasitic on line 4. A fuller version would have been "och kan ja få de fyra sista (siffrorna)" ("and can I have the last four figures of the child's social security number"). The mother's utterance in line 5, is of course similarly parasitic on line 4 and can be spelled out as "barnets personnummer (de) e åttifem elva tio" ("the child's social security number (it) is eighty-five eleven ten"). And similarly in other cases in this sequence.[10]

Traditionally, "elliptical" utterances have been derived from full sentential deep structures (underlying the same utterances), whereas in a dialogical grammar, a much more natural explanation is available; "elliptical" TCUs recover their "missing"[11] parts from prior utterances.

"Elliptical" utterances typically *take as given* parts of prior utterances and then do not repeat these parts. The reverse case (in some senses) is found in reactive utterances, in which the speaker takes up, repeats, some of the other's words and challenges them, talks back. Reactive utterances, which we have already introduced as a topic in section 3, are usually counter-utterances; they are parasitic on, or evoked by, the structure of preceding utterances, "repeating" or "quoting" parts of previous utterances. They involve (what may appear as) partial repetitions (Sacks 1992: partial repetitive tying). Examples are IRC and *x-och-x*, but there are of course innumerable others. Such utterances involve the re-employment of selected parts of the other's (or one's own) words and constructions in a prior utterance. On the form side, this is reflected in the position of the reactive utterance as a 'second' plus the fact that it is regularly prosodically orchestrated in a different way; it is reaccentuated. Accordingly, this is far from a case of copying; instead, we get a "re-doing", a new utterance act with its own interactional meaning.

Summing up this section, "elliptical" and reactive constructions, with their mutually opposite formal structures, represent two kinds of response and uptake. The "elliptical" ones signal acceptance of the other person's perspective on the local topic, and they comple-

---

[10] In (5), line 1, the self-presentation used by the social worker in answering the phone, could also be taken as an "elliptical" utterance. But it is not parasitic on prior utterances. Rather, it occurs in a well-defined slot and thus exploits the well-established local framing of the micro-situation.

[11] Gr. *elleipein* "to leave out". I use the term "elliptical" within inverted commas, because the traditional analysis (derivation from an underlying structure) does not fit the dialogical framework.

ment the other's communicative project, whereas the reactive ones signal some kind of problem with understanding and acceptance of the other's perspective, as this has been made manifest in the immediately preceding talk.

5. Elicitative constructions

Let us now move from responsive constructions and focus on what could be seen as their counterparts on the projective side, that is, all those construction types which *conventionally project* certain types of next utterances. We may call these *elicitative constructions*. Some interrogatives are good examples, and a particularly illustrative type is the slot-leaving interrogative (example 6: line 5):

(6)   (Tema K: P20:4) (police interrogation, P = police officer, S = suspect)

```
1.P:   you are working this summer?
2.S:   yes
3.P:   and where?
4.S:   the local education office
5.P:   the local education office in--?
6.S:   in Sandberga.

1.P:   du sommarjobbar?
2.S:   ja
3.P:   och var?
4.S:   skolkontoret
5.P:   skolkontoret i--?
6.S:   i Sandberga.
```

The slot-leaving interrogative (SLI) (and other syntactically incomplete utterances) projects, or invites, an "elliptical" response, in a local sequence which can be described in terms of "collaborative completion" (Lerner 1991; Bockgård 2001). At the same time, the SLI is itself often responsive, formally a continuation of the other's turn (though in (6), this turn (line 4) is overly laconic and "elliptical" in format).

Other interrogative constructions also project, or prefer, certain constructions as (minimal) answers: for example, a yes/no-interrogative projects "yes" or "no" (plus optional expansion), a wh-interrogative a phrasal answer (cf. lines 3, 5 above), and a why-interrogative a clause or multi-unit turn.

Many constructions are simultaneously both specifically responsive and specifically projective (elicitative). The IRC construction and *x-och-x* are examples of this, as well as, e.g., the slot-leaving interrogative (6: line 5) and the "elliptical" and-prefaced wh-question in (6: line 3: och var? "and where?").

6. Some general properties of grammatical constructions

In a dialogical grammar, a grammatical construction is a configuration of (two or) several syntactically and/or prosodically linked elements[12]. It is combined with a set of semantic, pragmatic or contextual conditions. In particular, it can have an outer syntax[13]. Grammatical constructions are form-based. They do not have correspondingly specific meanings or functions. Rather, we should think of their semantic-pragmatic side in terms of semantic-functional potentials, in analogy with the meaning potentials of lexical items (Linell 2002; Lähteenmäki 2001).

A grammatical construction is not a concrete, situated utterance. It is abstract in the sense that it transcends the individual situations of use. It belongs to the language system, understood as emergent (Hopper 1998) from the speakers' accumulated and sedimented experiences of utterances with mutually similar structures (Anward 1999). At the same time, however, grammatical constructions are generalised, or typified, utterances, rather than some sort of abstract, underlying structures, from which utterance types can be derived (generated). In this sense, constructions are concrete. Technically, this would mean that the grammatical analysis is monostratal, rather than generative.

In mainstream linguistics, the major function of language is seen as representational in nature, and notions like proposition and predication are basic. Thus, a syntactic construction is a sentence that involves the coupling of a composite linguistic expression with a set of truth conditions pertaining to states of affairs in the world talked about. In a dialogical theory, notions like communicative action and interaction, and intervention in the world, rather than representation of the world, are more basic. We can think of a grammatical construction as a generalised way of responding to and transforming a micro-situation, or as an intervention in the world of the concrete communicative situation. Alternatively, we

---

[12] The relations between syntax and prosody are complex. To some extent, they are clearly integrated and interdependent, but they can also be used as partly independent expressive devices (Auer 1996; Szczepek 2000).
[13] Without going into technical detail, we may some affinities between this and so-called construction grammar (Fillmore et al. 1988, Michaelis & Lambrecht 1996).

can say that utterances are instructions to the other (and to oneself) to pay attention to, to highlight and to conceive of something in a particular way. Grammatical constructions are, together with lexical items, expressive resources used in such instructive actions. Each new utterance, each new instruction, involves some attempt at modifying something in the apperception of the micro-situation in focus (even if these attempts at modification can be very small, of a temporary nature, often provisional and sometimes unsuccessful).

Let me return to *x-och-x* for a few moments. Is not *x-och-x*, after all, an unfortunate example, if one wishes to discuss the nature of grammatical constructions? Indeed, is *x-och-x* a *grammatical* construction at all? After all, it has received little or no attention in traditional as well as generative frameworks. Maybe there are good reasons for this marginalisation? Let us briefly look at some arguments that could be raised for depriving it of the status as a grammatical construction.[14]

First, *x-och-x* has an impoverished syntax (provided 'syntax' is taken in the conventional sense of 'inner syntax'); it is a simple conjunction of two copies of the word X, and the whole thing is not integrated in any close-knit syntactic combination. In fact, *x-och-x* typically occurs prosodically demarcated as a pre-front field constituent. Sometimes, it has indeed been treated as a peculiar (distributive) use of *och* ("and"). But as I have shown, it has an outer syntax. Thus, from a dialogical point-of-view, one must insist on the point that formal and semantic constraints on the use of linguistic expressions, including the use of grammatical constructions, must be described within a framework that is capable of handling relations across traditional sentence boundaries. (Incidentally, sentences, in general, have a dubious status in spoken language.) Grammatical constructions do not just have an inner syntax (intrasentential syntax), but many also have an outer syntax.

Secondly, the meaning of *x-och-x* cannot be compositionally derived from "and" and "X"; as Lindström (2001a) has pointed out, it is a formal or lexically open idiom in the terms of Fillmore et al. (1988). As such, it is, however, quite productive in modern conversational Swedish. In general, the border-line between lexical items and grammatical constructions is not always and everywhere as sharp, as many modern theories of language have assumed.[15]

Thirdly, it might be argued that *x-och-x* is propositionally empty and that "real", full-fledged grammatical constructions express propositions or parts of propositions. To this

---

[14] One must note, however, that the main reason for excluding *x-och-x* from a traditional grammar of Swedish is probably the fact that it belongs almost exclusively to conversational language. But I leave this argument aside in this context, since I take for granted that we are nowadays seriously interested in living spoken language.

[15] A full-fledged grammatical construction should not be dependent on specific (full) lexical items. Yet, as Fillmore et al. (1988) have argued, phrases like English *let alone* has its specific outer syntax. (Cf. also Clift 2001, on the grammar of *actually*.) However, *x-och-x* builds upon the function word *och* "and", and is therefore closer to the requirement just stated.

one may remark that while *x-och-x* may not express a proposition in and by itself, what it does is to point backwards towards something propositional, and to point forwards (i.e. project) another propositional version of the world. It does something particular in the production of propositional content, and it does something different from other units or construction that could occur in pre-front field.

In conclusion, I find, using a dialogical framework, that *x-och-x* does have many interesting properties *qua* grammatical construction. *x-och-x* is a grammatical resource of precisely the kinds that one would expect to find in talk-in-interaction.

7. Conclusions I: Grammatical constructions

I would now like to summarise some of the points made so far.

Grammatical constructions have an *outer syntax*; both *responsive* and *projective* (elicitative) relations are potentially indexed by the formal features of constructions. The grammar is not exclusively a matter of the internal formal composition of sentences. Grammatical constructions may be seen as *methods for transforming micro-situations* into other such situations. *Pragmatic properties* such as presuppositions and givenness (identifiability and activation) status etc are *dialogically engendered* over sequences.

Only these points have been topicalised in this paper. There are of course many other points pertaining to a dialogical grammar and its conception of grammatical constructions. Briefly, these might include the following:

- Constructions are organised so as to fit into *fields* (pre-front field, front field, core field, end field), which in turn have a loose coupling to the phases of (complex) turn construction (cf. Schegloff 1996; Lindström 2001b).
- Constructions are often loosely coupled with *activity contexts*.
- Grammatical regularities are *partly locally organised*; there is no empirical basis for the search for maximal generalisations that many mainstream linguistic theories have engaged in.
- Semantically, constructions are *abstract functional potentials*.
- There are often fuzzy boundaries between *lexis* and *grammar*, or between phraseology and grammar.
- Syntax and *prosody* (paralanguage) are partially integrated.

8. Conclusions II: A dialogical grammar?

It is the discursive practices in situ which are dialogical. The grammar of a language is dialogical in a somewhat extended (metaphorical) sense, namely that it has to be accommodated to, or even designed for, dialogical conditions in language use: "Must we not understand the structures of grammar to be in important respects adaptations to the turn-at-talk in a conversational turn-taking system with its interactional contingencies?" (Schegloff 1989: 143).

A dialogical grammar goes against autonomous syntax on several points:

- It cannot deal with exclusively with the internal formal composition of sentences and their transforms.
- It must bring in contexts, sequential contexts as well as activity-type contexts.
- It is *not exclusively* form-based, but brings in semantics in terms of functional potentials of grammatical constructions.
- It partially obliterates the boundaries between lexicon and grammar.

In a dialogical theory, it is assumed that cognition and communication are largely about sense-making. These processes (or practices) are not primarily seen in terms of abstract information processing or as syntactic algorithms. Nor is meaning intrinsic to language as an abstract system. On the other hand, it is not intrinsic to situated discourse itself either, i.e. it is not a discursive construction in situ *tout court*. A dialogical position holds that meaning is dialogically constituted between participants in a given situated interaction. This also involves a "dialogue" with the affordances of the empirical, i.e. physical and social, world, and a "dialogue" with sociocultural practices and the partially systematic organisation of language as parts of such sociocultural traditions (continuity of practices). Language and meaning are embodied and embedded, existing in the interface between the individual with his body and mind, the others and the sociocultural practices.

References

Allwood, Jens (2000): Talspråksfrekvenser. Frekvenser för ord och kollokationer i svenskt tal- och skriftspråk. (Gothenburg Papers in Theoretical Linguistics, S 21.) – Göteborg: Department of Linguistics.

Anward, Jan (1999): Constructing an Interactionist Account of Constructions. – Paper presented at a Workshop on Construction and Interaction, Helsinki, Finland, September 6, 1999.

Bockgård, Gustav (2001): Responser på samkonstruerade enheter i samtal. – Ms. Uppsala: FUMS.

Cedersund, Elisabet (1992): Talk, Text and Institutional Order. (Linköping Studies in Arts and Science, 78). – Linköping: Department of Theme Research.

Clift, Rebecka (2001): Meaning in Interaction: The case of *actually*. – *Language* 77, 245–291.

Fillmore, Charles (1985): Frames and the Semantics of Understanding. – *Quaderni di Semantica* 6, 222–254.

Fillmore, Charles/ Kay, Paul/O'Connor, M.C. (1988): Regularity and Idiomaticity in Grammatical Constructions: The case of *let alone*. – *Language* 64, 501–538.

Goffman, Erving (1961): Encounters: Two Studies in the Sociology of Interaction. – Indianapolis: Bobbs-Merrill.

Gundel, Jeanette/Hedberg, Nancy/Zacharski, Ron (1993): Cognitive Status and the Form of Referring Expressions in Discourse. – *Language* 69, 274–307.

Hedberg, Nancy (2000): The Referential Status of Clefts. – *Language* 76, 891–920.

Hopper, Paul (1998): Emergent Grammar. In: M. Tomasello (ed.): The New Psychology of Language: Cognitive and functional approaches to language, 155–175. – Mahwah, N.J.: Erlbaum.

Jespersen, Otto (1937; ^{2}1969): Analytic Syntax. – New York etc: Holt, Rinehart and Winston.

Lähteenmäki, Mika (2001): Dialogue, Language and Meaning: Variations on Bakhtinian Themes. – University of Jyväskylä: Department of Russian.

Lambrecht, Knud (1990): "What Me Worry?" 'Mad Magazine sentences' revisited. In: *Proceedings of the 16th Annual Meeting of the Berkeley Linguistics Society*, 215–228.

Lerner, Gene (1991): On the syntax of sentences-in-progress. – *Language in Society* 20, 441–458.

Lindström, Jan (1996): Njae ... problem och problem: Om x och x-responser i svenskan. I: *Svenskans Beskrivning* 21, 183–192. – Lund: Lund University Press.

– (1999): Vackert, vackert! Syntaktisk reduplikation i svenskan. (Studier i nordisk filologi, 77). – Helsingfors: Svenska litteratursällskapet i Finland.

– (2001a): Constituent Order and Constructions in Conversational Turns: the case of the x och x construction in Swedish. Ms. – Helsingfors: Department of Nordic Languages.

– (2001b): Från satsschema till turschema? Förfältet i fokus. – *Språk och Stil* 11, 25–80.

Linell, Per (1998): Approaching Dialogue: Talk, interaction and contexts in dialogical perspectives. – Amsterdam: John Benjamins.

– (2002): En dialogisk grammatik? (http://www.nordiska.uu.se/samtal/ publikationer.html)

Michaelis, Laura/Lambrecht, Knud (1996): Toward a construction-based theory of language function: The case of nominal extraposition. – *Language* 76, 215–247.

Nordberg, Bengt et al. (2000): Samtalsspråkets grammatik. Projektplan inlämnad till Riksbankens Jubileumsfond. – Uppsala: Department of Nordic Languages.

Sacks, Harvey (1992): Lectures on Conversation. Vol. I., ed. by Gail Jefferson. – Cambridge: Blackwell.

SAG (1999) = Teleman, Ulf, Hellberg, Staffan & Andersson, Erik: Svenska Akademiens Grammatik. 4 vols. – Stockholm: Svenska Akademien.

Schegloff, Emanuel A. (1989): Reflections on Language, Development, and the Interactional Character of Talk-in-Interaction. In: M. Bornstein/J. Bruner (eds.): Interaction in Human Development, 139–53. – Norwood, N.J.: Ablex.

– (1996): Turn Organization: One intersection of grammar and interaction. In: E. Ochs, E.A. Schegloff, S.A. Thompson (eds.), Interaction and Grammar, 52–133. – Cambridge: Cambridge University Press.

Schegloff, Emanuel A., Ochs, Elinor and Thompson, Sandra A. (1996): Introduction. In: E. Ochs/ E.A. Schegloff/S.A. Thompson (eds.), Interaction and Grammar, 1–51.– Cambridge: Cambridge University Press.

Szczepek, Barbara (2000): Formal Aspects of Collaborative Productions in English Conversation. – *InLiSt* (= Interaction and Linguistic Structures, Universität Konstanz), 17.
Trask, R.L. (1993): A Dictionary of Grammatical Terms in Linguistics. – London: Longman.

Amy B. M. Tsui

What do Linguistic Descriptions have to say about Discourse?[1]

1. Approaches to discourse analysis

The term "discourse" has been understood from different perspectives based on disciplines with very different concerns. This results in very different approaches to discourse analysis, focusing on different facets of discourse. In this paper, I shall examine what has been considered as two opposing approaches to discourse analysis, referred to as the "descriptive" approach and the "critical" approach (see Fairclough 1995). The descriptive approach aims at *describing* discourse features which are exhibited in the discourse. They have been labelled "descriptive" by Fairclough (1995: 42) because their goals are not explanatory in the sense that they do not look for causes. Subsumed under this approach is the work of linguists who aim to produce a rigorous description of how language above the sentence is structured and organized (see for example, Sinclair and Coulthard 1975; Stubbs 1983; Labov and Fanshel 1977) and the work of ethnomethodologists whose work on conversational analysis (hereafter CA) aims at understanding the accomplishment of social order and social organization in talk as perceived and understood by participants (see the elucidation of CA in Schegloff 1991, 1992, 1997). The critical approach examines discourse as social action and focuses not only on how social contextual features affect how discourse is structured but also the effect of discourse on social practices, or "social formation"[2] (see Fairclough 1995: 43). It is an approach which has been described by van Dijk as "doing social analysis by doing discourse analysis" (1999: 4). It is ideologically and politically motivated (see Widdowson 1995a; Caldas-Coulthard and Coulthard 1996: xi).

---

[1] This paper was presented as a plenary paper at the IADA Conference held in Sweden, Gotenberg, 19-21 April, 2001. The author wishes to thank Karin Aijmer and the organizers of the IADA Conference for their invitation. She also wishes to thank John Sinclair for his insightful comments on several drafts of this paper.
[2] Social formation is used instead of "society" by Fairclough because the term "society" is too fluid and vague (see Fairclough 1995).

2. Object of research: descriptive versus critical approaches

In recent years, descriptive approaches to discourse have come under heavy attack by researchers who adopt a critical approach to discourse. They have been criticized for focusing too much on the micro context of discourse and largely ignoring the macro social contexts and the dialectical relationship between the two. Wetherell (1998: 402) portrays linguists working in the CA tradition as "rarely rais(ing) their eyes from the next turn in the conversation". Similarly, Linell (1998) criticized the work of CA for ignoring the sociocultural context, though linguists of this school do explore the cotextual and situational environments (see also Duranti 1997).

Descriptive approaches have also been criticized for aiming at only description and not explanation. According to critical analysts, descriptive analysts make no attempt to look for causes and effects beyond the immediate situation, at the higher level of social institution and social formation (see Fairclough 1995). By making "local" rather than global interpretation of discourse, they neglect the impact of power and inequality in discourse. Ideological propositions which are implicit in the discourse and often opaque to participants, are subsumed under "background knowledge". This, according to Fairclough, leads to the "naturalization" of ideological propositions as common sense (Fairclough1995: 28), thereby reproducing the ideological effects of discourse. For example, the implicit ideological representation of the unequal power relationship in classroom discourse between the teacher and the students is symbolized by the norms of interaction in which the teacher controls the amount of talk, the speaking rights as well as the meanings and relevance of utterances. By focusing merely on the description of the orderliness exhibited in the discourse, descriptive discourse analysts are reinforcing the status quo. According to Fairclough (1995), the neglect of power and inequality in discourse is further reinforced by the fact that the descriptions made of conversational data are mostly based on conversations among equals. Consequently, the conversational features and the norms of interaction that they describe, such as the turn-taking systems proposed by Sacks, Schegloff, and Jefferson (1974), the Cooperative Principle proposed by Grice (1975), and the "adjacency pair" proposed by Schegloff and Sacks (1973) are taken as the archetype of verbal interaction, giving the illusion that typical verbal interactions are symmetrical in terms of speaker rights and obligations and that speakers have equal control over the meanings of utterances, and what counts as true, relevant and adequate information. Fairclough (1995: 48) argues that there is no reason to give primacy to equal encounters and that if one focuses on unequal encounters, or the comparison of 'equal' and 'unequal' encounters, then the variation in norms of interaction is likely to be highlighted.

Linguistic Descriptions 27

From the criticisms made by critical analysts of the descriptive approach, one can see that there are differences in the objects of research. For linguistic descriptions of discourse, the object of research is clearly language and linguistic structure and organization. Sinclair and Coulthard (1975: 10) specify that what they were interested in was the linguistic structure of discourse. Stubbs (1983: 86) asks questions like "how similar is discourse to other levels of linguistic organization?", "Are discourse phenomena amenable to linguistic explanations?".

For CA, the object of enquiry is social order and social organization as perceived and oriented to by conversational participants. Schegloff (1998: 416) explains the aim of CA as follows: "it is the members' world, the world of the particular members in a particular occasion, a world that is embodied and displayed in their conduct with one another, which is the grounds and the object of the entire enterprise, its sine qua non". Language, though not the ultimate object of research, is given primacy because of the methodology of investigation adopted by conversational analysts. They insist on the principle that formal analysis of discourse should resort to social categories in the analysis only when there is evidence in the discourse that these categories have been oriented to by its participants (see Schegloff 1997).

For critical discourse analysis (hereafter CDA), the object of research is the social phenomenon under investigation, such as power relationship, gender dominance, racism and so on, in which discourse is seen only as a part. However, in contrast with CA, where there is evidence in the discourse that social categories are oriented to by the participants, CDA maintains that the effect of such categories on discourse and the effects of discourse on the macro social contexts are often not apparent to the participants. Therefore, upon identifying a contextual feature, they will use it to explore how this feature affects, or is affected by, structures of talk (see van Dijk 1999: 4). As Wetherell (1998) points out, the theoretical concepts and social categories put forward are often based on implicit assumptions about language and social life without adequate justification of how these concepts or categories are grounded in the fine-grained analysis of the very conversation from which extrapolations are made. For this reason, critical discourse analysts' work has been criticized as politically motivated rather than linguistically motivated (see Widdowson 1995a,b; Stubbs 1997).

Different disciplines have different objects of research and there is little cause for debate. The somewhat heated debate between the descriptive analysts and critical analysts in recent years seems to be motivated not so much by the different objects of research, but rather a more fundamental difference in the understanding of the role of language in semiotics, whether language is central or peripheral. As mentioned above, linguistic discourse analysis sees language as central, and considers that the way language is structured and organized is central to the understanding of how meaning is created and interpreted in discourse. As Sinclair points out, unlike other sign systems such as dress and gestures, the linguistic signs do not themselves create meaning by their occurrence. He states that it is "the whole apparatus of language (which) weaves the signs into highly complex clusters (sentences, moves). ... It is the way meaning is created that distinguishes language from other sign systems, which are all inherently simpler by a huge margin. ... language has its own rich set of axioms that are not shared by others." (personal communication) This strongly echoes Firth's view of linguistics which, according to him, is "a group of related techniques for the handling of language events" and "a group of disciplines designed for systematic empirical analysis" which are "autonomous in the sense that they do not necessarily have a point of departure in another science or discipline such as psychology, sociology or in a school of metaphysics." (Firth 1957: 181). Linguistics, in his view, can be "*brought into relations* with semiologie" which he defines as the "the study of the use and function of signs and words in the heart of our everyday life in society" (p. 17, my emphasis), but language has its own way of creating meaning which is different and much more sophisticated, precise and complex than other sign systems. This view is fundamentally different from that adopted by critical discourse analysts who maintain that language is only a part of discourse. "Discourse" has been defined by Chouliaraki and Fairclough (1999: 38) as "semiotic elements of social practices" which includes "language (written and spoken and in combination with other semiotics, for example, with music in singing), nonverbal communication (facial expression, body movements, gestures, etc.) and visual images (for instance, photographs, film)". According to Fairclough (1995), discourse, and any instance of discursive practice, is simultaneously a spoken or written language text, discourse practice (i.e., text production and text interpretation), and sociocultural practice. Discourse analysis, therefore, goes beyond the description of the language text to include the interpretation of the relationship between the discursive practices and the text, and the explanation of the relationship between discursive practices and social practices. Kress (1998; cited in Fairclough 1999) argues that we should distance ourselves from the primacy of language in looking at the interplay between different semiotic systems, for example, in a science classroom, language figures in the discourse just as one system among others, and is no more important than others.

Whether language is seen as central or peripheral to the creation of meaning, and whether interactive talk is seen as central to the understanding of how social order is perceived by participants determine how investigations of discourse are conducted. Linguistic discourse analysis (LDA) and CA share the common characteristic of basing their descriptions firmly on hard evidence in the data and making their descriptions explicit, despite the fact that the phenomena that they are elucidating are quite different.

CDA, on the one hand, emphasizes the importance of basing social criticism on detailed, explicit, systematic analysis of text *and* context (see Fairclough 1995, 1999; Fowler

1996; van Dijk 1990), but on the other hand maintains that language should not be given primacy. It is perhaps for this reason that close linguistic analysis of text has not been given much attention. The latter position is further reinforced by the view that the social determination and effect of discourse may not be transparent to the participants and therefore the extrapolation of social determinations and effects may not be retrievable from the discourse. The work of CDA has been criticized by descriptive analysts as lacking in rigor and for not basing the analysis on firm evidence. Widdowson (1995b) criticizes CDA for being driven by a political agenda and allowing interpretation in support of belief to take precedence over analysis in support of theory. In a similar vein, Stubbs (1997: 102) observes that the analysts "find what they expect to find, whether absences or presences". Schegloff (1997: 167) used the term "theoretical imperialism" to describe how CDA imposes its own preoccupations on the discourse instead of trying to understand how it is perceived and understood by the participants.

The aim of this paper is not to establish the superiority of one approach over the other but rather to argue that rigorous linguistic analysis of discourse is essential to the analysis of any form of discourse. It demonstrates how by applying rigorous descriptive criteria to the analysis of data, linguistic descriptions of discourse have yielded insights into how meaning is created in discourse which may have otherwise been lost. It maintains that this kind of analysis is a prerequisite to critical studies of discourse (see Schegloff 1997). Nevertheless, it acknowledges that as critical discourse analysts rightly point out, in identifying the functions of discourse categories, the context is often largely restricted to the immediate linguistic and extra-linguistic contexts in which the very discourse takes place, and that there is scope for relating the discourse description to the larger social context. For this reason, the work of critical discourse analysis and descriptive discourse analysis should be seen as complementary rather than competitive.

3. Linguistic descriptions of discourse

The first linguistic description of spoken discourse based on naturally occurring spoken data was that made by Sinclair and Coulthard (1975), using classroom discourse as their data set. Subsequently, there were a number of linguistic descriptions of other genres of spoken discourse based on their work, such as dialogues in Harold Pinter's play (Burton 1980), doctor-patient conversations (Coulthard and Montgomery 1981) and classroom discourse and committee meetings (Stubbs 1983), quizzes (Berry 1987) and casual conversation (Tsui 1994).

Sinclair and Coulthard (1975: 15–17) laid down a set of minimal criteria for an adequate linguistic description:

- the descriptive system should be finite in number, otherwise one is saying nothing at all, but merely creating the illusion of classification;
- the symbols and terms in the descriptive apparatus should be precisely relatable to their exponents in the data so that the classification is replicable and clear;
- the whole of the data should be describable; the descriptive system should be comprehensive;
- there must be at least one impossible combination of symbols.

The first criterion specifies that there should be only a limited number of systems and each system is by definition "closed". This means that within a system, there is only a limited number of terms or choices, and they are mutually exclusive. The addition of one term to the system changes the meaning of the other terms in the system. (See Halliday 1961.) For example, in classroom discourse, when the teacher initiates the interaction with students, he or she is either giving them a piece of information or eliciting a response from them or directing them to do something. In other words, there is a system of "initiating move" in which there are three terms (or choices): informing, eliciting and directing. If the number of choices is infinite, that is, an open set, then one is not making a classification at all but simply giving an illusion of classification. This criterion forces the analysts to clarify what they mean when they wish to set up a category to account for data and to clarify their thinking with regard to whether utterances are describable in terms of discourse categories, whether utterances have multiple functions, or whether they are ambiguous and ambivalent.

The second criterion specifies that for each descriptive category, there should be explicit criteria for identification and each category should be relatable to their exponents in the data. Otherwise, the description is not replicable and different descriptions will be made of the same piece of data (see Firth 1935; Halliday 1961). This is one of the criteria which CDAs have been most heavily criticized for not being able to fulfill. Stubbs (1997) lists the criteria for evaluating CDA's textual analyses, amongst which are explicitness and replicability, and points out that CDA never explicitly spells out how their interpretation relates to the formal features of texts, and that their descriptive claims are often unclear. Interestingly, systematicity, explicitness and relating descriptions to linguistic data are also the criteria that critical discourse analysts used in the critique of their own work. Fairclough (1995) himself echoes van Dijk's calls for explicit and systematic analysis of text and context which is based on serious methods and theories and not just limited to mere paraphrases or quotations. Fowler (1996: 8), a critical linguist, expresses his concern over the fact that CDAs "take too much for granted in the way of method and of context", and

Linguistic Descriptions 31

that few "employ anything approaching a standard, consistent apparatus" in their analysis of data. He points out, "there is a need for published analyses to be more explicit, less allusive, about the tools they are employing ... we need to be more formal about method, ... in order to improve the analytic technique..." (ibid., p. 9).

The third criterion specifies that the descriptive system should be able to account for all data under analysis, and not just a fragment. Sinclair and Coulthard (1975) started with a piece of classroom discourse where the beginning and end of data could be easily identified, and their description aimed to account for all utterances which occurred within the data. This is a criterion which is not easy to satisfy, especially when one tries to apply it to discourse data as complex as casual conversation because a description which seems to adequately account for certain parts of the data may fall apart when applied to the rest, and analysts are often tempted to and do ignore "inconvenient facts" (Stubbs 1983: 61). It is precisely for this reason that this criterion is the ultimate test of the robustness, rigor and power of one's description. It forces the analyst to rethink and refine the descriptive system. As Sinclair and Coulthard have pointed out, if 95% of the data goes into a ragbag category, then there is something wrong with the description. In this respect, CDA suffers the weakness making descriptions which are "fragmentary" and "exemplificatory" (see Fowler 1996: 8).

The fourth criterion states that any descriptive claims about linguistic structure must specify the constraints on how the components of a structure can be combined. If there are no constraints, then there is no structure. This criterion can be easily understood when applied to syntactic structure. However, it is not immediately apparent that this criterion can be applied to spoken discourse, especially in casual conversation, in which it is impossible to put any constraint on what the next speaker will say. However, as we shall see, applying this criterion to discourse data has provided insights into how discourse organization and coherence are governed by structural constraints, how these constraints help interlocutors to interpret the meanings of utterances and what meaning is generated when they are violated.

In the rest of this paper, I shall discuss how the application of the above criteria to the linguistic description of casual conversation has helped us to gain a better understanding of how discourse works. Because of limited space, I shall focus only on aspects of conversational description which have been considered problematic in the literature.

4. Classifying conversational acts and identification criteria

One of the major problems in conversational descriptions is that there seem to be so many categorial labels to describe the functions of utterances, and very often the same function has been given different labels and vice versa. Moreover, it has been argued that in a single utterance, a speaker seems to be performing more than one speech act at a time, and that very often the meaning of an utterance is ambiguous and can be interpreted in different ways. This has led to the conclusion by some analysts that it is impossible to delimit a finite set of speech act types and to identify an utterance as performing a specific speech function (see for example, Levinson 1983; Leech 1983). This position has been widely accepted and any attempt to formalize the characterization of speech act types is likely to be accused of representing a rigid view of language, being "positivistic" and imposing the analysts' categories on data. However, it is curious that the views of these analysts do not seem to be shared by conversationalists. They do not seem to have problems understanding each other. They do not find each other's utterances ambiguous and most of the time they can determine the meaning quite quickly. There are occasions when ambiguities do arise, and interlocutors have to resort to repair mechanisms in conversation to seek clarification. However, this does not happen very often and even when it does, the ambiguities are usually resolved very quickly. Why is this the case? Schegloff (1978: 100) argued that this is because most of the examples that were provided in the discussions were conjured up. In actual conversation, the ambiguities proposed in these invented examples never actually arise because "actual participants in actual conversations do not encounter utterances as isolated sentences, and ... they do not encounter them in a range of scenarios, but in actual detailed single scenarios embedded in fine grained contexts". He observes that the function of an utterance is often quite straightforwardly interpretable and analyzable, and that even though there are "empirically ambiguous" utterances, they do not constitute the majority (ibid.). Otherwise, human communication would be very frustrating, if not impossible.

I would like to suggest that besides the insightful observation made by Schegloff, there is a further reason, namely that the analysis of utterances is not based on consistent and explicit criteria for identification; the labels used are not clearly defined, they are not labels in the same system and they are therefore not mutually exclusive. Let us take some classic examples of multiple functions, such as:

(1) "Would you like another drink?"

(2) "What are you doing tonight?"

(1) is considered as performing both a question and an offer, and (2) as performing a question and "pre-invitation". These categorial labels, however, have not been defined and there are no explicit criteria of identification. Presumably, it is because (1) and (2) are both interrogative in form and they both require a response from the addressee. However, if we look at the nature of the response expected, the first one is not asking for just a verbal response in the same way that (3) does:

(3) "What is the capital of Sweden?"

A positive response from the addressee would commit the speaker to give the former a drink. In other words, (1) is a speech act that involves a non-verbal action consequent to a positive response, and it is fundamentally different from a question like (3) which simply elicits a piece of information. Similar to (3), (2) also elicits a piece of information. It is the sequential organization of the conversational routine of extending an invitation which enables the addressee to interpret it as implying an upcoming invitation. That is to say, the label "pre-invitation" is a discourse sequence label. It is a term that belongs to a different system of choices than those to which speech acts like request, question, and offer belong.

5. Prospective classification

So, what are the explicit criteria that we can use to identify speech act types? Sinclair and Coulthard (1975: 12) proposed the concept of "continuous classification" and asserted that "the meaning of an utterance is its predictive assessment of what follows". In other words, in spoken discourse involving more than one party, it is the response that is prospected by an utterance that contributes to its meaning. This has been referred to as "prospective classification" (Sinclair and Coulthard 1975). Tsui (1994) applied this concept to the analysis of conversational data and made a first distinction between utterances that elicit obligatory verbal responses or their non-verbal surrogates and those that elicit an obligatory non-verbal response and an optional verbal response. For those that elicit an obligatory verbal response, a second distinction was made between those which elicit information and require a verbal response which provides the information, and those which provide information and simply require a minimal acknowledgement of receipt. For those requiring an obligatory non-verbal response, a distinction was made between those which prospect compliance and those that give the options of compliance and non-compliance. On this basis, four macro speech act types were identified. They form a system of choices and they are mutually defining. Table 1 represents how the classification produces the four macro speech act types.

On the basis of this classification, a "question" which expects the addressee to provide a piece of missing information would be classified a kind of Elicitation. An offer which allows the addressee to accept or to decline the offer would be classified as a Requestive since the acceptance of an offer would put the speaker under the obligation to carry out the proferred action. Given these identification criteria, (1) cannot possibly be performing both a kind of Elicitation and a Requestive at the same time.

Table 1   Four macro speech act types by prospective classification (see Tsui 1991a)

	Initiating Utterance			
Prospected response	Verbal		Non-verbal	
Response type	missing information	acknowledgement	+ option of non-compliance	- option of non-compliance
Class of initiating act	Elicitation	Informative	Requestive	Directive

6.   Structural location

While prospective classification is an important criterion, Sinclair and Coulthard (1975) maintain that it is the structural location of an utterance which finally determines its meaning. Hence, in determining what act the utterance performs, the questions that they asked were "whether it is intended to evoke a response, whether it is a response itself, whether it is intended to mark a boundary in the discourse, and so on" (ibid., p. 14). Therefore, in determining the meaning of an utterance, we need to ask where it occurs in the discourse structure. Tsui (1994) used exchange structure as a starting-point for classifying speech act types, and proposed that the four macro speech act types typically occur in the Initiating Move of an exchange. If they were to occur in another structural location, the function that they perform would be quite different. The importance of this criterion can be best seen in utterances whose functions are entirely dependent on their sequential or structural location. For example,

(4)   [Tsui 1994: 15]
    A: What's the time?
    ⇒ B: It's nearly three.

(5)   [ibid.]
        ⇒ A: It's nearly three.
          B: Oh my god!

The arrowed utterance in (4) would be a response to an elicitation providing the missing information whereas that in (5) would be an Informative providing a piece of information which probably served as a reminder, depending on the context.

As Schegloff and Sacks (1973: 299) point out, "Finding an utterance to be an answer, to be accomplishing answerhood, cannot be achieved by reference to phonological, syntactic, semantic, or logical features of the utterance itself, but only by consulting its sequential placement, e.g., its placement after a question".

The two criteria used for classification of utterances show a dialectical relationship between text and context. In order to determine the kind of response prospected, one must take into consideration the context in which the discourse occurs. For example, in the classroom, what looks like an Elicitation may have the function of a Directive. An example in Sinclair and Coulthard's data is "What are you laughing at?", said by the teacher, which was interpreted by a pupil as a Directive to shut up. The same utterance occurring in casual conversation is not likely to be interpreted in the same way. Once an utterance is produced, it becomes part of the context for the interpretation of what precedes and what follows, opening up or closing down options which are available to the next speaker. In the following example, G, a colleague of S, was telling S that she was very upset by a certain person referred to as "he". In the course of the conversation, she has not revealed the identity of this person.

(6)   [C:4:B:1:69]
        1   G: Is he here in Hong Kong?
        2   S: Oh I don't want to talk about who he is.
    ⇒   3   G: No I wouldn't <u>ask</u> you but I just <u>wondered</u> if he worked here um

In the above except, G performed an Elicitation and was expecting a response from S to provide the missing information. However, S challenged the presupposition in G's utterance that she was willing to provide the information, indicating that the knowledge was not shared. This challenging move shaped the discourse that followed: it led to the production of a rejoinder from G in which he reclassified the illocutionary force of his initial utterance from "ask" to "wondering". Although the word "wonder" is often used by people to elicit a response, in this case the juxtaposition of "ask" and "wonder" obviously means that "wonder" is "not ask", that is, it does not require a response. We can see that not only can interlocutors prospectively classify what is expected to follow so that whatever utterance that follows will be interpreted in that light, they can also retrospectively classify what went on before, hence assigning a new meaning to the utterance.

7. Discourse structure and utterance interpretation

In the preceding section, I have demonstrated, I hope, the importance of applying consistent and explicit criteria when classifying speech act types and what the possible criteria are. As we try to establish more delicate categories, other explicit criteria have to be set up in order to account adequately for the distinctions among the subclasses (for more delicate subclasses, see Tsui 1994). I hope I have also demonstrated how the categories in the system are mutually exclusive or mutually defining.

In this section, I will focus on structural descriptions of discourse, focusing on the exchange structure, and how the interpretation of utterances is made possible by an understanding of the discourse structure. I will also show how an attempt to account for all the data has generated new insights into conversational structure.

In their description of classroom discourse, Sinclair and Coulthard (1975) proposed that classroom exchanges are typically made up of three moves which are related to each other in a certain way such that an "initiating move" sets up the expectation of a "responding move" and a "follow-up move". These three moves constitute the elements of structure of an exchange. The unmarked form of an exchange consists of three parts whereas one which consists of two parts is "marked" and the third part is withheld for strategic reasons. An obvious example is socratic questioning in which the teacher withholds an evaluation of the student's response when it is wrong, and initiates a series of questions for the student to respond to in the hope that he or she will arrive at the correct answer. Sinclair and Coulthard's argument is that if a teacher withholds a third part frequently, it is likely to arouse discontent from pupils (see Sinclair 1982).

Sinclair and Coulthard's proposal of a three-part exchange as a basic interactional unit has been criticized as too classroom specific and it has been argued that it therefore cannot be generalized to the organization of discourse genres such as conversation where the power relationship is equal and one party does not have control over the other in terms of speaker rights and what counts as an adequate and relevant contribution to the discourse. It has been suggested that conversations are typically organized in terms of two-part exchanges or "adjacency pairs" (Schegloff and Sacks 1973). Burton (1980) argues that the occurrence of the third part in encounters outside the classroom is deviant.

(7)   [Burton 1980: 63]
        A: What's the time please?
        B: Three o'clock.
    *   A: Well done.

Coulthard and Brazil (1981: 90), upon noticing the occurrence of the third part in conversational exchanges, suggest that such occurrence is "marked" and is produced to achieve a certain effect. For example,

(8)   [Coulthard and Brazil 1981: 90]
        [Wife to husband]
        Wife: What time did you come home last night?
        Husband: About midnight.
    ⇒   Wife: No you didn't.

In this exchange, the occurrence of the follow-up move is "marked" because it is deliberately produced to show that the husband is lying. In a sense, this conversational exchange bears a strong similarity to a classroom exchange in that the wife asks a question to which she already has an answer. The follow-up move that she produces, similar to that produced by a teacher, is evaluative. The only difference is that in unequal power encounters such as classroom discourse, an evaluative follow-up move is "unmarked". Subsequently, there were attempts to apply three-part exchanges to discourse genres such as quizzes to explore the descriptive power of this structural category. The conclusion was that three-part exchanges typically occur in asymmetrical discourse where one party has power or knowledge over the other. In situations like this, the third element is obligatory. Otherwise, the third element is optional even if it occurs (see for example Berry 1987).

Tsui (1994) analyzed the structural organization of a corpus of conversational data among peers[3] by applying both "adjacency pairs" and "three-part exchanges" and found plenty of instances of three-part exchanges in which the third part is in no way evaluative or face-threatening. For example,

(9)   [Tsui 1994: 29]
    I   B: Where where is he staying?
    R   A: He's staying at the ah the Chung Chi Guest House.
    ⇒ F   B: Oh I see.

B's follow-up is simply to acknowledge that A's response has been heard and understood but it does not seem to be optional. Similarly, Heritage (1984) has found that the prevalent occurrence of the conversational particle "oh" after a piece of information has been pro-

---

[3] I am deliberately avoiding the word "equals" because there is a possibility of unequal gender relationships in some of the data even among peers.

vided to indicate a change of state of the knowledge. He points out that the questioner, upon receiving the information, is obliged to produce an 'oh'-receipt to indicate a change of knowledge state. In other words, the third part is obligatory and not optional.

If we say that the third element is obligatory, what evidence do we have apart from the fact that it is actually found in the data? How do we account for the fact that there is no lack of conversational exchanges where the third element is absent? Are we running into the danger of imposing the analyst's interpretation on the data?

Sacks (1972), in justifying the strong relationship between the first pair part and the second pair part in an "adjacency pair", proposed the notion of "noticeable absence", that is, if the second pair part is absent, it will be noticeable and actually noticed by the participants as absent. In other words, the "absence" of the second pair part is not something that the analyst imposes on the data. There will be evidence in the discourse data that such absence is oriented to by the participants. Sacks provided the following example.

```
(10)    [Sacks 1972: 341]
        1 WOMAN:    Hi
        2 BOY:      Hi
        3 WOMAN:    Hi, Annie
    ⇒   4 MOTHER:   Annie, don't you hear someone say hello to you?
        5 WOMAN:    Oh, that's okay, she smiled hello.
    ⇒   6 MOTHER:   You know you're supposed to greet someone, don't you?
    ⇒   7 ANNIE:    [hangs head] Hello.
```

Sacks points out that the absence of a second pair part to the greeting by the woman in line 3 is "noticed" by the mother. The obligatory nature of a return-greeting is further confirmed by the woman's saying that Annie "smiled hello" in line 5 and by the fact that in line 7, Annie does indeed return the woman's greeting by saying "hello".

Similarly, Tsui (1994) found in her data that when the third element in a conversational exchange is missing, it was "noticed", or oriented to, by the participants. The following is an example from her data. In this piece of data, B and C are peers just graduated from the university. B got a job as a bank manager and C is still unemployed.

```
(11)    [Tsui 1994: 33]
            1   B:  Mind you it's not bad really, banking business, I suppose, it's a clean job.
        R   2   C:  Yeah, it's that kind of image. I don't really go for that, you know.
    ⇒           ((2 sec))
        I   3   C:  Do you know what I mean though, I mean it suits you.
        R   4   B:  Yeah.
        I   5   C:  I mean, I'm not being insulting or anything, but I can't see myself
            6       being a bank manager.
```

```
       R    7   B:    ((laughs)) Oh I can see myself being a bank manager.
   ⇒ F     8   C:    You could, yes, that's what I mean.
```

In the above excerpt, there was clearly an expectation that after line 2, B would produce a third part after C's response. This can be seen by the two-second silence indicating that C was waiting for B to take his turn. The clarification made by C of what he meant in the previous move (line 3) was evidence that he felt that the interaction might have been infelicitous in the sense that B might have been offended by his utterance. This was further reinforced by the fact that C's clarification, "I mean it suits you.", was only responded to by a minimal acknowledgement (line 4), instead of a more elaborate response from B indicating that things are now in order. This led to a further clarification from C that he was "not being insulting" (line 5). It is only then that B responded more enthusiastically, indicating that the miscommunication has been repaired (line 7). The production of the third element of the exchange by C in line 8 shows that a satisfactory outcome has been achieved and that the interaction has been felicitous.

Apart from discourse evidence such as the above, the obligatory nature of the third element of an exchange can also be supported theoretically. Conversation is jointly constituted by the participants. As such, the meanings of utterances are subject to negotiation between the participants. Therefore, after the production of the first move by the first speaker, the second speaker demonstrates his or her interpretation of the initiating move by producing a response. However, whether the second speaker has correctly interpreted the first speaker's utterance, and whether the response is acceptable is not known until the first speaker produces a follow-up move to indicate that there is no miscommunication and the response is an appropriate one (see also Heritage and Atkinson 1984; Linell 1998).

Sometimes, when the first speaker intends to achieve a specific outcome, he or she will withhold the follow-up move until the intended outcome has been achieved, or until he or she agrees to accept the outcome. The following piece of data is by no means atypical:

```
(12)    [Tsui 1994: 40]
    I    C:   Are you sure you don't want a cigarette?
    R    B:   No I couldn't take your last but one.
    I    C:   Well the last one actually – that would be my last one.
    R    B:   No, no I'm not having it. I'd feel too bad.
 ⇒ F     C:   Okay.
```

In the first exchange, the follow-up move is absent because C does not accept the negative outcome of his offer and he therefore re-offers in the second exchange. The production of the follow-up move in this exchange indicates that he accepts the outcome.

The above discussion shows that it is in the process of repeatedly applying both "adjacency pairs" and "three-part exchanges" as units of interaction to the analysis of a range of conversational data, and trying to account for all moves in the data that it was found that though an "adjacency pair" is commonly found in the data, a "three-part exchange" is a more powerful description of conversational organization.

It is interesting that three-part exchanges can account for the organization of discourse genres as different as classroom discourse and casual conversation. The former is, in CDA terminology, an unequal encounter where there is an asymmetrical power relationship between the participants. The teacher not only has control over who has the right to speak, but also over the meanings of the utterances, sometimes even what the students mean, and what constitutes a correct and appropriate contribution to the discourse. Casual conversation, especially among equals, is one where the power relationship is symmetrical, at least in the conversational corpus examined, despite the fact that there could be asymmetry in gender. Yet, it was found that the organizational unit in the conversational corpus is basically the same. It is only the functions of the moves that are different. This suggests that there are certain descriptive categories that are basic to spoken discourse and it is important to develop a rigorous and systematic description of these categories.

8. Discourse structure and discourse coherence

In this last section, I shall address the question of how valid it is to describe conversation in terms of discourse structure since one can easily find data where an initiating move is not followed by a responding move, or a first pair part is not followed by a second pair part. I shall also discuss how in the process of trying to satisfy the criterion of having at least one impossible combination of categories we have gained some understanding of how coherence in discourse is achieved.

The observation that it is not uncommon to find that a question is not followed by an answer and a request is not followed by a compliance or non-compliance has been commonly cited as evidence that spoken discourse cannot be described in terms of structural expectations. This observation confuses what is "expected to occur" and "what actually occurs" (Tsui 1991b: 115). A statement of structure specifies what is expected to occur but not what will actually occur. It specifies that what actually occurs will always be interpreted in the light of this expectation. This means that an utterance following a question will always be interpreted as a possible answer to the question (see Berry 1982; Coulthard and Brazil 1981; Tsui 1991b). As Berry (1982: 38) points out, a rule such as "A predicts B" is "not inviolable from the point of view of what will actually occur, but it is invariant in that the existence of the rule will always be assumed for the purpose of interpreting what occurs".

Although the expectancy rule may be violated, one cannot therefore conclude that anything can follow anything in conversation because when a piece of discourse is coherent, we are able to recognize it immediately (see also Mey 2001).

Let us take the following example in which A and B share an office and A, who does not have a watch with him, asks B, "What's the time?" The following are possible next utterances provided by B.

(13) [Tsui 1991b: 118]
    A: What's the time?
    B: (a) Eleven.
       (b) Time for coffee.
       (c) I haven't got a watch, sorry.
       (d) How should I know?
       (e) Ask Jack.
       (f) You know bloody well what time it is.
       (g) Why do you ask?
       (h) What did you say?
       (i) What do you mean?

As I pointed out in Tsui (1991b), B's utterances in (a) to (i) are all coherent with A's question, but only (a) and (b) are the second pair parts to the first pair part, which is an Elicitation. What is it that accounts for the coherence? Tsui (1991b) proposed that in order for an utterance to form a coherence sequence with the first pair part, it must either fulfil the illocutionary intent of the first pair part, in which case it is a second pair part or it must be related to the pragmatic presupposition of the utterance in a certain way. In (13) above, (a) fulfills the illocutionary intent of A's Elicitation in providing the required piece of information. (b) will be interpreted in the light of A's Elicitation and, assuming that A and B have shared knowledge what time the coffee break is, (b) constitutes a second pair part as well. If, however, the knowledge is not shared, (b) will not be interpretable and the sequence will be considered incoherent by A, who is likely to repair the break-down in communication. (c) to (i) do not fulfil the illocutionary intent of A's Elicitation, but they are related to its pragmatic presuppositions which are as follows:

(i)   The speaker does not have the information and (sincerely) wants to have the information.

(ii)   The speaker has the need and the right to ask for the information.

(iii)   The speaker has reason to believe that the addressee has the information.

(iv) The speaker has reason to believe that the addressee is willing to supply the information (see Lakoff 1973; Labov & Fanshel 1977; Searle 1969; cf. Keenan 1983:79).

(v) The addressee can hear what the speaker says.

(vi) The addressee can understand the meaning conveyed (see Searle 1969: 57).

The first four presuppositions pertain specifically to Elicitation whereas the last two pertain to all speech acts. All utterances from (c) to (i) challenge the presuppositions of A's Elicitation. (c) and (d) challenge the presupposition that B has the information or is able to supply the information. (Whether (c) constitutes an answer is debatable in the same way as "I don't know" is.) (e) re-routes A to another source of information. The re-routing could be because B does not have the information, in which case it challenges presupposition (iii) or because B is not willing to supply the information, in which case it challenges presupposition (iv). (f) challenges the presupposition (i), and (g) challenges presupposition (ii). Finally, (h) and (i) challenge the presuppositions (v) and (vi) which pertain to the communication aspects. The list of possible next utterances listed in (13) is by no means exhaustive, and different utterances can be challenged in different ways. As a result of trying this out on many instances of coherent discourse sequences which are not adjacency pairs or three part exchanges, it seems to me that there are constraints governing what can follow a first pair part in a coherent sequence, viz., "it must either fulfil the illocutionary intention of the first pair part or challenge its pragmatic presuppositions". Again, the rule governing discourse coherence can be violated. When it is, there will be a breakdown in communication and interlocutors will try to repair it so that conversation can proceed normally. The social consequence of the violation of this rule is highly context-dependent, as we shall see in the concluding section.

9. Linguistic and critical discourse analyses: Complementary or competitive?

In this paper, I have argued for the need to subject discourse data to rigorous, systematic and explicit linguistic description. Because of limited space, I can only single out certain aspects of discourse description to illustrate attempts that have been made to produce linguistic descriptions of spoken discourse, moving from classroom discourse to casual conversation. This focus has been on how the criteria for a linguistic description can be applied to the analysis and how they force the analyst to refine the descriptive system. My aim is not to provide a model of linguistic description, but rather to argue that, as Labov pointed out almost three decades ago in his work on therapeutic discourse, formalization is a useful process because it sharpens the questions and promotes the search for answers (see Labov and Fanshel 1977).

The fact that a linguistic descriptive model which was initially based on classroom discourse, which is a classic case of asymmetrical discourse in which one speaker has almost absolute control over almost every aspect of the discourse could be applied to largely symmetrical discourse among peers suggests that there are certain formal aspects of discourse which are common to all discourse genres. We do not yet have a full understanding of these formal aspects and we do not have a rigorous apparatus as yet to adequately capture these aspects. Critical discourse analysis, by placing the discourse in the larger macro-social contexts will enable analysts to make a richer interpretation of the discourse which may be lost otherwise. Yet on the other hand, unless we firmly base our description on linguistic evidence in the data, we risk the danger of making "interpretations" of data that are governed by our ideological bias. I would like to end this paper by illustrating how these two approaches can be brought together to provide a rich analysis.

```
[BCET:D:15]
C is female and D is male. They are peers. < > stands for interrupted moves.
 1   I     D:    We don't want academics, especially arts students, they think and that's not
 2               good (tapping noise) That's what that book by Margaret O'Dennell's about,
 3               where the women weren't allowed to think.
 4  <R>   C:    Mind you don't you think if there's a need for
 5   I     D:    You remind me of one of those French whores of the late nineteenth century
 6               that you see running around with Louis the fourteenth. It's sort of the hair,
 7               sort of curls like that and straight into the air, you know, sort of - [
 8        C:    .hhh
 9   I     C:    What was I saying? I was saying something.
10   R?   D:    I don't know mate.
11   I     C:    What was I saying?
12   R?   D:    I don't know.
13   I     C:    You interrupted me.
14   R    D:    I'm sorry, I wasn't listening.
15  <I>   C:    Yeah, that was what I was going to say -
16   R    D:    I see, yes, very interesting.
17  <I>   C:    I was going to say –
18   R    D:    That's good. Yes, really
19   I     C:    I was going to say if there aren't, if there isn't any need for labour any more,
20               then academics are the only people who are going to keep themselves
21               amused.
```

Applying the linguistic descriptions discussed in this paper, the following observations can be made. Firstly, there are several instances where the exchanges are incomplete in the sense that either the Initiating move (lines 15, 17) or the Responding move (line 4) was interrupted. Secondly, the second Initiating Move performed by D (lines 5–7) not only interrupted C's response but also violated the Coherence Rule by producing an utterance which is neither related to the illocutionary intent or the pragmatic presupposition of C's incomplete response. Thirdly, in lines 10 and 12, the responses provided by D were marginal "answers" to C's Elicitation which proclaimed that he did not know what she was saying. Both responses from D challenge the presupposition that D should have the information. They are face-threatening because interlocutors should have paid attention to each other's contributions. However, D gave a "bald-on-record" declaration of ignorance without any hedges or redressing. It was not until C "criticized" D for interrupting her that D admitted that he was not listening and apologized. Finally, despite the repair, the discourse did not resume its normal course of development because C was interrupted again in lines 15 and 17. Before C completed her Informatives (in lines 15 and 17), D provided prospected responses (in lines 16 and 18) which acknowledged the receipt of information and provided comments on C's Informatives. Although D's responses would normally be prospected by Informatives, the very fact that they were produced before C had performed the "head act" of informing shows that D was retrospectively classifying C's Informatives as though they had already been completed. This violation of the structural constraints governing the exchange structure, or the adjacency pair, generates the conversational implicature that D was not interested in what C had to say.

The description of the conversational features given above will get another interpretation when we consider the data from a CDA perspective and consider the gender and dominance in conversation. From the fact that the female interlocutor, C, was the one who was being interrupted three times, and the male interlocutor was the one who demonstrated no interest in what C was saying or had to say, together with D's sexist remark on C's hair, we could interpret this as an unequal encounter exemplifying male dominating over female. On the other hand, we can see that C resisted D's domination in lines 9, 11, 15, and 19 by persistently re-initiating her own topic of talk. In line 13, she even drew D's attention to his violation of the Coherence Rule and forced an apology out of him. We could say that it is a case of a conversational tug-of-war between C and D involving gender domination.

10. Conclusion

The above analysis is very crude but I hope that it serves as an example to illustrate how applying linguistic descriptive criteria helps us to understand how interlocutors create meaning and manage the discourse by exploiting the possibilities and constraints which are available in the apparatus of language. Interpreting the data in the larger social context enables us to take into consideration social and cultural dimensions which shape the discourse. The two approaches are therefore complementary and not competitive. Nevertheless, as Schegloff (1997: 183) points out, "getting the formal aspect right" is a prerequisite to getting into a position where one could bring the concerns of critical discourse analysts to bear on the analysis.

References

Berry, Margaret (1982): Review article: M.A.K. Halliday (1978) Language as Social Semiotic: The social interpretation of language and meaning. – In: *Nottingham Linguistic Circular* 1, 64–94.
– (1987): Is Teacher an Unanalyzed Concept? – In: M.A.K Halliday/R. Fawcett (eds.): New Developments in Systemic Linguistics, Vol. I., 41–63. London: Frances Pinter.
Burton, Deidre (1980): Dialogue and Discourse.– London: Routledge and Kegan Paul.
Caldas-Coulthard, Carmen/Coulthard, Malcolm (eds.) (1996): Texts and Practices: Readings in Critical Discourse Analysis.– London: Routledge.
Chouliaraki, Lilie/Fairclough, Norman (1999): Discourse in Late Modernity – Rethinking Critical Discourse Analysis. Edinburgh: Edinburgh University Press.
Coulthard, Malcolm/Brazil, David (1981): Exchange Structure.– In: M. Coulthard/M. Montgomery (eds.): Studies in Discourse Analysis, 82–106. London: Routledge and Kegan Paul.
Coulthard, Malcolm/Montgomery, Martin (1981): Studies in Discourse Analysis. London: Routledge.
Duranti, Alessandro (1997): Linguistic Anthropology. – Cambridge: Cambridge University Press.
Fairclough, Norman (1995): Critical Discourse Analysis. – London: Longman.
– (1999): Linguistic and Intertextual Analysis within Discourse Analysis. – In: A. Jaworski/ N. Coupland (eds.): The Discourse Reader, 183–212. London: Routledge.
Firth, J.R. (1935): The Techniques of Semantics. – In: J.R. Firth (ed.): Papers in Linguistics 1934-195, 7–33. London: Oxford University Press.
– (1957): Papers in Linguistics: 1934–1951.– London: Oxford University Press.
Fowler, Roger (1996): On Critical Linguistics.– In: C. R. Caldas-Coulthard/M. Coulthard (eds.): Texts and Practices: Readings in Critical Discourse Analysis, 3–14. London: Routledge.
Grice, Paul (1975): Logic and Conversation.. – In: Cole, P./ Morgan, J. (eds.) Syntax and Semantics Vol. 3:Speech Acts, 41–58, New York: Academic Press.
Halliday, M.A.K. (1961): Categories of the Theory of Grammar. – *Word*, 17(3), 241–92.
Heritage, John (1984): A Change-of-State-Token and Aspects of Its Sequential Placement.– In: J. Atkinson/P. Drew (eds.): Structures of Social Action, 299–345. Cambridge: Cambridge University Press.
Heritage, John and Atkinson, Maxwell (1984): Introduction. – In: J. Atkinson/P. Drew (eds.): Structures of Social Action, 1–16. Cambridge: Cambridge University Press.
Keenan, Elinor Ochs (1983): Conversational Competence in Children.– In: E. Ochs/B. Schieffelin (eds.): Acquiring Conversational Competence, 3–25. London: Routledge and Kegan Paul.
Kress, Gunther (1998): A Satellite View of Language. Some lessons of a science classroom.– United Kingdom, Institute of Education Working Papers.

Labov, William/Fanshel, David (1977): Therapeutic Discourse.– New York: Academic Press.
Lakoff, Robin (1973): Questionable Answers and Answerable Questions. – In: B.B. Kachru (ed.): Issues in Linguistics: Papers in honour of Henry and Renee Kahane, 453–467. Urbana: University of Illinois Press.
Leech, Geoffrey (1983): Principles of Pragmatics.– London: Longman.
Levinson, Stephen (1983): Pragmatics.– Cambridge: Cambridge University Press.
Linell, Per (1998): Approaching Dialogue. – Amsterdam/Philadelphia: John Benjamins.
Mey, Jacob (2001): Pragmatics. – Oxford: Blackwell.
Sacks, Harvey (1972): On Analyzability of Stories by Children. – In: J.J. Gumperz/D. Hymes (eds.): Directions in Sociolinguistics, 329–45. New York,: Holt, Rinehart and Winston.
Sacks, Harvey/Schegloff, Emanuel/Jefferson, Gail (1974): A Simplest Systematics for the Organization of Turn-taking for Conversation.– *Language* 50(4), 696–753.
Schegloff, Emanuel (1978): On Some Questions and Ambiguities in Conversation. In: W. Dressler (ed.): Current Trends in Textlinguistics, 81–102. Berlin: de Gruyter.
– (1991): Reflections on Talk and Social Structure. – In: D. Boden/D. Zimmerman (eds.): Talk and Social Structure: Studies in ethnomethodology and Conversation Analysis, 44–70. Cambridge, Polity Press.
– (1992): On Talk and its Institutional Occasions.– In: P. Drew/J. Heritage (eds.): Talk at Work, 101–136. Cambridge: Cambridge University Press.
– (1997): Whose Text? Whose Context? – *Discourse and Society* 8(2), 165–187.
– (1998): Reply to Wetherell. – *Discourse and Society* 9(3), 413–416.
Schegloff, Emanuel/ Sacks, Harvey (1973): Opening up Closings.– *Semiotica* 7(4), 289–327.
Searle, John (1969): Speech Acts. – Cambridge: Cambridge University Press.
Sinclair, John (1982): Teacher Talk. – London: Oxford University Press.
Sinclair, John/Coulthard, Malcolm (1975): Towards an Analysis of Spoken Discourse. – London: Oxford University Press.
Stubbs, Michael (1983): Discourse Analysis. – Oxford: Blackwell.
– (1997): Whorf's Children: Critical comments on CDA. – In: A. Ryan/A. Wray (eds.): Exploring Models of Language, 100–116 Milton Keynes: Multilingual Matters.
Tsui, Amy B.M. (1991a): The Description of Utterances in Conversation.– In: J. Verschueren (ed.): Pragmatics at Issue, Vol.I, 229–247. Amsterdam/Philadelphia: John Benjamins.
– (1991b): Sequencing Rules and Coherence in Discourse. – *Journal of Pragmatics* 15, 111–29.
– (1994): English Conversation. – London: Oxford University Press.
van Dijk, Teun (1990): *Discourse and Society*: A new journal for a new research focus. – *Discourse and Society* 1(2), 5–16.
– (1999). Critical Discourse Analysis and Conversational Analysis.– *Discourse and Society* 10(4), 459–460.
Wetherell, Margaret (1998): Positioning and Interpretive Repertoires: CA and post-structuralism in dialogue. – *Discourse and Society* 9(3), 387–412.
Widdowson, Henry (1995a): Discourse Analysis. A critical view. – *Language and Literature*. 4(3), 157–172.
– (1995b): Review of : N. Fairclough Discourse and Social Change. – *Applied Linguistics* 16(4), 510–16.

Chapter 2
Misunderstanding as a Dialogical Phenomenon

Sorin Stati

Misunderstanding – A Dialogic Problem

1. Introduction

Misunderstanding is a typically interdisciplinary phenomenon and consequently the only method which fits this fundamental characteristic is a multi-dimensional approach. Researchers agree in placing it at a kind of crossroads where philosophy meets psychology, linguistics, speech pathology, pragmatics, semiotics, stylistics, literary criticism and so on and so forth. The present paper will discuss some features of misunderstanding against this background in order to throw some modest light on, and especially to measure, the dimensions of our ignorance.

Famous examples of misunderstanding in a literary work can be found in "Alice in the Wonderland", compare:

> ...the twinkling of the tea.
> The twinkling of what? said the King.
> It began with the tea.
> Of course twinkling begins with T, said the King sharply. and
> "Have some wine – the March Hare said.
> Alice looked all around the table, but there was nothing on it but tea.
> I don't see any wine – she remarked.
> There isn't any, said the March Hare.

To cite but one example of contemporary research concerning the literary aspects of misunderstanding, we can mention the problem of obscure style. In July 2002 a conference dedicated to this argument was organized by the universities of Padua and Trento at Bressanone in Italy. As is well known, "avoid obscurity of expression" is one of the principles of Grice (see Grice 1975). From a different point of view, misunderstanding is investigated by scholars who are interested in foreign language acquisition (cf. Allwood & Abelar 1984).

But first of all misunderstanding is a dialogic problem. This statement is the first proof of our ignorance since its vagueness is evident. All we do when speaking is to engage in dialogue. To vagueness we need to add confusion; we mean (a) the frequent confusion between misunderstanding and incomprehension (cf. Weigand 1999; see also Allwood & Abelar 1984), (b) the confusion between misunderstanding and what I call 'le dialogue des sourds'; the latter is only a kind of polemical verbal interaction, hence a kind of misunderstanding: two people expound their opinions on a certain subject; each one maintains his position and a witness concludes that the contrast is unbridgeable since each speaker is incapable of understanding the other and refuses to accept even a single one of the antagonist's ideas.

A few examples will clarify the concept of misunderstanding: the polemics between generativists and non-generativists in linguistics, as well the polemics between phonologists and phoneticians; the recurrent conflict between atheists and people of religion. How could we forget the wars of religion and, also to some extent – the conflict between science and religion, between materialism and idealism and so on and so forth? The participants in this kind of polemics often give the impression that they do not want to listen to one another, and popular wisdom has coined the proverb "There is no person deafer than he/she who does not want to hear".

The 'dialogue des sourds' is an extreme case of lack of cooperativity, and as such a an extreme case of Dialogue; in fact, the respect for a minimal set of cooperative principles is compulsory for Dialogue. If we consider the 'dialogue des sourds' as a species of dialogue this is for several reasons: suffice it to quote the polemic activity of two speakers, the presupposed presence of a judge (who may be a reader) etc. Since Aristotle rhetoricians have stressed the particular relevance of a judge, in a broad sense of the term, with reference to the three kinds of discourse.

Henceforth, we shall discuss misunderstanding *lato sensu*. Here are the issues we intend to develop: The definition of misunderstanding; favourable conditions for the production of misunderstandings: we mean the 'langue' conditions and the 'parole' conditions. Essentially, misunderstanding is a 'parole' phenomenon; it concerns utterances and not sentences. A 'langue' condition concerns the lexicon and precisely the existence of homonyms. On the contrary, on the 'parole' level a relation of coreference between two text words may be questionable and accordingly produce misunderstanding. Other issues are the levels or layers of the content of an utterance; the extraordinary complexity of the phenomenon 'the understanding of an utterance'; code-based decoding as opposed to inference-based interpretation; intertextuality.

2. The definition of misunderstanding

The need to start from a clear definition of misunderstanding is proved by the extensive literature on the subject. Literary problems, as for instance, stylistic ambiguity, the theatre of the absurd, are still at the center of attention, and the same may be said about the cinema and the activity of some 'monstres sacrés' like Ingmar Bergman. Certainly 'absurdity' and 'misunderstanding' are not synonyms, but they are akin; we are thinking of some famous examples of absurdity which produce misunderstanding, cf. "The present king of France is (not) wise" or "Colourless green ideas sleep furiously". And also significant is the number of papers announced at the present IADA conference dealing with various aspects of misunderstanding, both in oral and written speech. A very illuminating treatment of this phenomenon is due to Marcelo Dascal (see his "Introduction" to the special issue of *Journal of Pragmatics* on misunderstanding (1999)). Misunderstanding appears to be a phenomenon:

- typically belonging to speech reception,
- occurring on the semantic and pragmatic levels of communication,
- having to do with involuntary rather than non-literal meaning (of pieces of discourse).

If misunderstanding is so frequent this is because a text could never be completely explicit; a certain amount of information remains hidden among the semantic markers and has to be detected and discovered by the recipient. This process presupposes a certain amount of cooperativity, and Dascal states that cooperative communication is exceptional (Dascal 1999 : 758).

When the immediate co-text is not sufficient to avoid misunderstanding, this role is taken by the dialogue, first of all with regard to pragmatic features. Literary texts are full of examples which show how dialogue clarifies and rectifies the interpretation of ambiguous and difficult discourse. Here are two examples: "A: Il n'est plus bien loin, n'est-ce pas Electre?/B: Elle n'est plus bien loin./A: Je dis il. Je parle du jour./B: Je parle de la lumière." (Giraudoux 1987:75); "A: Ne venez plus jusqu'ici pour me faire des misères./B: Moi, je vous fais des misères?/A: Je ne dis pas que vous m'en faites. Mais vous voudriez bien m'en faire." (Pagnol 1989: 37).

We propose four principles for the interpretation of texts: (a) semantic and pragmatic information is often implicit; (b) people communicate more information by means of implicatures and inferences; (c) non-standard cases of misunderstanding (for the standard case see Weigand 1999) are not marginal or sporadic, but rather central and frequent; (d) the recipient may never be sure that he has detected all the implicit information, nor that he has given the right interpretation to the explicit signs or signals.

In order to achieve a felicitous communication these principles have to be added to those we shall call 'the morality principles', for instance, the principle of 'passive avoidance' of any lexical choice and of any syntactical scheme that could produce misunderstanding.

According to Weigand (1999: 765), research has to keep separate 'difficulty to understand', 'non-understanding' and 'misunderstanding'. She quotes the skeptical and the pessimistic opinions of those who consider miscommunication not as a failure but as part and parcel of the act of communication. Hence, conversation failure appears to be the rule rather than the exception. To all these features Weigand adds that the interlocutor who misunderstands is not aware of it. On the contrary, someone who is subject to non-understanding or has difficulties in understanding, is aware of it.

Here are some other definitions:

- Non-coincidence between the speaker's meaning and the interlocutor's interpretation.

If voluntary, misunderstanding is a strategic choice and presupposes certain stratagems. The latter label has nothing to do with the stratagems elaborated by Schopenhauer (1991). More useful than a definition are the classes of phenomena called misunderstandings; they are almost all of a semantic and pragmatic nature:

- the concept hidden in a lexeme is controversial, obscure, vague;
- the error of interpretation is due to intercultural differences;
- in the given situation of utterance the identification of a referent is doubtful, as in "A: We are going to speak to Mary./B: Which Mary?";
- a text word is polysemous;
- a text word belongs to a pair or a set of homonyms, cf. It. "di" the preposition and the imperative; a parallel example, in Romanian "zi".

Such examples are generally not a threat to the felicity of communication, just as the so-called 'false friends' are not; some additional examples: It. *Ha l'ora?* vs. *Allora?*; *Giovanni ed io* vs. *Giovanni e Dio*. (Some nuances of pronunciation can be ignored).

- pragmatic misunderstanding, as in "A: Est-ce que tu sais où se trouve le journal?/B: Je vais te le chercher./A: Non, c'est bon, dis-moi seulement où il est" (Trognon & Saint Dizier 1999).
- misunderstandings due to intertextuality. If, for example, the target text is clear for "Traduire c'est trahir un peu" or "Mourir c'est partir un peu", a considerable number of examples (especially literary ones, which presuppose a rich personal encyclopedia on the part of the recipient) are difficult to interpret. We know that the notion of difficulty of a text is relative and subjective: a text is difficult for person WX in circumstances YZ. But these remarks concern rather the difficulty to understand

than misunderstanding; we have quoted them because the reader is very often aware of the fact that the decoding of a text needs an intertextual reference.

The syntactic scheme allows for more than one decoding on the syntactic level.

3. The content levels of an utterance

The analysis of concrete cases of misunderstanding takes into account layers of significance especially at the pragmatic level of the utterances. Dascal describes the layers of significance by means of four questions (Dascal 1999: 773): What did he say?; What was the story about?; Why did he bother to say it?; Why did he say it in the way he said it?

In the following, we shall present our conception of the content strata (layers or levels) of an utterance (see Stati 1990).

Every utterance placed in a discourse has a content articulated as follows:

(a) a sequence of lexical meanings;

(b) a sequence of syntactic functions (subject, predicate, direct object, complement of time etc.): naturally the question may arise about the 'content character' of the syntactic functions, which is uncontroversial except for the circumstantial complements;

(c) a modality; the speaker expresses his attitude concerning the content represented by the preceding two strata; he may declare it certain, possible, desired, obligatory, etc.. The modality is expressed by means of modal adverbs, modal verbs, the modes of the verbs and also by means of the para-linguistic signals called intonation;

(d) a pragmatic function equivalent to illocutionary force. The pragmatic function is obligatory, in the sense that there is no utterance without such a function;

(e) an argumentative role; this content feature is present only in some utterances; the roles are frequent in argumentative texts, as well as in texts where argumentation is a dominant feature; in other texts, they could alternate with descriptive and narrative utterances.

Misunderstanding may appear at each level.

The simultaneous presence of pragmatic and argumentative characteristics is shown by examples such as the following: an utterance is at the same time a question (pragmatic function) and an objection (argumentative role). The distinction between the last two content strata is not a clearcut one, since argumentative roles could be included among the pragmatic functions. In addition to the four above-mentioned levels, misunderstanding may appear in the process of interpretation of the relationship with regard to the reference of the entire utterance or of one piece of it (for instance, identifying the referent of a nominal group).

A last type of misunderstanding regards the cases of errors in the identification of the text to which our text is in the relationship of intertextuality.

4. The crisis of the code-based interpretation

Traditional ('old-fashioned') as well as structural linguistics has accustomed us to the methodological principle according to which if a discourse gives us certain information this is expressed by a signal; and if it is evident that the number of signals detected is smaller by far than the number of items of information expressed, the linguist could reply that there are also phenomena of amalgamation, coalescence, syncretism, ellipsis and so on. This is the code-based model of discourse interpretation.

Code-based approaches treat communication as involving a set of observable signals, a set of unobservable messages and a code, i.e. a set of rules or procedures pairing messages with signals. Successful code-based communication results in duplication of messages : the message encoded is identical to the message received. Grice's works in the late sixties showed that communication is possible without the use of a code. For the criticism of the code-based interpretation of discourse see Deirdre Wilson (1997).

As far as misunderstanding is concerned, we should take into account the cases of difficulty or impossibility to detect the original intentions of the author when adequate signals are missing.

Code theories have been replaced by inferential theories inspired by the works of Paul Grice (see, for instance, Grice 1975) which treat utterances merely as evidence concerning the speaker's intentions. Intentions are not decoded but inferred. The existence of numerous pieces of information without a material basis or pivot gives credit to the opinion that "anything that can be communicated can be encoded". An argument favourable to inference theory (constructed by Dan Sperber and Deirdre Wilson; their conception is best known as the "relevance hypothesis", see Jucker 1995) is the fact that context dependance fits better with an inferential theory than a code-based approach. Further research in this field will establish the proportions of signalled and of inferred pieces of information at each level of the utterance content. Obviously, attention should be also paid to the situations in which inferred information is corroborated by signalled information.

5. Conclusion

Misunderstanding is a real, practical phenomenon which can, in principle, result in serious impediments to the transmission of messages. Nevertheless, we shall not adhere to the aphorism "Communication is inherently miscommunication"; its importance must not be overestimated inter alia because people dispose of other means of communicating and the simultaneous production of verbal and non-verbal signs corroborated with information transmitted by means of the situational context and/or contained in the interlocutors' encyclopedia compensate for the failure of the verbal code. "Incommunicability" exists as a philosophical and epistemological problem, about which writers and dramatists may be passionate but it has little relevance in practical communication and small chat. Therefore, I have only mentioned the phenomenon. In addition, I have formulated a kind of moral principle: be careful and avoid possible sources of misunderstanding! This guideline applies to interpretation errors due to the 'langue' system, as well as misunderstanding when the 'parole' conditions are favourable. The risk of being misunderstood persists in spite of our care to be clear and precise in the choice of lexemes and syntactic schemes. Eventually we shall have to resign ourselves to the inevitability of misunderstanding. Not everything can be expressed explicitly.

Apparently, Dialogue has been forgotten in favour of other features of misunderstanding. In effect, it has always been present, from the very first to the last page of this paper. The common denominator of all the features which have been discussed is Dialogue.

References

Allwood, Jens/Yanhia Abelar (1984): Lack of Understanding, Misunderstanding and Language Acquisition. – In: Extra & Mittner (eds.): Proceedings of the AILA Conference, Brussels, 1984.
Dascal, Marcelo (1999): Introduction: Some questions about misunderstanding. – *Journal of Pragmatics* 31(6), 753–762.
Giraudoux, Jean (1987): Electre, Paris.
Grice, Paul (1975): Logic and Conversation. – In: P. Cole/J. L. Morgan (eds.), Syntax and Semantics 3, 41–58. New York: Academic Press.
Jucker, Andreas (1995): Discourse Analysis and Relevance. – In: F. Hundsnurscher/E. Weigand (eds.), Future Perspectives of Dialogue Analysis, 121–146. Tübingen: Niemeyer.
Pagnol, Marcel (1989): Angèle, Paris.
Schopenhauer, Arthur (1991): L'arte di ottenere ragione esposta in 38 stratagemmi, Italian translation. Milano: Adelphi. (orig. 1864).
Stati, Sorin (1990): Le transphrastique, Paris: PUF.

Trognon, Alain and Valérie Saint-Dizier (1999): L'organisation conversationnelle des malentendus: le cas du dialogue tutorial. – *Journal of Pragmatics* 31, 787–815.

Weigand, Edda (1999): Misunderstanding: the Standard Case. – *Journal of Pragmatics* 31, 763–785.

Wilson, Deirdre (1997): Linguistic Structure and Inferential Communication. Paper Presented to the 16th International Congress of Linguists, Paris 20–25 July 1997.

Anita Fetzer

Infelicitous Communication or Degrees of Misunderstanding?

1. Introduction

Communication and miscommunication are frequently interpreted as representing discrete categories. If communication is successful, we talk about felicitous communication, and if it is unsuccessful, we talk about infelicitous communication or miscommunication. But can the notions of felicitous communication and understanding, and infelicitous communication and misunderstanding really be used as synonyms? That is to say, is the concept of understanding really binary or is it rather scalar? Are there degrees of understanding and degrees of misunderstanding? And how do they manifest themselves in discourse?

The goal of this contribution is to investigate the concepts of understanding and misunderstanding and their manifestations in discourse in the framework of the dialogue act of a plus/minus-validity claim. It is anchored to an integrative approach to dialogue and argues in favour of a dynamic conception of understanding, which refers to both the process of explicitating an utterance's contextual references and the product resulting from calculating their communicative meaning. Thus, infelicities result from inconsistencies regarding the explicitation of contextual references and the calculation of communicative meaning. In dialogue, however, these inconsistencies are generally negotiated and repaired and are thus an integral part of the dialogue. Sections I and II examine the dichotomy of understanding and misunderstanding in the frameworks of speech act theory and conversation analysis. Section III systematises the results obtained and supplements them with John Gumperz's conception of conversational inference. Section IV introduces the dialogue act of a plus/minus-validity claim and explicates understanding and misunderstanding as dialogical concepts. Section V concludes by comparing and contrasting understanding and misunderstanding in institutional and noninstitutional contexts.

2. Understanding and misunderstanding in speech act theory

In speech act theory, the minimal unit of investigating felicitous communication or understanding is the speech act. The meaning of a speech act is anchored to the intended effects on the hearer and calculated with regard to (1) what the speaker means, (2) what the sentence uttered means, (3) what the speaker intends, and (4) what the hearer understands. Or, to employ Searle's terminology: "S intends to produce IE [intended effects, AF] in H by means of getting H to recognize S's intention to produce IE" (1969:47). As regards felicitous communication in speech act theory, the understanding of a speech act can go wrong in each of these categories. Yet miscommunication and infelicitous communication can not be used as synonyms: miscommunication is anchored to the cognitive domains of inference and decoding, and manifests itself in the literal interpretation of indirect speech acts, such as taking the speaker-intended rejection of an invitation, *I have to go to the dentist*, literally. Infelicitous communication is anchored to a speech act's felicity conditions and manifests itself in the speaker's inappropriate performance of a speech act. It is categorised by Austin (cf. Austin 1980:18) into misfires, i.e. misinvocations and misexecutions, which are defined in the frameworks of conventions, coparticipants and the complete and correct performance of a speech act, and abuses, which are defined with regard to the coparticipants' attitudes, viz. sincerity and responsibility. In misfires the act is purported but void: it is 'misinvocated' and thus disallowed, or it is 'misexecuted' and therefore vitiated. In abuses, the act is professed but hollow, as the coparticipants do not have the necessary attitudes. For instance, the act of promising can go wrong because the coparticipants do not have the sincere attitude of wishing to perform a future act, because they promise some act which has already been performed, or because they promise some act which is not beneficial to the hearer.

To summarise and conclude, misunderstanding in the research paradigm of speech act theory is anchored to the miscalculation of the speaker-intended meaning regarding the dichotomy of direct and indirect speech acts, and to inappropriate felicity conditions. In the following section, misunderstanding is investigated in the realm of conversation analysis.

3. Understanding and misunderstanding in conversation

Contrary to speech act theory's philosophical approach to language and communication, conversation analysis examines authentic data and is thus firmly anchored to empiricism.

In this setting, language is not investigated in isolation but always in context. As a consequence of this, the meaning of an utterance does not exist in isolation. Rather, it is interactionally organised and intrinsically linked to the coparticipants and their employment of the turn-taking system, to interruptions and repair. Thus, neither understanding nor misunderstanding represent discrete phenomena. Rather, they are anchored to the immediate social and linguistic contexts where they manifest themselves in the coparticipant's employment of an acknowledgement signifying understanding or a request for clarification, if there is a lack of understanding. For this reason, understanding and misunderstanding are always local and retrospective. The concept of misunderstanding is further refined by Blum-Kulka & Weizman (1998) with regard to its negotiated and non-negotiated status, and by Grimshaw (1980) and Hinnenkamp (1998). Allen D. Grimshaw adopts the local and retrospective perspective and supplements it with the premise that social actors act in a rational and intentional manner. He categorises the outcomes of communicative events as (1) understanding as intended, where no misunderstanding occurs, (2) nonhearings, i.e. no acoustic signal is received, (3) no (or partial or ambiguous) understanding, viz. an acoustic signal is received but the hearer deliberately chooses to ignore it, (4) mishearings, that is the hearer believes that s/he has heard and interpreted an utterance in the speaker-intended manner, when this is not the case, and (5) misunderstanding, where the hearer is able to infer either the speaker-intended variant or the non-intended variant, and deliberately chooses the latter. Grimshaw thus extends the traditional frame of reference, which assumes that coparticipants have the intention of understanding utterances in the speaker-intended manner, by introducing the parasitic element of deliberate misunderstanding, which is employed in a strategic manner.

To summarise and conclude, misunderstanding has been described as both a social and a cognitive phenomenon, which is manifest in the discursive strategies of reformulation, i.e. self- and other-reformulation, and repair, viz. self- and other-repair, and in mishaps in the allocation of turns, such as overlaps or interruptions. Thus, misunderstanding and understanding are local and retrospective by definition.

4. Understanding, misunderstanding & conversational inference

From the examination of understanding and misunderstanding in speech act theory and in conversation, it has become apparent that both understanding and misunderstanding represent scalar concepts with fuzzy boundaries. For this reason, it seems more appropriate to talk about degrees of understanding and degrees of misunderstanding. Furthermore, it has been shown that understanding and misunderstanding can only be accounted for if linguistic and social contexts are seen as integral parts of natural-language communication. Because of this extension of the contextual framework, a context-bound process of interpretation is required, namely conversational inference, which John Gumperz defines as follows:

> 'Conversational inference', as I use the term, is the 'situated' or context-bound process of interpretation, by means of which participants in a conversation assess other's intentions, and on which they base their responses. (...) Conversational inference, (...), is part of the very act of conversing. One indirectly or implicitly illustrates one's understanding of what is said through verbal and nonverbal responses, by the way one builds on what one hears to participate in a conversation, rather than through talking about it in abstract terms. (Gumperz 1977:191)

Contrary to the individual-centred conception of inference in the research paradigm of cognitive science, conversational inference is a dialogical concept par excellence: it is anchored to the coparticipants and their calculation of communicative meaning, which is not restricted to local contexts but rather extends to speech activities, communicative projects and discourse genres, and the expectations about thematic progression, constraints on content and turn-taking. As a consequence of this, understanding and misunderstanding – or the contextualisation and "miscontextualisation" of utterances – are constitutive parts of conversation, as is illustrated by the examination of the following dialogue adopted from Levinson (1983:292):

A-1: I have a fourteen year old son
B-1: Well that's all right
A-2: I also have a dog
B-2: Oh I'm sorry

Here the two speakers A and B produce and exchange two utterances each. Speaker A refers to her/himself by the indexical *I* and predicates that she or he has a fourteen year old son in A-1, and that she or he has a dog in A-2. As regards the setting, the referent of the indexical *I* is retrieved through a process of inferencing, in which s/he is identified as the source of the utterance, i.e. the speaker A. This also obtains for the employment of the indexical *I* in the utterance B-2, which also refers to the source of the utterance, namely speaker B. Analogously, the communicative meaning of the indexical *that* employed in the utterance B-1 is retrieved and identified as the previous utterance. In contrast to this individual-centred viewpoint, a conversational-inference perspective takes the analysis one step further by integrating the speech event and the social and linguistic contexts. As a consequence of this, the discursive meaning of the indexicals *I* and *that* is retrieved and calculated in the framework of the speech event of interviewing a potential tenant. In this setting, the indexical *I* does not only refer to the source, viz. the speaker A or B, but rather to the source and their social and interactional roles, i.e. landlady or landlord and a potential tenant. Moreover, the utterance A-1 does not only express an assertion, i.e. a self-reference and predication, but this assertion simultaneously functions as a query whether a family would qualify as a tenant of the apartment. The response B-1 gives an affirmative answer to the implicit yes/no-question and prompts speaker A to produce a further question regarding the qualification for apartment tenancy, namely whether having a dog would also be allowed. This is declined by speaker B. In this specific context the rejection also functions as the initiation of a conversational closing.

Yet natural-language communication is not only a context-dependent and dialogical activity anchored to speaker, hearer and their interactional roles. Rather, the notion context can be differentiated into an immediate context, viz. adjacent utterances, and more remote contexts, such as a communicative project, discourse genre and institutionalized communication. For this reason, the investigation of understanding and misunderstanding requires a framework which accounts for dialogue and context. Such a frame of reference, the dialogue act of a plus/minus-validity claim, is introduced in the following.

5. The dialogue act of a plus/minus-validity claim

In his *Theory of communicative action* (1987) Jürgen Habermas defines communication as speakers postulating validity claims which are ratified by the hearers' acceptance or rejection. In this setting, the hearer's ratification of a postulated validity claim is a necessary condition for felicitous communication and therefore a constitutive part of a communicative action. In spite of the fact that Jürgen Habermas's approach is primarily macro or top-down, the dialogue principle of ratification can be adapted to the investigation of micro settings. As regards the conversation examined above, speaker A postulates the validity claim A-1, which is ratified and accepted by speaker B in the utterance B-1. Then speaker A postulates a further validity claim A-2, which is thematically linked to A-1 by the adverbial *also* and the indexical *that*. This is ratified by speaker B and the utterance B-2, which from a linguistic-surface viewpoint realises an apology but has the communicative function of a rejection. But does the dialogue act of a plus/minus-validity claim really provide new insights?

The dialogue act of a plus/minus-validity claim does not only refer to the actual surface structure of an utterance but rather gives a principled account of its embeddedness in context (Fetzer 2000, 2002). More precisely, validity claims are anchored to an interactive tripartite system of objective, subjective and social worlds and their presuppositions, as is schematised by figure I:

Figure 1:

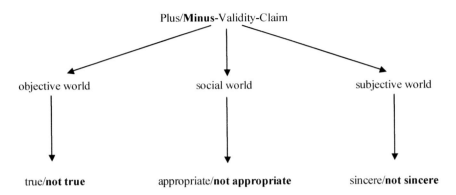

In this dialogue setting, the postulation of a validity claim is intrinsically linked to its linguistic representation and cannot be separated from it. The constitutive system of objective, subjective and social worlds is defined as follows:

- The objective world is determined by the dichotomy of true / false. References to this world are characterised by theoretical claims represented in the propositional format, i.e. reference and predication. Their mode of linguistic representation is direct / explicit, *I have a fourteen year old son*, for example. The non-acceptance of a validity claim's references to the objective world is represented by syntactic and semantic negation, *you do not qualify for apartment tenancy*, for example.

As regards the conversation examined above, validity claims referring to the objective world are realised by *speaker has a son, that is all right, speaker has a dog* and *speaker is sorry*.

- The subjective world is determined by the premise of sincerity, i.e. speaker's communicative intention(s) meant as uttered, and interpreted as meant. References to this world represent emotive information and their mode of representation is non-linear, i.e. simultaneously explicit / implicit, e.g. non- and paraverbal behaviour. While the acceptance of a validity claim's references to the subjective world is manifest in sincere communication, their non-acceptance is generally referred to as lying.

The subjective-world premise of sincerity is also implicit in Recanati's concept of a reflexive intention which is defined by default reflexivity and therefore refers to *not* a certain type of intention, e.g. deception or insincerity (Recanati 1986:234). Furthermore, it is implicit in the ethnomethodological principle of the sanctioned use of doubt (Garfinkel 1994).

Infelicitous Communication

As regards our dialogue, references to this world have not been accounted for explicitly. In general, they are realised by the interlocutor's tone of voice and other paralinguistic and nonverbal signals.

- The social world is determined by the paradigm of appropriateness. References to this world are represented both explicitly and implicitly.

As regards our dialogue, validity claims referring to this world are realised by the actual utterances A-1, B-1, A-2 and B-2.

The social world can be categorised into another tripartite system of textual, interpersonal and interactional presuppositions, as is schematised by figure II:

Figure II:

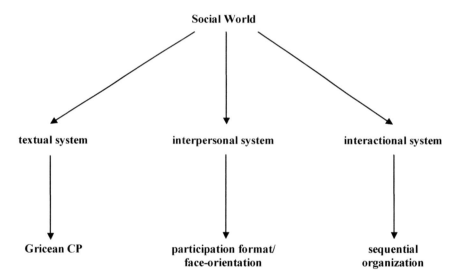

- The textual subsystem is governed by the Gricean CP (Grice 1975), the maxims and the implicatures derived from them. It covers both explicit and implicit modes of linguistic representation. While an explicit representation does not infringe on the maxims of quality, quantity, relation and manner, an implicit representation infringes on one or more of the maxims thus generating a conversational implicature.

As regards our conversation above, validity claims referring to the textual system are realised explicitly by *I have a fourteen year old son* and implicitly by *also*.

- The interpersonal subsystem is determined by the production and reception format (Goffman 1974; Levinson 1988) and the participants' face wants / needs (Brown and Levinson 1987).

As regards our conversation above, validity claims referring to the interpersonal system are realised by the indexical *I* referring to the individual interlocutors and their status in the participation format as speaker and hearer, and their participant roles. They are also realised by the predications *be all right* and *be sorry* which refer to the participants' face wants. While the rather informal expression *all right* indexes the participant's positive face by establishing solidarity, the latter indexes the participant's negative face and conveys respect.

- The interactional subsystem is governed by the sequential organisation of discourse. It is based on the principles of conditional relevance and adjacency (Levinson 1983), and is only explicitly referred to in a negotiation-of-validity sequence.

As regards our conversation examined above, validity claims referring to the interactional system are realised by the indexicals *well* and *oh*, which refer to the prior communicative contributions A-1 and A-2 thus establishing local coherence; and they are also realised by the sequential positioning of the individual contributions.

In natural-language communication, interlocutors postulate, ratify and negotiate the communicative status of validity claims anchored to the three worlds and their presuppositions. Contrary to Jürgen Habermas's conception of the postulation and ratification of a validity claim, which can consist of a single reference to the objective world only, interlocutors in natural-language communication postulate at least three validity claims in their communicative contribution and thus refer to the objective, social and subjective worlds, and each validity claim requires ratification. In the case of accepting all of the references to the three worlds, the overall validity claim is assigned the status of a plus-validity claim and attributed to the interlocutors' discourse common ground. Moreover, it is not only the overall validity claim, which is attributed to the discourse common ground but also the validity claims referring to the individual worlds and their presuppositions. In the case of rejecting one or more references to the three worlds, the overall validity claim is assigned the status of a minus-validity claim and not attributed to the discourse common ground. Instead, a negotiation-of-validity sequence is initiated, in which the non-accepted claims are made explicit. Only then is it possible to negotiate and reject or accept them. Once agreement has been reached about their status, it is possible to re-establish the discourse common ground and attribute the accepted claims and their presuppositions to it.

In the validity-claim of reference, understanding is intrinsically linked to misunderstanding. Moreover, misunderstanding is understood both as process and product. For this reason, misunderstanding can occur in the process of assigning contextual references, and it can be the product of the ratification of a validity claim. Thus, misunderstanding is a product of something having gone wrong in the process of contextualisation. But is contextualisation only linked to the actual micro level? Let us return to our dialogue about children and dogs, where having a fourteen-year-old son is accepted whereas having a dog is met with implicit rejection. Without any further contextual information this exchange seems quite odd. But does it qualify as some kind of misunderstanding?

In the four adjacent utterances, there is no reformulation, no repair and there do not seem to be any problems regarding the allocation of turns. For this reason, we cannot really classify this exchange as some sort of misunderstanding. But still, the exchange seems somehow strange despite the number of cohesive links employed, such as *also*, despite the identity of the speakers and despite the speech act of acceptance. So, which further criteria do we need as leading to understanding or misunderstanding?

So far, a context-dependent conception of communication as dialogue has been identified as a necessary condition for the investigation of understanding and misunderstanding. But is this a sufficient condition? To answer this question, the notion of context-dependence requires to be refined upon, as context can, in principle refer to anything and everything. So what is context? Firstly, there is the differentiation between linguistic context and social context. Secondly, coparticipants do not really exchange utterances only – or postulate and ratify validity claims. Rather, they exchange validity claims in a particular frame, discourse genre or communicative project. For this reason, the frame and setting, in which validity claims are exchanged, is of crucial importance for the investigation of understanding and misunderstanding. That is, if we frame our dialogue as some kind of small talk, the response B-2 seems quite inappropriate and would be classified as misunderstanding, which would have to be negotiated. If we frame the conversation as an interview about the qualification for apartment tenancy, the response B-2 makes perfect sense.

As a consequence of this, an investigation of understanding and misunderstanding requires both a bottom-up and a top-down approach to communication. The relevance of a top-down approach to discourse has been put forward by a number of researchers, such as P. Linell (1995, 1998) who regards communication as a communicative project and of S. Sarangi and S. Slembrouck's work on bureaucratic discourse (1996), which is elaborated on in the following section.

6. Understanding and misunderstanding in institutional contexts

Understanding and misunderstanding have been defined as scalar phenomena, which are context-dependent by definition. Furthermore, it has been shown that the complexity of these phenomena can only be captured in supplementing a bottom-up approach to communication with a top-down frame of reference. While the former focuses on the retrieval of immediate contextual information in order to be able to calculate conversational implicatures and communicative meaning, the latter requires conversational inferencing. From a bottom-up perspective, the communicative meaning of the questions *how many children do you have* or *where do you live* are contextualised or interpreted as a request for information regarding the size of family, marital status or availability and may thus be negotiated. From an institutional-communication viewpoint, which is top-down by definition, their communicative meaning is not negotiable. Here, they are contextualised with regard to specific communicative goals, such as the qualification for social security benefits, as convincingly argued for by Sarangi and Slembrouck: "Turns and contributions receive interpretations which are different from 'standard' conversational practices" (1996:43). As regards the interpretation of contextual references to the social world, their interpretation is predetermined by different presuppositions: in the framework of the interactional presuppositions the initiating moves are generally allocated to the bureaucrat while the responsive moves are allocated to the client. In the framework of the interpersonal presuppositions the coparticipants' face-wants are fairly neutral regarding the positive face, but quite high regarding the bureaucrat's negative face. In the framework of the textual presuppositions the calculation of conversational implicatures follows, according to Sarangi and Slembrouck, subservient procedures: "Also, whatever information clients volunteer is not interpreted in terms of expressive contents load, but only in terms of procedural routines. You cannot rely on letting your utterance speak, because the information contained in the utterance itself is subservient to procedures" (1996:45). As a consequence of this, "[t]he same linguistic structure may mean different things in different institutional contexts and may thus affect the talk in different ways depending on the mode the talk is embedded in" (1996:64).

To summarise and conclude, natural-language communication is characterised by degrees of understanding and degrees of misunderstanding. Communication does not occur in a void, but rather in linguistic and social contexts. In this setting, coparticipants are rational and intentional agents, who negotiate the communicative status of a validity claim by explicitating its contextual references. For this reason, understanding a validity claim is both process and product. As regards its status as process, understanding is synonymous with the contextualisation of an utterance, which is a necessary condition for the calculation of the product: its communicative meaning. Degrees of understanding and misunderstanding can occur in the process of calculating the communicative meaning of a validity claim, and they can occur with the product, the ratification of a validity claim.

References

Austin, John L.(1980): How to do Things with Words. – Cambridge: Cambridge University Press
Blum-Kulka, Shoshana/Weizman, Elda (1988): The Inevitability of Misunderstandings: Discourse ambiguities – *Text* 8(3), 219–241.
Brown, Penelope/Levinson, Stephen (1987): Politeness. Some universals in language usage. Cambridge: Cambridge University Press.
Fetzer, Anita (2000): Negotiating Validity Claims in Political Interviews – *Text* 20 (4), 1–46.
– (2002). Micro Situations and Macro Structures: Natural-Language Communication and Context – *Context in Context. A Special Issue of Foundations of Science* 7 (3), 255–291.
Garfinkel, Harold (1994): Studies in Ethnomethodology. Cambridge: Polity Press.
Goffman, Erving (1974): Frame Analysis. – Boston: North Eastern University Press.
Grice, H. Paul (1975): Logic and Conversation. – In: P. Cole/J.L.Morgan (eds.): Syntax and Semantics, vol. 3, 41–58. N.Y.: Academic Press.
Grimshaw, Allan D. (1980): Mishearings, Misunderstandings, and other Nonsuccesses in Talk: A plea for redress of speaker-oriented bias. – *Sociological Inquiry* 50, 31–74.
Gumperz, John J. (1977): Sociocultural Knowledge in Conversational Inference. – In: Saville-Troike, M. (ed.): Linguistics and Anthropology, 191–211. Washington D.C: Washingten University Press,.
– (1991): Contextualization and Understanding. – In: Duranti, A./C. Goodwin (eds.): Rethinking Context, 229–252. Cambridge: Cambridge University Press.
Habermas, Jürgen (1987): Theorie des kommunikativen Handelns. – Frankfurt: Suhrkamp.
Hinnenkamp, Volker (1998): Missverständnisse in Gesprächen: eine empirische Untersuchung im Rahmen der interpretativen Soziolinguistik. – Opladen: Westdeutscher Verlag.
Levinson, Stephen C. (1983): Pragmatics. – Cambridge: Cambridge University Press.
– (1988): Putting Linguistics on a Proper Footing: Explorations in Goffman's concepts of participation. – In: Drew, P./Wootton, A.(eds.): Erving Goffman. Exploring the Interaction Order, 161–227. Cambridge: Cambridge University Press.
Linell, Per (1995): Troubles with Mutualities: Towards a dialogical theory of misunderstanding and miscommunication. – In: Marková, I./Grauman, C./K. Foppa (eds.): Mutualities in Dialogue, 176–213. Cambridge: Cambridge University Press.
– (1998): Approaching Dialogue. – Amsterdam: Benjamins.
Recanati, Francois (1986): On Defining Communicative Intentions – *Mind & Language* 1(3), 213–242.
Sarangi, Srikant and Slembrouck, Stef (1996): Language. Bureaucracy & Social Control. – London: Longman.
Searle, John (1969): Speech Acts. – Cambridge: Cambridge University Press.
Watts, Richard. W., Ide, Sachiko and Ehlich, Konrad (eds.)(1992): Politeness in Language. Berlin: de Gruyter.
Weizman, Elda (1998): Individual Intentions and Collective Purposes: the Case of News Interviews. – In: Chmejrková, S., Hoffmannova, J., Müllerova, O., Svetla, J. (eds.): Dialoganalyse VI, 268–280. Tübingen: Niemeyer.

Ernest W. B. Hess-Lüttich

Understanding Misunderstanding: Kafka's *The Trial*

1. Conversation, Kafkaësque

Kafka's novel *The Trial* has been recently described as a satirical burlesque, unmasking absurdities of contemporary Austrian law (Ziolkowski 1996), or as a psychoanalytical case study of paranoia (Schmidhäuser 1996), resulting from a guilt complex of a Jewish lawyer unable to accept his homosexuality (cf. Mecke 1982). In this paper, I shall propose a different perspective taking a closer look at the specific structure of dialogue presented in the text.

The novel begins with the famous sentence "Jemand mußte Josef K. verleumdet haben [...]".[1] The indefinite pronoun and modal verb set the stylistical tone of indeterminacy and uncertainty, which is characteristic for the novel from this point on.[2] This is neither to be achieved through the "objectivity" of "omniscient" narration, the multi-perspective "single subjectivities", nor through a "unidimensional" self of identification ["Identifikations-Ich"]. Certainties are, however, the basis of every non-pathological communication. Two of the fundamental conditions are singled out here, derived from perception psychology and logic of interaction: the psychological condition of an object's consistency ["Objektkonstanz"] and the condition of communicative norms of action.

---

[1] Franz Kafka, *Der Process*. Historisch-kritische Ausgabe, ed. Roland Reuß in Zusammenarbeit mit Peter Staengle. – Frankfurt am Main: Stroemfeld 1998. An electronic edition is available from Chadwyck-Healey since 2000ff. As this paper does not pursue any philological interests, I am quoting from the following edition: Franz Kafka, *Gesammelte Werke*, ed. Max Brod, 7 vols. Frankfurt am Main: Fischer 1976: vol. 2, 7. An earlier draft of this paper appeared in *Journal of The Kafka Society of America* 15. 1–2 (1991): 37–52 ("The rhetoric of Misunderstanding in Kafka's *The Trial*"). Most recently, Strelka (2001) devoted a booklength study to the comparison of "Kafkaësque elements" in Kafka's novels with special attention to his use of parabolic narrative.

[2] A topos of Kafka research: cf. Allemann (1963: 259); Krusche (1974: 35). Ziolkowski (1996: 335) gives a very precise account of the contemporary discussion of law and law philosophy in Austria and Germany. He argues that the first sentence explicitly refers to Austrian law ("Verleumdung", cf. §§ 209–210 Österreichisches Strafgesetz 1852) as opposed to German law ("falsche Anschuldigung", cf. §§ 164–165 RStGB [Reichsstrafgesetzbuch] 1871).

According to Piaget, the requirement for the orientation of a person in the world is the development of "objective" invariants of perception structures.[3] Certainties of the identification of ego and alter, space and time, classification and causality are constants which are derivative thereof. If ego and alter communicate, they mutually presuppose the function of conventionalized expectations of normal interaction patterns ["Normalformerwartungen"]. If ego perceives the object x as x at time t and at place 1, it expects and presupposes that, given the same pragmatic conditions, alter will perceive x as x. If x is a stable object, perhaps an artefact, ego then assumes that the perceived object x at time t_1 will still be x at time t_2. Expectations of interactional logic are based on the stability of routine experience (idealisation of iterative ability ["Iterierbarkeitsidealisierung"]). Communicative understanding cannot succeed without dependence on assumptions of regularity ["Regelmässigkeitsannahmen"]. If the rules are transgressed, compatible patterns of reinterpretation, which explain the deviation and establish a new stability of action, must be available.

The entire first section of the novel is a series of infractions of such expectations of normal interaction patterns. Possibilities for reinterpretation are not offered. First the rule is named – "die Köchin der Frau Grubach, seiner Zimmervermieterin, die ihm jeden Tag gegen acht Uhr früh das Frühstück brachte", then its transgression – "kam diesmal nicht. Das war noch niemals geschehen" (7). The neighbor observes him "mit einer an ihr ganz ungewöhnlichen Neugierde"; instead of the expected cook a man arrives "den er in dieser Wohnung noch niemals gesehen hatte". K.'s questions go unanswered and explanations are not offered.

Later K. is forced to realize that his typifications of objects ["Objekttypisierungen"] have become so precarious that dependable expectations are no longer possible. He cannot find the law court, which is actually well-known to him, the street is longer than he remembers, and the house is bigger than expected; he asks for an arbitrary name of the carpenter Lanz (36) so that he will appear inconspicuous (!), just to find that this is what the wife of the bailiff has been expecting. The anticipation of "normal" reactions proves to be increasingly false. This, in turn, leads to a distrust of the possibility and certainty of such anticipation with respect to objects in the environment as well as to his dialogue partners.

The dissolution of objective invariants leads, however, inevitably (thus some critics' impression of "Ohnmacht" and "necessity") to the dissolution of logical categories. The self-evident becomes questionable, the obvious ambivalent. This dissolution leads to a communicative conflict which cannot be resolved within the process, because, due to their relativity, the silent assumptions of the dialogue partners can no longer be the shared basis for understanding. For this reason the stereotypical literary terminology of the "paradoxical

---

[3] Piaget (1963); Furth (1972: 318).

structure of the Kafkaësque" is not precise enough.[4] It is not a matter of the surprising reversal of logically concordant circumstances, but rather the logical conventions of thought themselves are called into question. Fritz Schütze offers a sociological explanation in his examinations of the interaction postulates of everyday dialogues:[5]

> Wenn sich die Normalformerwartungen innerhalb eines Satzes oder Textkontextes widersprechen, dann muß dieser Widerspruch als eine schlüsselsymbolische Anweisung für eine höhersymbolische Reinterpretation der verketteten Wörter und ihrer konkreten Gebrauchssituation wahrgenommen werden. Auch das ist ein generelles wechselseitiges Unterstellungsprinzip für die Anwendung von Wissensbeständen. Seine Mißachtung kann nur als Bruch grundlegender Kooperationsprinzipien oder als Symptom für einen geistigen Defekt verstanden werden.[6]

The principle of cooperation, (that is, the interaction postulate of mutual readiness for understanding between dialogue partners) which is based on shared knowledge and an inventory of rules, is violated repeatedly without explanation or indication (key symbolic instruction ["schlüsselsymbolische Anweisung"]) for a reinterpretation from a logical meta-level, which is again concordant to a logical discordant level of communication. K. is Frau Grubach's "best and most-loved tenant". Nevertheless she simultaneously refuses him the handshake which would seal this empathy; Fräulein Bürstner tolerates his touch, but avoids eye contact and verbal agreement; Leni demonstrates good will to him, but does not ratify the schema of action which he has offered; the wife of the bailiff caresses him, but turns to the student; the prison chaplain in the cathedral does not fulfill K.'s expectations, but antipathy cannot be attributed to him due to simultaneous friendliness.[7]

Such internally contradictory sign-clusters in direct dialogue have been seen, according to an approach in communication psychology which has become popular,[8] as an integral part of the aetiology of schizophrenic syndromes. The definition of schizophrenia as the non-acceptance of communication on the basis of a hypersensitive perception of the envi-

---

[4] Cf. exemplary Kobs (1970), chapter A ("Die Dichtung des Paradoxen"); Politzer (1978), Chapter IV ("Parabel und Paradox"); to a critique cf. Neumann (1973: 464ff.) et passim.

[5] Cf. Schütze (1978).

[6] Schütze (1980: 74): "If the expectations of normal interaction patterns within a sentence or context of a text contradict each other [...], then this contradiction must be perceived as a key symbolic instruction for a higher symbolic reinterpretation of the word chain and its concrete situational use. This is also a general and mutual presupposition for the application of knowledge. The disregard of this principle can only be understood as a rupture of fundamental principles of cooperation or a symptom of a psychic defect."

[7] Binder (1976b) has contributed an extensive amount of material on the nonverbal behavior of dialogue figures in the novels (above all, as mentioned, in *Der Verschollene* and *Das Schloß*, without devoting the appropriate amount of attention to fundamental (for text interpretation) semantic contradictions of semiotic signals in dialogue.

[8] I am referring to the Bateson School: cf. Bateson et al. (eds.) (1975); Watzlawick (1973); to a biographical link of paradoxical structures of communication (in the psychological, not in a logical sense) in the novels with Kafka's familial socialization cf. Kreis (1976).

ronment, in favor of the formation of a personal "logic" (Wittgenstein: "private"; Lacan: "metaphorical"), can be relevant with respect to critical interpretations in literary study of the isolation of the perspective figure, the solitude, the hermeticism, the ruptures in understanding, etc.

Such a hypersensitive perception of the environment ("Überempfindlichkeit" is, by the way, K.'s own ironic explanation for his tendency toward misunderstandings) does not, however, arise from an ontological approximation, but may be defined by the analysis of communication structure. At the beginning of most occurrences of interaction into which K. enters, there exists a seemingly insignificant "misunderstanding" which one immediately forgets again. After the first such misunderstanding, however, understanding does not simply normalize itself, but remains problematic.[9] This begins with the misunderstandings in the dialogues with Frau Grubach and Fräulein Bürstner and ends with the interrogation of the "investigation". K. misinterprets the words of Hasterer ("Du bist ja selbst *schuld*, daß ich dich heute morgen überfalle") in the light of the reprimand of the director and a guilt he is not prepared to acknowledge. "Diesen Vorgang gewissermaßen von innen heraus mitzuerleben, ermöglicht Kafka dem Leser durch ein kunstvoll inszeniertes Mißverständnis des K., dessen Produkt dem Leser nur in einer völlig einseitigen Erzählperspektive aus der Sicht des K. zugänglich gemacht wird".[10] Here a misunderstanding, as a category of communication conflict, can be explained by the strategic function of "forced communicative" asymmetrical dialogues, as Fritz Schütze's empirical studies of institutional speech types, such as examination, interrogation, protocol, and hearing, illustrate.[11]

These fallacies of interactional logic which seem to be insignificant at first sight, and which in nonpathological communication are easily compensated for by "practical idealizations" in the sense of Alfred Schütz[12] lead, because of a much stricter application of rules as in normal everyday conversation, to a deficit of trust with respect to our own competence of perception and typification of a situation. This uncertainty leads, in turn, to an even more extreme and sensitive perception of the environment, which, as reflected in the syntactical structure, carefully registers a plurality of observations of partner behavior even in the most fleeting conversations. In this way the anticipated discrepancies within sign clusters emerge microscopically enlarged and gain dysfunctional importance in comparison to the norm. Already we are in the midst of – in and of itself, just as in some plays of

---

[9] Krusche (1974: 37 and 54ff.) makes this observation in his analysis of the novel *Amerika*, however the "technique" of misunderstanding is slightly different, due to possibilities for a higher symbolical reinterpretation, which leads Krusche to a "glimmer of hope" ["Schimmer von Hoffnung"] (58).
[10] Schmidhäuser (1996: 350); cf. Beißner (1983: 37).
[11] Cf. Schütze (1978).
[12] Schütz (1971).

Ionesco, logically progressive – *circulus vitiosus*, which the critics have always sensed, and which, in my opinion, even surpasses Büchner's *Lenz* in its precision of the portrayal of the increasing loss of everyday communicative encounters.[13] Here the doubt, that gives rise to a failure of understanding, becomes vivid; it is a failure which pushes the possibility for identity through communication with others even further into the distance: "[...] ein Mensch, dünn und schwach in der Ferne und Höhe..." (192).[14]

2. Violation of Interactional Rules

The causes for the impression on the reader of repeated misunderstandings seems to be insufficiently explained in a philologic sense with most ontological (Beissner, Emrich, Ide, Hillmann, Pongs, Weinberg, etc.) or materialistic (Richter, Lukacs, Benjamin, Reimann, Hermsdorf, etc.) categories of Germanistic Kafka research.[15] "Solitude", "desolation", and "monadic existence" result from a series of communicative mistakes. These "mistakes" in K.'s interaction with his environment exist, as shown, foremost in the transgression of rules of interactional logic, such as:

- *The violation in the principle of cooperation* ["Kooperativitätsprinzip"] (Grice), e.g., in the dialogue with Frau Grubach or Fräulein Bürstner, as mentioned earlier; in *The Castle* this technique is even more strongly accentuated, e.g. in the dialogue with Bürgel.[16]
- *A lack of "practical idealizations"* ["praktische Idealisierungen"] (Schütz), e.g., an infraction of the rule for idealisation of iterative ability ["Iterierbarkeitsidealisierung"] in the dissolution of object consistencies or a violation of the rule of idealisation of reciprocity in the insufficient adaptation of mutual systems of relevance; for instance, the selective perception of which semiotic mode, in a multimedial process, bears the most relevant information: i.e., if a discrepancy between the meaning of these modes is not bridged in practical dialogue, this will lead to a so-called "paradoxical" communicative crisis.

---

[13] Cf. Hess-Lüttich (1981: 187–227).
[14] Cf. the symbolism of regression in Kafka!
[15] Cf. Caputo-Mayr/Herz (1987): Franz Kafka: Eine kommentierte Bibliographie der Sekundärliteratur (1955–1980, mit einem Nachtrag 1985); Beicken (1974).
[16] Cf. Krusche (1974: 58ff.) ("Prästabilierte Disharmonie") and 62ff. ("Der Mensch als Monade").

- *Breaks in the formal organization of dialogue and mutual insurance of understanding* (Sacks): (see below the analysis of phasal structure in the dialogue with Titorelli).

- *Uncertainties in the constitution of dependable typification of actors* (Piaget), e.g., analogous to the dissolution of object consistencies ["Objektkonstanzen"] – the disintegration of interactional routines on the basis of a growing loss of trust towards the characters and the personal experience with them: old acquaintances seem suddenly threatening to K., like the young man in the hallway; or routines in old relationships like that with Elsa fading into the periphery.

- *Divergences in the selection of respective schemata of action* (Schütze), e.g., the dialogues between K. and the law court officials, in part also those with Titorelli, cannot lead to mutual understanding. The latter argue strategically within the institutional framework of the court, while K. argues morally within a mundane framework of his personal situation.[17] The total senselessness and inefficiency of K's argumentation results from this divergence. Within a strategic scheme of action, strategic reaction, if it is not made into the object of "discourse" on the metalevel itself, is a condition of argumentative success, and any attempt to transcend the discourse level will itself be subject to strategic interpretation. An illustrative example is K.'s attempt at self defense in the first interrogation, which remains completely fruitless for these reasons. The repeated experience of the futility of personal efforts leads to the (for K.) unexplainable, but accurately described (with "empirical precision", as it were) symptoms of exhaustion, of suffocation, the experience of degradation, and of alienation.

- *Differences in the mutual pragmatic (situation related) and semantic (theme related) definitions of signs*, e.g., K. is forced to take notice of the most irritating discrepancy between the interpretations by his dialogue partners and himself of his situation as someone "being accused". The various comments which the individual dialogue partners attribute to the "trial" share a common feature; they take its potential danger much more seriously than K. is prepared to do. Even in the utilization of legal jargon significant differences exist between K., on the one hand, and all of his dialogue partners on the other.[18] This begins with the misunderstanding of the term "arrest" and its consequences, and ends with the identification of "accusation" and "guilt", objective law and mythical "respect for the written word" in the cathedral dialogue.

---

[17] Cf. Allemann's differentiation between "juridical" and a "completely different" justification (1963: 255ff.); cf. also Schütze (1980) on strategical schemata of action.

[18] Cf. Abraham (1985), especially chapters 1 and 2.

- *Violation of the essential condition of vagueness in colloquial communication* (Garfinkel), e.g., group specific metaphorical concepts are taken literally; this example may be derived from the point above and leads back to the first: the principle of cooperation. With 'Kohlhaasian' obstinacy K. holds onto an everyday use of notions associated with the court; notions which have long been displaced in their semantic content and have become metaphors (accusation, law, guilt, court, right, examination, etc.). He does not enter into the jargon of the mysterious court, which is strange and uncontrollable to him and, therefore, unmanageable, disconcerting, and restrictive. In its place, he utilizes his chain of argumentation, which is, in and of itself, rational, logical, and literal, but with which he maneuvers himself, even linguistically, to the periphery and to a hermetical remoteness.

This series of conditions for Kafkaësque conflicts of communication in the dialogues of *The Trial* is neither exhaustive nor systematic. Its only function is to explain the specific rhetorical structures of the novel within a communication-sociological framework. That is, instead of attempting to explain these structures as a somewhat mythical "dream logic", as some critics have done, or to place the action as a "psychic reflection" in K.'s inner world,[19] it supplies a draft of some linguistic causes for the particular effect of the novel on its readers: a framework for the rhetoric of misunderstanding in *The Trial*.

3. The Dialogue K. / Titorelli – A Phase Structure Analysis

So far, these observations have been displayed systematically. They can, however, also be derived from the macrostructural analysis of concrete phases of conversation. This possibility should be mentioned in the following sketch.

I have excluded one dialogue from the previous discussion: the dialogue K. / Titorelli, based on the fact that Titorelli occupies a unique place in K.'s surroundings. This contrasts him with the other figures with whom K. communicates. Presumably this is also why he has received particular notice in Kafka research.[20] Uyttersprot even bases his argument for the reorganization of the chapters in *The Trial* on the "wahrhaft beherrschende Gestalt dieses Initiierten".[21] The attention that this particular dialogue has attracted in literary scholar-

---

[19] Cf. Allemann (1963: 224); Emrich (1970: 264f.); Schmidhäuser (1996: 345ff.).
[20] Cf. Emrich (1970: 285–297); Sokel (1976: 399–415); Politzer (1978: 325ff.); Frey (1965: 79–95); Hillmann (1973: 56–68).
[21] Uyttersprot (1957: 33f., 54ff. et passim).

ship motivates me to have a closer look at it.[22] In the following sketch, it is taken as an example and as paradigmatic material for the application of new methods of dialogue analysis. Since there is no room here for extensive quotation, I have divided the dialogue into turns marked by the speaker's initial (T1 = first turn of the painter Titorelli (123); K48 = K.'s last turn (141)).[23]

          Even before the dialogue begins, the expectations of normal interaction patterns ["Normalformerwartungen"] remain unfulfilled in the manner described above. K. asks a girl about the painter, and gives possibly the most accurate answer to the question of what he wants from him: "Ich will mich von ihm malen lassen" (122). With this, however, he evokes an unexpected astonishment, "als hätte er etwas außerordentlich Überraschendes oder Ungeschicktes gesagt" (122).

          The beginning of the dialogue also deviates from the usual introductory phases of conversation, with the characteristic adjacency pairs of the greeting ritual.[24] Instead of responding to the painter's introduction

T1   "Kunstmaler Titorelli" by introducing himself and then stating his intention, K. first refers to the pragmatic context, the girls who are scurrying

K1   around the painter: "Sie scheinen im Hause sehr beliebt zu sein" (123). Titorelli uses this occasion to provide a thorough commentary on this set-

T2   ting.[25]

K2   K. only initiates the reason for his visit after this. He does so not explicitly, but rather through a brief reference to the manufacturer's letter of introduction, which is supposed to explain the reason for his visit to the painter. K. is obviously trying to avoid explanations of his own, which constantly provoked undesired reactions in the previous dialogues. Besides, he can only make assumptions about the exact contents of the letter, which causes him to react rather than act in order to avoid any dis-

---

[22] For theoretical background and methodology, cf. Ungeheuer (1977); Hess-Lüttich (1981); id. (2000).
[23] The following emerged, in part, from seminar discussions in which new methods of conversation and dialogue analysis were tested. At this time it arose in the practical demonstration that a simplified version of the procedure of the analysis of phasal structure was similarly applicable in instruction, just as Glinz's procedure of content related text analysis through thematic paraphrase. Cf. Glinz (1969) (application to Kafka); id. (1977/78); Kobs (1970); Ungeheuer (1977); id. (1980) (application to Lessing).
[24] Cf. Schegloff (1968); Berens (1976).
[25] An interpretation of intratextual context from semiotic points of view remains absent due to limited space; perhaps for the purposes of this framework the commentaries of Gesine Frey (1965, especially 79–95) to the theme "space" and "figure" in *The Trial* would be sufficient.

crepancies. The logically expected reference to the letter does not occur
however. Instead, Titorelli asks K. if he would like to have his portrait
painted. Because of the vagueness of the previous turn (= K2) this is semantically and pragmatically compatible, or logically plausible, and repeats the explanation K. gave the girls (see above). However, it runs counter to his basic expectations. K. reacts accordingly "astonished" (nonverbally) and lets him puzzle about the presupposed contents of the letter (125, 10).

Instead of clarifying this discrepancy through reinterpretation on a metalevel and making explicit his motivation for action (to gain information about the status of his trial and to enlist the help of Titorelli), he diverts attention again by referring to the surroundings: "Sie arbeiten gerade an einem Bild" (125, 16). The logical coherence with the painter's question is preserved by the lexeme "painting" (Bild); however, it deviates semantically from K.'s plan of action. In order to follow it, he must therefore use the semantic distraction as a strategic implicature. He operates on two levels: on the first, he explicitly states an interest in Titorelli's artwork; on the second, he implicitly introduces the topic of the court, at which his plan of action is directed. The logical stringency is preserved by the theme of the painting, the portrait of a judge.

But also in this phase of the dialogue, mutual understanding can hardly be reached, despite the reference to concrete objects in the setting. The attributes of "Justice", portrayed allegorically, rather fit the description of a "Goddess of Victory"; the apparent mimetic realism is revealed as pretention; the rank of the judge is lower than had been supposed; the alleged freedom of artistic expression is subject to, as is repeatedly emphasized, a complicated canon of rules of legal provisions and judicial orders; the attempt to define the allegorical figure more sharply distances it further and makes it appear, suggestively, as a goddess of the hunt.

K.'s strategy miscarries: "Schließlich aber machte er sich Vorwürfe, daß er so lange schon hier war und im Grunde noch nichts für seine eigene Sache unternommen hatte" (126, 37–38). His attempt to come to the point by asking the name of the judge, which should lead thematically away from the painting once again to the court, miscarries as well because Titorelli pleads confidentiality and nonverbally signals disinterest in continuing the dialogue. The inconsistency of Titorelli's behavior irritates K.: first charming verbosity, then brusque rebuff, then once again, after K.'s tactical insertion referring to the painter, nonverbal effusive friendliness.

K12
T13
This is semiotically simultaneous with verbally unmasking K.'s conversational tactic as a transparent maneuver (which bluntly violates the principle of cooperation), and is followed again, when K. wants to explain, by sharp rejection. Even less sensitive individuals would experience a crisis of interaction when confronted with such an alternation of contradictory sign clusters that violate a number of the above mentioned rules of normal conversation, but that through their immediate reinterpretation ("Sie konnten ja nicht wissen...") force the dialogue to progress on the same level of communication, leaving no room for arguments on a meta-communicative level.

K13

T14
K14

T15
Once again, K. renounces metacommunicative explanation, as well as a connection to the opportunity presented to him thematically by Titorelli to reveal his true motive for the conversation. Instead, he again refers to Titorelli's two-sided relationship to the court[26] – on the one hand, confidant, on the other independent from it: "Ist das eine öffentlich anerkannte Stellung?" Titorelli's answer cuts off – again in violation of the principle of cooperation – any continuation of the dialogue, in that he makes no semantic addition to his curt "No", to which K. could refer in his response. The latter must therefore persist, in order to maintain the dialogue, upon which the former, completely unexpectedly ("mit zusammengezogener Stirn"), reveals that he has long since been informed about K.'s "case" by the manufacturer. (Incidentally, this leaves the relationship between the painter and the manufacturer equally ambivalent, since both purport to be doing the other a favor.) However, this reveals his reaction to K.'s attempted distraction maneuver as likewise strategic, since he can thus contrast his prescience of K. with the latter's behavior in the dialogic situation, in a manner not dissimiliar to a game of "cat-and-mouse".

After a new episodic insertion, which is devoted to the divergent definitions of the situation – Titorelli interprets K.'s nonverbal signals concerning the oppressive room temperature (intentionally?) incorrectly as coziness, and forces him against his will to settle into the pillows on his bed – Titorelli poses the first relevant question into the awkward obscurity of the situation: "Sie sind unschuldig?"

With this the topic which had been intended from the beginning is finally broached. Agreeing on the same topic, however, in no way guarantees mutual understanding. Both partners in the dialogue have a com-

---

[26] To an interpretation of this contradiction cf. Emrich (1970: 288).

K16 pletely different notion of "innocence", without arguing the concept on a metacommunicative level. K.'s attempts to do this miscarry as in other dialogues (with Leni, with Fräulein Bürstner, etc.), because no one wants to enter into the moral discussion. This question, it seems, was answered by issuing the indictment in the first place; every reaction to it must start from this given and unquestionable assumption, and it can only be a tactical move. What is denoted by the term cannot be argued or clearly defined, measured by shared norms, or semantically objectified. For K. "guilt" is a fact "to be proven", for Titorelli it is fate "proven" a priori. The alternative is not acquittal and freedom – that is K.'s illusion and misunderstanding – but rather a *modus vivendi* under the verdict of his own confession. This, however, would require the relinquishing of his norm-structure, his semantic system, his identity, his self-defined existence.[27]

With this, the next turns of the conversation are already anticipated. They lead to K.'s resigned awareness of the fundamental rules of the judicial communication system at the end of this phase, after the notion of guilt has been dissipated. Titorelli accepts K.'s innocence without questioning the court's accusation, which implies guilt. The court defines justice because it has the power (in which Justitia becomes Diana), but it is not the incarnation of justice as K. understands it. The power is confirmed immediately: "...alles [gehört] zum Gericht" (129, 31). The court's ubiquity suffocates the "others", the recalcitrants and outsiders. His agents (T20: "Auch diese Mädchen gehören zum Gericht") pull the noose tighter and tighter ("[...] eines hatte einen Strohhalm durch eine Ritze zwischen den Balken gesteckt und führte ihn langsam auf und ab" [129, 36f.]).

T21

T22
K22
T26
K26

The feeling of helplessness is systematically reinforced by his partner in the dialogue: if anyone at all could help him, it would be he alone, Titorelli – he leaves it open how. K. insists in vain on specification and is therefore at first puzzled when Titorelli finally enumerates the alternatives for action, then becomes suspicious again because of the contradiction between the supposed free choice of alternatives and the painter's own premises, according to which at least the "definite acquittal" – which is the only acceptable reaction to "innocence" for K. – is excluded a priori. K. proves that Titorelli's argumentation reveals gaps in its logic: indices

---

[27] In this sense Allemann is completely correct when he connects K.'s subjugation under the verdict of guilty to the question of his right to exist.

K27	which could testify to the accused's innocence would not influence the court; however, the judges would be, under certain circumstances, open to such viewpoints in unofficial discussions in the corridors; an innocent person would not need the help of third parties at all; on the other hand, there could be no definite acquittal through the "proof" of innocence. Titorelli's
T28	ostensible solution to the contradiction – to differentiate between theory and practice – only makes the situation more hopeless, because it does not help K. at all practically if he should be right theoretically, that is, morally. His conclusion is as consistent as it is fatalistic: "Ein einziger Henker
K28	könnte das ganze Gericht ersetzen" (123, 34).
T29	Once again the painter immediately obscures the clarity of this conclusion. He mentions the relativity of personal experience and of the general history of the court (there may have perhaps been acquittals), of legends and of a "probable truth" ("gewissen Wahrheit") which they "probably" ("wohl gewiß") contained (133, 7). K. gives up. His central motivation
K31	for this conversation is destroyed. If true freedom is not possible, it is useless to discuss it. Having just recognized clearly the arbitrariness based on power, and also the ostensible a prioristic asymmetry of the dialogue between the initiated one and the one in need of help, K. now misinterprets Titorelli's interactional trap as simply "opinion".
	He accepts the choice between two equally undesired alternatives, the "ostensible acquittal" ("scheinbare Freisprechung") and the "indefinite postponement" ("Verschleppung"), instead of arguing the choice itself. In this crucial phase of the dialogue, K.'s moral position is dismantled piece by piece – not by better argument, but rather by formal tricks of conversational strategy. The digression once again to the suffocating atmosphere of the musty chamber is no longer surprising at this point. The apparently friendly verbosity of Titorelli's description of exactly this constriction becomes for K., in his claustrophobic anguish, increasingly threatening.
	This is reinforced by the repeated discrepancy between semiotic modes in the following sequence: K., restricted in his capacity to act freely to an undesired choice between two equally objectionable alternatives ("schein-
T35	bare Freisprechung" and "Verschleppung"), must infer from Titorelli's
K35	nonverbal behavior ("In dem Blicke des Malers lag es wie ein Vorwurf..." [135, 13f.]), which contradicts his "friendly" words, that this choice as
T35	well, under the arbitrary verdict of guilt, is not truly free. Every nascent hope which is awakened by the painter's effusion is immediately dashed: "...verbürge mich für Ihre Unschuld" (135, 11); "es ist dann für den

T36	Angeklagten die Zeit der höchsten Zuversicht" (135, 35); "Der Richter [...] kann Sie unbesorgt freisprechen" (136, 1); "Sie aber treten aus dem Gericht und sind frei" (136, 3). Every glimpse of light is immediately darkened by the subsequent sentence. Teasings of hope and blows of futility alternate constantly until K. is "ein wenig zusammengesunken" (137, 12). His verbal contributions become shorter and more monosyllabic in direct proportion to the increase in his partner's pedantic and vain verbosity. He tightens the screw of acquittal and non-acquittal to the point of open cynicism: "Der scheinbare Freispruch scheint Ihnen offenbar nicht vorteilhaft zu sein [...] vielleicht entspricht Ihnen die Verschleppung
T40	besser" (137, 32f.). K., at this point, is no longer capable of a verbal response: "K. schwieg" (137, 31); "K. nickte" (137, 35). Titorelli's vivid depiction of the consequences of the postponement finishes him off:
T42	"Schon während der letzten Worte hatte K. den Rock über die Arme gelegt und war aufgestanden" (139, 7f.). K.'s willingness to converse is exhausted, the conclusion of the dialogue has been drawn, the "Hilfsmetho-
K40	den" of the court's painter "verhindern die wirkliche Freisprechung" (139, 19), which was his sole concern. He wants to get out of the clutches and chamber of this ambivalent helper, who is at the same time the agent of his opponent, but Titorelli will not yield. The girls from the court flock in front of the door, behind him the painter plagues him with a series of
K47	desolate heathlandscapes. He is too weak to resist him; his answers are short to the point of brusqueness, but he responds, he comments, inquires about the price, and is only released after he buys all the paintings. He
K48	stumbles into supposed freedom and finds himself surrounded by law offices. Meanwhile, he is shocked by his own astonishment:

Als eine Grundregel für das Verhalten eines Angeklagten erschien es ihm, immer vorbereitet zu sein, sich niemals überraschen zu lassen, nicht ahnungslos nach rechts zu schauen, wenn links der Richter neben ihm stand – und gerade gegen diese Grundregel verstieß er immer wieder. (141, 22–26).

This is not the only basic rule that K. breaks repeatedly (see above). But Titorelli also follows few of the conversation postulates which Grice established for everyday communication.[28] He does not correspond to K.'s expectations for information, either quantitatively ("make your contribution as informative as is required", "do not make your contribution more informative than is required") or qualitatively ("do not say that for which you lack adequate evidence"); his remarks are neither directly relevant to K.'s goals of action ("be

---

[28] Grice (1975, especially 45ff.).

relevant"), nor are they precise and clear ("avoid obscurity of expression"; "avoid ambiguity", "be brief", "be orderly").

What is decisive, however – indeed, the dialogue occupies a key place in the novel for this reason – is that communication does not fail here due to a "prästabilierte Disharmonie",[29] but rather due to the systematic violation of the rules of conversation. The possibility for understanding exists from the beginning, as Emrich noted correctly;[30] Titorelli is not trying to deceive his dialogue partner, he knows the "truth of the court" ("Wahrheit des Gerichts") and voices it; he is independent, but not an outsider: "K. erkannte: hier, wenn irgendwo, war der Durchbruch möglich."[31] The breakthrough is a negative one: with each round of conversation another hope is destroyed; every slight hope is repeatedly rejected. The principle of gradual reduction[32] finalizes the failure. It is based upon mistakes made on both sides – but different types of mistakes respectively: Titorelli's paradoxical ambivalence, which suspends the validity of routine certainties of behavior and with it the intersubjectively shared basis of understanding, is placed in contrast to K.'s "logical" precision, which disregards essential conditions for vagueness of mundane conversation and is not able to reinterpret, from a metacommunicative perspective, the fundamental difference between the semantic and pragmatic rules applied. The misunderstanding can therefore not be clarified as such, but rather becomes an independent axiom of "Kafkaësque conversation".

K.'s goal, the "real acquittal", is at the same time a condition for his lack of communication: it is, as an ideal, not real.[33] Only the alternatives offered by Titorelli enable "real" communication, which has more to do with exertion and observation, with rule and discipline, with organization and compromise, than with "truth" and the absolute, with freedom and a monadic existence, which (K.'s "logical" conclusion) ends in silence and death.

---

[29] Krusche (1974) uses the expression associated with Musil for characterization of (for him presupposed) a priori impossibility of understanding in the "irrational-mythical quality of the castle world" (58).
[30] Emrich (1970: 287f.).
[31] Characteristically, however, Kafka cut this section (in the "Haus" fragment): op. cit.: 210.
[32] Cf. Walser (1968: 79ff.) (where he speaks of the principle of *Aufhebung*), then programmatically Ramm (1971); Deleuze & Guattari (1976), chapter II.
[33] To the possibilities for interpretation, which may be added here, cf. Sokel (1976, Chapter 21: 399–415).

References

Abraham, Ulf (1985): Der verhörte Held. Verhöre, Urteile und die Rede von Recht und Schuld im Werk Franz Kafkas. – München: Fink.
Adorno, Theodor W. (1955): Aufzeichnungen zu Kafka. – In: T.W. Adorno: Prismen. Kulturkritik und Gesellschaft. – Frankfurt/M.: Suhrkamp.
Allemann, Beda (1963): Kafka. *Der Prozeß*. – In: Benno von Wiese (ed.): Der deutsche Roman. Vom Barock bis zur Gegenwart. Vol. II. – Düsseldorf: Bagel.
Argyle, Michael (1974): Soziale Interaktion. – Köln: Kiepenheuer und Witsch.
Bateson, Gregory et. al. (eds.) (1975): Schizophrenie und Familie. – Frankfurt/M.: Suhrkamp.
Bauer, Gerhard (1969): Zur Poetik des Dialogs. – Darmstadt: Wiss. Buchges.
Beicken, Peter U. (1974): Franz Kafka. Eine kritische Einführung in die Forschung. – Frankfurt/M.: Athenaion.
Beißner, Friedrich (1958): Kafka der Dichter. – Stuttgart: Kohlhammer.
– (1983): Der Erzähler Franz Kafka und andere Vorträge. – Frankfurt/M.: Suhrkamp.
Benjamin, Walter (1966): Franz Kafka. – In: W. Benjamin: Schriften. Vol. 2. – Frankfurt/M.: Suhrkamp.
Berens, Franz-Josef (1976): Bemerkungen zur Dialogkonstituierung. – In: F.J. Berens et al., 15–34.
– et al. (1976): Projekt Dialogstrukturen. – München: Hueber.
Beutner, Barbara (1973): Die Bildsprache Franz Kafkas. – München: Fink.
Binder, Hartmut (1966): Motiv und Gestaltung bei Franz Kafka. – Bonn: Bouvier.
– (1976a): Kafka, Kommentar zu den Romanen, etc. – München: Winkler.
– (1976b): Kafka in neuer Sicht. Mimik, Gestik und Personengefüge als Darstellungsformen des Autobiographischen. – Stuttgart: Metzler.
Bloom, Harold (ed.) (1987): Franz Kafka's "The Trial". – New York: Chelsea House.
Brod, Max (³1954): Franz Kafka. Eine Biographie. – Frankfurt/M.: Fischer.
Caputo-Mayr, Maria Luise / Herz, Julius M. (1987): Franz Kafka: Eine kommentierte Bibliographie der Sekundärliteratur (1955–1980, mit einem Nachtrag 1985). – Bern: Francke.
Corngold, Stanley A. (1988): Franz Kafka: The Necessity of Form. – Ithaca/NY: Cornell University Press.
Deleuze, Gilles / Guattari, Félix (1976): Kafka. Für eine kleine Literatur. – Frankfurt/M.: Suhrkamp.
Emrich, Wilhelm (1970): Franz Kafka. – Frankfurt/M.: Athenäum.
Frey, Gesine (1965): Der Raum und die Figuren in Franz Kafkas Roman "Der Prozeß". – Marburg: Elwert.
Furth, Hans G. (1972): Intelligenz und Erkennen. Die Grundlagen der genetischen Erkenntnistheorie Piagets. – Frankfurt/M.: Suhrkamp.
Glinz, Hans (1969): Methoden zur Objektivierung des Verstehens von Texten, gezeigt an Kafka: Kinder auf der Landstraße. – *Jahrbuch für Internationale Germanistik* 1, 75–106.
– (1977/78): Textanalyse und Verstehenstheorie. 2 Vols. – Wiesbaden: Athenaion.
Grice, H. Paul (1975): Logic and Conversation. – In: Peter Cole / Jerry L. Morgan (eds.): Syntax and Semantics. Vol. III: Speech Acts, 41–58. New York etc.: Academic Press.
Hemmerle, Rudolf (1958): Franz Kafka. Eine Bibliographie. – München: Lerche.
Hermsdorf, Klaus (1961): Kafka. Weltbild und Roman. – Berlin: Rütten und Loening.
Hess-Lüttich, Ernest W.B. (ed.) (1980): Literatur und Konversation. Sprachsoziologie und Pragmatik in der Literaturwissenschaft. – Wiesbaden: Athenaion.
– (1981): Grundlagen der Dialoglinguistik (= Soziale Interaktion und literarischer Dialog. Vol. 1). – Berlin: Erich Schmidt.

- (1985): Zeichen und Schichten in Drama und Theater – Gerhart Hauptmanns "Ratten" (= Soziale Interaktion und literarischer Dialog. Vol. 2). – Berlin: Erich Schmidt.
- (2000): Literary Theory and Media Practice. – New York: CUNY.

Hillmann, Heinz (^{2}1973): Franz Kafka. Dichtungstheorie und Dichtungsgestalt. – Bonn: Bouvier.

Ide, Heinz (1957): Franz Kafka, 'Der Prozeß'. Interpretation des ersten Kapitels. – In: Jahrbuch der Wittheit zu Bremen. Vol. 6, 19–57.

Järv, Harry (1961): Die Kafka-Literatur. Eine Bibliographie. – Malmö: Cavefors.

Kafka, Franz (1976): Gesammelte Werke in sieben Bänden, ed. Max Brod. – Frankfurt/M.: Fischer.
- (1998): Der Process. Historisch-kritische Ausgabe, ed. Roland Reuß in Zusammenarbeit mit Peter Staengle. – Frankfurt/M.: Stroemfeld.
- (2000ff.): Werke. Kritische Ausgabe auf CD-Rom und im WWW. Fischer & Chadwick-Healey. http://kafka.chadwyck.co.uk; http://kafka.chadwyck.com.

Koelb, Clayton (1989): Kafka's Rhetoric: The Passion of Reading. – Ithaca/NY: Cornell University Press.

Kobs, Jörgen (1970): Kafka. Untersuchungen zu Bewußtsein und Sprache seiner Gestalten. – Bad Homburg: Athenäum.

Kreis, Rudolf (1976): Die doppelte Rede des Franz Kafka. Eine textlinguistische Analyse. – Paderborn: Schöningh.

Krusche, Dietrich (1974): Kafka und Kafka-Deutung: Die problematisierte Interaktion. – München: Fink.

Lacan, Jacques (1975): Schriften. Vol. I. – Frankfurt/M.: Suhrkamp.

Mecke, Günter (1982): Franz Kafkas offenbares Geheimnis. Eine Psychopathographie. – München: Fink.

Mölk, Ulrich (ed.) (1996): Literatur und Recht. Literarische Rechtsfälle von der Antike bis in die Gegenwart. – Göttingen: Wallstein.

Neumann, Gerhard (1973): Umkehrung und Ablehnung: Franz Kafkas "gleitendes Paradox". – In: H. Politzer (ed.) (1973): 459–515.

Piaget, Jean (1963): Le langage et les opérations intellectuelles. – In: Problèmes de psycholinguistique, 51–61. Paris: Symposium de l'Association de psychologie scientifique de langue française.

Politzer, Heinz (1978): Franz Kafka. Der Künstler. – Frankfurt/M.: Fischer.
- (ed.). (1973): Franz Kafka (= Wege der Forschung 322). – Darmstadt.

Pongs, Hermann (1960): Franz Kafka. Der Dichter des Labyrinths. – Heidelberg: Rothe.

Ramm, Klaus (1971): Reduktion als Erzählprinzip bei Kafka. – Frankfurt/M.: Athenäum.

Reimann, Paul (1957): Die gesellschaftliche Problematik in Kafkas Romanen. – *Weimarer Beiträge* 3, vol. 4, 598–618.

Richter, Helmut (1962): Franz Kafka. Werk und Entwurf. – Berlin: Rütten und Loening.

Richter, Peter (1975): Variation als Prinzip. Untersuchungen an Franz Kafkas Romanwerk. – Bonn: Bouvier.

Sandbank, Shimon (1989): After Kafka: The Influence of Kafka's Fiction. – Athens/GA: University of Georgia Press.

Schegloff, Emanuel A. (1968): Sequencing in Conversational Openings. – *American Anthropology*, 70, 1075–1095.

Schlieben-Lange, Brigitte (1975): Linguistische Pragmatik. – Stuttgart: Kohlhammer.

Schmidhäuser, Eberhard (1996): Kafkas "Der Prozeß". Ein Versuch aus der Sicht des Juristen. – In: Mölk (ed.) (1996): 341–355.

Schütz, Alfred (1971): Das Problem der Relevanz. —Frankfurt/M.: Suhrkamp.

Schütze, Fritz (1978): Interaktionsfreiheit und Zwangskommunikation – oder Interaktion konversationsanalytisch. – Mimeograph Bielefeld.

– (1980): Interaktionspostulate – am Beispiel literarischer Texte. – In: Hess-Lüttich (ed.) (1980): 72–94.
Sokel, Walter H. (1976): Franz Kafka. Tragik und Ironie. Zur Struktur seiner Kunst. – Frankfurt/M.: Fischer.
Strelka, Joseph P. (2001): Der Paraboliker Franz Kafka. – Tübingen, Basel: Francke.
Trost, Pavel (1964): Franz Kafka und das Prager Deutsch. – *Philologica Pragensia* VII, Nr. 3, 29–37.
Ungeheuer, Gerold (1977): Gesprächsanalyse und ihre kommunikationstheoretischen Voraussetzungen. – In: Wegner (ed.) (1977): 27–65.
– (1980): Gesprächsanalyse an literarischen Texten. In: Hess-Lüttich (ed.) (1980): 43–71.
Uyttersprot, Herman (1957): Eine neue Ordnung der Werke Kafkas? Zur Struktur von "Der Prozeß" und "Amerika". – Antwerpen: De Vries-Bouwers.
Walser, Martin (^{3}1968): Beschreibung einer Form. Versuch über Franz Kafka. – München: Hanser.
Watzlawick, Paul et al. (^{3}1973): Menschliche Kommunikation. – Bern, Stuttgart, Wien: Huber.
Wegner, Dirk (ed.) (1978): Gesprächsanalysen. – Hamburg: Buske.
Weinberg, Kurt (1963): Kafkas Dichtungen. Die Travestien des Mythos. – Bern, München: Francke.
Ziolkowski, Theodore (1996): Kafkas "Der Prozeß" und die Krise des modernen Rechts. – In: Mölk (ed.) (1996): 325–340.

Silvia Bruti

Modal Competence and Misunderstandings in *The Merry Wives of Windsor*

1. Introduction

Research in pragmatics, especially within the province of speech act theory, has shown how human interaction is based on sequences of actions that strictly depend on speakers' intentions, beliefs, wants and status. To this aim, the notion of speaker needs to be investigated and defined in order to account for how his/her role in communication can model the construction of meaning. In this paper I would like to demonstrate how an analysis of the modal competence of speakers and of the transformation it undergoes within a speech act framework may effectively contribute to better define the roles of interactants and the power relationships in dialogic interaction and in dramatic dialogue in particular.

After briefly illustrating the theoretical framework I refer to (cf. 2–6 below), I will show that despite the dominance of a specific illocutionary force at a macro-level (the exercitive, in this case), the plot is made up of many different micro-oscillations that are closely intertwined with changes in the characters' modal competence. Thus power and roles are negotiated in the modal transformations implied by all illocutionary types. Moreover, these changes do not affect deontic modality only but also affect epistemic modality to a large extent. It is in fact epistemic modality that triggers off many of the strands in the plot, especially when knowledge gaps favour a planned form of misunderstanding (Weigand 1999: 764–765).

1.1 Dramatic dialogue

Because of its quality of interactional mimesis, dramatic dialogue resembles in many respects spontaneous conversation as a series of doings that presupposes a configuration of interactants, a turn-taking system, the performance of speech acts, the relation speakers have with their own acts (intentions, commitment, success in performance), and the effects of these acts on other participants.

Indications of status and role, as well as all the implicit norms of social behaviour, are therefore inscribed in dramatic dialogue. The status of a character exerts a considerable influence on his/her actions and on the discursive roles he/she can take on in the unrolling of the plot. Yet, characters often disregard rules and act according to roles that do not match their status. On other occasions, the role of a single individual may be modified by his/her interactants in such ways that it no longer fits his/her original status (Falzon Santucci 1983). Roles in discourse are subject to a continuous evolution, to the point that a complete understanding of the dynamics of interaction is only possible if a record of discourse development is kept.

1.2 Speech act theory and modal predicates

I would like to integrate the performative logic of speech act theory (Austin 1962; Searle 1969) with the notion of modal competence (Kiefer 1987; Sbisà 1989; Bertuccelli Papi 1996) and its transformations with the ultimate aim of shedding light on intersubjective relationships, specifically on the dynamics of roles and on the discursive creation of subjectivity (Birch 1991: 113–114). Modal predicates attributable to speakers, as pointed out in Bertuccelli Papi (1996), are not only useful to identify and rank illocutionary force but also to account for the different ways in which speakers decide to couch their messages.

1.3 The Falstaff plays

I will limit the investigation to some scenes of *The Merry Wives of Windsor* (hence MWW), one of the so-called *Falstaff plays*.[1] In this comedy illocutions play a primary role, as humour is more often secured by language than by situations. The play pivots in fact on jargons belonging to colloquial English, on eccentricity and idiosyncrasy, on invention and register shifting. Falstaff, a born comedian and a witty "corruptor of words", is the catalyser of comic, a seducer who triggers a series of events but ends up being himself "seduced".

The active role of language in comedy, and in Shakespearean comedy in particular, has often been recognised (Elam 1984: 1 and 5). It has also been noticed that this genre is characterised by the massive use of the directive (Searle 1969; or "exercitive" in Austin

---

[1] This label undergirds four different plays, i.e. three history plays, *Henry IV Part One*, *Henry IV Part Two*, *Henry V* and the comedy I have just mentioned (Elam 1986; Salmon and Burness 1987).

1962) or by illocutionary type (Ohmann 1971; Elam 1984: 201), whereas tragedy displays a more varied range of speech act types. The prevailing use of the exercitive[2], often employed in peremptory orders, mirrors a configuration of roles and a hierarchy of modal competence that is typical of comedies (cf. Elam 1984: 202).

2. Theoretical framework

2.1 Austin's speech act classification

I will briefly illustrate the elaboration of Austin's speech act typology put forward by Marina Sbisà (1989), which I will refer to in analysing modal variation. Austin's model is preferred to other typologies for the importance it attaches to two crucial illocutionary effects: firstly the securing of uptake, i.e. the recognition of both the meaning and the force of the act, which is a necessary condition for the act to be carried out; secondly, the response that each act elicits. Austin emphasises that acts occur as a sequel and not as single token utterances as Searle advocates (Searle 1969: 23; Sbisà 1995: 499). As Sbisà points out, Greimas's narrative programme (1970, 1983) can effectively explain the sequential ordering of speech acts (cf. 2.3. below).

2.2 Modal competence

In order to account for the requirements of certain speech acts, such as assignments of obligations or rights, the category of illocution should be flanked by that of modality. Each participant in an interaction has his/her own modal competence (cf. Kiefer 1987; Palmer 1979), which can be defined by means of some modal predicates. These modal attributes can variously be modified, either by the subject himself/herself, or by his/her interlocutors. Modal competence can therefore be evaluated at each stage of a sequence of performed speech acts. Describing a character's modal competence is equal to describing his/her epistemic, deontic and volitional status as a subject (Sbisà 1989: 103). A similar conception is contained in Austin's study, where it is noticed that illocutionary acts may prove infelicitous when the necessary prerequisites for their accomplishment are not fulfilled: these

---

[2] At least when counting the lexicalised occurrences (Elam 1984: 201).

cases are called "misapplications" (1962: 17).[3] In particular, according to Sbisà, modality is accounted for by three modal predicates, CAN, MUST and KNOW. The two former predicates relate to deontic modality. CAN specifies the power, the capacity or authority which entitles the speaker to perform an act (cf. Palmer's (1979) notion of "dynamic" modality). MUST identifies instead the duty of a speaker to perform a speech act. The predicate KNOW, to be understood in an epistemic sense, denotes some cognitive aspect of the subject ("the burden of the proof" the locutor is expected to provide in assertive acts; cf. Searle 1979: 40). The competence implied by KNOW impinges on the contiguous domain of CAN, because to know may mean "having the skill to do something" and consequently "being able to do something" (having the aptitude, the right or the authority to do something). Likewise "letting somebody know something" is equal to endowing him/her with a certain degree of power, here to be understood as aptitude, right, or authority.[4]

2.3 Greimas's actantial model

To explain modal transformations, Sbisà (1989) employs the actantial model devised by Greimas (Greimas 1970, 1983; Greimas and Courtés 1979). The actantial couple sender (S) and receiver (r) can explain how the performance of an illocutionary act not only depends on the speaker's status but also affects the modal role of the addressee (Bazzanella *et al.* 1991). Sbisà splits however the role of the receiver into two distinct roles, receiver 1 (r1) and receiver 2 (r2). This distinction is specifically introduced to account for commissive speech acts, where the sender lays a duty on himself/herself: the function of S (+CAN) and that of r2 (+MUST) are performed by the same person. R1 is instead given the right to expect a future action of the sender. This separation proves to be illuminating also in other

---

[3] Searle also meant to lay down some conditions for the successful performance of speech acts (1969: 57–61), the rule of the propositional content, the preparatory rule, the sincerity rule and the essential rule. Both the preparatory and the sincerity condition cover some aspects that have to do with modal roles, namely the requisites for the performance of an act, and the intentions, beliefs, and feelings of a speaker. Bazzanella *et al.* (1991) also recognise that preparatory conditions establish what entitles a speaker to perform a given illocutionary act. For certain acts, linguistic and communicative competence are enough, whereas for others some specific authority or capacity is required.
[4] Sbisà disregards the predicates WANT and BELIEVE because she advocates that the former must be perceived as a manifest attitude of the will of the subject and is not negotiated; the latter is somewhat similar to the modal predicate KNOW, with which it shares the feature of specifying the epistemic status of the subject but it is only a personal conviction, whereas KNOW always entails the practical demonstration and the recognition that the subject knows something. In the present study I will only consider the modal predicates indicated by Sbisà, even though all modal predicates should be considered to better define the pragmatic roles of speakers.

speech act types. A typology of modal predicates can be identified for each speech act type, as the following table shows.[5]

TYPE	S	r1	r2
EXERCITIVE	+CAN	±MUST	±MUST
COMMISSIVE	+CAN	+CAN	+MUST
VERDICTIVE	+CAN	+KNOW	+MUST
BEHABITIVE	+MUST	+KNOW	+CAN

3. Modal predicates and speech act types

Exercitives are defined as those acts in which a sender who is endowed with a certain degree of power either imposes a duty on somebody or lifts a duty from somebody. This class encompasses both institutional acts such as naming, baptising, etc. and real exercitives like orders and questions, as well as those language uses which presuppose some authority (e.g. doctor's advice and the like, where there is incongruity in knowledge/competence between sender and receiver). A second receiver is justified by the fact that imposing a duty on somebody necessarily entails passing a complementary duty to somebody else (the same holds for lifting the duty from somebody and passing it to somebody else). For example, with an order a task is assigned to a particular person. It is therefore implied that the same task is not to be carried out by somebody else, the sender of the order *in primis*. The sender later evaluates how the receiver has carried out the order.

Commissives are those acts in which a sender endowed with the attribute (+CAN) transfers power to r1 and imposes a duty on r2. In this case s/he performs two roles, i.e. that of the sender and that of r2. So s/he assigns himself/herself a duty and authorises r1 to expect such a course of action.

Verdictives are acts in which a sender who has a certain power (+CAN) assigns some knowledge to r1 and a duty to r2. As is the case with commissives, two actantial roles may be performed by the same subject. Let's take for example the case in which a sender who has the competence to express some knowledge also has the role of r2, i.e. the one who answers for the truthfulness of that knowledge (either by providing evidence or by referring to some external authority). R1 actually inherits some knowledge, either in the form of an official evaluation or of informal criticism.

---

[5] Expositives are not considered by Sbisà (1989) because she does not envisage pronounced differences between this class and that of verdictives.

In behabitives the sender himself/herself has a duty and consequently assigns knowledge to r1 and power to r2. The sender is not assigned the duty by any institutional authority and in fact this duty would be better conceived as proper social behaviour. So the speaker gives vent to his/her feelings, and as r2, expresses his/her right to be acknowledged and to be shown a due reaction. The knowledge of r1 does not rest on truthfulness/falsity but is conventionally determined by agreed norms of social behaviour.

4. Effects on sender and receivers

All types, except behabitives, presuppose some power for the sender, which is authority in the case of exercitives, aptitude for commissives, and competence for verdictives. The similarity between these modal qualifications makes shifts between types likely and frequent. The only type in which the sender has no power is the behabitive; as has briefly been hinted at, in this type the sender is not required any special competence but needs only to be recognised as a member of the social community. Thus the language of those who do not have great prestige or are recognised as having special authority is geared towards the expression of opinions or impressions. So, for example, when a locutor is denied his/her competence, an assertion turns into the expression of opinion.

As for the effects on the receivers, in both commissives and verdictives, r1 receives some power or knowledge because there is a r2 who undertakes a matching obligation. The relationship between r1 and r2 can best be explained through transformations in modal competence. In verdictives and exercitives the main transformation applies to r1 and requires respectively the knowledge and the power that s/he is assigned. The perlocutionary aim of these acts is in fact to make somebody believe or do something. The most striking feature of commissives is r2's obligation, whereas in behabitives both the effect on r1 as knowledge and on r2 as power are relevant (the performance of an act of apology may be aimed at obtaining forgiveness).

The modal status of the receiver is modified at various stages of the ongoing interaction, whereas the sender's status does not need to be negotiated. The status of the sender – as either power, knowledge or skill at doing something – may have been acquired in the same situation of utterance; it may depend on institutional factors or may have been negotiated with the same or other interlocutors in previous speech acts, but it can also derive from extra-linguistic actions or events. In some cases it is not immediately verifiable but is silently accepted by participants. Sometimes it happens that the prerequisites, i.e. the necessary modal competence, for the performance of certain acts are not fulfilled. In uttering an order the sender may not have the necessary power to impose on the receiver. The act is still an exercitive, but if the receiver can ascertain the lack of competence of the sender, s/he can reject the act by denying its uptake (Austin 1962: 116–117; Sbisà 1989: 84). However, if one considers a sequence of acts and not a single speech act, the status of the sender may variously be modified by the receivers' reactions.

5. Mixed illocutionary forces

In dialogic interaction, acts usually follow one another in pairs like question-answer according to the logic of action-reaction. So an order is typically followed either by an acceptance, a rejection, a commitment to undertake a course of action or by an evaluation of the future action.

Speech acts are rarely pure in speech, so shifts or mixed illocutionary forces are the rule rather than the exception. Behabitives provide a good case in point: whenever the sender's modal competence is watered down, an act may turn into a behabitive, which is the type requiring the lowest degree of competence. However, the shift towards the behabitive type is not always triggered by a decline in power; sometimes the locutor may choose to perform an act which shows little power because this is part of a strategic scheme, e.g. one to avoid being sanctioned or being accused of untruthfulness.

Verdictives and behabitives are very close to each other because they both assign r1 some knowledge, but the roles of S and r2 are reversed. In verdictives the perlocutionary aim is to make somebody believe something, but r2 also has the duty to provide evidence for what s/he knows. Behabitives also tend to make somebody do or believe something, but the effect on r2, who is the same person as S, is positive and desirable: a behabitive act like a greeting may ratify the beginning of an exchange, whereas an apology may enable S to recapture social solidarity by asking his/her interlocutor to do something for him/her.

What is relevant, though, is the global effect produced by a speech act, although it may be obtained by adding various partial illocutionary effects of different types. I am here referring to the notion of "macro-illocution", or global speech act, enacted as a sequence of local-level utterances (Fotion 1971; van Dijk 1977). In exercitive strategies, which are aimed at getting the receiver to do something, the sender may cunningly employ commissive and verdictive illocutions. An instance of a global exercitive strategy is the manipulation acted out by Mistress Quickly in MWW (cf. 7.3. below). Quickly achieves her super-goal by dismissing her perlocutionary aim and putting on a deferential attitude: she gives up explicit directivity in favour of "weaker" illocutionary forces, such as behabitive acts, which are not demanding for the receiver, and often also undertakes obligations with commissives.

6. Sequences of manipulation and sanction

In order to understand the force of an illocution it is necessary to locate it within a sequence of actions. Some illocutionary types tend to occur as sequence initiators, or in Greimas's terms (1983) as manipulative acts: they are especially exercitives and commissives, which are logically prior to the actions anticipated by their illocutionary aims. By contrast, there are reactive acts that most typically appear as sequels to other acts and are called sanctioning acts.

The concept of manipulation includes both two distinct moments and subjects; it is in fact made up of the manipulative act of the sender who pushes the receiver to accept a "bond", and an act which the receiver must perform. In Greimas's typology the combination of four modal predicates (CAN, KNOW, MUST and WANT) gives rise to four different manipulative tactics: "temptation" and "intimidation", based on the power of the sender, and "provocation" and "seduction", based on the knowledge of the sender. If we consider instead the modal competence of the receiver, the same tactics may be grouped differently: "intimidation" and "provocation" assign the receiver an obligation, whereas "temptation" and "seduction" spur him/her to want something (Greimas/Courtés 1979: 220–221; Sbisà 1989: 224).

The tactics refer to modal roles, yet they do not correspond to fixed illocutionary types. Manipulation is mainly an opening move, whereas sanction is usually a reactive move that concludes a sequence. With the latter the sender judges the action performed by the receiver either positively or negatively. Being backward oriented, this function is preferentially fulfilled by acts that refer to something that has already happened, i.e. verdictives and behabitives (Sbisà 1989: 233). To sum up, manipulation is the cause of a sequence of actions and sanction the ensuing verbal or non-verbal reaction. Greimas's narrative scheme accounts for the dynamic quality of speech act sequences and establishes an adequate segmentation of the sequence (cf. Sbisà 2000).

7. Modality and micro-illocutions in MWW

The plot of comedies usually hinges on epistemic gaps. This does not rule out the possibility that other modal transformations are grafted onto the epistemic dimension. Conversely, the management of power and the negotiation of discursive roles are not only exhausted in exercitives but are actually the product of transformations on all levels. It is also true that plots are triggered by some tactics aimed at achieving perlocutionary effects that at times prove to be effective but may also be totally disastrous. As I have anticipated above, communication is often tricky and may engender misunderstanding.

Misunderstanding is generally conceived of as an involuntary phenomenon. It has however been recognised that on some occasions speakers who are aware of the mechanism deliberately use utterances that can lead to misunderstanding (Weigand 1999: 764). This may entail using deceiving speech acts but also disguising one's real modal competence, and thus camouflaging one's pragmatic role. Indirect illocutionary acts have also been connected with misunderstanding, but I agree with Weigand (1999: 765), who claims that they are not necessarily deceptive. The kind of misunderstanding that I refer to is instead linked to the speaker's manipulative design thus it is intentional but needs to be kept hidden for the strategy to be successful. In the following sections I will show how this mechanism works both by pointing out the tactics which set the action in motion and the modifications in the characters' modal competence.

7.1 Falstaff

Towards the beginning of MWW, Falstaff explains his ideas to Pistol:

> Fal. No quips now, Pistol. Indeed, I am in the waist two yards about, but I am now about no waste: I am about thrift. Briefly, I do mean to make love to Ford's wife. I spy entertainment in her: she discourses, she carves, she gives the leer of invitation; I can construe the action of her familiar style, and the hardest voice of her behaviour, to be Englished rightly, is, 'I am Sir John Falstaff's'. (I, iii, 38)

This plan does not apply to Mistress Ford only, for Falstaff intends to pursue the same objective with Mistress Page (I, iii, 54). In a commissive act Falstaff reveals his future aims, but in making predictions concerning other people he shows what he plans to do:

> Fal. [...] I will be cheaters to them both, and they shall be exchequers to me: they shall be my East and West Indies, and I will trade to them both. Go bear thou this letter to Mistress Page; and thou this to Mistress Ford: we will thrive, lads, we will thrive. (I, iii, 65 ff.)

With such a declaration he discloses his manipulative programme in the form of seduction. Seduction obtains, in fact, when a sender has a cognitive vantage-point, whereas the receivers – here Mistress Page and Mistress Ford – are driven to "wish" something (Greimas/Courtés 1979). The real goal of seduction is not clearly explicit, nor does Falstaff mention the stages of his plan. Falstaff's commitment is often weak and changeable, because he takes life as a game where rules and moves can always be changed.

Seduction is usually accomplished by exhorting, praising or flattering the interlocutor so as to make him/her realise that s/he has the aptitude or the ability to do something and consequently stimulating his/her self esteem and will. This strategy is undeniably directive: as the Latin etymology of the verb itself shows, *seducere* means drive away, divert hence the sense of driving the addressee to do something (cf. Parret 1986: 104, although he envisages seduction as an involuntary tactic).

Falstaff's knowledge is mentioned when he says "I spy entertainment", and he confesses to Pistol that he caught a glimpse of encouragement in Mistress Ford's look. Falstaff's strategy, though, is mentioned later on, in II, i, 4, when Mistress Page reads the letter she received from him. His argumentation is indeed based on the competence that he gained from attentive observation. So his modal competence or power takes here the form of knowledge:

> Ask me no reason why I love you, for though Love use Reason for his precision, he admits him not for his counsellor. You are not young, no more am I; go to, then, there's sympathy. You are merry, so am I; ha, ha, then, there's more sympathy. You love sack, and so do I; would you desire better sympathy? Let it suffice thee, Mistress Page—at least, if the love of soldier can suffice—that I love thee. I will not say pity me—'tis not a soldier-like phrase—but I say, love me. [...]' (II, i, 4–12)

Shortly after the initial exercitive, which contains however behabitive aspects as an open display of his feelings (he courts the woman by declaring his love to her), there are three verdictives, which enable Falstaff to draw some generalising conclusions concerning the presumed similarity and kinship between himself and Mistress Page. Thanks to the power derived from his knowledge, Falstaff weaves the plot for a conquest, but his modal competence will soon be modified because of an encounter between his two intended victims. The knowledge on which his plan is based will however prove to be imperfect and faulty.

7.2   The merry wives

The seeds of the failure of Falstaff's tactics are sown in the first scene of the second act, when Mistress Ford visits Mistress Page and shows her the letter she received from the knight in order to comment on his impudence (he is courting both of them at the same time). Before they meet, the two women's competence is equal and both are in a subordinate position in comparison with Falstaff. His strength, which is the power derived from his knowledge, crumbles to pieces:

> Mrs. Page. Letter for letter, but that the name of Page and Ford differs! To thy great comfort in this mystery of ill opinions, here's the twin brother of thy letter (II, i, 67–70).

At the beginning of the exchange Mistress Page is in a position of superior knowledge because she is aware of the letter she received from Falstaff and she learns that her friend received a similar letter. Her competence consists of power as knowledge and also as aptness, which entitles her to perform a series of verdictives and commissives, two types which require the commitment of the locutor to the truth of what he/she says and to his/her future behaviour:

> [...] but let thine [letter] inherit first, for I protest mine never shall (commissive). I warrant he hath a thousand of these letters, writ with blank space for different names -sure, more- and these are of the second edition (verdictive).[...] I had rather be a giantess, and lie under Mount Pelion. Well, I will find you twenty lascivious turtles ere one chaste man (commissive) (II, i, 70–78).

This harangue bridges Mistress Ford's informative gaps: this is once again a variation in modal competence in which a character moves from a position of –knowledge to +knowledge as the addressee of verdictives. Because of her position of addressee of commissives, Mistress Ford is also assigned some power, which she decides to share with her friend while agreeing to her proposal. Their agreement is ratified and it is even verbally reinforced by the adoption of the same naval metaphor which Mistress Page used before to describe how they could reply to Falstaff's "boarding":

> Mrs. Ford. 'Boarding' call you it? I'll be sure to keep him above deck.
> Mrs. Page. So will I: if he come under my hatches, I'll never to sea again.
> [...]
> Mrs. Page. Let's consult together against this greasy knight. (II, i, 87–90 and 105)

Falstaff suspects that the two women might plot against him when Mistress Quickly tells him about the two messages one after the other:

> Fal. But I pray thee tell me this: has Ford's wife and Page's wife acquainted each other how they love me?
> Quick. That were a jest indeed! (II, ii, 103–106)

But Quickly's answer puts an end to his right speculations.

In Act 3, the wives' competence reaches its climax: they uncover Falstaff's plot, secure his page's assistance, and instruct Mrs. Ford's servants to act according to their plan. As Elam observes (1984: 67), "situations [are] deliberately set up to trap or deceive some unknowing and unrehearsed outsider". The machinations used by the merry wives against

Falstaff are thoughtfully contrived in such terms. Verdictive and exercitive illocutions dominate in their speech:

> Mrs. Page. [to Falstaff's page Robin] Thou'rt a good boy: this secrecy of thine shall be a tailor to thee, and shall make thee a new doublet and hose (III, iii, 29–31)

Sometimes exercitives are disguised as commissives, but it is clear that the duty is not imposed on the sender:

> Mrs. Page. I will lay a plot to try that [her husband's jealousy], and we will yet have more tricks with Falstaff: his dissolute disease will scarce obey his medicine.
> Mrs. Ford. Shall we send that foolish carrion, Mistress Quickly, to him, and excuse his throwing into the water, and give him another hope, to betray him to another punishment?
> Mrs. Page. We will do it: let him be sent for to-morrow eight o'clock to have amends. (III, iii, 176–184)

True commissives are also used for promises that concern the future, i.e. to assert the resolution to do something that has negative consequences for r1 and imposes no heavy obligation on r2. After the wives trick and punish Falstaff for the second time (he is thrown in the river and is beaten), they are resolved to tell their husbands the truth:

> Mrs. Ford. Shall we tell our husbands how we have served him?
> Mrs. Page. Yes, by all means – if it be but to scrape the figures out of your husband's brains. If they can find in their hearts the poor unvirtuous fat knight shall be any further afflicted, we two will still be the ministers. (IV, ii, 200–206)

Falstaff's attempt at seducing the two women is a failure and he becomes the real victim of a strategy of manipulation, a mixture of temptation and seduction based on the power and knowledge they have acquired in their meeting.

7.3 Mistress Quickly

Another interesting example where the modal competence of a subject determines future events is contained in Mistress Quickly's manipulative design, which is sometimes enacted as temptation, other times as seduction at Falstaff's expense. In both cases, regardless of the speech act she performs, she is in a position of superiority both with regard to power and knowledge. Unlike Falstaff, she also achieves her perlocutionary aims because as a sender she is perfectly aware of her competence and knows how to best take advantage of it. She contrives to disguise her competence and often pretends to have none, thus inducing her interlocutors to judge her power as less significant than it actually is and not to expect her to perform exercitives.

She acts as a go-between, both for the wives and for Page's daughter Anne and her numerous suitors. In I, iv Mistress Quickly promises Simple to recommend his master Slender to the girl. Shortly afterwards Doctor Caius arrives home and Quickly is excessively obliging and respectful to prevent him from finding out that Simple is there. It is only in an aside to the audience that she reveals that she does not intend to keep her promises, but that she has a particular goal in mind. When Simple leaves, Doctor Caius tries to force Quickly to keep her promises:

> Caius. [...] Do not you tell-a me dat I shall have Anne Page for myself? [...] By gar, I will myself have Anne Page. (I, iv, 110–114)

It can be observed that she overuses her competence as a sender, committing herself to two contrary courses of action, i.e. pleading Caius's and Slender's cause with Anne, certain that she will not do anybody any harm. In fact, as she tells Simple in an aside "[...] Anne's mind – [that]'s neither here nor there" (I, iv, 100–101). When her master menaces her ("By gar, if I have not Anne Page, I shall turn your head out of my door"; I, iv, 118–119), Quickly understands that it is convenient for her to look defeated, so she asserts something that she does not believe, as becomes clear when she remains alone onstage:

> Quick. You shall have An- [Exeunt Caius and Rugby] – fool's head of your own. No, I know Anne's mind for that; never a woman in Windsor knows more of Anne's mind than I do, nor can do more than I do with her, I thank heaven. (I, iv, 121–125)

When Anne's third suitor arrives, Quickly does her utmost to take advantage of him and promises that she will help him with the girl.

> Fent. [...] Let me have thy voice in my behalf; if thou seest her before me, commend me.
> Quick. Will I? I'faith, that we will; and I will tell your worship more of the wart the next time we have confidence; and of other wooers. (I, iv, 150–154)

Later Quickly makes it clear that she is not on such familiar terms with Anne Page: "For I know Anne's mind as well as another does" (I, iv, 157–158). In taking advantage of the three suitors' gullibility, Quickly plays with power in two different ways. First she feigns an authority derived from her knowledge of the girl. Secondly she assigns herself obligations she does not intend to carry out. In talking she conceals her real power; she abstains from peremptory orders, and commits herself to a certain behaviour. In particular, in her role of go-between with Mistress Ford, Mistress Page and Falstaff she adopts a humble, deferential attitude, especially towards Falstaff (II, ii, 31 and ff.), performing a series of behabitives, the only acts which require no special authority on the part of the sender (Sbisà 1989: 157). She greets him and blesses him before delivering the two women's message.

> Quick. Give your worship good morrow.
> Fal. Good morrow, goodwife.
> Quick. Not so, and't please your worship.
> Fal. Good maid, then. (II, ii, 31–36)

In his first love debacle Falstaff is thrown into the river with dirty linen (III, iv), but Quickly succeeds in persuading him to arrange another meeting with Mistress Ford. The manipulative design is the same as has been used earlier. The sender tries to hide her power and to hide the directive perlocutionary aim from the addressee. So she acts mainly through politeness, proceeds to justify Mistress Ford's deeds (with verdictives), and then to guarantee the truth of her own assertions (with commissives). With commissives r2's task is certainly more demanding than r1's. Quickly's rhetorical skill consists however in constructing her turns so as to upgrade the perlocutionary effect on r1 and downgrade instead r2's obligation (her own, in this case). Summarising briefly, Quickly's discursive strategy is coherent throughout the play: she minimises the competence of the sender and emphasises the effects of the modal transformations on one of the addressees. She avoids performing exercitives because they entail assigning or eliminating obligations, which in turn would betray her aim of making somebody do something. In using verdictives she amplifies r1's modal competence, because s/he receives some knowledge, whereas in commissives she highlights the obligation which she herself undertakes. With behabitives there is no need to hide her modal competence, both because the sender has no special modal attribute, and because these acts often serve as strategic moves for the positive effect they have on r1 (consider, for example, the role of excuses in obtaining forgiveness, or greetings and expressions of admiration, which are aimed at winning the interlocutor's favour).

8. Conclusion

Bach and Harnish's (1979) classification of collateral acts may serve to clarify misunderstanding, in particular the kind which is brought about by modal competence and tactics in MWW. They claim that various conversational acts are performed along with illocutionary acts and call them "collateral acts". Like perlocutionary intentions, the intentions of these acts may or may not be intended to be identified: the two types are labelled respectively as "overt" and "covert" (1981: 97). Some collateral acts need in fact to be recognised as such by the hearer, e.g. storytelling, joking, and punning. By contrast, covert collateral acts are performed with intentions that are meant not to be recognised: "These are acts of manipulation, including such devious acts as innuendo, deliberate ambiguity, and 'sneaky presupposition'. [...] They succeed only if their intent is not recognised, or at least not recognized as intended to be recognized, [...] whereas an indirect speech act is performed with an intention that can be reasonably expected to be recognized" (1981: 101).[6] In our case, thus, the intentions behind single illocutions are overt and the receivers usually interpret them correctly, whereas those lying behind collateral acts, i.e. manipulation, seduction or other tactics, are hidden. The receivers therefore rarely discover the manipulative design that lies behind the illocutionary network.

References

Austin, John L. (1962): How to Do Things with Words. – Oxford: Clarendon Press.
Bach, Kenneth/Harnish, Mike (1979): Linguistic Communication and Speech Acts. – Cambridge (Mass.): M.I.T. Press.
Bazzanella, Carla,/Caffi, Claudia/Sbisà, Marina (1991): Scalar Dimensions of Illocutionary Force. – In: Igor Z. Zagar (ed.): Speech acts. Fiction or reality?, 63–76. Ljubljana, IPrA distribution Centre for Yugoslavia.
Bertuccelli Papi, Marcella (1996): Semantic Roles, Pragmatic Roles, and Text Modalities. – *Rassegna Italiana di Linguistica Applicata* 2, 19–34.
Birch, David (1991): The Language of Drama. – Basingstoke/London: Macmillan.
Dijk, Teun A. van (1977): Text and Context. – London: Longman.
Elam, Keir (1984): Shakespeare's Universe of Discourse: Language-Games in the Comedies. – Cambridge: Cambridge University Press.
– (1986): La grande festa del linguaggio. – Bologna: Il Mulino.
Falzon Santucci, Carmelo (1983): Status, ruolo e l'interazione drammatica. – In: Guy Aston et al.(eds.): Interazione, dialogo, convenzioni. Il caso del testo drammatico, 103–113. Bologna: Clueb.
Fotion, Nicholas (1971): Master Speech Acts. – *Philosophical Quarterly* 21, 232–243.
Greimas, Algirdas J. (1970): Du Sens. – Paris: Seuil.
– (1983): Du Sens II. – Paris: Seuil.
Greimas, Algirdas J./Courtés, Josef (1979): Sémiotique. Dictionnaire raisonné de la théorie du langage. – Paris: Hachette.
Kiefer, Ferenc (1987): On Defining Modality. – *Folia Linguistica* XXI, 67–94.
Ohmann, Richard (1971): Speech-Acts and the Definition of Literature. – *Philosophy and Rhetoric* 4, 1–19.
Palmer, Frank R. (1979): Modality and the English Modals. – London/New York: Longman.
Parret, Herman (1986): Les passions. Essai sur la mise en discours de la subjectivité. – Bruxelles: Mardaga.
– (1994): Indirection, Manipulation and Seduction in Discourse. – In: Herman Parret (ed.): Pretending to Communicate, 223–238. Berlin/New York: De Gruyter.
Sbisà, Marina (1989): Linguaggio, ragione, interazione. Per una teoria pragmatica degli atti linguistici. – Bologna: Il Mulino.

---

[6] Cf. Parret (1994: 230): "the discursive act of manipulation is a maimed discursive act: its intentionality cannot be uncovered nor admitted".

– (1995): Speech Act Theory. – In: Jef Verschueren,/Jan-Ola Östman/Jan Blommaert (eds.): Handbook of Pragmatics, 495–506. Amsterdam/Philadelphia: John Benjamins.
– (2000): Cognition and Narrativity in Speech Act Sequences. – Paper presented at the 7th International Pragmatics Conference, Budapest, 7–14 July 2000.
Salmon, Vivian /Burness, Edwina (eds.) (1987): A reader in the Language of Shakespearean Drama. – Amsterdam/ Philadelphia: John Benjamins.
Searle, John Ross (1969): Speech Acts. – Cambridge: Cambridge University Press.
– (1979): Expression and Meaning. – Cambridge: Cambridge University Press.
Weigand, Edda (1999): Misunderstanding: The standard case. – *Journal of Pragmatics* 31, 763–785.

Monika Dannerer

Misunderstandings at Work

> "Miscommunication is an interesting and slippery concept – perhaps interesting initially because it is slippery."
> Coupland/Wiemann/Giles (1991: 1)

My aim is to look at misunderstandings in workplace-meetings, i.e. misunderstandings in face-to-face communication in a specific institutional setting. After a short definition of "understanding" and "misunderstanding" I will look at the problems of identifying misunderstandings in a multi-party conversation in an authentic setting. The main part of the paper consists of an analysis of different types of misunderstandings that occur in my data. The main questions will be how misunderstandings arise, how they are identified and dealt with, or even cleared up, within the group, and what importance can be attributed to power and underlying conflict as well as to differing knowledge and conception of the task.

1. Understandings and misunderstandings

Misunderstandings are often regarded as the result of a lack of communicative competence, as something that must not happen and that does not happen if both parties are speaking "clearly" and are listening carefully enough. Most practical communication guides treat misunderstandings and miscommunication as "aberrant behaviour which should be eliminated" – and can be avoided with some sort of training (Coupland/Wiemann/Giles 1991:1).

But now that linguistics has turned away from simplistic sender-receiver-models or conduit models of communication (cf. e.g. Coupland/Wiemann/ Giles 1991: 8; Eisenberg/Phillips 1991: 246f.), it seems necessary to define "understanding". I am going to use the term in its interactional, functional and cognitive sense. Therefore I regard it as important to consider the fact that discourse partners are always co-constructing a mental representation of what they hear; they interpret, they make presuppositions, they take into account the situation, the context, and their knowledge about the topic, the partner, the type of situation, the type of interaction and about any former interactions with the partner, etc.

(cf. also van Dijk/Kintsch 1983: 4–8).[1] Closely associated with the cognitive aspect of what we do when we try to understand is the pragmatic or functional point of view that defines understanding in relation to the aims and goals of conversational partners in the actual communication situation.[2] Thus I agree with the definition of understanding, that is given by Kindt/Weingarten (1984: 194) who say that understanding is the

> "[...] Prozeß, der dazu dient, daß Interaktionsteilnehmer zu einem ihren Erwartungen entsprechenden und am Interaktionsziel orientierten Maß an Ähnlichkeit der Bedeutungszuschreibung zu vorgegebenen Objekten gelangen." (cf. also Selting 1987: 15)

> [Translation M.D.]: [...] process, that leads the participants to a similarity in the semantic interpretation of given objects that corresponds with their expectations and their interactional aims.

Both of these concepts, the cognitive and the pragmatic, make it evident that understanding is to be seen as a dynamic process in two ways:

1. There is no dichotomy between understanding and misunderstanding: we do not either understand or not understand the meaning of an utterance, but we often understand/or misunderstand parts of an utterance and we probably do not understand all the nuances it has for the speaker. Moreover the degree of (mis)understanding shifts constantly within a conversation.

2. Understanding and misunderstanding are not necessarily interpreted in the same way by the different discourse partners or by the observers (cf. also Fiehler 1998: 102).

---

[1] Considering the complexity of these mental processes there are approaches that even deny that "understanding" is possible. Doubt about the possibility of understanding the emotions and intentions of another individual dates from the early 19th century, the period of Romanticism (cf. Lorenz 1997: 110f.) and it is also a hermeneutic position. J.G. Droysen (1977: 433; cit. acc. to Lorenz 1997: 99) writes: "Wohl versteht der Mensch den Menschen, aber nur peripherisch; er nimmt seine Tat, seine Rede, seine Miene wahr, aber immer nur diese eine, diesen Moment; beweisen, daß er ihn richtig, daß er sie ganz verstanden [hat], kann er nicht". [Translation M.D.]: "Man does understand man, but only peripherally; he perceives his action, his speech, his countenance, but only at one single moment; he cannot prove that he has understood him correctly and completely".

[2] Cf. also Kindt/Weingarten (1984: 194) about miscommunication. We may assume that understanding is achieved, when communication enables the conversational partners to attain their aims and goals.

2. Discovering misunderstandings

Misunderstandings can be discovered if signalled metacommunicatively or if there is a lack of coherence between the utterances of different speakers. When there are only two discourse partners, misunderstandings are quite easy to detect, but within multi-party-discourse where not everybody reacts verbally to the contributions of another member of the group, we cannot be sure whether everybody "understood" an utterance. According to the Latin proverb "si tacuisses, philosophus mansisses" we should not assume that people will ask for clarification any time they do not understand or have doubts about their understanding. For the linguist there is probably very little chance to be able to analyse these "silent misunderstandings" in empirical data.

But even when there are metacommunicative indicators that misunderstandings have occurred, we should still take into account the possibility that these hints might be misleading. People might pretend not to understand or to misunderstand for a number of strategic reasons. And moreover, discourse partners sometimes "impute to each other" – especially in situations of conflict – a lack of willingness to co-operate and thus to understand. As this imputation might also be for strategic reasons, it illustrates the problem of recognising misunderstandings. Thus I am fully aware that the lack of "willingness to understand" is a problematic assumption, and must be treated very carefully.

We can conclude that if we are dealing with authentic data that is not gathered in an experimental setting,

- we cannot discover all the misunderstandings, and

- we cannot always separate real misunderstandings from pretended or strategic misunderstandings or from the strategic imputation of a misunderstanding of the conversational partner even if there are contextual and linguistic signs.[3]

---

[3] Recorded data and its transcription help the observing linguist to go into details that are far beyond what participants might do during a face-to-face interaction. Nevertheless, the linguist's understanding of the situation is the result of interpretation and therefore can only be a partial understanding.

3. Examples

In my corpus there is a considerable amount of self-initiated repair and repair initiated by others that shows that there are problems of understanding or misunderstanding; participants quite frequently use different means to ensure comprehension, e.g. reformulations as described for German in Bührig (1996) or questions (e.g. Rost-Roth 2000).[4] What I think is especially interesting in an institutional setting is the question of how misunderstandings are regarded and dealt with, because this reveals much about relationships and tasks and the conception that the participants have about their roles and tasks within an enterprise or within a certain project.

3.1 The data

My corpus consists of eight videotaped meetings with a total length of 12 hours. They all took place in a large Austrian company that mainly develops and constructs new products in the field of engineering. The type of meeting investigated is not a regular one held daily or weekly, but these meetings are organised whenever there is a problem to solve or new ideas that need to be explained and discussed within the group. It is important to stress that all these meetings are authentic, i.e. they were neither role-play nor arranged situations with given topics.[5]

The meetings took place in two different groups, each of them consisting of six people from three or four different departments. From each group I registered/filmed and analysed four meetings.

The group that I have called "RESEARCH group" has been working together constantly for more than one year on the task of developing a new measuring device. As they have to consider the needs of the market as well as their technical capabilities, three departments are engaged in this project: the electronic department, the measuring department and the marketing department for new products.

The second group I have called "SOFTWARE group". They have the task of improving a newly installed software that is used internally for marketing, distribution and controlling (company-internal software). In this case members of the department of logistics (to which also belongs the head of the project and its main executor) work together with various

---

[4] I am not going to give a systematic list of all forms of misunderstandings that occur in my material.
[5] For detailed analysis see Dannerer (1999).

Misunderstandings at Work 107

other departments. When I was collecting my data they cooperated with two different marketing departments and the department that deals with the processing of orders.

As we will see, inter-departmental co-operation is an excellent source for investigating misunderstandings as different viewpoints and different interests seem to provoke such misunderstandings more frequently than in other settings.

3.2 Misunderstandings due to divergent departmental viewpoints

Martina Rost-Roth (1994) closes her paper with the following words:

> "Ich gehe [...] davon aus, daß die beste Grundlage für eine gute Verständigung gemeinsame Interessen sind. Daraus folgt die Frage, in welcher Weise sich konfligierende Interessen auf den Prozeß der Verständigung und die Verständigungsbereitschaft auswirken." (39)
>
> [Translation M.D.]: "[...] I assume that the best ground for good understanding is common interest. This poses the question of how conflicting interests influence the process of understanding and the willingness to understand."

In agreement with this position I would like to show in my first example how differing departmental viewpoints influence the understanding, or cause misunderstanding, and how a whole team gets involved and interferes, in order to help to overcome the misunderstanding.

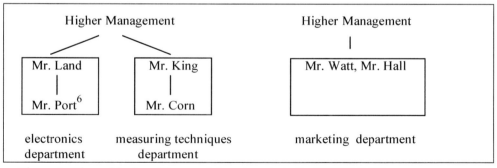

Figure 1: Hierarchical positions and departments in the RESEARCH-group

This example will be taken from the "RESEARCH group", whose members belong not only to different departments, but also hold different hierarchical positions as shown in figure 1.

In the following extract, where all members are present – except for Mr. Corn – they are discussing the general configuration of a the new measuring-device: under discussion are

---

[6] Leader of the project.

different sensors that are available and their prices which seem much too high. Mr. King, an elderly and very experienced technician, poses a question about the price of a type of sensor that has not yet been discussed: *approximately what is the price of * the injection-line-sensor.*[7] Mr. Hall from the marketing-group answers him, that *that is * the biggest luxury that we have in / for the moment * in the whole package. * that is very clear.* The situation of dissent that results from this utterance and that is to be seen in the transcription is the result of a misunderstanding that comes from the different interpretations of the word "luxury".

RESEARCH-1

```
K      wenn uns jetzt schon die Auspufftemperatur solche
       if the exhaust-temperature causes already such
L  aber es is
   but it is
```
479
```
K  Schwierigkeitn bereitet, * wie liegt dann preislich * der
   problems for us          * approximately what is the price of * the
```
480
```
H                          das is * der größte Luxus den
                           that is * the biggest luxury that
K  Einspritzleitungssensor. **
   injection-line-sensor. **
```
481
```
H  wir in / derzeit * in dem ganzn Paket drinnen habn. * das
   we have in / for the moment * in the whole package. * that
```
482
```
H  is ganz klar.
   is very clear.
K                i würde net sagn daß des a Luxus is.
                 I would not say that this is luxury.
```
483
```
K  also * die Einspritzung zu überwachn, * das habn Sie hier
   well * to monitor the injection,      * you've worked it out
P            (glaub i auch net)
             (I don't believe either)
```
484
```
K  richtig herausgearbeitet, is also eine Notwendigkeit.
   correctly here,           is a necessity.
```
485

---

[7] For transcript notations see appendix.

K	weil dort die häufigstn	Fehler
	because there the most frequent	problems
L	na. im Sinn vom Preis.	na. Sie habn
	no. in the sense of costs	no. now you've
W		im Sinn (wenn wir)
		in the sense (if we)

486

H	ja ja
	yes yes
K	auftretn (können).
	(can) occur.
L	ihn jetzt * Sie habn ihn jetzt mißverstandn ( )
	* you've got him wrong now ( )

487

H	Luxus im Sinne von von größter Preisanteil das is <u>der</u>
	luxury in the sense of of the biggest part of the costs that is <u>the</u>
W	der größte Preis<u>an</u>teil. ja.
	the biggest <u>part</u> of the costs yes.

488

H	große Preisbrockn. *
	big chunk of the costs. *
K	**ja,**
	yes,
L	daß er <u>not</u>wendig is, * des * glaubn S'ihm *
	that it <u>is</u> necessary, * this * you believe him *

489

H	<u>wert</u>voll is er. richtig. **
	it is worth a lot. correctly. **
P	also i glaub halt
	well I mean

490

Whereas Hall uses the term "luxury" to express that the injection-line-sensor is something very expensive, King (mis)understands the term "luxury" as signalling something that is superfluous. Therefore he starts his argumentation about the necessity of this sensor (score area 483–487).

Mr. Port, the leader of the project and a very well regarded engineer in the electronic department, supports King (484), while the others try to clear up the misunderstanding: Mr. Land, who is the leader of the electronic department, starts with a clarification of the meaning: *in the sense of costs* (486) and continues with a metacommunicative comment on the misunderstanding (486f.: *you've got him wrong now*). He is supported by Hall and Mr. Watt, who works with Hall in the marketing department. Hall himself makes an explicit clarification: *luxury in the sense of of the biggest part of the costs * that is the big chunk of the costs.* *. Since King still does not agree, Land asks Hall to confirm that they share the same opinion about the necessity of the sensor (489: *that it is necessary, * this * you believe him *).* By putting *necessary* (that is a partial repetition of what King said in 485) in front of the main-clause, he puts great stress on it. The signal of agreement uttered by King is high pitched and pronounced with rising intonation (*yes,*). However it cannot be interpreted as a ratification of the misunderstanding, as it immediately follows the fronted sub-clause and is not repeated at the end of Land's utterance. – King once again takes the opportunity to stress his opinion that the sensor is necessary. With Hall's agreement (490) it is clarified that "luxury" means something that is valuable and necessary at the same time.

In this example, the misunderstanding is clearly a semantic problem and it is only blamed on the hearer, King. The first recognition of a misunderstanding comes neither from Hall nor from King, but from a "third party". There is a correction in elliptic form, then a meta-communicative declaration of the misunderstanding followed by a reformulation; it is only at this point, that the former speaker comes in and helps to repair the misunderstanding.

Some minutes later, after having calculated roughly the price of these injection-line-sensors, which is indeed very high, Hall comes back to his earlier formulation:

```
H            ja deswegn mein ich. * es sin diese
             yes therefore I think. * these sensors
L       hm. **
P  nichts. *
   nothing.
598
```
```
H  Sensorn eindeutig der größte Preisbrockn. *     die Frage
   are definitely the biggest chunk of the costs. * the question
L                                             (        )
599
```
```
H  is ob wir uns das für alle Zylinder leistn können. *
   is whether we can afford that for all of the cylinders. *
?W                                                         hmhm,
600
```
```
H                                    ja,
                                     yes,
K  ja aber das wär ja das Attraktive. *      Luxus. * wenn wir
   yes but that would be the attraction. *   luxury. * if we
?                                            hmhm,
601
```
```
H                                 im a / im im im   gutn Sinn
                                  in a / in in in a good sense
K  es schon so bezeichnen.
   are calling it that.
L                    (die mal) auch für'n Kundn ein Luxus. net,
                     ( ) also for the customer a luxury. isn't it,
602
```
```
H        im gutn Sinn Luxus. ja. *
         luxury in a good sense. yes, *
L                                 und auch und auch die /
                                  and also and also the /
W  hmhm,                          gut aber jetzt    ja,
   hmhm,                          well but now      yes,
603
```

This time Hall avoids using the word "luxury" once again. He speaks more clearly about the *biggest chunk of the costs* (599). But now it is King who comes back to the expression "luxury" by defining it again – this time making it a synonym of something "attractive". Thus at this moment he ratifies the clarification of the former misunderstanding. The additional remarks of Hall and Land help to indicate that there is now consent in this question.

The fact that this misunderstanding arises, reveals a lot about the problems in this group. The construction engineers (King, Port and Land) think that a high technical standard is necessary, while the members of the marketing department (Watt and Hall) are also interested in a good quality monitoring-system. They also believe that a low price is necessary in order to be competitive. King is afraid that the low price could become the most important argument and that the marketing department is not aware of the necessity of certain technical features. Thus there is a more general disagreement underlying King's first interpretation of the word "luxury".[8]

3.2 Misunderstanding due to conflict

Misunderstandings also reveal underlying conflicts *within* departments. In another meeting of the RESEARCH group a misunderstanding arises between Mr. King and Mr. Corn, his inferior, about a task to be done. Corn had to contact a student from the university who had agreed to do part of the research-work. Land, the superior of King and Corn asks to be briefed about the progress in this field (554–557):

```
L   dieses Billigaufklemmgebers habn Sie mir gestern gsagt, daß *
    this sensor x               you told me yesterday, that  *
                                to Corn
```
554
```
L   und Sie auch * daß es einen Herrn gibt, der * doch * von der
    and you too  * that there is somebody, who * indeed * from the
        zu King
```
555
```
L   Hochschule, * der bereit wäre eine Studie zu machn über *
    university, * who would be ready to do a study about  *
```
556

---

[8] Moreover this monosemantic interpretation might be strengthened by the fact that King is the oldest member of this group and that he sees – more than the others – luxury as something that is pleasant, but not necessary.

```
C                                    ja genau, * was is da
jetzt,
                                     yes indeed, * what is there
now,
L  Auswertbarkeit von Druckverläufen * (    )
   evaluation of pressure-signals   * (    )
```
557
```
C   ah der Herr *                           nana, also die
    ah, Mister *                            no no, well the
K              nja Sie habn die Aufgabe ghabt.  (        )
                   well you have got the task.
```
558
```
C  er hat / er hat /              ja des hab i
   he had / he had /              yes indeed (or: yes, I
did)
                                  # - - - - nods - - - -
K  dann dort die     dort nachzufragen       schaun daß
   to                to ask there            to have a look
that
```
559
```
C            dieser Herr Egg,      ja. * dieser Herr
             this Mister Egg,      yes. * this Mister
     nods  #
K   * Sie * ihn zum Gespräch bekommen.
    * you * can get him to talk with you.
```
560
```
C   Egg ah * macht    zur Zeit ebn Diplomarbeit, * und er hat
    Egg ah * is presently doing his thesis,     * and he had
```
561

Corn begins his answer with a rhetoric question addressed to himself *(yes indeed, * what is there now, ah, Mister *)* but before he is able to come to the point, he is interrupted by King, who refers to the question that Corn posed, which he took as a real question (*well you have got the task.*). Corn is afraid that King would start to load all the work (not only contacting the student) on him. Thus he immediately interrupts him strongly denying that it was his task to do this work (*no no, [...]*). It is only when King is able to finish his utterance (*to ask there to have a look that * you * can get him to talk with you.*) that Corn realizes the misunderstanding and that he starts to report on what he did.

In this case the misunderstanding is cleared up by the two discourse partners themselves. It is neither metacommunicatively named as a misunderstanding nor is there any face-work or an apology relating to the false, but still face-threatening, assumptions. The tension that arises is rapidly overcome when it becomes evident that King correctly remembers that Corn only had to do a part of the task, and when King realises that Corn has done his job.

This time the misunderstanding is not due to a semantic problem, but arises because King and Corn each think they know what the other would like to say. The misunderstanding hints at an underlying conflict, which comes to the surface when the participants interrupt each other. The consciousness of the participants is focused in such a way that they anticipate the meaning of the ongoing turn according to the image they have of the other individual: The superior (too easily) supposes that his junior has forgotten to do what he was supposed to do and the latter has the impression that everything is being blamed on him.

In the two examples examined up to now the misunderstandings were easy to recognise. However, if there are no metacommunicative indicators, the identification of misunderstandings is not always that simple. Misunderstandings and dissent are often difficult to distinguish – it seems to be the case that participants disagree because they do not understand correctly and that they later agree because they achieve a (better) understanding.

Stalpers also says that "corrections of misunderstanding are often treated as the expression of dissent by the hearer" and that in empirical data the distinction between misunderstandings and dissent is not always clear, neither to the linguist (Stalpers 1995: 175f.) nor to the participants: disagreement can be treated as a misunderstanding by one participant and at the same time as dissent by the other.

3.3 (Pretending) misunderstanding as a means of reducing conflict

The fact that disagreement and misunderstanding are so closely related is also used strategically to reduce conflict.

An example that illustrates this function is taken from a meeting of the SOFTWARE group, where three members of the group were discussing the best way to improve the software. Mr. Pen, head of one of the marketing departments, wanted Mr. Fast, a junior software-engineer, who was also head of the project, to make improvements to the software itself. Fast, as well as Mr. Salt, the member of another marketing department, are of the opinion that the problem does not lie in the software but in the way it is used by the employees.

A conflict arises when Pen directly attacks Fast as being unwilling to co-operate or change the software. Although Salt disagrees, Pen insists, but when Fast also denies this, Pen suddenly relents and apologises. He declares the dissent to be a misunderstanding (16):

```
P   verbessern, oder zu ändern. *               jawohl i hab
    improve, or to change.      *               yes indeed I
S                                    dess glaub i net. des
                                     I don't believe this. this
```
14

```
F                    also wenn S'ma des attestiern, Herr Pen,  dann
                     well when you believe that, Mister Pen,   then
P   des scho so verstandn.
    understood it like this.
S                                                    na
                                                     no
15
F   muß i sagn, na, des kann net stimmen
    I have to say, no, that can not be true
P   tschuldigung, dann hab i Sie falsch verstandn, hab i Sie
    excuse me, then I misunderstood you, I
S                                                    na
                                                     no
16
F                            ich      ich stell nur in Zweifel, an
                             I        I only doubt about, about
P   falsch verstandn,
    misunderstood you,
S                            des * glaub i net.
                             I don't believe that.
                             # - very low - - - - #
17
```

This sudden compliance is very astonishing and as the meeting continues it can be seen that he does not stop accusing Fast of not being co-operative. Thus we have to interpret his initial reaction as strategic. To declare something as a misunderstanding and to blame it on oneself is an easy and face-saving way of putting an end to a conflict, of withdrawing a reproach.

Schwitalla (1987) analysed different means of reducing conflict and, amongst others, he listed apologies and the reinterpretation of the incident which led to the conflict. We can see here that declaring something to be a misunderstanding also serves as an appropriate way of calming things down.

3.4   Strategic or undiscovered misunderstandings

As already indicated in Section 2, it is not always possible to distinguish strategic or pretended misunderstandings from real misunderstandings. This holds true not only when misunderstandings are explicitly named but also when misunderstandings seem to be evident only to the linguist analysing them.

As an illustration I will quote another example from the SOFTWARE meetings where it is the context in which the word "benefit" is used by the conversation partners that causes misunderstanding and that is exploited to achieve a topic shift.

Mr. Salt is speaking about what a "benefit" it would be for the whole enterprise, if the improvement of the software would start with the problems of his own department:

> wo Sie gesagt habn wir solln die Prioritätn <u>dort</u>hin legn. net der der am lautestn schreit, * sondern dort wo der größte **Nutzn** zu erwartn ist. * und letztlich <u>machn</u> wir im Systemgeschäft einen Großteil des FIRMA-<u>Um</u>satzes.

> you said we should put the priorities there. not to the one who cries loudest, * but to the one where the biggest **benefit** is to be expected. * and finally we make in our department quite a big part of the turnover.

Mr. Star, head of the logistics department, agrees with him (a good strategy to get the next turn) but turns the topic around by sticking to the keyword "benefit" and using it in the context he is dealing with – the "benefits" of the new software in general:

> Sie habn völlig recht Herr Salt.[...] deswegn gehn ma ja jetzt über die Schiene wo is der **Nutzn**, und wo stehn ma in der Erreichung unseres **Nutzns**, * aber da brauch ma natürlich klarerweise Ihre Mithilfe.

> you are completely right Mr Salt [...] therefore we now take the track where is the **benefit**, und where are we in the way to reach our **benefit**, * but naturally it's clear we need your help.

By exploiting the word "benefit" in these two different contexts, Salt and Star manage to shift the topic three times. Each of them tries to talk about the benefits he sees but does it in a way so as to suggest it is the same point of view and the same argumentation as the other has brought up. By using the same word, they pretend to create a coherent dialogue but they manage to come back to their own topic through this surface cohesion.

I suspect that in this case the question of whether there is a misunderstanding or not can hardly be answered objectively. It might be that both participants recognise the misunderstanding but that they do not speak about it since it helps both of them to continue speaking about "their" topic. But as they are from different departments and have very different perspectives on the software and its improvement, it might also be the case that they do not realise at all that there is only cohesion but no coherence between their utterances, that they are talking about different topics and using the word "benefit" in different contexts.

4. Conclusions

From these few examples of empirical data, the following conclusions about detecting, treating misunderstandings in a multi-party talk can be drawn:

(1) In a multi-party talk we have to assume that there are a number of "silent misunderstandings" that cannot be revealed as not every participant has to react (immediately) to every utterance.

(2) Misunderstandings show what image we have of the other participant as well as about the different positions and perspectives of groups and about any underlying tensions which exist between them.

(3) Revealing, or pretending to reveal, a misunderstanding can be used (strategically) to de-escalate dissent situations.

(4) There are sometimes hints in the context about whether misunderstandings are real or only pretended; nevertheless we cannot always be sure that we are detecting strategic misunderstandings.

(5) Misunderstandings can be solved by the two participants primarily involved, but there is also the possibility that a whole group cooperates to clear up a misunderstanding.

(6) As far as misunderstandings are the result of divergent perspectives between work groups or departments, they are an interesting key to the analysis of workplace communication.

References

Bührig, Kristin (1996): Reformulierende Handlungen. Zur Analyse sprachlicher Adaptierungsprozesse in institutioneller Kommunikation. – Tübingen: Narr.
Coupland, Nikolas/Wiemann, John M./Giles, Howard (1991): Talk as "Problem" and Communication as "Miscommunication". In Integrative Analysis. – In: Coupland, Nikolas/Giles, Howard/Wiemann, John M. (eds.): "Miscommunication" and Problematic Talk. 1–17. Newbury Park, London, New Delhi: Sage Publications.
Dannerer, Monika (1999): Besprechungen im Betrieb. Empirische Analysen und didaktische Perspektiven. – München: iudicium 1999 (=Studien Deutsch Bd. 26).
Droysen, Johann Gustav (1977): Historik [historisch-kritische Ausgabe P. Leyh]. – Stuttgart, Bad Cannstatt.
Eisenberg, Eric M./Phillips, Steven R. (1991): Miscommunication in Organisations.– In: Coupland, Nikolas/Giles, Howard/Wiemann, John M. (eds.): "Miscommunication" and Problematic Talk. 244–258. Newbury Park, London, New Delhi: Sage Publications.
Fiehler, Reinhard (1998): Verständigungsprobleme und gestörte Kommunikation. Einführung in die Thematik. – In: Ders. (Hg.): Verständigungsprobleme und gestörte Kommunikation. 7–16. Opladen: Westdeutscher Verlag.

- (Hg.) (1998): Verständigungsprobleme und gestörte Kommunikation. – Opladen: Westdeutscher Verlag.
Kindt, Walther/Weingarten, Rüdiger (1984): Verständigungsprobleme. – In: *Deutsche Sprache* 12 (1984). 193–218.
Lorenz, Chris (1997): Konstruktion der Vergangenheit. Eine Einführung in die Geschichtstheorie. – Köln, Weimar, Wien: Böhlau.
Rost-Roth, Martina (1994): Verständigungsprobleme in der interkulturellen Kommunikation. Ein Forschungsüberblick zu Analysen und Diagnosen in empirischen Untersuchungen.– In: *Zeitschrift für Literaturwissenschaft und Linguistik* 93 (1994). 9–45.
- (2000): Formen und Funktionen von Interrogationen im gesprochenen Deutsch. Habil, Freie Universität Berlin, noch unveröff. Manuskript.
Schwitalla, Johannes (1987): Sprachliche Mittel der Konfliktreduzierung in Streitgesprächen.– In: Schank, Gerd/Schwitalla, Johannes (Hgg.) (1987): Konflikte in Gesprächen. 99–175. Tübingen: Narr.
Selting, Margret (1987): Verständigungsprobleme. Eine empirische Analyse am Beispiel der Bürger-Verwaltungskommunikation. – Tübingen: Niemeyer.
Stalpers, Judith (1995): The expression of disagreement. In: Ehlich, Konrad/Wagner, Johannes (eds.): The Discourse of Business Negotiation. 275–290. – Berlin, New York: Mouton de Gruyter (=Studies in Anthropological Linguistics 8).
van Dijk, Teun A/. van Kintsch, Walter (1983): Strategies of discourse comprehension.– New York, NY: Academic Press.

Appendix: Transcript notation (selection)

General rule: every participant has a line on his own, indicated by the initial letter(s) of his surname at the beginning of the line. Within a score area utterances that occur one beneath the other were spoken at the same time.

*	= short pause up to one second
**	= longer pause (up to two seconds)
***	= pause up to three seconds
good,	= rising intonation
good.	= falling intonation
<u>and</u>	= stressed
is:s	= expansion
(and)	= supposed word/utterance
( )	= unrecoverable word/utterance
?L	= speaker is probably L
?	= speaker can not be identified
/	= cut-off (within a word or a construction)
fat	= important passage for interpretation

Chiara M. Monzoni

Do Italians 'Prefer' Disagreeing? Some Interactional Features of Disputational Talk in Italian Multi-Party Family Interaction

1. Disputing and Preference Organization

The analysis of disagreements and disputes in talk-in-interaction has focused on the ways speakers perform these actions, especially in relation to the forms which agreements take, and the preference organization through which speakers orient to maximizing social solidarity and social support (Heritage 1984). If we consider agreements and disagreements, then, speakers usually orient to maximizing social solidarity through actions such as agreements, rather than conflict as with disagreements (Levinson 1983; Heritage 1984; Pomerantz 1984). According to much previous research, which has been based largely on Pomerantz's work (ibidem), a preference organization is operative for agreements rather than disagreements, so that agreements are composed exclusively of agreement components and delivered in unmarked next position, and thus preferred. By contrast, disagreements display more complex and marked formats: they may be delayed by silences, agreement prefaces or reluctance markers (Levinson 1983; Heritage 1984; Pomerantz 1984; Sacks 1987; Bilmes 1988; Schegloff 1988). Because of these more elaborated forms disagreements take, we say that they are dispreferred.

Even though during disagreements speakers seem overall to avoid outright contrast and either minimize or mitigate conflictual positions through delays and other markers, once they find themselves disagreeing, they may progressively drop modulated responses and use less mitigated formats. Let us consider, for instance, the following case of a disagreement. In the first turn, C. is criticizing D.'s relationship with his partner (l. 1–3).

This extract, taken from a telephone call, is useful to highlight both the way disagreements are performed in a marked fashion, and how although at first the preference organization is fully operative, as the disagreement continues and develops the preference organization is gradually relaxed.

Extract 1. (Connie & Dee. Goldberg: 2: 18)
```
       1    C:   .hh definitely fo:r the fifteen years I:ve known you,
       2         (.3) yiknow you've really bo:th basic'ly honestly gone
       3         yer own ways.
  =>   4         (.8)¹
  =>   5    D:   essentially:: except we've hadda good relationship at
  =>   6         home yihknow
  =>   7    C:   ye:s but I mean its a relationship whe:reuh: yihknow
  =>   8         pa:ss the butter dear, hh
       9         (.5)
      10    C:   yihkno[w make a piece of toa:st dear this type'v' thing.
  =>  11    D:         [no not really
      12         (.)
      13    D:   we've actually hadda real health- I think we've hadda
      14         very healthy   relationship y'know.
```

The excerpt begins at a point when C. criticises the relationship of D. with his partner (l. 1–3). This turn is not immediately followed by a remark by D. but by a quite long gap (l. 4: 0.8 seconds), after which a first disagreeing turn is produced by D. (l. 5–6): it is characterized by an agreement preface ('essentially') which further delays the disagreeing component in the turn. The disagreement ('we've hadda good relationship at home yihknow', l. 5–6) is performed through a favourable assessment of his relationship which counters the critical position that C. has previously taken (Pomerantz 1984). This first disagreeing turn, then, is marked and thus dispreferred, since the disagreement component is delayed and pushed further back in the turn both by the gap and by the agreement preface which mitigates it. The subsequent move by C. (l. 7–8) is characterized by an agreement token ('ye:s', l. 7) immediately followed by a contrastive marker ('but', l.7), through which she introduces the disagreement ('I mean its a relationship whe:reuh: yihknow pa:ss the butter dear, hh', l. 7–8).

In both these turns, through the use of dispreference markers and agreement prefaces, speakers display an orientation to a preference organization where disagreements are marked and thus dispreferred. Nonetheless, these markers are subsequently dropped and give way to successively more direct formats (see, for instance, the outright rejection in l. 11). Therefore, even though speakers mitigate their utterances, when producing the first disagreeing turns, once they find themselves in opposition, they subsequently assume less mitigated positions: in this way, the preference organization gets relaxed, and in those cases when even more aggravated utterances are performed, a reversal of it becomes operative (see especially Kotthoff 1993).

---

[1] This datum is taken from Pomerantz (1984: 72, ex. 40), in her transcription between l. 2 & 3 (l. 3 & 5 in our transcript) no pause is noted; however, by listening to the data a .8 sec. gap is detectable.

Some Interactional Features of Disputational Talk 121

Preference organization and disagreements have been the focus of much previous research, whilst less attention has been devoted to outright conflict (with the exception of Garcia 1991; Kotthoff 1993; Hutchby 1996; Dersley 1998; Dersley & Wootton 2000). These latter studies have highlighted the fact that when speakers enter a disagreement, disagreeing turns still take a marked format; but once the dispute evolves and speakers continue maintaining oppositional stances, they may give way to less mitigated moves and even aggravated ones. In this way, a preference organization where disagreements are dispreferred is progressively relaxed and then reversed, so that disagreeing turns take a 'preferred' format later in the dispute.

2. Disputing in Italian Multi-Party Family Interaction: a 'preferred' Activity?

During the analysis of Italian family multi-party[2] interaction[3] it emerged that when disagreements arise and then develop into disputational talk, the system underlying these activities seems to be organized differently from what emerged in previous studies. Let us consider the following case, where Li. is intervening with a disconnected interjection (l. 3) during Ve.'s narrative (l. 1–2). The interjection, which is an assessment of the meat ('*cotechino*', l. 3) they have been eating, is addressed to Me., since Li. is looking at him while producing this turn and the assessment is followed by 'you know' ('you', 2nd person singular). (See extract 2.)

Here Li. is delivering a positive assessment of the '*cotechino*'[4] they have been eating ('*cotechino* was gOOd', l. 3). The addressed recipient (Me.) does not immediately respond to it: Li. elaborates her turn first through '*sai*' ('you know', 2nd person singular, l. 3), then she continues with a T.C.U. that seems to be orienting to a forthcoming criticism or disagreement by Me. ('it's NOT that it is', l. 3 and 5). At this point, Me. interjects her talk and disagrees with her (l. 6, 'it's too fat.'). This turn is formed by an assessment which introduces an opposition to the prior one by Li.: '*troppo grasso*' ('too fat', l. 6) – where the adverb 'too' strengthens the contrastive adjective 'fat'. Note that Me.'s turn is not formed

---

[2] In these interactions the number of participants ranged from four to ten.
[3] This study represents a portion of my doctoral dissertation completed at the Department of Sociology, University of York (U.K.) under the direction of Dr. Paul Drew, to whom I am indebted for his guidance and for his insightful comments on the analysis. Remaining problems are solely mine. I am also grateful to the E.U. Marie Curie Fellowship which funded this research.
[4] '*cotechino*' is a particular kind of meat (pork).

by reluctance markers or agreement prefaces, but it is composed exclusively of a contrastive assessment; thus it is produced in an unmitigated and unmarked fashion.

```
    Extract 2. (CMM:BOX3:Cotechino:13–21)
       1   VE:   .... allora ci ho pensato per una
                 .... so I've thought about it for a
       2         settimana ne ho parlato con Dani.=
                 week I've talked about it with Dani.=
=>     3   LI:   =(       ) cotechino [era bUOno.(? sai. non è)]=
                 =(       ) cotechino [was gOOd. (?you know. it's not)]=
       4   VE:                        [>anCHE PERChé ne avevamo già ordinato UNO!<]
                                      [>alSO BECause we had already ordered ONE!<]
=>     5   LI:   = che sia-  (to ME)=
                 = that it is-  (to ME)=
=>     6   ME:   =è troppo grasso.=
                 =((it'))s too fat.=
       7   VE:   =che-=
                 =that-=
=>     8   LI:   =no::::! questo è molto molto c- cosato⁵ NO::::!
                 =no::::! this one is very very th- thinged NO::::!
```

Moreover, even though this disagreement is not immediately forthcoming, but is first withheld and delayed, it is not clear whether the delay is dependent on an orientation of the speakers to the disagreement as a dispreferred action. Note that Li.'s turn (l. 3 and l. 5) is a disconnected interjection,[6] and Me. responds to Li. after Ve. has finished speaking in overlap with Li. (l. 4). In other words, even though Me.'s disagreement is delayed, the delay might be related to the fact that Li. has intervened in the interaction between Ve. and Li., more than to a preference organization where disagreements are dispreferred. In those instances when a speaker intervenes, while another interactant is speaking, the recipients addressed by the interjector may at first withhold their responses and show an orientation to the interaction which is in progress. Therefore, the delays – which might at first be interpreted as indices of a preference organization where disagreements are marked and thus dispreferred – may be related to other phenomena associated with multi-party interaction. In other words, if the same exchange had occurred during a conversation between Li. and Me. only. Me. would display an orientation to a preference organization where disagreements are dispreferred. However, it is not possible to make the same assumption in the more complex interactional environment of multi-party talk. In this conversational context, in fact, Me. might have withheld his disagreement because of the contingent talk by Ve.

After Me. has delivered the first disagreement in an unmitigated fashion, Li. responds to him immediately through a disagreeing turn which is aggravated since it is prefaced by an

---

[5] '*cosato*' (literally, 'thinged': past participle of the verb '*cosare*') is a slang expression which replaces any verb one does not remember or one does not know.

[6] This interjection is disconnected since it is not topically and pragmatically coherent with the immediate prior turn.

outright rejection ('=no::::! this one is very very th- thinged NO::::!', l. 8). In this way, she heightens the contrast with Me.'s position.

The formats which the first disagreeing turns take differ from the ones which characterized the oppositional moves found in the first case we considered (ex. 1). As we noted, in (1), the first disagreeing turns are mitigated by agreement components and other dispreference prefaces, so that it is clear that in that case speakers orient to a preference organization where disagreements are dispreferred. In the extract from Italian data (ex. 2), by contrast, interactants do not seem to orient to such an underlying organization: disagreements are performed in an unmitigated and even aggravated fashion, so that if a preference organization is operative at all, we could say that disputational moves are 'preferred', rather than dispreferred. In other words, in the second extract, disagreement is not mitigated but conflictual stances are performed through particularly oppositional unmitigated and aggravated moves.

The second extract is a prototypical representation of the way speakers engage in disagreements in our corpus. They do so by performing outright and unmitigated moves from the very first disagreeing turn. Therefore, the organization underlying speakers' actions in the data is different from the preference organization found in other corpora – where the first disagreeing turns are marked and thus dispreferred. In our corpus, the first turn in which the speaker takes issue with a previous utterance (an assessment or an assertion) is always constituted exclusively by disagreeing components; thus it is unmitigated[7] and it is not usually withheld and delayed.[8] Since the very first disagreeing turn is not marked, then, we can not talk of a reversal of the preference organization: in other words, in this corpus a preference organization, as it has been described in the literature, is *not* operative from the very beginning of the disagreement.

Such a difference, between what emerges from our data and what has been so far described in the literature, seems to be connected to the different nature and interactional context of our corpus. The corpora analysed in previous research are mostly taken from adult two-party interactions (both telephone and face-to-face: Pomerantz 1984; face-to-face: Dersley & Wootton 2000 and 2001), institutional two-party (telephone calls: Hutchby 1996; face-to-face: Kotthoff 1993) or three-party talk (Garcia 1991). In none of these corpora do we find multi-party interactions (with four or more participants) in a particularly

---

[7] Note that in some instances it may even be aggravated, through the use of outright rejections as a preface to the disagreeing turn (see extract 2, l. 9), or even as free-standing oppositional turns (see below: extract 5).

[8] In some instances, the first disagreeing move is delayed. However, in the vast majority of these cases, the delay is linked to other phenomena connected to the multi-party context. For example, the first disagreeing turn may be withheld at first, in those cases when another concurrent interaction is under way (see ex. 2). For a further discussion about delays, see also below.

informal setting (family talk). Therefore, the different organization of disagreements in our corpora might be strongly influenced by the specific interactional setting where it occurs.

Let us consider, for instance, the following case, where Ga. is talking to Cl. about a religious play (see l. 1)[9], Ma. is a by-stander:[10]

```
Extract 3. (CMM: TR98:4:Assisi:28–41)
      1    GA:   hai mai visto 'forza venite gente'?
                 have you ever seen 'forza venite gente'?
      2          (1.6)
      3    CL:   °no°.
      4          (.4)
      5    GA:   la commedia.
                 the play.
      6    GA:   ah::: stupenda,
                 ah::: wonderful,
      7          (1.2)
=>    8    GA:   perché (.4) mo' va oltre il fatto religioso.
                 because (.4) now it goes beyond the religious fact.
      9          (.)
      10   GA:   bellissimo °da vedere°.=
                 very beautiful °to see°.=
=>    11   MA:   =mo' guarda caso un'altra volta con 'sti fatti reli°g°-=
                 =now look by sheer coincidence one more time with these
                 reli°g°- facts=
=>    12   GA:   =ho de[tto (     )
                 =I've sa[id (     )
=>    13   MA:        [UE':::! NON FATEME ESAURIRE! EH! PER CORTESIA!=
                      [C'MO:::N! DON'T EXHAUST[11] ME! EH! PLEASE!=
=>    14         = >NON COMINCIARE ANCHE TU[12]<
                 = >DON'T YOU BEGIN IT AS WELL<
```

Here Ga. has asked Cl. if she has seen a (religious) play (l. 1). After the minimal response by her recipient (l. 3), Ga. continues first by specifying that it is a play (l. 5), then by positively assessing it (l. 6), and by explaining the reason why she thinks it is so good ('because (.4) now it goes beyond the religious fact.', l. 8). After this turn a micropause (l. 9) is produced, after which she delivers a further assessment of the play ('very beautiful to see', l. 10). After this second assessment, a non-ratified participant (Ma.), intervenes to argue with her ('now look by sheer coincidence one more time with these reli°g-° facts', l. 11). This first oppositional turn is not mitigated insofar as it is formed exclusively by disagreeing components; thus does not show any orientation to the preference organization as we know it. Note, first of all, that Ma. does not disagree with Ga.'s second assessment but he takes issue with the fact that she has been speaking about 'religious facts', which is what

---

[9] Note that this extract is taken from a set of data taped in a period of time when the members of this family have been extensively discussing religion and the Church.
[10] I.e. a non-ratified participant at this point of the interaction.
[11] 'you' second person plural.
[12] 'you', second person singular.

she introduced in the turn prior to the assessment (l. 8 'because (.4) now it goes beyond the religious fact'). Therefore, his oppositional turn is delayed. However, in this case we cannot state with certainty that the delay shows an orientation to a preference organization where disagreements are dispreferred: the delay may be connected to the fact that he is a non-ratified participant intervening in the talk.

In general, then, the delays during the delivery of the first disagreeing turn may not be solely and univocally related to an orientation of the interactants to disagreement as a dispreferred action. By contrast, they may be explainable also in the light of other factors connected to multi-party talk, such as the fact that other interactions are under way (see extract 2), and the fact that a non-ratified participant intervenes in a participation framework of which he is not part at that point of the talk, to disagree with one of the ratified participants (see extract 3).[13]

Furthermore, in these instances, once a silence takes place after an assertion, this does not lead to a revision by the speaker that uttered the first utterance. Compare the following case, taken from dyadic talk:

```
       Extract n. 4 (Pomerantz 1984: 76: ex. 50: JS:II:48)
=>   1    L:   D'they have a good cook there?
=>   2         (1.7)
=>   3    L:   Nothing special?
     4    J:   No. - Every- everybody takes their turns.
```

Here the first question – which displays a positive assessment – is not immediately responded to by the recipient (l. 2). After quite a long gap (l. 2), the first speaker revises and reformulates the question through a backdown (l. 3). According to Pomerantz, backdowns may be produced "when recipients *potentially* disagree" (Pomerantz 1984: 76, emphasis added). In other words, the fact that the recipient withholds his response is interpreted by that interactant as a move that potentially leads to disagreement. At this stage, then, by revising his position through a backdown, the first speaker maximizes the chances of an agreement being produced, rather than a disagreement.

However, multi-party interaction seems to be more complex than dyadic talk, when it comes to issues such as the interpretation of silences by the interactants. As we have said, earlier in the previous extract (3) Ga. is speaking to Cl., who is thus a ratified recipient of her talk, and Ma. is a by-stander (among other participants). Since Cl. is the ratified recipient of Ga.'s talk, the gaps throughout this stretch of talk (l. 1–10) are interactively produced by those two speakers only. In other words, even though the silences might be indices of some problems in the talk, Ga. could not possibly have interpreted them as indices of an upcoming disagreement by a third non-aligned and non-ratified participant (Ma.) at

---

[13] See also ex. 5 (l. 4).

that point in the conversation. It follows then that some of the resources that speakers have to avoid conflict in dyadic interaction are not available during multi-party talk, insofar as the current speaker may not foresee an upcoming disagreement which might be later produced by a bystander, in the same way as he can do in dyadic talk, when the current speaker and his recipient are also the only ratified participants in that interaction.

In our corpus we have also found instances where a speaker may invite a revision of the first disagreeing turn. Nonetheless, once interactants deliver a first oppositional move, they keep pursuing disagreement rather than agreement, as exemplified in the following case:

```
    Extract n. 5 (CMM:TR98:7:4-Priest:15–26)
=>   1    PR:    no vede oggi e:: la donna in carriera come si dice è un
=>   2           problema sa::.=
                 no you see today a::nd career women as people say¹⁴ are a
                 problem you¹⁵ know::.=
     3    LI:    = eh [(?veramente)
                 = eh [(?really)
=>   4    CL:         [no no no! NO! ¹⁶=
=>   5    PR:    =eh?
                 =what?
=>   6    CL:    no no!=
=>   7    PR:    =eh?
                 =what?
     8    TE:    °non è d'accordo.°=
                 °she doesn't agree.°=
=>   9    CL:    =FINAL[MENTE! FINALMENTE! ci avete oppress(h)o(hh.)=
                 =AT   [LAST! AT LAST! you¹⁷ kept us und(h)e(hh.)r =
     10   LI:         [°no°-
=>   11   CL:    = per tant(h)i(h.)millenni! s.v.
                 = for so man(h)y(h.)millenia! s.v.
```

In this case, Pr. has been telling Li. about his niece and the problems she has to reconcile her job and her family needs (data not shown). In his turn in l. 1–2 he makes an assessment about career women in general. While Li. immediately agrees with him (l. 3), a by-stander (Cl.) intervenes after a slight delay and rejects this assertion through a turn which is exclusively formed by rejection tokens ('no no no! NO!' , l. 4)[18], through which she displays an aggravated opposition to Pr.'s stance. Pr. reacts to it through a repair initiator 'eh?' (l. 5). As we have previously noted, according to Pomerantz (1984), when an assessment has been delivered, recipients may react through silences, questioning repeats, requests for clarifications, or other repair initiators, after which the first speaker may revise his utter-

---

[14] 'as people say' refers to the expression 'career women', not the 'problem'.
[15] 'you' second person singular (formal use).
[16] Note that the whole cluster is uttered with animated intonation; moreover, the four 'no's are performed with different tones: the first 'no' is uttered with a very low tone, in each next one the tone progressively increases.
[17] 'you' second person plural.
[18] See note 16.

ance and produce backdowns from their previous turns. In this way, agreement is collaboratively pursued and maximized. Similarly, in this case the repair initiator may have the function of inviting a revision and repair of Cl.'s aggravated first oppositional move.

Cl. responds to the repair initiator through 'no no!' (l. 6). Even though formally this turn is designed as a repair of her prior utterance, since she utters just two 'no's' with a tone which is lower than the one previously used,[19] pragmatically the essence of her turn does not change: in other words, she still rejects Pr.'s first assertion in an unmitigated fashion. Therefore, she does not revise her position, but reasserts it. In other words, she still pursues the disagreement. Subsequently, Pr. produces another repair initiator ('eh?', l. 7), through which he invites again a revision of the oppositional stance taken by Cl.

After the repair initiator, Te. intervenes and makes explicit Cl.'s position through a meta-pragmatical comment ('she doesn't agree', l. 8). After Te.'s intervention, Cl. produces an outright accusation ('AT LAST! AT LAST! you kept us und(h)e(hh.)r for so man(h)y(h.) millennia!', l. 9 & l. 11), through which she expresses her oppositional stance and engages Pr. in conflict in a more forceful way.[20]

In the previous instance taken from a dyadic interaction (ex. 4), the use of repair initiators after a first assessment leads to a revision and backdown of it, so that in that extract speakers pursue agreements, rather than disagreement. By contrast, in the example we have just considered (ex. 5), the interactant who produces the first oppositional move disregards the opportunities – created by her co-participant through the use of repair initiators – to revise her aggravated position: in this way, she pursues disagreement, rather than agreement. This occurs regularly in our corpus: once speakers have taken an oppositional stance to a prior turn, they maintain that position and pursue disagreement from the very start, even in those cases when the speaker they disagree with provides at first the possibility for a revision or backdown through the use of repair initiators. In these instances, then, interactants do not display an orientation to the preference organization documented in the research literature: rather, disagreement is pursued in an outright fashion from the very beginning.

---

[19] The first utterance, by contrast, was produced by increasing the tone of each 'no' (see note n. 16).
[20] Note that through the accusation she makes relevant a response by Pr. (Atkinson & Drew 1979; Garcia 1991).

3. Concluding Remarks

Through the analysis of disputational talk in Italian multi-party family interactions, we have seen that disagreeing and disputational utterances take a particularly unmitigated and even aggravated format. This seems to indicate the operativeness of an organization where disagreements are unmarked from the very beginning of disputational talk. This is in contrast with previous studies which underlined the existence of a preference organization where disagreements are dispreferred (see, especially, Pomerantz 1984); or where the preference organization is reversed later in the dispute: the first disagreeing turns take a dispreferred format, but when the dispute progresses, disagreements – rather than agreements – become preferred (Bilmes 1988; Garcia 1991; Kotthoff 1993; Dersley 1998; Dersley & Wootton 2000). In our cases, we cannot speak of a preference organization where disagreements are dispreferred, not even of a reversal of a preference organization, because there is no orientation to such a system from the very start. As we noted, the main difference between our data and the ones from previous research is that our corpus is composed of multi-party interactions taking place in a particularly informal setting. Hence, it might be the very nature of these data and their interactional context which allow for such different practices for disagreements. In other words, there might be a subset of practices which operate in this specific kind of setting. As we have seen, the very multi-party context seems to be more complex than a dyadic one, with regard to certain actions: for instance, silences might be more difficult to interpret as associated with an up-coming disagreement, in those cases when a by-stander is going to disagree.

Moreover, as far as disagreements and disputational talk are concerned, the preference organization, as it has been described, seems to be in some cases unsatisfactory. Preference organization has been described as a tool speakers have to promote social solidarity and avoid conflict (Levinson 1983; Heritage 1984). Even if this is the case for other kinds of actions and for disagreements in different social and interactional settings, it does not seem to be true for our corpus. The final aim of disagreements and arguments does not seem to be the one of promoting social solidarity: by contrast, by taking such oppositional stances, the final goal these speakers pursue is to 'advance' their position and/or convince the other of their stance. During these exchanges the final goal of the interactants is to assert and defend their position, rather than promoting social solidarity: from the very beginning, they avoid mitigated moves (such as agreement prefaces), and once they have expressed oppositional stances, they do not revise them. Speakers, then, avoid those very moves that they should pursue, if a preference organization would be operative.

References

Atkinson, Maxwell/Drew, Paul (1979): Order in Court: the organization of verbal interaction in judicial settings. – London: Macmillan.
Atkinson, Maxwell/Heritage, John (eds.) (1984): Structures of Social Action. – Cambridge & New York: Cambridge University Press.
Bilmes, Jack (1988): The Concept of Preference in Conversation Analysis. – *Language in Society* 17, 161–181.
Button, Graham/ Lee, John R. E. (eds.) (1987): Talk and Social Organization. – Clevedon: England: Multilingual Matters.
Dersley, Ian (1998): Complaining and Arguing in Everyday Conversation. – Unpublished D. Phil. dissertation, University of York, U.K.
Dersley, Ian/Wootton, Anthony J. (2000): Complaint Sequences within Antagonistic Arguments. – *Research on Language and Social Interaction* 33(4), 375–406.
– (2001): In the Heat of the Sequence: Interactional features preceding walkouts from argumentative talk. – *Language in Society* 30, 611–638.
Garcia, Angela (1991): Dispute Resolution without Disputing: How the interactional organization of mediation hearings minimizes argument. – *American Sociological Review* 56, 818–835.
Heritage, John (1984): Garfinkel and Ethnomethodology. – Cambridge: Polity Press.
Hutchby, Ian (1996): Confrontation Talk: Arguments, asymmetries and power on talk radio. – Mahwah, N.J.: Lawrence Erlbaum Associates, Inc..
Kotthoff, Helga (1993): Disagreement and Concession in Disputes: On the context sensitivity of preference structures. – *Language in Society* 22, 193–216.
Levinson, Stephen (1983): Pragmatics. – Cambridge & New York: Cambridge University Press.
Pomerantz, Anita (1984): Agreeing and Disagreeing with Assessments: Some features of preferred/dispreferred turn shapes. – In: M. Atkinsons, J. Heritage (eds.) (1984), 57–102.
Sacks, Harvey (1987): On the Preferences for Agreement and Contiguity in Sequences in Conversation. – In : G. Button, J. R. E. Lee, (eds.) (1987), 54–69.
Schegloff, Emanuel A. (1988): On a Virtual Servo-mechanism for Guessing Bad News: a single case conjuncture. – *Social Problems* 35, 442–457.

Sara Cigada

The Logical Structure of Dialogue and the Representation of Emotions: An Example from Hitchcock's *Notorious*

> "Talking is a special case or variety of purposive, indeed rational, behavior"
> Grice (1975)

In the analysed text – some sequences from Alfred Hitchcock's *Notorious* (1946) – linguistic tools are combined with images to create the representation of a highly emotional situation. The *páthos* effects are reached through the use of inferential structures which determine a growing tension in the dialogue.

1. Theoretical Frame

Rigotti (1993), Rigotti/Rocci (2001), Rigotti/Cigada (forthcoming) give guidelines for an analysis of speech acts in terms of "communicative event", and outline the methodological issues involved in examining textual utterances from a functional point of view.[1]

---

[1] "In che senso diciamo che l'atto comunicativo è un evento? Un evento è una qualunque cosa che accade, meglio, che ci accade. In altre parole, si parla di evento quando si ha a che fare con qualcosa 1.che accade e 2.che, più o meno direttamente, ci tocca, ci cambia, ci sposta. Quando un evento comunicativo si compie, esso produce un cambiamento nel destinatario e questo cambiamento è il "senso" della avvenuta comunicazione. Il fatto di parlare di evento comunicativo sottolinea il fatto che, dal punto di vista del destinatario, il messaggio 'arriva' come sollecitazione a lasciarsi coinvolgere (nelle diverse maniere in cui un messaggio può coinvolgere: informa, rallegra, rende destinatari di una promessa, richiede una risposta, pone nella condizione di dover obbedire o disobbedire... ecc.). Il coinvolgimento del destinatario, il suo cambiamento, rappresentano un elemento del senso, ciò che fa dell'atto comunicativo, appunto, un evento comunicativo. Ciò non toglie che il messaggio abbia già un senso 'proprio' in quanto testo coerente e in quanto atto linguistico adeguato all'intenzione comunicativa del mittente". (Rigotti/Cigada, forthcoming). "What do we mean by saying that a communicative act is an event? An event is anything that happens, or better, that happens *to us*. In other words, we speak of event when we are dealing with something which, 1.happens, and, 2.somehow touches, changes or moves us. When a communicative event takes place, it produces a change in the hearer and this change is the "sense" of the communicative event. To speak of communicative event means that the message comes to the hearer as a request for involvement (in any of the different ways, in which a message may in-

In a recent article Karl N. Renner proposes an analysis of text/visual cooperation in television programs. The visual part of television represents "Realitätsausschnitte" (Renner 2001: 28). In fact the meaning of verbal interaction is created by the visible presence of situations which are not verbally referred to, but which are necessary to "build up" the sense of the text. For example, on a freezing December morning Andrea meets Stefano, who is arriving at the university wearing a T-shirt, and asks him:

—Aren't you cold?!

The same question would be senseless in another situation, on a hot afternoon six months later for example.

The switching from the description of verbal communication components – like the one we have just illustrated – to the attribution of textual functions, however, does not seem justified. For this reason we keep Renner's paper in the background of our analysis, as a possible source of stimuli.[2]

2. Methodological Issues

In order to determine the object of our analysis, it is important to focus on the interaction between the characters in the plot. This being a fictional interaction, however, the actual one, which takes place between the director and the audience, cannot be left aside. This is why we sometimes refer to actual interaction in order to better understand the development of the scene we examine.

The scene chosen is analysed by means of Rigotti's "Congruity Theory" (Rigotti forthcoming). The scene – a film sequence – is divided into minimal utterances (cf. Rigotti 1993: 46), which correspond to minimal meaningful steps in the communicative interaction. Each of these steps is dominated by a Connective Predicate (CP from now on), which

---

volve: by informing, cheering up, promising, asking for answers, forcing to obey or disobey, etc.). The hearer's involvement and the change produced in him are part of the 'sense'. They are indeed what turns a communicative act into a communicative event. Nonetheless the message already has a sense of its own, as it is coherent and consistent with the speaker's communicative intention".

[2] In the last part of his paper, Renner proposes the following hypothesis: in texts constituted by verbal texts and images, images represent the topics while verbal parts represent the focus. He provides some simple examples from his corpus. Even if this assumption appears to be naïve from the text-analytical point of view, it would be interesting to use it to examine portions of some texts.

represents the communicative function[3] of that specific portion of the text. It is possible to assign a definite function to each utterance, as utterances fulfil textual functions by definition.

From a semantic point of view, the CP has a predicative structure, i.e. it determines a series of related objects (arguments): Speaker, Hearer/s, Utterance/s. Inside the utterance the specific functions of topic and focus are determined by the CP itself (cf. Tschida 1995), which directs the interest of the interlocutors to a particular aspect of their shared experience and controls the communicative tension.

The CP can be represented in the following way:

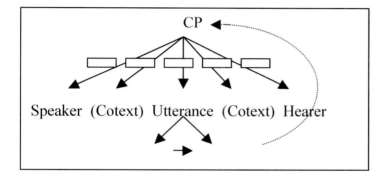

The analysis of real dialogue utterances meets with considerable difficulties; for this reason we consider this work only as an attempt to analysis. The representation itself poses a number of problems: one of the most difficult aspects is the conversational implicature, which often remains completely implicit even if it is an essential element of the meaning. Nevertheless it seems worthwhile to submit this model to further discussion.

3. The Text Examined

We analyse a sequence of the film *Notorious*, starring Ingrid Bergman and Cary Grant. The plot is the following: the CIA asks Miss Alicia Huberman to spy on Alexius Sebastian. Mr. Sebastian, an old friend of Alicia's late father, is the head of a Nazi organisation in

---

[3] For the relationship between this model and the illocution-perlocution models, see Rigotti forthcoming. In the representation of CP, the smaller boxes on the arrows show the specific presuppositions for each argument.

Rio. Devlin, a CIA agent, falls in love with the girl and takes it upon himself to redeem her. But when Mr. Sebastian proposes to Alicia, Devlin, blinded by jealousy, abandons her. Alicia is discovered by Mr. Sebastian, whom she has married in order to spy on him, and he tries to poison her. Fortunately Devlin is unable to forget the girl and comes to Alicia's rescue, destroys the Nazi organisation and... happy ending comes. The analysed sequence coincides with a meaningful breakthrough in the plot.

Alicia's arrival is announced to the CIA agents in the department. As she is supposed not to go there lest she be identified as a spy, they express their disapproval of her behaviour before she enters the room, mentioning her past habits. Devlin stands up for her.[4]

> The door opens and a dazed Alicia is shown into the office.
> PRESCOTT How do you do, Miss Huberman?
> ALICIA How do you do?
> PRESCOTT (introduces the others) This is Mister Beardsley and Señor Julio Barbosa. Care to sit down?
> ALICIA (sits) Thank you.
> BARBOSA You have the esteem of my government, Señorita.
> BEARDSLEY But we are worried about you visiting this office.
> ALICIA I promise not to break the rules again, but I need some advice and I couldn't find Mister Devlin. In fact, I need it before lunch.

In the first part of the sequence some formal exchanges are performed: greetings, introduction, offering a seat, thanking. Beardsley refers to Alicia's unexpected visit with the euphemism "we are worried" and Alicia replies explaining that she has been obliged to break the rule since she urgently needs advice from Mr. Devlin. She must have expected to find him there, as this is the case. The expressions of courtesy performed contrast with the mistrust expressed before she enters.

		Frames	*Dialogues*
(1)	camera framing Alicia	PRESCOTT (1a) Something happened? ALICIA (1b) Yes, / (1c) something rather confusing. (1d) Mister Sebastian has asked me to marry him.
	camera on Devlin, amazed; short pause	BEARDSLEY (1e) What? PRESCOTT (1f) Well, well.
	Alicia	ALICIA (1g) He / he wants me to marry him right away / (1h) and I am to give him my answer at lunch. (1i) And I didn't know what the department might think
	she looks at Devlin	about such a step.
	Devlin, shocked	

---

[4] This is the meaning of the scene from an internal point of view: we already know why she is going to the department, as the director has just shown us Alexius Sebastian proposing to her.

	(same)	PRESCOTT (1j) Are you willing to go
	Prescott and Alicia	this far for us, Miss Huberman?
	(same) Alicia turning to Prescott	ALICIA (1k) Yes, / if you wish.
(2)	Prescott turning to Devlin	PRESCOTT (2l) What do you think of this, Devlin?
	Devlin, motionless	DEVLIN (2m) Oh, I think it's a useful idea.
	Beardsley to Devlin	BEARDSLEY (2n) Well, you know the situation better than any of us.

DEVLIN (to Alicia) May I ask what inspired Alex Sebastian to go this far?
ALICIA He's in love with me.
DEVLIN And he thinks you're in love with him?
ALICIA (more to Devlin than the others) Yes, that's what he thinks.
BARBOSA (delighted) Gentlemen, it's the cream of the jest.
ALICIA (looks straight at Devlin) Then... then, it's all right? (Prescott sees the look pass between Alicia and Devlin but doesn't know what to make of it.)
PRESCOTT Well. Yes, I-I'd say so. Of course, it's a perfect marriage... for us.
DEVLIN There's only one thing. Won't it delay us a bit?
PRESCOTT What do you mean?
DEVLIN Well, Mister Sebastian is a very romantic fellow, isn't he, Alicia?
ALICIA Yes.
DEVLIN Then he'll probably want to take his bride away for a long honeymoon. Won't that hold us up?
BEARDSLEY Devlin's got a point there.
PRESCOTT Oh, I don't know. I think we can rely on Miss Huberman to get back into the house, quickly.
ALICIA (quietly) Yes, I think I can manage that.
(Devlin abruptly gets up to leave the room to cover his emotion.)
DEVLIN Well, everything seems to be nicely arranged. I don't think you need me here anymore, do you, Captain Prescott?
(Devlin closes the door on his way out, leaving a drained Alicia with the others.)[5]

Two "main utterances" – (1) and (2) – are recognisable in the passage (which lasts 32 seconds in all). The change from (1) to (2) is indicated by a gesture of Prescott, by a change of prosody and by a frame switch from 'Prescott and Alicia' to 'Prescott and Devlin'. The function of (1) as a whole is complex enough: in fact "Alicia asks Devlin for help"; at the same time, she shows she is ready to do anything in order to help her country and this substantiates her moral integrity as a patriot, even if her availability to marry a man she does not love verges on despair. The function of (2) is also complex. Refusing to give her his help because of his jealousy, Devlin proves to be a mean man in spite of the importance of his job. In the development of the plot, Devlin's omission is the hero's mistake, which represents a turning point in the story. Let us zoom in now.

---

[5] The script is available at http://www.geocities.com/Hollywood/Cinema/3761/notorious.html; http://www.script-o-rama.com/filmtranscripts.shtml (Sept. 2001).

4. Utterance Analysis

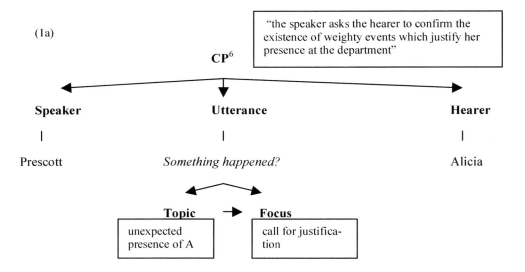

As the function of a question may be represented as "call for answer" (cf. Gobber 1999: 17ff), questions have been considered as strategies for the management of the speaker/hearer relationship: what the speaker says demands an answer from the hearer.

In this context, the expected question would be "What happened?" (an open question indeed), because it is a contextual presupposition that Alicia must not go to the department and, in a 'normal'[7] relationship between speaker and hearer, the quoting of presupposition breaks Grice's second rule in the category of Quantity.[8] The infraction of a rule usually indicates that another sense-effect is produced: "Something happened?", in fact, shows Prescott's mistrust as a secondary sense-effect. As the presumption of this question is a positive one, its general meaning becomes "It is better for you to prove that something important happened" (cf. Ilie 1993).

Notice that the topic of the utterance is neither constituted by a part of the text nor by inferences from the text, but by the fact that Alicia went to the department.

Questions as "call for answer" determine in general a change of turn: they establish the hearer's commitment to answer to the question itself. Alicia's answer is highly coopera-

---

[6] In the representation of each utterance the Connective Predicate is made explicit in the box at the top right.
[7] 'Normal' means here 'based on reciprocal trust'. Cf. Rigotti (1998).
[8] Grice (1975, 45): "Do not make your contribution more informative than is required". The subject should be discussed, but we have no room here.

tive: without considering the expression of mistrust, she confirms the existence of a weighty event and she starts telling *what* is going on.

(1b)

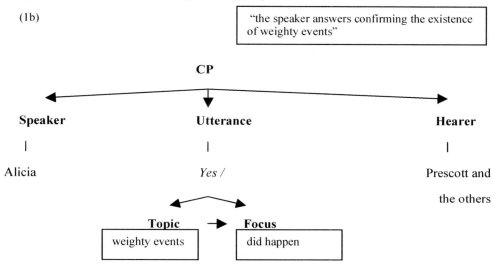

Alicia answers the question as it has been posed, leaving aside the implicit threat expressed in Prescott's previous turn: she confirms that something unexpected has happened and explains the events. As it is a contextual presupposition that something unexpected has happened – otherwise she would not be there – this linguistic behaviour represents a new infraction of a communicative rule. Again a sense-effect is produced: she gives us (but not the internal hearers, who still do not know) an impression both of humility and of great strength and deep calm, in spite of her evident and comprehensible confusion, with the result that she appears to be morally superior.

The first utterance in Alicia's turn is cataphoric: the indefiniteness of "something" still needs to be fulfilled and this creates a suspence. That is why we decided to divide Alicia's turn into three different utterances. Marked prosody seems to indicate the outlined steps.

(1c)

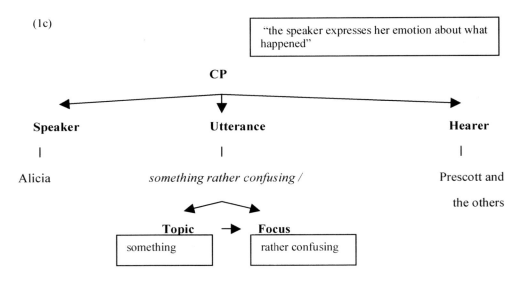

Again this second part of Alicia's turn is cataphoric; suspense grows in the action. Towards the spectators, Alicia's self-control in relating what we already know shows her courage.

(1d)

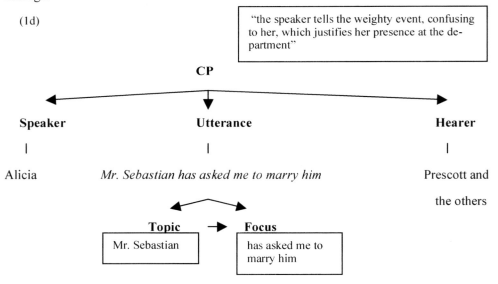

In this sequential step Devlin is a special hearer. To him, the sense of Alicia's last words should also contain the following implication: "As you proposed to me as well, I ask you whether your proposal is still valid. If this is the case, as I hope, I will not marry Mr. Sebastian".

The Logical Structure of Dialogue and the Representation of Emotions 139

Three emotional reactions follow Alicia's words: two of them are expressed in Beardsley and Prescott's turns; in the cinema construction they follow each other, while they could be contemporary in a real action. The third reaction is expressed by an image: while Breadsley and Prescott speak, Devlin's dumb amazement is shown in frame (focus in frame) rather than in the dialogue.

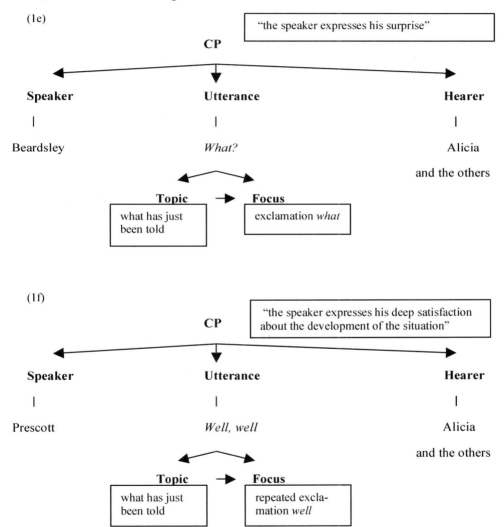

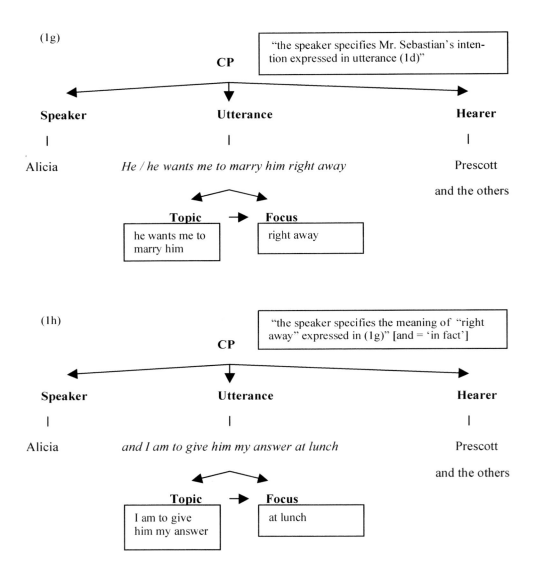

The deontic expression "I am to give…" is an implication following the proposal. Devlin continues to be a particular hearer of what Alicia says.

The indirect interrogative structure in the next utterance (1i) contains an indirect speech act, i.e. a request to the department to define its position. Alicia's request presupposes her decision to act according to the department's judgement and it consequently implies that she needs to know the answer. At this point of the dialogue she has answered Prescott's former suspicion about her unadvised coming to the department: yes, something has happened which justifies her going there in spite of danger. The following utterance (1j) shows Prescott's change of opinion.

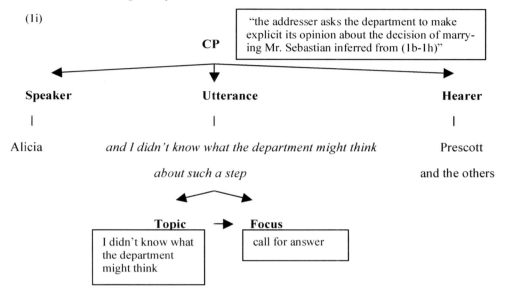

The phrase "about such a step" seems to be a thematic transition, i.e. an anaphoric part of the utterance. Alicia pronounces these last words looking at Devlin: this is an indication for the interpretation of (1k), after Prescott's turn of speech. In fact the frame moves now to Devlin who looks upset. He does not utter a word, but his visible emotion forms part of the general sense of the utterance (against Renner, in this utterance the image shows the focus).

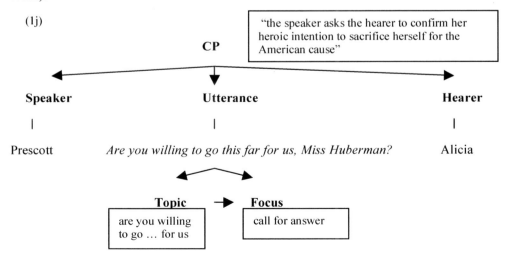

The adverb "this far" seems to be anaphoric for "such a step"; i.e. it constitutes a thematic transition.

Notice the opposition between "for us" and "Miss Huberman": Alicia's German family name reminds us of her Nazi father and contrasts with "for us" underlining the speaker's admiration. He now realises that Alicia is a patriot.

In the next utterance polysemy produces a multiplicity of emotional effects. The kind of analysis we are conducting permits us to represent this polysemy.

(1k)[A]

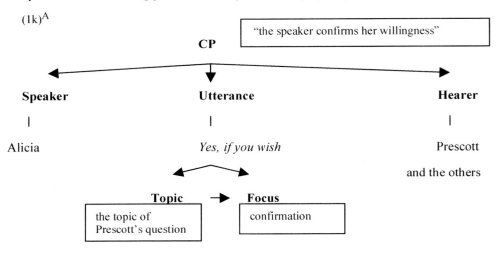

In the text addressed to Prescott, "if you wish" may be considered as a transition. In fact, it has already been inferred from Alicia's discourse that she has decided to do whatever the department judges to be appropriate. She is just waiting to know whether they will consider it useful for her to marry Mr. Sebastian.

But the same text is addressed to Devlin too. In the second case, the utterance has to be split into two sub-utterances:

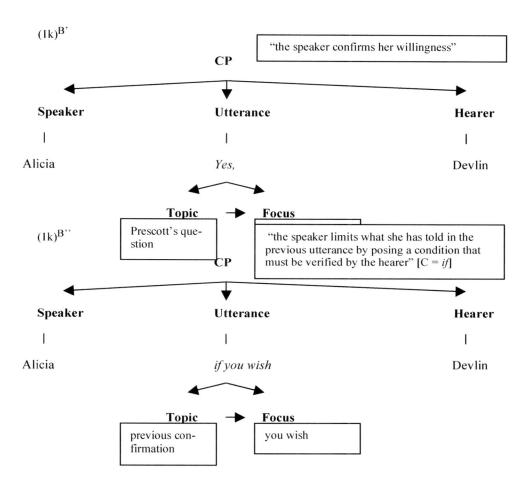

Devlin's wish to marry Alicia is shared knowledge between the two of them. With this request, Alicia starts to behave in accordance with the ancient *éndoxon* "amare est idem velle et idem nolle":[9] she proves that she loves him in any case, even if he will not understand it until the end of the story. The condition $(1k)^{B''}$ is confirmed by the hearer, who keeps silent in spite of pressure – Devlin should say something as he is the CIA member in charge of Mr. Sebastian's case.

---

[9] "Loving is to want and not to want together with another one". Sallust uses a part of this proverbial saying for the first time in *Cat* 20,4 (*Idem velle atque idem nolle ea demum firma amicitia est*), recalling the Aristotelian concept of friendship (*Rhet* 1381 a 9–11). After Sallust the concept can be found in Minucius Felix (*Octavius* 1,3), Jerome (*Ep* 130,12), Apollinaris Sidonius, Donatus, Seneca (*De ira* 3,34). Other authors use the same idea in a theological (Ambrose, Colombanus, John of Salisbury, Rosvita) or a political (Apuleius) context. Many thanks to Maria Bettetini for providing me with this information.

At this point Alicia's position is clear. Both the department and Devlin must react. The shift from the first group of utterances (1, a-k) to the second (2, l-n) coincides with Prescott's intervention where he asks Devlin to give his opinion.

(2l)

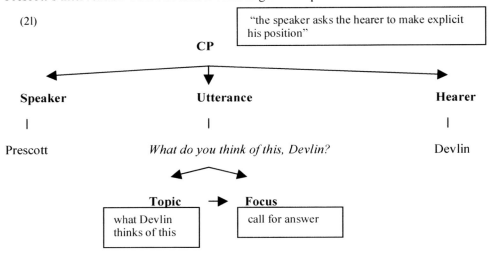

The answer is polysemic, too, in that hearers are changed in a different way by the utterance:

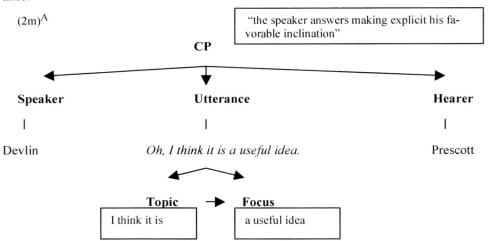

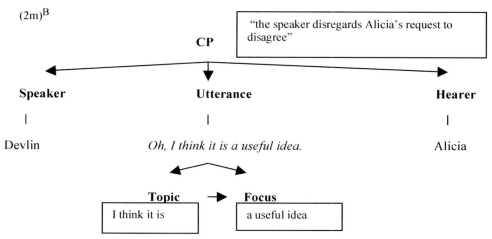

In this utterance Devlin fulfils his betrayal of Alicia, whose sacrifice is said to be "useful". He knows the situation better than anybody else in the department, so his statement is considered as definitive. This is confirmed by the following:

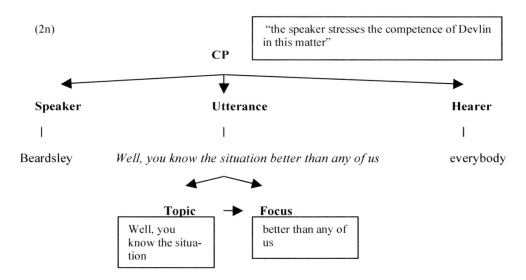

This statement is the second premise of a chain of two enthymemes:

A. Whoever knows the situation better than the others can judge in a better way;
   (2n) *You know the situation better than the others*;
   You can judge in a better way.

B. It is good to act in accordance with the opinion of the one who can judge in a better way;
You can judge in a better way;
(conclusion) *We will act in accordance to your opinion.*

5. Concluding Remarks

The analysis of this short interaction in *Notorious* shows that it is possible to analyse the content of a dialogue by means of the Congruity Theory, i.e. through connectives which describe the semantic-pragmatic function of each utterance in its relationship to the speaker and the hearer. In the sequence we analysed it is interesting to remark in particular that even a highly emotional situation can be examined by means of this methodology, highlighting the logical structure of dialogue.

In conclusion, it is meaningful to note that the *páthos* effects themselves are created through the use of reason, as we have detected by the application of a strict semantic-pragmatic analysis.

References

Gobber, Giovanni (1999): Pragmatica delle frasi interrogative. Con applicazioni al Tedesco, al Polacco e al Russo. – Milano: ISU.
Grice, H. Paul (1975): Logic and Conversation. – In: P. Cole, J.L. Morgan (eds.): Syntax and Semantics. Vol. 3: Speech Acts, 41–58. New York: Academic Press.
Ilie, Cornelia (1994): What Else Can I Tell You? A Pragmatic Study of English Rhetorical Questions as Discursive and Argumentative Acts. – Stockholm: Almqvist & Wiksell International.
Plantin, Christian (1997): Les raisons des émotions. – In: M. Bondi (ed.): Forms of Argumentative Discourse. Atti del Convegno Bologna 12–13 Dicembre 1996, 3–50. Bologna: CLUEB.
Renner, Karl N. (2001): Die Text-Bild-Schere. – *Studies in Communication Sciences/Studi di Scienze della comunicazione* 2, 23–44.
Rigotti, Eddo (1993): La sequenza testuale: definizione e procedimenti di analisi con esemplificazioni in lingue diverse. – *L'analisi linguistica e letteraria* I/1, 43–148.
– (1998): Zur Rolle der *pístis* in der Kommunikation. – In: S. Chmejrková et al. (eds.): Dialogue Analysis VI. Proceedings of the 6th IADA Conference Prague 1996, 77–83. Tübingen: Niemeyer.
Rigotti, Eddo and Cigada, Sara (forthcoming): La comunicazione verbale, vol. I. – Lugano: Università della Svizzera italiana.

Rigotti, Eddo and Rocci, Andrea (2001): Sens – Non-sens – Contresens. Tentative d'une définition explicative. – *Studies in Communication Sciences/Studi di Scienze della comunicazione* 2, 45–80.
Rigotti, Eddo and Rocci, Andrea (forthcoming): Congruity, Connective Predicates and Theme-Rheme Articulation. – In: P. Schulz (ed.): Semiotics and Communication Sciences. Toronto. University of Toronto Press.
Tschida, Alexander (1995): Kontinuität und Progression: Entwurf einer Typologie sprachlicher Information am Beispiel des Französischen. – Wilhelmsfeld: Egert.

Andreas H. Jucker and Sara W. Smith

"He hired who?": Problems in Reference Assignments in Conversations[1]

Abstract

Conversationalists use referring expressions to create mental images of referents for their interlocutors. In contrast to traditional analyses which assume that referents must always be clearly identifiable for the addressees, we maintain that such images are often vague and fuzzy because more precision would incur unwarranted processing effort and is not needed for the purposes of the current conversation. Speakers must therefore assess in every case how much precision is needed and which referring expression could best achieve the required level of precision for the addressee. They also must assess to what extent at any given moment a referent is in focus for the addressee. We analyze cases in which such assessments turn out to be mistaken, attempting to explain both why the reference was problematic and the means employed for repair. We conclude that neither syntactic nor semantic considerations can fully account for these cases; rather, speakers are taking into account the hearers' expectations about the level of vagueness to be employed for characters with different types of status in the discourse.

1. Introduction

For communication to be successful conversationalists must be able to evoke for their interlocutors appropriate mental images of all the entities they want to talk about. Such images may either be evoked on the basis of shared relevant background assumptions or as a

---

[1] This paper is part of a larger research project on "Reference assignment strategies in English" funded by the German Science Foundation, with additional financial support from the Department of Psychology and from the Scholarly and Creative Activities Committee at California State University, Long Beach. We gratefully acknowledge assistance from our colleagues Simone Müller and Anja Janoschka and from the following students: Steven Andrews, Daniela Bergner, Barb Breustedt, Pat Hiromi Noda, Andrea Simon, Marissa Subia, Britta Watz, and Marja Zibelius.

result of the conversation in which they are engaged. It is important to stress that the mental images that the interlocutors entertain of a certain discourse entity need not be identical. Traditional approaches to reference assignment regularly assume that communication can only be successful if the addressee can uniquely identify each discourse entity. But we argue that speakers only aim to individuate discourse entities to a degree that is sufficient for current purposes (see also Smith, Jucker and Müller 2001). Each referring expression that they use must therefore give as much information as is needed for this task, but no more.

How much individuation is needed depends on the situation and the discourse entities involved. In some situations and for some discourse entities it is essential that the addressee can identify the intended referent uniquely. In many cases, however, an intermediate level of vagueness may be more appropriate. That is, the hearer needs to know something about who or what is being talked about but need not be able to identify the referent exactly. While the speaker may well be capable of identifying the referent in a semantically and/or syntactically precise way, she may not find it worth the processing costs or useful in advancing the discourse. Finally, there are some cases in which the hearer may have the basis to construct only a vague and generic representation that is quite adequate for the purposes of the discourse. That is, she may want to talk generically about people or situations. Even though she has a particular example in mind, that may not be the point. We believe this is not a mistake on the part of the speaker but rather an important strategic aspect of referring expressions.

Generally it is of course difficult for the analyst to determine on the basis of conversation protocols how precise the speaker intends the mental image of a certain discourse entity to be for the addressee. As long as the conversation proceeds smoothly, we may assume that the addressee managed successfully to access appropriate mental images, but we have no way of establishing how precise or fuzzy they are. On some occasions the mental images may even be entirely wrong but without disrupting the conversation. The addressee may be able to make sense of the speaker's words even if this is not the sense intended by the speaker. The discrepancy may become apparent later in the conversation, or it may never be noticed.

Thus it is particularly interesting for the analyst to analyze situations in which the interlocutors themselves notice that their mental images of discourse referents may not be appropriate. In this paper we want to focus on precisely such situations. We will analyze sequences from protocols of interactions between California students that took part in an experiment in which one participant was asked to tell the second half of a short movie to a partner who had only seen the first half. But before we can do this, we will briefly present the essentials of our approach to reference assignment.

2. Previous Findings

Interlocutors use a combination of syntactic, semantic, lexical and pragmatic information to establish the intended referent of any given referring expression. Names, such as *Charlie Chaplin*, and descriptions, such as *the woman from the boat*, convey mainly semantic and lexical information. Personal pronouns, on the other hand, do not encode any lexical information, but they indicate whether a single referent or more than one referent is intended (singular versus plural pronouns), and they may indicate the gender of the intended referent (*he* versus *she*). Syntactic information is often induced in the case of anaphora resolution, that is to say the intended referent of a pronoun is established on the basis of syntactic criteria. All these processes have often been described and they are fairly well understood (e.g. Chesterman 1991; Epstein 1998, 1999; Hawkins 1978; Lyons 1980; 1999; Reuland and ter Meulen 1989).

However, interlocutors often rely on pragmatic information in order to establish or disambiguate the intended reference of a referring expression. In a relevance theoretic perspective, for instance, it is assumed that pronominal referring expressions often cannot be disambiguated on the basis of syntactic, semantic and lexical information alone.

(1)   I put the butterfly wing on the table. It broke.
(2)   I put the heavy book on the table. It broke. (Blakemore 1987: 112–113)

There is no linguistic rule which would determine the correct identity of the referent of the pronoun *it* in the second sentence. Pragmatically it is clear on the basis of the preceding sentence that in the first case the butterfly wing and in the second the table is meant, because this is the only interpretation that makes intuitive sense.

We agree that reference assignment is often based on pragmatic principles rather than on syntax and semantics. However, in contrast to Blakemore we do not rely on intuited data but on realistically elicited conversational data. In this data it can be shown that interlocutors not only regularly rely on pragmatic means of reference assignment but that reference assignment often remains a fuzzy and vague process, which does not establish a unique referent for the addressee but only a fuzzy mental image. We argue that speakers use expressions that allow *sufficient* identification, because *unique* identification is often not needed. Speakers in our conversation protocols regularly use expressions whose referent can only be established pragmatically, because they are syntactically, semantically and lexically not specific enough.

It is important, however, to distinguish between vague linguistic expressions on the one hand and vague mental images of discourse referents on the other. A linguistic expression may be vague for one of two reasons. First, it may be vague, or potentially ambiguous, because the intended discourse referent is obvious and precise individuation is therefore not needed. In this case the pragmatic information available to the interlocutors overrides all other information and reference assignment is unproblematic. Second, the speaker may wish to convey only a vague mental image because the discourse referent is not particularly important for current purposes. It is a background entity that does not warrant a higher individuation effort, and she chooses a linguistic expression that conveys this vague mental image.

Elsewhere (Smith and Jucker 1998) we have argued that all referring expressions are inherently interactive. By this we mean that speakers are sensitive to hearers both in terms of their long-term shared knowledge (e.g. Clark 1996) and also in terms of the current status or accessibility of concepts (e.g. Ariel 1988, 1991, 1996). Further, with Simone Müller (Smith, Jucker and Müller 2001), we have also argued that the degree of individuation of characters is calibrated to the degree of salience of an entity in the discourse and thus to the accessibility the speaker believes the hearer should maintain for that entity. We identified four levels of salience that were reflected in the referring expressions used to introduce characters. At the lowest level of salience, some characters were frame-induced and remained in the role of props in that frame. This includes waiters who played only their role as waiters, other customers, etc. These characters were not individuated in their introduction but rather referred to in terms of their generic roles. Some characters previously introduced as props became individuated in order to play a more salient and individual role in the narrative. This includes the waiter who harassed Chaplin and another customer who got beat up because he was 10 cents short. Some characters will play a secondary role, and they need to be kept accessible throughout a subplot or perhaps the whole narrative. Speakers signal their salience through introductions that individuate their characteristics and actions. Finally, the central character(s) such as Chaplin are understood to be salient and as such remain accessible throughout the narrative. Speakers are licensed (pragmatically) to refer to Chaplin as *he* throughout the whole narrative, independent of syntactic constraints that might select another male referent.

3. Data

Our data consist of recordings of pairs of students who watched a silent Charlie Chaplin movie (*The Immigrant*, 1917[2]). After the first half of the movie, we asked one of the par-

---

[2] We thank Kino's International for their kind permission to use this video.

ticipants to leave the room and to narrate what he or she had seen so far. Once the second participant had finished watching the movie, he or she told the second part to the partner. And finally the participants discussed the movie.

The use of such movie narratives for linguistic research has a long history. The most famous example is probably the Pear Story study carried out by Wallace Chafe and associates (Chafe 1980; but see also Redeker 1986, 1987 for a similar experiment). Informants were asked to retell the contents of a silent movie to the researcher, even though it must have been clear to the participants that the researcher knew the story much better than they did. And it is obvious that many of the recordings that were analyzed suffered from this artificial situation. Our recordings also rely on a laboratory situation. The participants know that they are taking part in an experiment and that they are being recorded. However, they engage in what we believe to be a realistic every-day situation. They fill somebody in on a part of a movie which this person has missed. In addition to the realism of the situation, our experiment has the advantage that we as analysts know how much common ground the participants share (the first half of the movie), and which discourse entities must be new for one of the participants (those that appear only in the second half of the movie).

The movie tells the story of a group of immigrants – among them Charlie Chaplin – who travel on an ocean liner to the United States. The first part ends with the arrival of the boat in New York. The second part starts with the disembarkation scene and then switches to a restaurant, where Chaplin is reunited with a young woman whom he had befriended on the boat. The scenes in the restaurant involve several waiters, either as individuals or as a group, several diners and a rich artist. Chaplin loses the coin he had found, but he is rescued by the artist, who takes a keen interest in Chaplin and his lady friend, hires them as models, and inadvertently pays for their meal.

The data used for this analysis consists of 11 recordings of pairs of students (9 all-native, 1 ESL with near-native skills, and 1 mixed pair (A=EFL, B=native)). For the present paper only the dialogic narratives were analyzed. Participant A is the one who only watches the first half of the movie. Participant B watches the entire movie and afterwards narrates the second part.

4. Analysis

As background, we will first discuss some examples in which vague or ambiguous referring expressions are used without leading to a disruption of the conversational flow. Next we will discuss examples of self-corrections, that is to say, cases in which the speaker perceives some potential problem in the reference assignment for the addressee. Finally we will discuss cases in which the addressee asks for clarification as to the identity of a particular referring expression.

4.1 Unproblematic vague or ambiguous referring expressions

Speakers use a large number of referring expressions that turn out to be vague, potentially ambiguous or even mistaken if they are scrutinized on the basis of the conversation protocols and with the analyst's intimate knowledge of the movie that they are talking about. Speakers use referring expressions that are "mistaken", either because they do not remember the film adequately (memory problems) or because they do not use the right words (linguistic problems). In some cases, the vagueness is unproblematic, and we may assume that the addressee draws the right conclusions on the basis of pragmatic plausibility. In other cases, the emergent stories turn out to be incoherent or implausible, and one may wonder why the addressee accepts the story without protest. Does he not care sufficiently whether the story makes sense or not? Does he not pay sufficient attention to detect the implausibility in the story? Or is he intimidated by the experimental set up in which these interactions were recorded and therefore does not dare to reveal his own lack of understanding?

Referring expressions may be vague because a more precise individuation is not warranted on the basis of the relative insignificance of the discourse referent. Consider for example extract (3).

```
(3)   B:   OK.
           .. after you left--
           ((door slamming))
           erm ...(1.8) it was where .. Charlie Chaplin and they're &
           & ... gonna re- get ready to get off the boat,
      A:   uh huh,
      B:   and so they got e=rm .. the--
           .. they let the two o'em off first,
           and then they let him off,
           .. s- .. later,   (pair 001)
```

This extract represents the beginning of B's narrative. She uses the personal pronoun *they* several times with varying reference. In the first occurrence it refers vaguely to the immigrants that both interlocutors are familiar with from the first half of the movie. The second occurrence is in an unfinished sentence and remains unclear. The third occurrence of *they* refers to the immigration officials in charge of disembarkation procedures. *They* let two of *them* off first. On the basis of the first half of the movie and what speaker B has said so far, it is virtually impossible for B to identify whom they let off first. In fact, A is referring to the young woman and her mother. The last occurrence of *they* refers again to the immigration officials. What emerges is a fairly imprecise account of the first scene of the second half of the movie. It is not clear who gets ready to get off and who lets who off first. However, participant A does not express any uneasiness about the lack of precision, and in fact it seems plausible that this vague account is quite sufficient for his current purposes. It provides a transition from the boat to the city, where the rest of the movie is set.

In other cases, the story line may disambiguate referents that would otherwise be unclear. In extract (4) speaker B uses the pronoun *he/his/him* in a potentially confusing way. The relevant referring expressions have been indexed. Expressions indexed as 1 refer to Charlie Chaplin, while expressions indexed as 2 refer to another customer described as *this other bum*.

```
(4)    B:  (H) erm ..so the=n,
           (H) he(1)'s trying to figure out &
           & <X while X> this other bum(2) walks in,
           and he='s(2) got a coin in his(2) hands,
           sits next to him(1) figures out &
           & that you know it's probably .. HIS(1) coin,
           (H) so= he(1) [tries] to get HIS(2) attention, (pair no 002)
```

While there seems to be no syntactic basis for identifying each referent of the pronouns, based on pragmatic grounds participant A was probably able to reconstruct a sufficiently clear situation. *This other bum* walks in with a coin in his hand and sits down next to Charlie Chaplin, who tries to catch his attention in order to get the coin back. The narration continues without interruption and without any apparent problems on the part of participant A. This example is typical of many cases in which speakers use the pronoun *he* for Charlie Chaplin, even if on syntactic grounds alone a pronoun does not sufficiently individuate him. He is the most salient character throughout the narration, and therefore seems to be always available for pronominalization. The other characters, on the other hand, are less salient. They can be pronominalized only if pronominalization is syntactically licensed. We will show below how this can lead to confusion if the speaker uses the syntactically licensed pronoun *he* for a minor male character and the pragmatically licensed pronoun *he* for Charlie Chaplin in situations in which the story line does not sufficiently specify who acts and to whom things happen.

In this section we have shown that in some cases vague expressions are adequate because it is sufficient for the addressee to have a fuzzy and imprecise mental image of the intended referent. The speaker herself, in fact, may have a very imprecise mental image only. In other cases, the speaker relies on the addressee's ability to establish the identity of the intended referent pragmatically. A more explicit referring expression is not needed, because it is clear from the context and on the basis of pragmatic plausibility who is meant.

4.2 Reformulations: when the speaker detects a potential problem

Frequently, the speaker would begin with one form of a referring expression but, before completing the utterance, would reformulate it. First, these cases are of interest in regard to the present topic because they provide evidence that the speaker is continuously monitoring the referring expression for adequacy from the addressee's perspective. Second, the context of the problematic expression and the nature of the self-editing should provide evidence as to the nature of the speaker's concerns.

We will first look at three examples in which the reformulations are exactly as we would expect, but the reasons for them vary. In the fourth case, we will find the reformulation itself puzzling but revealing. In the first example, extract (5), the speaker uses a semantically vague expression *the guy*, but then before completing the utterance replaces it by a semantically more explicit one, *the waiter*.

```
(5)    B:    (...)
             so anyway,
             Charlie decides he's gonna pay.
             so the guy brings him--
             the waiter brings the bill.
             (H) erm he gives him the coin to pay,
             and the waiter puts it in his mouth and it be=nds
             so it's totally fake. (pair 004)
```

In this case, the waiter was featured prominently in the previous scene. However, when the speaker introduced a new segment, she apparently realized that the addressee might not have kept the waiter in sufficient focus to be accessible via a vague expression such as *the guy*.

Extract (6) is virtually identical to example (5) in some ways and quite different in others. The speaker again uses the vague expression *the guy* and immediately replaces it with a semantically more explicit expression, *the artist*. The artist is salient at this point of the narrative, so the speaker presumably was not concerned about the degree of accessibility. Rather, in this case the context would not be sufficient to select between several accessible male characters as the referent for *the guy*.

```
(6)    B:    (...)
             the artist offered to pay for the bill,
             and Charlie kept saying <Q oh no Q>.
             and pretending like he could pay.
             and he did it so many times that the artist finally said oh &
```

```
              & OK.
              you pay for it <@ yourself @>.
              so what he ended up doing is he ended up--
              th- the guy,
              the artist when he sat at their table .. erm put down HIS &
              & money to pay,
        A:    right, (0)
        B:    (0) and Charlie grabbed it,
              paying for his check with his money anyway. (pair no 022)
```

In extract (7), the vague and underdetermined pronoun *he* is replaced by a more specific expression, *the waiter*.

```
   (7)  B:   (...)
              and erm .. he--
              .. the waiter when he came to pick up the &
              & ...(1.2) the quarter .. from him,
              erm he dropped it,
              .. and so he was trying to like--
              trying to get th- get the quarter,    (pair no 001)
```

At first it seems strange that the speaker would initially pronominalize this character at this point. While the waiter had been in focus during an earlier segment, he had not been mentioned directly for 35 lines, while three other male characters were introduced. So syntactically *he* would not be licensed as the waiter. However, on closer inspection, the waiter can be seen as present implicitly in recent segments – first as a member of the group of waiters who beat up another customer and then as the intimidating presence behind the unpaid bill. Thus the speaker has herself kept him in mental focus enough to pronominalize him. However, she apparently realizes that the addressee may not have done so, and so she corrects herself with the more explicit expression *the waiter*.

Extract (8) is particularly interesting. Here the speaker has trouble finding a referring expression for the artist character. She introduces him with two vague expressions *this other like hefty guy or something* and *he's like an artist or somethin'*. Then, in the midst of talking about three men, the speaker needs to refer to him again. She first refers to him with the pronoun *he*. Syntactically, there are three possible referents – the waiter, Chaplin, and the artist. However, it is highly implausible that the waiter offers to pay. Thus *he* can potentially refer either to Chaplin or to the artist. She then replaces *he* by *the man*.

```
   (8)  B:   this other like hefty guy or something
              comes over and sits by 'em,
              and he's like an artist or somethin',
              they are talking or whatever,
              a=nd .. like e=rm the waiter brings out the the bill again.
              .. and he the man offers to pay,
              and Charlie's like <Q oh no no no Q>,
```

At first sight this reformulation of *he* as *the man* would not seem helpful, as both expressions seem equally vague. Syntactically and semantically, they are identical; each encodes only the gender of the referent and the fact that a single referent is intended. However, pragmatically, they are distinct in that they convey different information about the salience of the character referred to. We have seen elsewhere that the pronoun *he* can stand either for a salient character or for a background character. The expression *the man*, on the other hand, ordinarily implies that no more precise description is available; in other words it can only stand for a background character. In this case, it therefore must refer to the artist. Thus the expression *the man* is disambiguated by pragmatic considerations rather than semantic ones.

In the analyses above, we find evidence of constant monitoring of the referring expression in terms of its probable interpretation by the addressee. The speaker attempts to take into account the current accessibility of a referent for the addressee. Many of the reformulations were designed to increase the precision of an expression that appeared to be too vague for the context. It is important to note, however, that the reformulation did not necessarily produce a semantically unique expression but rather one that was pragmatically motivated.

4.3   Requests for clarification: when the addressee admits to a problem

In this section, we analyze cases in which the addressee asks for clarification. Apparently the speaker's assessment of how much precision is needed to achieve the required level of salience for the addressee turns out to be mistaken. We are interested in identifying the contexts in which such confusion occurs, the formal structures involved, and the speaker's repair strategies.

In most cases, problems arise when the addressee is unable to use syntactic or semantic cues to disambiguate a pronoun's reference from among several competing referents. We have noted that the addressee often does not appear to be concerned about ambiguous pronouns. However, it is interesting to note those cases in which the addressee does find them problematic. In the excerpt below, the addressee initially does not indicate any problem with the speaker's repeated reference to *them*. Either he hopes that further information will clarify the reference or else he believes it is not important to know who is being employed or engaged. However, when the speaker indicates the conclusion of the episode, the addressee at that point admits confusion as to who is referenced by *them*.

```
(9)   B:    (...)
            so Charlie Chaplin takes the tip,
            and puts his check on top of it,
```

```
           and then gives it to the waiter,
           (H) and so the waiter gets upset cause he assumes the artist &
           & guy didn't leave him a tip.
           (H) a=nd--
           ...(1.5) then they leave,
           a=nd the artist guy says he wants to= .. employ them now,
           starting tomorrow,
           or engage them now he says.
           so he is--
           he hired them,
           and .. there was [trouble],
      A:                   [he hired who]?
      B:   Charlie Chaplin and his girlfriend. (pair 006)
```

Presumably the addressee became concerned because it is important at the end of the narration to learn how it all ended, and this includes the information as to who was hired by the rich artist.

In terms of formal story structure, the use of the personal pronoun *them* in excerpt (9) should not be problematic. The narration in the immediately preceding context concerned the three main characters; the artist, Charlie Chaplin, and the young woman. If in this situation the artist is mentioned separately and in opposition to a group of people that can be referred to by *they*, this group must consist of Charlie Chaplin and the young woman. Clearly the speaker had a precise referent in mind and assumed the addressee would also. So what went wrong? While in the speaker's mind the girlfriend was presumably still with Chaplin during recent scenes, she was no longer salient in the narrative. For the addressee, it is as though the girlfriend had dropped out of focus and was therefore no longer available to be included in *them*.

Extract (10) looks similar in that Speaker B uses a vague pronoun and participant A asks for the identity of the people referred to. But in this case it is plausible to assume that the speaker did not have a very precise mental image of the intended discourse referent. The scene included several backgrounded characters, along with the central characters.

```
(10)  B:   (...)
           and (H) .. what happened was erm,
           they're on the boat,
           and he's like got the girl and the mom,
           .. but all of a sudden they get to America.
           (H) and they pull out this rope,
           and they tie them to the boat.
           it's kind of [weird like]--
      A:                [tied] who to the boat.
      B:   all the people are standing there like this,
      A:   uh huh.
      B:   and they take this thing,
           and they just like ... rope 'em up.
```

```
              basically put a rope,
              so they can't walk,
              they can't leave,
         A:   uh huh,
              [o=h],
         B:   [and what they do] is erm--
         A:   (H) so they kept them s- IN the boat. (pair no 142)
```

It is interesting to note that speaker B does not really provide more information as to the identity of the intended discourse referent. She says *all the people*, which is only marginally more helpful than *they*. But she specifies more clearly what the situation is like and in what sense this group of people is "tied to the boat". As will be discussed further below, we believe that examples such as this provide evidence that it is not so much the identifiability of the discourse referents that is at issue in spite of the question asked by A. Rather the addressee seeks to clarify their role.

In excerpt (11) below, as in (9) above, the source of the problem seems to be the addressee's lack of mental access to characters who have been introduced earlier but who are not salient at that point in the narrative. The episode described in (11) causes problems for several partners. Another customer pays his bill but then is beat up by the group of waiters. Chaplin's waiter explains that the patron was 10 cents short. Chaplin checks his pocket and is horrified to find a hole instead of his coin. This motivates several scenes that follow, in which Chaplin tries to figure out how to pay the bill.

In this part of the narrative, A's confusion is understandable because Chaplin seems the most plausible candidate for the pronoun *him*.

```
(11)     B:   (...)
              they show this strong guy.
         A:   yeah.
         B:   and he gives his money for the bill.
              and then there's this waiter,
              that doesn't like Charlie anyway.
              who's like got--
              a big fat guy with funny .. d- er   dracula &
              & .. eyebrows. (0)
         A:   (0) @@@, (0)
         B:   (0) and then he beats the shit out of [him],
         A:                                        [@@@@]
              [[<@ out of Charlie @>]],
         B:   [[because]]--
              yeah.
              [no out] the guy,
         A:   [@@]
         B:   who pays his bill,
              cause he was ten cents short. (pair no 63)
```

It is easy, in hindsight, to see how speaker A became confused. The description given by B *they show this strong guy and he gives his money for the bill* neither makes the character salient nor gives any hint that there should be a problem. And, at the same time, the speaker notes that the waiter does not like Charlie. So there appears to be motivation for the waiter to beat up Charlie, but no motivation for him to beat up the man who just paid. Thus, the speaker gives no basis for keeping the character introduced as *this strong guy* in focus. As a result, he apparently is no longer accessible when referred to as *him*.

We have argued above that Charlie Chaplin, as the main character of the narration, is almost always available for pronominalization on pragmatic grounds, while for the other characters pronominalization has to be syntactically licensed. Here the pronoun *he* may either refer to Charlie Chaplin, or to a male character who is only temporarily prominent. This creates ambiguous cases, where the story line would make both Chaplin and the other male character plausible referents. The addressee apparently assumes that Chaplin is, by default, the referent unless the referent is clearly licensed on syntactic or semantic grounds. For this reason, several requests for clarification (e.g., excerpts 11, 12, and 13) were variants of the form: "was that Charlie Chaplin"?

In the conversation below (12), the speaker seems to make the other customer more salient through repeated mentions of him and reference to his insufficient money: *another waiter goes up to someone else, and the guy doesn't have enough money* and *they like yell at the guy, and they beat the guy up*. Yet when he ends the scene with a pronoun *they're all hitting him*, the hearer also tries to confirm his interpretation, that the victim is Chaplin *uh huh Charlie Chapman*.

```
(12) B:  and then he .. orders another bowl of beans.
     A:  @@@,
     B:  <@ so he put the bowls of beans @> and they're eating,
         (H) an' er,
         ... they're watching in the restaurant.
         .. another waiter goes up to someone else,
         ... and .. the guy doesn't have enough money.
     A:  [uh huh].
     B:  [so he] goes back he's like--
         tells the main guy.
         you know he don't have enough money.
         (H) so a=ll the waiters come out.
         (H) and they ... they like yell at the guy,
         and they beat the guy up.
         they're all .. HITting him [XXXX].
     A:                             [uh huh Charlie] Chapman.
     B:  no.
         the other guy.
         Charlie an' his girlfriend are eating.
     A:  uh huh,
```

```
             [oh they] beat up the other guy who left, (0)
        B:   [this is]--
             (0) yeah.
             ... no no it's just another guy.
        A:   oh OK.
        B:   they just flash to it.
             [all of a sudden] there is another [[customer]].
        A:   [uh huh]                           [[mhm]],
        B:   (H) and so they--
             he gets beat up,
             and then ... the waiters all walk back in the back.
        A:   [mhm]. (pair no 142)
```

From a structural point of view, the story told by participant A is clear. She relates how Charlie Chaplin is eating while a scene unfolds in which another customer, whom she describes first as *someone else*, and then as *the guy*, gets beaten up by the group of waiters because he does not have enough money. But apparently the lack of a specific designation for the character makes it hard for the addressee to give him the appropriate level of salience. Moreover in the sequence she refers to two different waiters. Participant A, therefore, gets confused and cannot keep track of the different characters. Having lost track of the potential referents, the hearer apparently falls back on the default assignment, that it is Charlie Chaplin referenced by the final *him*.

Again in excerpt (13), the addressee loses confidence in his ability to reconcile conflicting evidence about who is being referenced. Again, he indicates that his default assumption is that the problematic reference is to Chaplin.

```
   (13)  B:   OK.        er you left when they went to--
              <@ when they @> got to New York.
              right?
         A:   right.
         B:   OK.
              at that point they put a little rope up ... erm .. &
              & to hold everybody back,
              and like the immigration guy came in and--
              or whatever.
              and approved them all to go through,
              and the lady an' her mother went first,
              he went back in,
              and [he kicked the guy on his way] out,
         A:       [was that Charlie Chaplin]?
         B:   huh?
         A:   Charlie?
         B:   yeah.
              Charlie Chaplin went back in, (pair no 022)
```

In this case the extract is taken from the very beginning of B's narration. She has not in fact mentioned Chaplin directly when the confusion occurs, but rather she has assumed his presence. She had introduced the immigrants as a group with the pronoun *they*. First, she is making the general assumption that they will be salient enough from the first half of the movie. Presumably she also assumes that Chaplin will remain salient to the addressee as the central character. To make matters more difficult for the addressee, the speaker has also introduced the immigration officials. It is impossible to know when the addressee's confusion begins. The first use of *he* would be syntactically licensed to refer to *the immigration guy* four lines earlier and so may have seemed unproblematic. However, the addressee expresses his confusion after the following line, in which there are two vague expressions, *he* and *the guy*. In fact it is difficult to be sure what the speaker intends, as Chaplin and the immigration official have exchanged kicks. The expression *he* would be syntactically licensed to refer to the immigration official and pragmatically licensed to refer to either. And the noun phrase *the guy* seems too specific to refer to Chaplin and not specific enough to refer to the immigration official. Finally then the addressee seeks confirmation of his interpretation, *was that Charlie Chaplin?* In reply, the speaker reiterates an earlier part of the scene, confirming both that Chaplin was involved and also what his role was – *Charlie Chaplin went back in*. But it is interesting to note that the speaker never really answered the question itself, as to who kicked who. Rather the speaker clarified an earlier part of the episode, and apparently she assumed that the hearer would infer as much as would be needed to understand the overall point. While it still is not clear to the analyst exactly what was intended, the clarification seemed to serve the purposes of the addressee, and the narrative moved on.

5. Discussion

It is interesting to note that in most cases, the speaker defines the problem as a problem in understanding the scenario, not just in identifying the referent. That is, the speaker might have repaired the problem simply by giving a more precise description of the referent – that is literally what was asked, and that is what a model dependent on identifiability would assume. But instead the speaker takes pains to re-describe the larger context, and in fact she sometimes never directly identifies the referent. Her strategy implies that she sees the issue in terms of placing the referent in the context of the activities in the scene, not strictly in terms of identifying an individual. Her strategies also seem designed to place entities in some degree of focus in a context.

Vague expressions such as *he* or *the man* could not possibly work if the requirement were that they provide unique identification of a character. Rather they work to move the spotlight onto or off of the characters believed to be in focus in the hearer's representation. All the entities introduced into a narrative cannot be foregrounded simultaneously, so speakers must work from assumptions about what referents will or will not be accessible for the addressee. Thus *he* is interpreted from among referents in focus, based on either syntactic or pragmatic considerations. If a character is included in a scene, in terms of the formal story structure, but has not recently played an active role, he or she may become inaccessible as a referent for a pronoun. Further, vague expressions are interpreted in terms of contrast with other referring expressions that might be syntactically or semantically legitimate but which are not pragmatically as apt.

6. Conclusion

In this paper we have shown that reference assignment is often pragmatically based, that is to say that speakers provide semantically and syntactically underdetermined linguistic expressions and let addressees rely on pragmatic principles for the interpretation of the intended discourse referent. Linguistic expressions may be vague and potentially ambiguous because more precision would be unwarranted by the relative insignificance of the intended discourse referent. A fuzzy mental image is all that is needed, and a more precise designation would have assigned an unwarranted degree of discourse saliency to the discourse referent. In other cases a linguistic expression may remain vague or potentially ambiguous because the situation is sufficiently clear and allows unproblematic reference assignment on pragmatic principles.

For the most part, hearers are able to make good-enough reference assignments, based on these pragmatic principles. However, we found that this remains a problematic part of conversations. Speakers constantly monitor and reformulate their referring expressions, in hopes of facilitating the partner's assignment. Sometimes the monitoring is not successful, and the hearer finds himself confused and in need of clarification. In some cases, the confusion may be resolved with a brief reformulation, but in many cases some negotiation of meaning may be required.

Speakers do not attempt to make referring expressions uniquely identifiable based on either syntactic or semantic constraints. Rather, they depend on pragmatic constraints to guide the hearer in interpreting vague expressions. One pragmatic strategy is to use expressions whose level of precision matches the level of salience in the discourse. They avoid using expressions that imply more precision in identification than is needed for the purposes of the conversation. Another strategy is to repair referring expressions by re-establishing the scenario as a whole rather than simply adding to the precision of the referring expression. Speakers apparently hold an implicit model to the effect that reference is based on understanding the role of a referent in the discourse as a whole. Speakers also appear to take into account the presumed level of focus of a referent for the addressee. These strategies provide evidence of intersubjectivity in the formulation of referring expressions – that is, speakers are sensitive to hearers' processing needs and also to their understanding of the discourse.

References

Ariel, Mira. (1988): Referring and accessibility. – *Journal of Linguistics* 24.1, 65–87.
– (1991): The function of accessibility in a theory of grammar. – *Journal of Pragmatics* 16, 443–463.
– (1996): Referring expressions and the +/- coreference distinction.– In: T. Fretheim, J. K. Gundel (eds.). Reference and Referent Accessibility. (P&BNS 38). Amsterdam: Benjamins, 13–35.
Blakemore, Diane. (1987): Semantic Constraints on Relevance. – Oxford: Blackwell.
Chafe, Wallace L. (ed.). (1980): The Pear Stories. Cognitive, Cultural, and Linguistic Aspects of Narrative Production. (Advances in Discourse Processes 3). – Norwood, N.J.: Ablex.
Chesterman, Andrew. (1991): On Definiteness. A Study with Special Reference to English and Finnish. (Cambridge Studies in Linguistics 56). Cambridge: Cambridge University Press.
Clark, Herbert H. (1996): Using Language. – Cambridge: Cambridge University Press.
Epstein, Richard. (1998): Reference and definite referring expressions. – *Pragmatics & Cognition* 6.1/2, 189–207.
– (1999): Roles, frames and definiteness. – In: K. van Hoek, A.A. Kibrik and L. Noordman (eds.). Discourse Studies in Cognitive Linguistics. Selected Papers from the Fifth International Cognitive Linguistics Conference. Amsterdam, July 1997, 53–74. Amsterdam/Philadelphia: Benjamins.
Hawkins, John A. (1978): Definiteness and Indefiniteness. A Study in Reference and Grammaticality Prediction. – London: Croom Helm.
Lyons, Christopher G. (1980): The meaning of the English definite article. – In: J. van der Auwera (ed.), The Semantics of Determiners. 81–95. London: Croom Helm,
– (1999): Definiteness. (Cambridge Textbooks in Linguistics). Cambridge: Cambridge University Press.
Redeker, Gisela. (1986): Language Use in Informal Narratives. Effects of Social Distance and Listener Involvement. (Tilburg Papers in Language and Literature 105). – Tilburg: Univ. of Tilburg, Dept. of Language and Literature.
– (1987): Introduction of story characters in interactive and non-interactive narration. – In: M. Bertuccelli-Papi, J. Verschueren (eds.). The Pragmatic Perspective: Selected Papers from the 1985 International Pragmatics Conference. (Pragmatics & Beyond Companion Series 5), 339–355. Amsterdam: John Benjamins.
Reuland, Eric J., and Alice G.B. ter Meulen (eds.) (1989): The Representation of (In)definiteness.– Cambridge, Mass.: The MIT Press.
Smith, Sara W., and Andreas H. Jucker (1998): Interactive aspects of reference assignment in conversations. *Pragmatics & Cognition* 6.1/2, 153–187.

Smith, Sara W., Andreas H. Jucker and Simone Müller (2001): "Some artist guy": The role of salience and common ground in the formulation of referring expressions in conversational narratives.– In: N.T. Enikö (ed.). Pragmatics in 2000: Selected Papers from the 7th International Pragmatics Conference, Vol 2. Antwerp: International Pragmatics Association, 528–542.

Chapter 3
Signposting in the Dialogue

Simone Müller

The Discourse Marker *so* in Native and Non-native Discourse[1]

1. Introduction

The research presented in this paper is part of a bigger research project (Müller, in prep.) intended to investigate the use of a number of discourse markers (DM; in the widest sense of the term) by German speakers of English as a Foreign Language (EFL) as compared to their use by American native speakers (NS) of English. In this paper, the use of *so* will be described and analyzed.

2. Research question

In some previous research with a smaller data set and a range of discourse markers (11 native speakers, 28 EFL speakers, 19 DMs), I found that the natives used the discourse marker *so* more than twice as much as the EFL speakers. *So* (DM) accounted for 1.58 per cent of the total words per native speaker and 0.69 per cent per EFL speaker. Why should that be the case? *So* as a connective is part of the typical vocabulary taught in school, at least in Germany, and it occurs as such in the first or at the latest in the second year of learning English. Therefore, it might be expected that the usage of *so* will have become part of the speakers' L2 competence.

Paul Hays (1992) takes the same stand. He carried out a study with Japanese students speaking English (in Japan) and elicited his data in free conversation interviews with an instructor as the interviewer (1992: 27f). In his analysis, Hays follows Schiffrin's model of planes, in which the discourse markers on the ideational plane include *so*. Based on this model and on the results of his study, he concludes that "semantic words, and therefore ideational discourse markers [e.g. *so*] are to be expected earlier, because they are overtly

---

[1] I would like to thank Rosemary Bock and my supervisor, Andreas H. Jucker, for helpful comments on this paper. Of course, all remaining mistakes are my own.

taught. (…) [Markers on other planes] would not be expected unless there has been exposure to that discourse community" (Hays 1992: 29).

This argument is plausible. However, Schiffrin distinguishes various functions of *so*, on the ideational plane as well as on other planes (see section 3). So my hypothesis concerning *so* was that native speakers and EFL speakers use the various functions of *so* to different degrees.

Before I delve into these functions of *so*, I shall give a short overview of some literature dealing with *so* and a description of our experiment and the data I used.

3. *So* in literature

There are several approaches to *so* and different terms for it. Fraser, for example, excludes a number of other expressions from the class of 'discourse markers' which other authors clearly include, but treats *so* as a member of this class (e.g. Fraser 1988; 1990). He approaches DMs from a grammatical-pragmatic perspective and characterizes a DM as a linguistic expression which "signals the relationship that the speaker intends between the utterance the DM introduces and the foregoing utterance" (Fraser 1999: 936).

Blakemore (1988) analyzes *so* within a relevance theoretic framework, where it functions as a constraint on relevance (1988: 185ff) and specifies the relation between two utterances (Blakemore 1992: 136). While she avoids giving *so* a name in the 1988 paper, she later terms it a 'discourse connective' (Blakemore 1992: 136); as do some other authors working within Relevance Theory (e.g. Blass 1990; Unger 1996). Neither Fraser nor Blakemore distinguishes the different discourse marker functions *so* might have, which, however, would be necessary to answer my research question.

Schiffrin (1987) includes the treatment of *so* in her book entitled *Discourse Markers*, in which she analyzes DMs as being multifunctional in a model of discourse consisting of several planes. According to her, DMs are contextual coordinates (p. 327) which contribute to coherence in conversation by allowing "speakers to construct and integrate multiple planes and dimensions of an emergent reality" (p. 330). On a structural level, *so* functions as a marker of main idea units (p. 191–201). It also "conveys a meaning of 'result'" and does so on three planes: Ideational Structure, Information State and Action Structure (p. 202). Finally, "[s]o functions in the organization of transitions in participation framework" (p. 217); it may be used to indicate that a transition is being offered, but it can also be used to introduce the utterance after the transition (p. 219). Even on this plane (participation framework), *so*, if used in an utterance-final position, can convey a notion of result: Here, "*so* instructs the hearer to recover a conclusion [...] which has already been presented, or which is otherwise mutually known" (p. 223). Much of Schiffrin's approach will be found again in the categories used in this paper.

Redeker (1990 and 1991) takes up the idea of a model with several planes within a coherence framework but reduces their number to two levels, the ideational and the pragmatic structure. The pragmatic level is further subdivided into rhetorical and sequential relations, a sequential relation being assumed "when two adjacent discourse units do not have any obvious ideational or rhetorical relation – while still being understood as belonging to the same discourse" (1990: 369). *So* can be used both as a "semantically rich connective" to mark ideational relations and as a "pragmatic connective" to mark pragmatic relations (1990: 372). Redeker's idea of a sequential function is lacking in Schiffrin's description, but nevertheless proved relevant for dealing with real data.

4. The data

The conversations for this research were collected as part of another project focusing on reference assignment. Therefore, the setup of the experiment was not specifically meant to elicit the whole range or all possible functions of discourse markers. Nevertheless, it provided the same setting and task for all participants, natives and non-natives alike, so that the resulting transcripts are perfectly comparable.[2]

In the experiment, pairs of university students (A and B) watched a 24-minute silent Chaplin movie, *The Immigrant*. Partner A was called out in the middle of the movie and asked to orally retell the first part of the story. Partner B saw the whole movie and was afterwards asked to tell his/her partner what had happened in the second part. Both partners then discussed the movie, often making use of some questions that they had been given as suggestions or a guideline for their discussion. When there was only one participant (= speaker C), he or she watched and retold the whole movie and expressed his/her opinion about it.

In addition, the participants answered questions about their relation to the movie and filled out a demographic questionnaire. For the non-native speakers, this questionnaire included data about how and how long they had learned English, the language(s) they use in

---

[2] Thanks to my supervisor, Andreas H. Jucker, and his Californian colleague Sara W. Smith, who allowed me to add to the experiment design according to my own needs and to use all the resulting transcripts for my research. Thanks also to all our student assistants who have faithfully transcribed more than forty hours of recording.

various contexts and how long they had been to the States or another English-speaking country.

The conversations/narratives took about fifteen minutes and were recorded on audio and video tape; the transcriptions were done at the Justus Liebig University, Giessen, Germany, basically following Du Bois' (1991) transcription design principles.

Of the over two hundred participants, I selected only those speakers who were either (American) native or German EFL speakers. This resulted in seventy recordings being analyzed; thirty-four of the participants being American NS and seventy-seven German EFL speakers.

5. Analysis of *so*

All instances of *so* were searched for by a computer program (written in PERL), looked at in context, categorized by hand, and counted according to categories by another computer program. The categorization process had been tested earlier by recoding a certain number of instances after one month, refining the categories and carrying out another recoding process. In this process, a recoding reliability of 86% was achieved. The results of the categorization were then submitted to a thorough statistical analysis using SPSS.

5.1. The categories

My original intention had been to use functions of *so* that had already been described in the relevant literature. In this respect, Schiffrin's (1987) treatment of *so* proved to be valuable; however, it soon turned out that her descriptions were not sufficient for the data at hand. Therefore, I had to add further categories according to the functions *so* apparently had in the transcriptions. The categories I finally used were the following:

Table 1: Overview of the categories of *so*

Level	Category	Short explanation of the function of so
Propositional level	RIN	marking result or consequence
Structural level	MIU	main idea unit marker
	SRE	summing up / rewording / giving an example
	SEQ	sequential
	BOM	boundary marker
Speech act level	SAM	speech act marker and opinion marker
	SAM_TRP	marking a request or question
Exchange level	TRP	transition relevance place
	IMR_TRP	implied result + TRP
Without level	RAG	indefinable
	NCA	no category applied/applicable
Non-discourse marker uses	ADM	adverb of degree or manner (*so big, so many*)
	PPS	expressing purpose, "so that", "in order that"
	EXP	in fixed expressions (e.g. *and so on*)
	OTH	other, e.g. substitute (*so did she; I think so*)
	TRL	direct translation of a German expression or usage (e.g. *and so*)

I fully agree with Schiffrin (e.g. 1987: 316) that discourse markers may perform more than one function at the same time. However, it did not seem to be useful to classify the instances of *so* according to **all** those functions; therefore, I chose the category that described the most salient one.

In the following, I will give more detailed explanations and typical examples from the transcripts for the categories that are not self-explanatory. Excerpt lines are preceded by line number; after the excerpt, the number of the transcript and the role of the speaker are given in brackets.

Propositional level:

RIN: result or consequence (also inferential)

This category is a combination of Schiffrin's 'result' (ideational, fact-based plane) and 'inference' (information-state, knowledge-based plane; Schiffrin 1987: 202). Initially, I had intended to keep 'result' and 'inference' apart, but her definitions of the two functions are neither precise nor different enough to allow for a practical clear-cut categorization. Therefore, RIN was used for any *so* that conveyed a sense of result or consequence.

The following example shows a typical usage of *so* as a result/consequence marker, where the beating of a restaurant customer is presented as a result of his failure to pay the full amount of his bill:

```
(1)    67            his waiter ...(1.1) gave some other guy a check.
       68            s- some other guy that he was waiting on a check.
       69     A:     mhm,
       70     B:     and the guy was short.
       71            ...(1.5) ten .. about ten cents on the check.
       72     A:     mhm,
       73 --> B:     and so they beat him up.
       (125B)
```

Structural level:

To organize their narrative and discussion, the speakers used *so* in four different functions: as a main idea unit marker (MIU), for summing up, rewording or giving an example (SRE), to introduce the next part of the story (SEQ), and as a boundary marker (BOM).

MIU: main idea unit marker

This category is taken from Schiffrin's description of *so* as a marker of main idea units (Schiffrin 1987: 191–203). It was applied whenever the speaker came back after a digression or explanation to the main thread of the narrative or to a topic or an opinion mentioned before and repeated or alluded to this main idea.

In example (2), speaker B has narrated almost the whole story line of the second part of the movie, which ends with Chaplin and his girl-friend entering a marriage license office. After attending to A's request for clarification who got married to whom, B resumes the main thread of the story using *so*.

```
(2)    258    B:     and the=n .. they= .. decided to get married.
       259    A:     ... how about Charlie.
       260    B:     ... they got MARRied.
       261    A:     oh yeah?
       262           [oh] OK.
       263    B:     [@].
       264           he was the guy.
       265           .. and the girl.
       266    A:     oh OK.
       267 --> B:    so they got married at the end.
       268           ... that's it,
       269    A:     ...(1.3) OK.
       (130B)
```

In example (3), B suddenly thinks of an event she had forgotten to include in the narrative so far. After supplying this information, B resumes the narrative at the point where she had interrupted herself.

```
(3)   49          (H) and ..(1.5) he was broke,
      50          and didn't have any money,
      51          and he was hungry,
      52          ... so= he went into a restaurant,
      53          and--
      54          ... or no.
      55          he found some money on the floor.
      56          (H) so he said OK I wanna go to a restaurant.
      57  -->     so he went to the restaurant,
      58          ...(1.5) a=nd he sat down an' .. got some beans,
      (009C)
```

SRE: Summing up / rewording / giving an example

Frequently, speakers would express the same propositional content as in a previous utterance but in different words, without a digression in between. Sometimes, the expression introduced with *so* comprised the whole propositional idea, sometimes it summarized this idea, and sometimes it gave an example of it, as in the following two examples.

Example (4) presents a rewording: line 200 expresses the content of line 199 in other words.

```
(4)   194         .. and he the man offers to pay,
      195         and Charlie's like <Q oh no no no Q>,
      196         and they go back and forth like two or three times,
      197         and then (H) finally the man's like &
      198         & <Q OK I .. oh all right .. you pay Q> you know,
      199         and Charlie is like <Q DANG Q>.
      200  -->    and so he's like I should've let him pay whatever.
      (008B)
```

In (5), speaker B gives an example of what Chaplin ordered (*more things*):

```
(5)   92          .. he <@ keeps ordering more things @>.
      93          like--
      94   -->    so he orders her co=ffee,
      (010B)
```

SEQ: sequential

This category was applied when the only function seemed to be the introduction of the next part of the story, as in example (6) below. This function was mentioned only by Redeker (1990: 369) and in the fourth edition of the Oxford Advanced Learner's Dictionary (OALD 1989).

```
(6)   100    B:   (H) so= h- .. er he got the--
      101         I think the waiter brought him his check,
      102         (H) and he .. dig in his pa=nts.
      103         and realized (H) that he didn't have the money,
      104         he was kind of scared.
      105  -->    so this old guy,
      106         this old--
      107         he go--
      108         I think he was homeless came in,
      109         and h- o- obviously he picked up the .. coin &
      109a        & from outsi=de.
      110    A:   mhm,
      (125B)
```

BOM: boundary marker

So as a boundary marker (BOM) is an interesting category that I had to add during the categorization process: Several speakers would listen to my instructions, acknowledge them (by *OK*, for example) and then start their narrative with *so* (see examples (7) and (8)).

```
(7)   4      C:   OK.
      5  -->      ...(1.5) so it's about ... Charlie Chaplin,
      6           he's an immigrant,
      7           ...(1.2) and erm--
      (141C)

(8)   26
      27 --> B:   so what happened when you went out was that they &
      27a         & arrived in America,
      28     A:   mhm.
      (046B)
```

Speech act level:

SAM: speech act marker and opinion marker

The category was applied when *so* introduced an opinion. SAM always contained an element of result: Through the use of *so*, the speaker presented the opinion as based on (previously mentioned) facts or ideas, as in example (9).

```
(9)   353    B:   (H) I I liked it too.
      354         because .. I never seen (H) .. erm .. a silent film?
      355         an' I never seen Charlie Chapl[in in] his films,
      356    A:                                 [mhm].
      357 --> B:  so (H) that's why I liked it,
      (140B)
```

SAM_TRP: speech act marker + transition relevance place

This category was applied whenever a question or request began with *so*, based again on Schiffrin. She describes one of the functions of *so* as marking "an action which has just been motivated", for example a request (Schiffrin 1987: 209). I have not accorded this function a category of its own but a combination of categories, since a request represents a speech act, and at the same time *so* + request or question always involved a speaker transition, as in example (10).

```
(10)   221       B:   yeah.
       222            it was kind of funny ... I guess.
       223       A:   yeah.
       224       B:   ...(1.4) so I guess we're supposed to discuss &
       224a           & this now?
       225       A:   yeah. ((reading the instructions))
       226 -->   B:   so do you understand what happened?
       (125B)
```

Exchange level:

TRP: transition relevance place; IMR_TRP: implied result + TRP

I have split up the function of *so* that Schiffrin describes in her section on "*So* and participation structures" (1987: 217ff) into two categories: TRP for situations where a speaker self-selected (often after a long pause), starting her/his turn with *so*, and IMR_TRP for cases of 'implied result' (cf. Schiffrin 1987: 223) where a *so* at the end of an utterance concluded the explanation of an opinion or an event and the speaker evidently, judging by his/her (often falling) intonation, considered it unnecessary to state the result/conclusion because it was inferable or clear.

Excerpt (11) illustrates a typical case of TRP, whereas excerpt (12) shows a case of an implied result (IMR_TRP), which might be formulated as "I cannot judge in general about silent films, as I seem to have just done (in line 229)".

```
(11)   508       B:   .. when they're in--
       509            when they're talking,
       510            they--
       511            right?
       512            ... <SV they were SV>--
       513            ...(1.8) they were moving their mouths SV>,
       514       A:   <SV OK SV>.
       515       B:   e=r,
       516 -->   A:   ...(2.6) so everything was .. over-emphasized,
       (022A)
```

```
(12)  229     B:   I don't really like .. erm .. silent films.
      230     A:   I don't either.
      231          ...(1.8) but--
      232          ... it was OK for .. as .. a silent film goes,
      233     B:   yeah.
      234 -->      well I've actually never seen one <@ so @>.
      235     A:   yeah.
      (001B)
```

Without level:

RAG: ragbag category, indefinable; NCA: no category applied/applicable

The ragbag category was applied when the utterance introduced with *so* was not finished or unintelligible, while NCA was used when it seemed impossible to establish which function that instance of *so* had, despite the co-text being intelligible.

5.2. The results

The following figure (Figure 1) shows the actual results, presented as averages of *so* per total words per speaker in each group (US native speakers and German EFL speakers). For this figure, the functions of *so* have been grouped into

- resultative *so*'s (RIN, SAM),
- structural *so*'s (MIU, SRE, SEQ, BOM),
- non-DM *so*'s (ADM, PPS, EXP, OTH, TRL)
- all *so*'s that involve TRP (SAM_TRP, TRP, IMR_TRP).

The two categories on the speech act level have been split up because the difference in the frequency of the SAM (speech act / opinion marker) function was similar to the one of the RIN (result) function (which seems plausible since, as I said before, SAM always contained an element of result), whereas the frequency difference for the SAM_TRP function (for questions and requests) was comparable to those of the TRP and IMR_TRP functions.

The resultative functions of *so* occurred with a frequency of 0.73 per cent in the transcripts of the American native speakers, while the German EFL speakers used it only 0.45 times in a hundred words. The difference is even more remarkable with the structural functions of *so*, which were used by the American NS almost three times as much as by the Germans (0.40% vs. 0.11%). *So* in its non-discourse marker functions, however, was used only half as much by the native speakers (0.13%) as by the German speakers (0.25%). The percentages of the *so* categories involving TRP and the ragbag categories were about the same in both groups (0.09% and 0.14/0.15%).

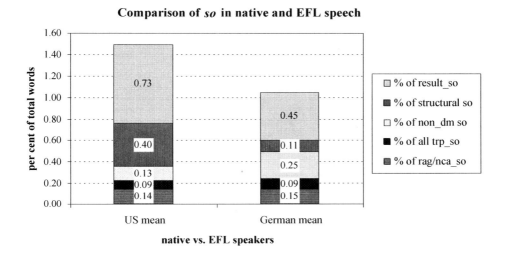

Figure 1: Comparison of the average usage of *so*, calculated as percentages of total words per speaker

The statistical tests showed that the differences between the native and the non-native speakers as illustrated in the figure were highly significant for *so* in general (t-Test, $p<0.001$), for resultative *so* (Kruskal-Wallis test, $p<0.000$) and structural *so* (Median Test, $p<0.000$), which means that it can hardly be by chance that the native speakers used these functions of *so* much more than the non-native speakers. For the non-discourse marker functions, the difference was also significant (Median Test, $p<0.016$), but in the opposite direction: the German speakers definitely use them more than the American NS.

Summarizing these results, we can say that:
The German EFL speakers used:

- fewer resultative *so*'s (RIN, SAM) than NSs,
- fewer structural *so*'s (MIU, SRE, SEQ, BOM) than NSs,
- more non-DM *so*'s (ADM, PPS, EXP, OTH, TRL) than NSs,
- all TRP *so*'s (SAM_TRP, TRP, IMR_TRP) as much as NSs.

Other observations about the results:

All categories were used by at least some of the Germans, and only 4 EFL speakers did not use resultative *so* at all. In the group of NS, the females used resultative *so* and structural *so* significantly more than the male NS. This tendency, however, cannot be shown for the EFL speakers, even though the percentage of females in each group was approximately the same (70% of the NS, 75% of the EFL speakers). Of the structural markers, SEQ was used at least once by more than two-thirds of the native speakers, but by less than a quarter of the EFL speakers. The same percentage of speakers in each group used BOM (once each). The relationship between the participants, friends or strangers, was not found to have a significant influence on the frequency of *so*, in contrast to the findings of other studies (cf. Redeker 1990; Jucker and Smith 1998).

6. Potential explanations for the results

It will probably never be possible to determine exactly the reasons for these results, but some potential explanations suggest themselves.

Influence of NS contact

I statistically analyzed the relationship between the frequencies of *so* in its various functions and the amount of informal contact the EFL speakers had with natives. It turned out that the German speakers who spent some time abroad and/or use English as a primary means of communication with friends used structural *so* twice as much as the speakers without (casual) NS contact. So it seems that non-native speakers of English learn how to use *so* for structuring discourse and narratives only in direct contact with natives. (For other functions, no significant correlation could be found.)

EFL teaching

Which of the functions of *so* do German students learn in school? To answer this question, I examined three English textbook series at the beginner's level which were in use at the time when our participants (age 19 through 31) must have been in the relevant grades. Two of the three series introduced *so* in (various) non-DM functions, which might indicate why the EFL speakers used them more. All three translated *so* as 'darum', 'deshalb', and/or 'deswegen', which might explain why 95% of the Germans used *so* in its resultative function; but it does not explain why they used it much less than natives. The type of discourse where SEQ occurs (retelling a story) is not part of the textbooks I looked at. They contain texts that are (mostly) either dialogs or pieces of literature, so that the sequential function of *so* may have been learned in school only if the teacher taught it, but not from the book. Two of the textbook series translate DM *so* as 'also', which can probably be used with the same functions as *so* except for SEQ. Thus, textbooks may explain the difference in the frequency of sequential *so*, but not necessarily the other results described above.

Influence of German so

The German EFL speakers frequently used *so* as equivalent to German 'so', both incorrectly (TRL) and (more or less) correctly (ADM). Even as an adverb of degree or manner, it seemed that *so* was often used in places where native speakers would use "such", as in example (13a), or would also use the expressions "very (good)", "that (much)" or "as (much)", as in examples (13b) through (13e):

```
(13a)              (speaker 56B)
234       and he had so .. strange habits to ea- to eat this.

(13b)              (speaker 22A)
360    A: but .. I I didn't think he looked .. like that &
360a      & quite so much,

(13c)              (speaker 41B)
527       ... (H) the acting in the first part was not so good,

(13d)              (speaker 41B)
544       [[but she didn't]] act so much.

(13e)              (speaker 42A)
614       there weren't so many big actors,
```

Influence of German also

Finally, it is possible that the use of *so* by Germans is also influenced by one of its German translations, 'also'. Meanwhile, I have recorded another set of narratives plus discussion with the same setup but conducted in German, so that I will be able to compare English discourse markers with their German equivalents.[3]

---

[3] Thanks to Martin Montgomery, who suggested this to me at the conference, and to Jesús Romero Trillo, who presented interesting findings in the same line from a comparison between English and Spanish corpora. Thanks a lot also to my supervisor, Andreas H. Jucker, who allowed me to conduct the extra set of recording sessions and have our student assistants transcribe them.

7. Conclusion

At the beginning of this paper, I suggested that native speakers of English and German speakers of English as a foreign language would use the functions of the discourse marker *so* to various degrees. Based on the results of an extensive categorization process, statistical analyses revealed that this is indeed the case. It was also expected that the EFL speakers would use ideational functions rather than functions on other planes of Schiffrin's (1987) model, because ideational relationships are supposedly taught first in school while pragmatic functions are not. This expectation, however, proved to be wrong: Even though *so* is presented as a marker of result in German textbooks of the English language, the German speakers did not use it as much as the native speakers, while they used functions involving TRP (corresponding to Schiffrin's Exchange Structure and Participation Framework, 1987: 316) as much as the American participants. Part of the answer may lie in the assumed fact that Germans tend to use English *so* in a similar way as its German counterpart 'also', an assumption that still remains to be investigated.

References

Blakemore, Diane (1988): 'So' as a constraint on relevance. – In: Kempson, Ruth M. (ed.): Mental Representations. The Interface between Language and Reality, 183–195. Cambridge: Cambridge University Press.
– (1992): Understanding Utterances. An Introduction to Pragmatics. – Oxford: Blackwell.
Blass, Regina (1990): Constraints on relevance. A key to particle typology. – *Notes on Linguistics* 48, 8–21.
Du Bois, John W. (1991): Transcription design principles for spoken discourse research. – *Pragmatics* 1, 71–106.
Fraser, Bruce (1988): Types of English discourse markers. – *Acta Linguistica Hungarica* 38, 19–33.
– (1990): An approach to discourse markers. – *Journal of Pragmatics* 14, 383–395.
– (1999): What are discourse markers? – *Journal of Pragmatics* 31, 931–952.
Hays, Paul R. (1992): Discourse markers and L2 acquisition. – In: Staub, Don and Cheryl Delk (eds.): The Proceedings of the Twelfth Second Language Research Forum, 24–34. Michigan: Papers in Applied Linguistics – Michigan.
Jucker, Andreas H. and Sara W. Smith (1998): *And people just you know like 'wow'*: Discourse markers as negotiating strategies. – In: Jucker, Andreas H. and Yael Ziv (eds.): Discourse Markers: Description and Theory, 171–202. Amsterdam: John Benjamins.
Müller, Simone (in preparation): Discourse Markers in Native and Non-Native English Discourse.
OALD (1989): Oxford Advanced Learner's Dictionary of Current English, A.S. Hornby, 4th ed. – Oxford: Oxford University Press.

Redeker, Gisela (1990): Ideational and pragmatic markers of discourse structure. – *Journal of Pragmatics* 14, 367–381.
– (1991): Review article: Linguistic markers of discourse structure. Review of Deborah Schiffrin (1987): Discourse Markers, Cambridge: CUP. – *Linguistics* 29, 1139–1172.
Schiffrin, Deborah (1987): Discourse Markers. – Cambridge: Cambridge University Press.
Unger, Christoph J. (1996): The scope of discourse connectives: implication for discourse organization. – *Journal of Linguistics* 32, 402–438.

Jesús Romero Trillo

Subjective and Objective Grounding in Discourse Markers: A Cross-linguistic Corpus-driven Approach[1,2]

1. Introduction

The analysis of language, either written or spoken, demands the correct understanding of the crucial axes that shape the cognitive framework of the language user, i.e., the deictic pointers that help to process discourse in relation to time, place, person, society, etc. (cf. Lyons 1977). These pointers, and their role in text coding and decoding information, have been profusely described in the past according to different linguistic traditions, ranging from the most "down-to-the-text" ones, e.g. Halliday & Hasan (1976), to the most cognitively oriented, e.g. Gernsbacher & Givón (1995).

The study of the relationship between the text and its meaningful understanding is what has traditionally been termed "coherence". This notion, according to the above mentioned traditions, may rely either on the interpretability of language in a given context –the Hallidayan tradition–, or rest on the cognitive understanding of arguments that are realized by propositions, i.e. "coherence as a mental entity" (Givón 1995: 61).

In my opinion, the difference between the two ways of analysing coherence lies in the concept of "grounding", which I shall define as: "the connections that are established between a text and other sources of knowledge that enable the recipient to create a network of concepts". In the Hallidayan tradition grounding is formalised by relations, called cohesive chains (Halliday & Hasan 1987), which relate to the overall coherence of the text. Without denying this essential component of discourse building, the second model puts the emphasis on the mental representation of the text, characterised by the existence of a mental text structure that constitutes the "chief guarantor of fast on-line access to episodic information during both text production and text comprehension" (Givón 1995:64)

In the present article, I will adopt Givón's approach to coherence and will concentrate on the grounding effects of discourse markers in the speech of native and non-native speakers of English.

---

[1] This research has been funded by the Comunidad Autónoma de Madrid, as a part of the *UAM-Corpus Project* (ref. CAM 06/0027/2001) (*in progress*).
[2] I am grateful to the editor for helpful comments on the final version of this article.

Traditional studies on coherence relations have mostly concentrated either on the deictic elements that establish the cognitive axes of discourse, or on the relationship between the ideas that build a mental text structure. In contrast, the present analysis will delve into the role of discourse markers as the elements that, often inadvertently, model the cognitive relationship between discourse content and the interlocutors in spoken language. The study will also describe how these markers function differently in English and Spanish, with the subsequent cognitive difficulty for non-native speakers of the language.

2. Subjective and objective grounding in speech

Ordinary spoken discourse is characterised by a continuous flow of elements that ground it to present or past experiences and events related to the speaker or hearer. In other words, everyday discourse often refers to the lives of its participants. This is the reason why sometimes discourse between relatives or friends lacks the elements that may make it comprehensible for an external audience, in what Bernstein defined "restricted code language" (1971).

Reference to the participant's cognitive status in spoken language is also related to the notion of authority. Many, if not all, our words are grounded on the authority that either the speaker or the hearer, as witness or experiencer of events, holds. In other cases, the authority is not overtly assigned to a person, but to common lore or agreed consensus.

Grounding, in this sense, is the tool by which the speaker relates his/her speech to the knowledge that is shared with the audience. I will describe the following categories of Grounding:

- "Subjective grounding": the discourse reference relates to the speaker's or hearer's personal beliefs, experiences or attitudes..

- "Objective grounding": the reference relies on a social or generally agreed cognitive status.

Previous studies on the role of subjectivity in discourse have concentrated on the description of lexical and grammatical elements in texts. For example, Sanders & Spooren (1997) classify this phenomenon under the general term of "subjective discourse". For them, subjective discourse relates to the cases when a certain topic is bound to a speaking or thinking subject of consciousness – which is not "objective" by nature. In their approach, any concept becomes subjective when the speaker connects it explicitly to himself or to another subject and does not rely on an objective description.

These authors further differentiate between the case when the connection relates to the speaker, "subjectification", and when the connection is linked to concrete or abstract persons other than the speaker, which they call "perspectivisation".

In their model, subjectification can be exemplified: "I believe Jan is in Paris", and perspectivisation: "Mary believes Jan is in Paris". As shown in their examples, the difference in both utterances has to do with the Referential Center in which the utterance is anchored assuming their cognitive network, "I" or "Mary", a difference that is largely dependent on semantic and lexical constraints.

In my description of discourse markers, however, I have preferred subjective grounding for all personal references in the construction of speech (either first person or second person), as opposed to the markers that indicate a neutral, social-bound origin of authority, i.e., objective grounding. The reason is that, in the case of discourse markers, all the personal references, even those that carry a second person, e.g. "you know", "you see", show the intention of the speaker to include the listener into his/her cognitive framework in order to make joint progress with the topic under discussion. Therefore, subjective grounding refers to an attitude or personal belief towards the predicated information by introducing the speaker/listener's consciousness, beliefs or evaluation. By using such markers, the speaker foregrounds him/herself to some extent and becomes an active part of the discourse. Subjective grounding, therefore, creates room for consent by the listener, especially when the second person elements appear, *(you know, you see)*, in what I have called elsewhere "the sympathetic circularity function" (Romero Trillo 2001).

Objective grounding markers, on the other hand, are linked to the external judgment of a fact or event, and do not often lend themselves to being challenged by the addressee of a message. These markers, e.g.: *in fact, of course, indeed,* etc. indicate the speaker's cognitive detachment of the content of the message, but also interest in its development (Lazard 2001).

3. Subjective and objective grounding in English and Spanish discourse markers

The hypothesis behind the study is that different languages organize subjective and objective grounding through lexical and grammatical options that are consciously selected by speakers, like pronouns, verbs, fixed expressions, etc. However, there are fewer conscious, or even unconscious options realised by discourse markers, which often escape speakers' linguistic control (Romero Trillo, 1997). In the present case, the markers represent a way to relate meaning and cognition, and are used and establish intellectual rapport in a language.

The classification of the subjective and objective grounding markers in English and Spanish under study is the following:

Subjective
- English
  I mean, I think, I believe, I know, you know, you see,
- Spanish
  Osea ('I mean'), *creo* ('I think'), *me parece* ('it seems to me'), *sabes* ('you know'), *ves* ('you see'), *es decir* ('that is to say')

Objective:
- English
  Really, of course, indeed, in fact, surely, certainly, actually
- Spanish
  Realmente ('really'), *desde luego* ('of course'), *de* hecho ('in fact'), *de verdad* ('in truth'), *seguro* ('surely'), *seguramente* ('for sure'), *ciertamente* ('certainly')

It is important to mention that the meanings of the selected markers in both languages are almost equivalent with regard to their lexical source. However, in the analysis the meaning of the markers is not taken into account, since what matters is the realization of the functions according to the context where they appear (Romero Trillo, 2001).

The first step in the analysis consists in the comparison of the realization of objective and subjective grounding in the English and Spanish corpora. Secondly, the analysis concentrated on the study of the realization of the English markers by advanced non-native speakers in order to see the extent to which the phenomenon of "pragmatic fossilization" (Romero Trillo, 2002) affects not only the use but also the conceptualisation of grounding in a foreign language.

4. Analysis of the data

4.1. Description of the corpora

The English data comes from the London-Lund Corpus of English Conversation. The section under study in this article consists of 50,000 words of natural face-to-face adult interactions in a university environment.

The Spanish data comes from the Corpus de Referencia del Español Actual (CREA) (1992), compiled at the Universidad Autónoma de Madrid, and consists of natural face-to-face adult conversations, with a total amount of 50,893 words.

The non-native English data comes from the UAM-Corpus (in progress), a collection of spoken EFL conversations collected on a longitudinal basis from pre-school children to university students. The section that has been used for this analysis consists of 24,648 words of advanced learners' conversation in the Department of English Philology at the Universidad Autónoma de Madrid.

4.2. Investigation

The first analysis tries to discover whether the speakers in the corpora showed a preference in the use of Subjective and Objective markers. For this purpose, I made a Paired T-test for dependent samples to compare the three corpora. The results were significant in the three cases, based on the relative frequencies shown in figures 1 to 3:

London-Lund: $t=6.63$ ($p=0.000096$)
CREA: $t=2.51$ ($p=0.0013992$)
UAM Corpus: $t=4.55$ ($p=0.027543$)

In the figure below (1 to 3) I show the use of objective and subjective markers in each corpus. The graphs show the higher proportion of subjective markers in the three cases.

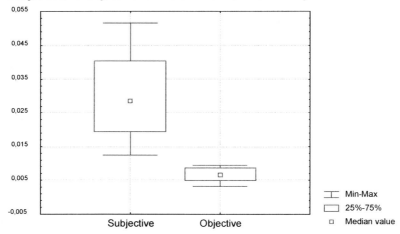

Figure 1. Box &Whisker Plot of the relative frequency of markers in the London-Lund

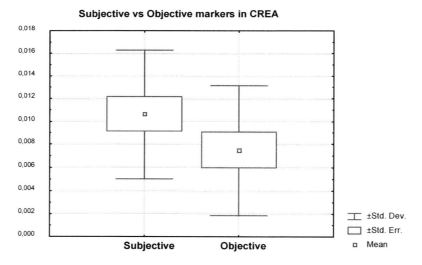

Figure 2. Box &Whisker Plot of the relative frequency of markers in the CREA

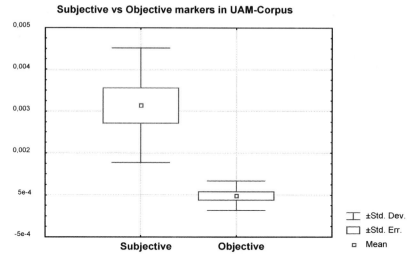

Figure 3. Box & Whisker Plot of the relative frequency of markers in the UAM-Corpus

These analyses indicate that English and Spanish prefer the use of subjective markers to the use of objective markers. This preference is also shared by the speakers in the corpus of non-native English (UAM-Corpus).

The second analysis that I carried out has the aim to discover the difference in the use of the discourse markers across the three corpora. In other words, my interest was to check if there was a significant higher or lower use of subjective and objective markers in the corpora.

The results of the analysis can be observed in the following pie-charts which represent the use of subjective and objective markers in the three corpora:

English Native speakers

Table 1. Use of subjective markers by native speakers

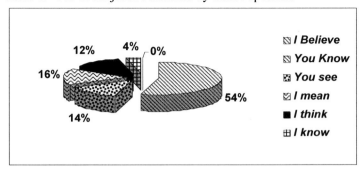

Table 2. Use of objective markers by native speakers

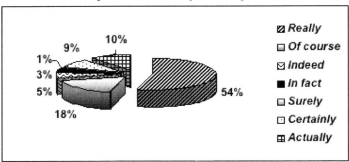

English Non-native Speakers

Table 3. Use of subjective markers by non-native speakers

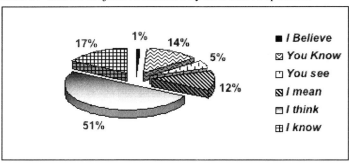

Table 4. Use of objective markers by non-native speakers

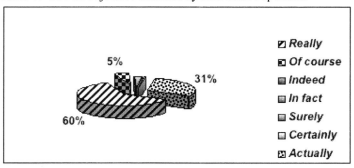

Spanish Speakers

Table 5. Use of subjective markers by Spanish speakers

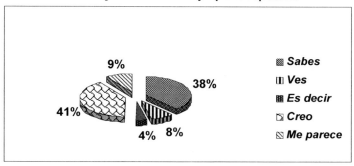

Table 6. Use of objective markers by Spanish speakers

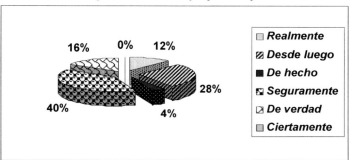

These results show that, with regard to subjective elements, Spanish markers are mainly first-person based and concentrated on the item *creo* (41%), whereas English markers are mainly second-person based with *you know* (54%) and *you see* (14%). This fact has clear consequences for the realization of the markers by non-native speakers as indicated by the overuse of first person markers: *I think* –the direct translation of *creo*– (51%) and *I know* (17%). On the contrary, the use of second-person markers by this group of speakers is infrequent: *you know* (14%) and *you see* (5%). This enormous difference in the ascription of the personal reference of the markers clearly produces a "dysfunction" in the involvement of the speakers, with probable pragmatic inaccuracies.

With regard to the use of objective markers, the situation is quite different because both native and non-native speakers use the element *really* in a consistent way (54% and 60%, respectively), in contrast with the limited use of the marker *realmente* by Spanish speakers (12%). What is noticeable, is the overuse of the element *actually* by non-native speakers

(31%) compared with native speakers (10%), a fact which is not explained by its Spanish translation *de hecho*, used only in 4% of the cases.

In order to check the overall pattern of use of subjective and objective markers in the three corpora, I made a one-way ANOVA test in the group of subjective markers with the following significant result: F(2,30), (p=0,0000). This result indicates that there is a significantly higher use of subjective markers in English compared with Spanish. Following this pattern, the analysis also reported a statistically significantly lower use of subjective markers by non-native speakers of English, i.e., Spanish speakers of English make a limited use of these elements in comparison with the native model, as seen in Figure 5:

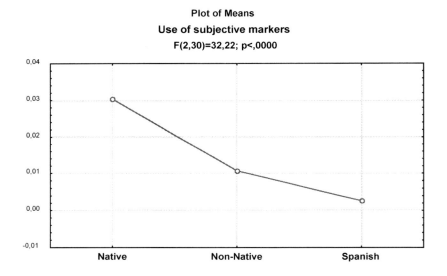

Figure 5.

The same one-way ANOVA test was conducted for objective markers with a significant difference, F(2,30) (p=0,0003) in the use of English and Spanish markers. In contrast with the previous analysis, the results showed no difference in the use of objective markers by native and non-native speakers of English. This indicates that non-native speakers are able to acquire the use of objective markers in a more native-like consistent way, as can be observed in figure 6:

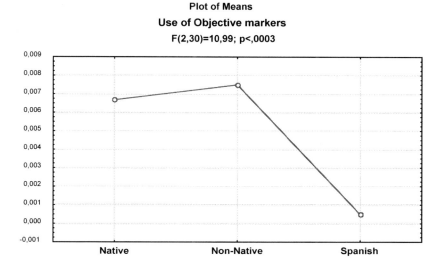

Figure 6.

5. Conclusions

The article has shown that languages differ in their organization of subjective and objective grounding. This difference does not only refer to the lexical and grammatical elements, but also to pragmatic elements such as discourse markers.

Specifically, the article has shown that English and Spanish globally favour the use of subjective vs. objective markers, probably because they contribute to establishing a more personal rapport between speakers, which is one of the features of spoken language.

However, our data has shown that English and Spanish show very different trends in the frequency of these elements, which may make this aspect of language difficult to learn for non-native speakers of English. This difficulty mainly applies to the acquisition of subjective elements, since learners of English are able to reach a native-like proficiency in the use of objective elements. The reason for this may be two-fold:

- The more transparent conceptual equivalence of objective markers makes Spanish learners of English more confident when they communicate in the target language.

- Subjective markers are not overtly present in the learning process, since they are more elusive to explain in terms of meaning, register and frequency.

My impression is that both reasons may explain the learners' difficulties with subjective markers.

In my opinion, this kind of research has a clear pedagogical implication in the acquisition of an L2, because discourse markers, which are essential to the cognitive modelling of discourse, are often beyond linguistic awareness and may show a different pattern in their frequency and distribution across languages.

In fact, the only way to establish a solid understanding of this phenomenon is through the analysis of a large-scale modelling of discourse particles in different corpora of native and non-native speakers of English, and to understand discourse variation across languages.

To sum up, the study has shown the relevance of the correct use and distribution of discourse markers to obtain a pragmatically-balanced speech in a non-native language, especially in the case of languages with such disparities in the use of objective and subjective grounding as English and Spanish.

References

Bernstein, Basil (1971): Class, Codes and Control, vol 1. London: – Routledge and Kegan Paul.
Gernsbacher, Morton A. and Talmy Givón (eds) (1995): Coherence in Spontaneous Texts. – Amsterdam: John Benjamins Publishing Company.
Givón, Talmy. (1995): Coherence in text vs. coherence in mind: in Gernsbacher & Givón (eds.) 59–116.
Halliday, M.A.K. and Ruqaya Hasan (1976): Cohesion in English. – London: Longman.
– (1987): Language, Context and Text. – Oxford: Oxford University Press.
Lazard, Gilbert (2001): On the grammaticalisation of evidentiality. – *Journal of Pragmatics* 33, 359–367.
Lyons, John (1977): Semantics (2 vols). – Cambridge: C.U.P.
Romero Trillo, Jesús (1997): Pragmatic mechanisms to obtain the addressee's attention in English and Spanish conversations. – *Journal of Pragmatics* 28, 205–221.
– (2001): A mathematical model for the analysis of variation in discourse. *Journal of Linguistics*. 37, 27–550.
– (2002): The pragmatic fossilization of discourse markers in non-native speakers of English. – *Journal of Pragmatics*. 34, 769–784.
Sanders, José and Wilbert Spooren (1997): Perspective, subjectivity and modality from a cognitive linguistic point of view. – In W.A. Liebert et al. (eds.) Discourse and Perspective in Cognitive Linguistics. 85–112. Amsterdam: John Benjamins.

The corpora

Marcos Marín, F. et al. (1992): Corpus de referencia del español actual. – Madrid: Universidad Autónoma de Madrid
Romero Trillo, J. et al. UAM-Corpus (in progress). – Madrid: Universidad Autónoma de Madrid
Svartvik, J and Quirk, R. (eds.) (1980): A Corpus of English Conversation. – Lund: Lund University Press.

Chapter 4
Exploring Dialogue in Academic Discourse

Anna Mauranen

Talking Academic: A Corpus Approach to Academic Speech

Spoken language has been a neglected area in the study of academic discourses. Following the tradition of analysing writing, the early explorations into academic speech have focused on monologic speech such as is found in lectures. Yet it is in the interactive or dialogic situations that academic speech differs most clearly from the written genres. The 'backstage' talk like disagreements, failures and irrelevancies, which can be likened to Gilbert/Mulkay's (1984) 'contingent' repertoires, move to the forefront when a variety of dialogic event types, such as seminars, group discussions, meetings and consultation hours are investigated. Such event types are well represented in the MICASE corpus. The focus in this paper is on conflictual discourse in academic speech, and the possibilities of corpus research in uncovering its characteristic expressions. A corpus approach turns out to be fruitful and yield observations which go beyond and complement other approaches to the elusive phenomenon of expressing negativity and conflict.

1. Introduction

Linguistic research into academic discourses has been heavily dominated by applied linguistics, thus mainly motivated by practical concerns, which may be one of the reasons why it has almost exclusively concerned itself with the study of the written text. Scientific speaking has constituted data for the sociology of science more than for linguistics. Nevertheless, the interest in academic genres has gradually broadened to include areas of less immediate applicability, such as historical research, and more recently also increasingly the spoken language. The latter has also begun to find its way to the applied domain, which may herald the beginning of a wealth of research interest, if the written mode is anything to go by.

As I have pointed out in other contexts, the relationship between speaking and writing can be likened to the distinction that the well-known sociologists of science, Gilbert/Mulkay (1984) drew between on the one hand formal, official, polished-up, accounts of research, following as it were from the very nature of the object of research, which they called the scientists' "empiricist repertoire", and on the other hand the "contingent" repertoire, which refers to the scientists' ways of describing professional actions and beliefs resulting from individuals acting on the basis of their particular social positions, personal inclinations, interests, etc. (Gilbert/Mulkay 1984: 56–7). Gilbert/Mulkay's scientists resorted to their contingent repertoire when engaging in informal peer discourses about their work, but the 'contingent repertoires' employed in everyday academic speaking in university settings comprise a much wider spectrum of discourses. Speaking in a university context quite routinely involves many kinds of 'backstage phenomena' that we normally do not write about. These discourses deserve more attention than they have received, not only as data about variable linguistic forms, but potentially also as discourses which are intermediate between direct experimentation and fieldwork on the one hand, and the finished, published products of the written genres of the academia on the other. In occupying this mediating position they may turn out to carry epistemological meanings of the kinds that Rowley-Jolivet (1999) invests conference papers with: bridging the gap between the laboratory and the research article, and contributing to a more balanced view on the dispute between realism and relativism by taking mediating steps on board. It is likely that the variety of spoken discourses academics engage in as part of their normal work provide important insights into the formation and maintenance of knowledge just as they do to the use of language.

The data that I use in this paper consists of a wide variety of university discourses recorded in their normal everyday contexts. It comes from the Michigan Corpus of Academic Spoken English (MICASE, see Simpson et al. 1999). The MICASE is one of two simultaneously but independently started projects compiling corpora of academic speech in the US in the late nineties. Both projects were motivated primarily by the practical need to develop appropriate tests and teaching materials for foreign students and teaching assistants in American universities, although researchers also had their eye on the databases from the start. One of these projects (T2K-SWAL) was in Arizona, Flagstaff, led by Douglas Biber and his associates, the other one at Michigan, Ann Arbor, directed by John Swales and Rita Simpson. The MICASE corpus, like its counterpart in Arizona, is based on a variety of speech genres (or, rather, event types) that characterise a university environment. So, in addition to the obvious lectures and seminars, the corpus covers thesis defences, student presentations, group discussions, meetings and consultation hours, etc. The corpus has also sought to distinguish between primarily monologic and dialogic event types, and strike a balance between the two.

One of the questions the MICASE project set itself at the outset was "is academic speaking more like conversation than academic writing". As the corpus has grown to a size allowing serious research, the basic answer to that question seems to be: much more like conversation (see, for instance Lindemann/Mauranen 2001, Poos/Simpson 2000,

Swales/Burke 2001). Similar findings were reported by Biber (2001) on the Arizona corpus, which he approached with his multivariate analysis of key features (see, e.g. Biber 1988): there seem to be more conversational features than features earlier found to characterise academic prose. The result may at first sight seem self-evident – clearly, speech must be like other speech. But this did not look quite so obvious before the findings were available.

For one thing, we do not seem to pay much conscious attention to the situational management talk which inevitably accompanies even quite formal events like large lectures, or thesis defences. So although especially the beginnings and ends of such events are linguistically quite different from that which counts as "the lecture itself", this talk appears to be filtered out not only from public accounts of such events but also from our mental representation of a lecture, and the kind of linguistic realisation that goes with it. To put it in slightly different terms, the 'transactional' or the generically salient characteristics of the situation overshadow the interactional aspects. McCarthy (2001:112–113) summarises research on the intermingling of relational and transactional features in several different genres; most of this work shows that interactional discourse varies in its degree of ritualisation, and that it occurs in fairly predictable phases in different genres. The study closest to the topic at hand is by S. Thompson (1997) on university research presentations, which emphasises the importance of serious facework in this genre: building an appropriate relationship between speaker and audience is an integral part of oral presentations. The kind of phasal structure that characterises for example service encounters thus also appears to apply to academic discourses.

For me, an intriguing issue relating to speech versus writing which was anything but obvious from the outset is the question to what extent academic speaking would be competitive, or conflictual. Academic writing is usually described with expressions evoking competition and conflict, often with battlefield metaphors. This inherent competitiveness and conflict presumably is what for example motivates the abundant use of hedges in academic texts (see, for instance Markkanen/Schröder 1997, Myers 1989, Varttala 1999). In contrast, descriptions of conversation normally emphasise the co-operative and consensual nature of face-to-face interactions (e.g. Aijmer 1996, Eggins/Slade 1997). So the question arose how is academic speech positioned in these terms? Is it conflictual rather than consensual?

2. Academic backstages

I shall look fairly briefly and generally into some backstage phenomena negotiated in academic speech events, and then in the next section move on to manifestations of conflict in a broad sense, with metadiscourse as the main focus. Typical backstage phenomena include for example various disclaimers as well as the metadiscourse of justifications for talking about things which might induce criticism on account of breaking some maxims of academic discourse etiquette, like being irrelevant to the topic (1), admitting you are unable to answer a question (2), or admitting to a memory lapse (3):

(1) i mention that just for those who are interested it is totally irrelevant to what i'm talking about.

(2) good question i_ i'll have to_ i'll email um one of the authors of this article
   A: mhm. Galtung in the course of his essay, there's this wonderful essay, i don't know if i told you about it by Galtung, about uh Saxonic Nipponic uh uh Gallic and Teuton- and Teutonic uh, styles of intellectual argument. it's it's just it's wonderful [it's just,] would be (fun) it's delicious uh, now
                                                              [B: oh that]

(3) what was i going to say about before oh <LAUGH> there's, i was gonna say before the Galtung um, the point that was just, on the table which is what?...
   C: <LAUGH"> apropos of aging
   D: <LAUGH> but you're getting worse [don't worry]
   E: [if you can't] remember we'll go on to the next (other) example
   D: <LAUGH>
   A: uh uh about uh thing but oh yes right no that that the uh that he starts his example, with the example of um of the, American professor

Others include very mundane problems with the physical environment (4), or uncertainties and negotiations about situational management as in (5), which is from an undergraduate seminar (A and B are students, and C the instructor).

(4)   A: ... and this gives us a way, a n- a new way in to trying to decide among these various theories of personal identity. <PAUSE :15 WHILE WRITING ON BOARD> <TRIPS OVER CORD> sorry excuse me (R:sorry,) there's no
   R: [other um, outlet, um]
   A: [no, maybe if we let it,] if we push it over this way, yeah (R: there we go.) um, and the second stage of the, of, the experiment is...

(5)   A: am i the only one who read?
   B: [i don't know if anyone (xx)]
   A: [so what exactly]   would you like us to discuss? (C: hm?) what exactly should we be discussing?
   C: um like, just to go through the the...

A special kind of backstage comment was triggered by the recording itself (6–8). These examples serve as useful reminders to researchers of the limitations of recorded data as representing naturally occurring speech. Recorded subjects remain conscious of the recording, and adjust their behaviour accordingly.

(6)   A: ...okay, so um, i guess we should, fill out these forms. yeah, i don't know if, i'm assuming that they will be here but
   B: corpus of academic spoken English
   A: i don't know.
   B: look at that. (PAUSE :06)
   A: oh i actually have to put my real name on here huh? on the pink form?

(7)   okay i'm gonna say something that is gonna sound really bad on tape but, they're...

(8)   you remind me sometime when we're not being taped i'll tell you a Feynman story

One of the notable characteristics of speech is laughter, which we obviously cannot represent in writing – whatever humour there might be in written academic text, it must be expressed by very different means. As a brief glimpse of how laughter is distributed across speech events, I present a quick overview of where Michigan university discourses involve laughter. Humour and laughter research has suggested there tends to be less of it in institutional, formal settings than in casual conversations. Thus, as one might expect, the least laughter was found in the speech event types closely associated with the institutional role of the university, viz. lectures.

least laughter /1000 words

event type	n of events
lecture	18
office hour	1
discussion	1

Some researchers have noted the polysemous nature of humour, which allows both a serious and a non-serious meaning to be recognised simultaneously. This again allows participants to claim that either the "serious" or the "non-serious" meaning was not intended, thus enabling "interactants to speak off the record, to make light of what is perhaps quite serious to them" (Eggins/Slade 1997:156). As Eggins and Slade put it, "humour arises as interactants make text in contexts which involve conflict, tension, and contradiction" (ibid:167). Academic discourses can be assumed to involve each of these elements to some degree, and one might expect these most frequently in contexts institutionally involving argumentation and criticism, like thesis defences, discussions, as well as possibly seminars, or departmental meetings. A look at the event types where most laughter in fact did occur does not confirm the assumption:

most laughter /1000 words

event type	n of events
colloquium	3
lab section	3
lecture	3
meeting	2
tutorial	2
seminar	2
interview	1
office hour	1
tour	1
advising session	1
discussion	1

From this list, it looks as if laughter occurred in mainly dialogic event types, that is, those most similar to conversation. Although the lecture appears to be the event type where even Americans laugh the least (the two events with zero amount of laughter were both lectures), there were three lectures where laughter was frequent. The most laughter occurred during a special lecture accompanying the presentation of an award for the Teacher of the Year at Michigan University. The event therefore resembled a floor show, and could easily be dismissed as exceptional, but the other two were more routine-like, with nothing else particularly remarkable about them. Without going into detail, I would just like to point out that most of the laughter was preceded by reference to some sort of discrepancy or incongruity – in the lectures the discrepancies often obtained between an abstract and a concrete interpretation of a term or concept. In the dialogic event types, a number of joking references were made to potentially embarrassing topics, like misunderstanding or inability to provide a good answer (examples 11, 21, 23 below), forgetting (as in example 3 above), as well as sensitive issues like age or gender.

The reason for laughter shared by those present may remain obscure to outsiders (9), as tends to be the case in conference presentations – speakers make reference to shared meanings, such as well-known theoretical approaches (*no colourless green ideas here*) that they can be confident are viewed by the audience in a certain way, and which in part serve to create social cohesion.

(9)   uh, well normally it's just a quick, run-through but i don't if people wanna do it on a on a you know just... in this, fashion common on the fourth floor <LAUGH> that's fine too. i don't know, what do people wanna do?

Laughter, then, at a superficial glance seems to have very similar functions to ordinary conversation, contributing to the impression of similarity between academic and other speech, but at the same time the lecture, possibly also other monologic speech events, appears to be different from the more dialogic event types.

While I cannot develop the role of laughter further here, the issue of the seemingly missing negativity and conflict in academic talk has already been touched upon. I shall turn to this next.

3. Criticism and disagreement

I wanted to pursue the expression of criticism and conflict, because recent work on this data seems to point to its elusiveness. Looking at evaluative expressions, I found (2000) that while positive evaluations abound in the data, negative evaluations were very hard to find. This was subsequently supported by Swales and Burke (2001), and it points to a certain consensus-orientedness, which in turn is a characteristic of conversation more than academic prose. In an attempt to locate criticism, disagreement and negative evaluation, which could broadly be termed conflictual discourse, I turned to transcripts of event types where criticism was most obviously inbuilt, that is, thesis defences. Since my aim is to uncover typical linguistic indicators of criticism, I shall limit the discussion to those conflictual instances which in Allwood's (1993:9) terms would be both 'actual' (as opposed to latent) and 'overt' (as opposed to covert) conflicts. These presumably are more in evidence in the actual linguistic output than their opposites, which may rely solely on introspection or content analysis for their recognition.

As first candidates, one might assume that expressions like *agree* and *disagree* would be common in academic contexts. Burdine (2001) found that *I disagree* occurred 31 times in her combined corpus of three genres of spoken American English (4 million words, including for example academic meetings) whereas *I don't agree* was more marked, with only 6 occurrences. However, the present, solely academic, data was different. *Agree* appeared over a hundred times in a million words, but mostly expressing agreement. It was used in *I don't agree* only six times, and *I disagree* merely four times. An interesting case was the qualified or partial agreement *I agree that X but...*, of which there were twelve in the data.

How was criticism expressed, then? The most commonly recurring expressions can be grouped in three main types, as listed below:

Criticism – thesis defence transcripts

- cognitive verbs: it seems to me, what puzzles me, I was wondering or similar expressions (**to me** A is like B...),
- reflexive discourse: say, argue, point,...
- others: but, why...

After this initial stage of extracting what looked like key expressions in the thesis transcripts, I searched for these in the whole corpus. I then reduced the data by focusing on the speech events where the expressions were used most consistently. I checked the use of the target items per 1000 words in terms of all files, and selected the top twenty event files for closer analysis. I look at examples from each of these types below.

3.1 Cognitive verbs

Among cognitive verbs the most commonly recurring expression was *(seems) to me.* After excluding irrelevant expressions (like *come and talk to me*), 74 instances were left, of which only three appeared to signal simply uncertainty or a speculative attitude without a clear stance.

(seems) to me	
context of criticism	41
context of other stance marking	30
speculative, not critical	3
total	74

In connection with the first person singular, *seems* appears to be primarily marking stance, and in well over half of the time (41/74) it was involved in criticism, quite typically preceding express criticism of the previous speaker (as in 10) – or otherwise the most obvious target like the candidate in a thesis defence or the presenter in a seminar. This example (10) is from a thesis defence, where A is the candidate's advisor, and B a committee member.

(10) A: uh this may be related to a conversation that, uh XX and i have had, um, periodically. i mean he /.../ (they're) very very different way of accounting for these phenomena and i i don't i don't know
[where you] stand on [that]
B: [well wouldn't]   [wouldn't,] yeah but i mean **it seem- it seems to me**, i mean i i i see that ambiguity i mean is there is is there i mean are there complex theories that somehow (are this) kind of thing, and hence i mean no matter what outcome, there is i mean you always find some (sequent) of the theory that fits.(A: right) or is there no theory at all? and all i do is is basically (A: right) reasoning in hindsight when i see that and ...

A mere *to me* + BE is used in a very similar way, as can be seen from an extract of the same defence a little later, where A is the candidate, and B a committee member (11):

(11) A: ... the argument is the same [the]   the, the numerals are different
[B: mhm]
B: yeah. well, uh, uh, right, but i mean it's like a world of difference **[to me]** right? when somebody says
                              [A: mhm]
two-five-one and i'm hearing, five-one-four [it's really different] so i think if you really do hear it that
                              [A: okay, right]
way i mean i i i'd be willing to let you hear it that way, that's fine, (A: <LAUGH>) but i think, the indication of something, i mean even to say in here something about the you know the the (A: yeah) Lydian A-flat ...

In cases where oppositional stance marking appeared without an obvious adversary, *it seems to me* still marked the speaker's stance with a strong polemical overtone, and could be heard as challenging the interactants, not only absent third parties, theories, or general principles of argumentation. This example is from a graduate students' seminar.

(12) B: right so [the claim the claim then is] is that is that is that the, the statement is false um,
A: [that's all i'm saying (xx)]
B: [if it's if it's] referring to something physical i'm not inclined to to think that it's referring to something physical, and if i- the the contention is that if i if i deny that then i'm committed to dualism assumptionist dualism. uh now may- maybe someone can convince me that in fact i should be committed to assumptionist dualism, (A: yeah yeah. yeah yeah.) but that's not a step that i i_ **it it seems to me** that i'm forced to take.
A: if you could, w- w- rewind just a couple sentences? (B: okay) you said this state is false if it refers to something physical?

Basically, *it seems to me* signals a stance, and by asserting a view the speaker inevitably sets up an opposition between that viewpoint and its actual or potential opposites. So in (13), indicating the speaker's view makes the question a challenge rather than just an inquiry or a prompt for the seminar panel team to say something.

(13) A: ... uh, does the audience have any questions they want to ask either of the teams? yeah, B?
B: um, i guess i would address this mostly to the jail group. um, and reflecting of what uh, XX said about this being part of a a wider political situation. Why is the universe of things that you could address as a social policy issue, in order to get at crime, would you target crack? i read a statistic that eighty percent of the people who commit crimes are under the influence of alcohol, by the legal standard. um, **it seems to me that** there's there's a lot behind the fact that crack is singled out as something to be addressed, that has to do with demonizing poor minorities. so, could you react to that?

Marking stance and being polemical or critical do not thus differ greatly. Although there were one or two positive cases, *it seems to me* appears strongly inclined towards negative evaluation or challenge. Despite the generally recognised hedging effect of *seem*, in the context of *to me* it works in a different manner – it would be stretching the interpretation implausibly far to see the conflictual stance marking as included in hedging. Once more, we are reminded of the association of specific meanings with particular forms or combinations that a given lemma enters into.

3.2 Metadiscourse

The next type of critical signal was metadiscourse. Example (14) illustrates a number of metadiscursive (or discourse reflexive) expressions in a somewhat heated seminar debate.

(14) A: ... affirming, the proposition of a red spherical ball, which doesn't seem to include, the phenomenal character of what in fact is going on and what i'm imagining.
B: okay i i i i hear that **claim**. (A: uhuh) um, uh i i um i understand that it's not that it doesn't seem to include, phenomena **i have to argue** and did a little bit last week (A: right right) and would have a little bit today **argued** that this explains, um phenomenality. but you don't yet have a reason to deny this **claim**. [if all you've said all you're saying] now is that that this is not_ e- even if you're right
[A: (yeah but i wi- i wi-)]
i don't think you are from what you're suspecting but even if you're right, this **claim** is, not um all your your **complaint** is that this **claim** is not the whole truth about the universe fine. i just wanna know whether it's true...

Metadiscourse plays an important role in secondary socialisation. It involves all three Hallidayan metafunctions, not only the textual, of which it is the obvious extension, or the interpersonal, with which it has also frequently been combined in the literature. Both of these aspects are obviously important – organising discourse as it unfolds (textual function), metadiscourse imposes the speaker's order on the discourse situation, and in this sense is acting out power relations (interpersonal function). This is particularly clear in evaluative modification of metadiscourse (*that's a very interesting remark/ good observation/ a really important point*) which also serves to socialise students into the discourse community. At the same time, such labels categorise referential content, the knowledge, into 'arguments', 'claims', 'points', etc, in this way setting up hierarchies, imparting value systems and making them explicit (*a very important issue, here's a flawed argument, that's not a criticism*). In Hallidayan terms, this then involves the ideational component.

Very frequent metadiscursive items that occurred with criticism were *claim* and *argue*, of the latter particularly the nominal form *argument*. These seem to play a role in secondary socialisation, where for instance *argument* is used for evaluative 'demonstration' in monologic speech as in (15), but also in an engaged, dialogical manner in criticism and argumentation (16).

(15) and, taken to its extreme form, that can be seen as a form of biological materialism that what our bodies need therefore determines what our culture will produce for us, or what we do. and so that's that's **that's it, the argument** in its extreme form. **it's flawed**, because it reduces the complexity of human thought and action, to one single factor.

(16) okay. well, that that, very well maybe true, but, **i think you can't make an argument that** no whites use, crack cocaine. however, um there has been no white

The socialising effect can also be detected on a scale of development from lower to higher steps on the academic ladder, if we look at the different user groups: both *claim* and *argue* are used most by senior faculty, followed closely by senior graduates – both of these groups are proportionally overrepresented using these items as compared to their average proportion of talking (Mauranen 2001).

An even more common, inconspicuous but frequently occurring vehicle of negotiating conflictual discourse was *say*. It has sometimes been described as the most neutral reporting verb, but however neutral it might be by itself, it certainly is frequently involved in argumentation. Its most characteristic form in this data in conflictual use was *saying* in the context of the pronouns *I* and *you*. Interestingly, Craig and Sanusi (2000) have similarly identified the *–ing* form as the carrier of an argumentative function in the use of *say*, and they also observed this use in the first and second person. Their analysis dealt with argumentative structure in two organised student debates. One of the uses in the present data of **you / I + BE saying** is negotiating or clarifying unclear meanings rather than debating (17):

(17) A: are you s- suggesting a, a link between the narrator and the street? is that what i'm, hearing or am i just?
B: a link between the narrator and,
A: the street, like, the conflicted, -ness of the narrator's (merged) the half of this_ half rubble. **are you_ were you saying that** or am i just hearing you, differently?
B: **i'm saying** that he is feeling conflict based on, what he sees in the street
A: oh okay.

However, the more interesting uses for the present purpose are those where **you / I + BE saying** is used more conflictually in argumentation and criticism or disagreement. The argumentative use also includes attempts to reach consensus, not only continuing or beginning disagreement, as in the following example (18) from a seminar:

(18) A: okay i don't know what you're_ if that's your conclusion we we_ if that if that really is your conclusion we don't disagree, because **all i'm saying is**, <LAUGH> **all i'm saying** so far there is, when you imagine when you visually ...

Despite a few occurrences of these less combative instances, a critical or overtly conflictual use was more than three times as common as the consensual (19 and 20):

(19) A: right, but but tha- uh [B: ah but then how][**what i'm trying to say**]
B: but how do i know that reading this? **if you're if you're saying**, look at the way, Jarrett's actual realization of the piece contrast with the way the piece was composed (A: okay) that's fine (A: yeah) but, that needs to be said [really] overtly because there's so many places where these chords symbols
[A: yeah]
[A: don't jive]
[disagree] with the [music]

(20) A: ... i think that there's a, um, that a lot of their, success and attention, has been pretty well deserved. i mean when they they
B: yeah but think of all those groups, okay but think of all those gazillion groups, that don't sell records
A: right but not, **what i'm saying** is not [everyone gets the]
B: [**are you saying** they don't deserve]success?
A: no. **what i'm saying** is is that not everyone gets the, the Video Vanguard Award.

Both speakers in (20) also make good use of *but*. Craig and Sanusi (2000) identified the use of *I'm just saying* and similar expressions as pragmatic devices by which speakers claim that they have all along held a consistent argumentative standpoint. While such consistency is more easily discernible in qualitative research with a detailed analysis of small data samples in their entirety, the present corpus approach was equally capable of detecting the argumentative use, and ascertaining its typicality across different speech event types in broadly academic, debative settings. Both research approaches are thus able to support the observation that a seemingly neutral metadiscursive item like *say* participates in an important way in negotiating disagreement and viewpoint differences. Clearly metadiscourse, or reflexive discourse, plays a crucial role in negotiating what it is we are talking about and what we mean even outside those written genres where it is particularly frequent and therefore much studied.

3.3 Why

The last recurrent category of conflictual indicators in the transcripts was the motley 'other', which included signals like *but* and *why*. The use of the adversative conjunction is very well known, and therefore I found the innocent-looking interrogative pronoun more intriguing. However, *why*, unlike the other critical markers illustrated here, was rather narrowly confined to a particular type of situational context: its main critical use was in thesis defences (examples 21 to 23), and very little appeared outside this event type. In all, only 20% of the *why* instances were critical.

(21) i i'm still curious **why**, um, you wanted to do the, thing you brought up just at the end about uh making, different cultures look, equally good since it didn't have anything to do with your thesis. i mean as far as i can tell. i i don't understand the connection, uh there and **i wondered why** <LAUGH> you wanted to, um do that.

(22) A: okay, here's another thing about keys. page seventy-two... uh, this piece... uh, seems to have practically no B naturals in it... (B: mhm) right?
B: right
A: now **why** is_ **why** didn't you just notate this with on E-flat then? is this is this, do you_ is this somehow a, a, a Lydian F or a Dorian D or something it doesn't sound anything like it to me

(23) A: **why** would you not take the Bayesian tack? which is, put your money where your mouth is. so, <B: LAUGH> give you some options if you really think this is gonna happen, then you choose A, if you don't you choose B why not take that that approach?
C: um, i can do that <LAUGH>
A: and you would expect that there would be differences?
C: i mean i'm not familiar with the Bayesian, approach so, i mean i feel, comfortable with, the conviction (rather than Bayesian) but...

As these examples show, *why* in defences tends to be used in rather strong, even devastating criticism, dealing with basic questions like selecting methods (22, 23) or dealing with certain issues at all (21). As already mentioned, this conflictual *why* was used much more sporadically in other speech event types, even though some instances were found in for example seminars (24):

(24) ... i think that that's, huh, an indicator of success that's, you know, that has never been matched by treatment programs. so i don't understand **why** you're claiming that we should move prog- or move money to programs that offer us, you know, that we don't know what they offer us. ...

Why is thus more specific than the other conflictual markers, and in its characteristic context of thesis defence, spells hard times for the candidate.

4. Conclusion

Academic speaking seems to deal with its typical backstage phenomena much like ordinary conversation, for example by using laughter to negotiate discrepancies or embarrassments. These backstage phenomena occur even in generally monologic event types like lectures, although they are apparently mostly restricted to certain phases of the speech event (like beginnings and ends), or else they are interpretable as asides, and thus remain outside the main body of the talk.

Although markers of conflictual discourse were hard to find, their recurrent characteristic expressions lent themselves to corpus-based scrutiny very well after initial clues from reading transcripts of whole events. The difficulty in detecting them derives from at least two factors: first, the markers of criticism tend to be so banal as to escape notice –like *it seems to me* or *what you're saying*. This is in stark opposition to expressions of praise (*good, great, nice*), which present themselves readily without the researcher's having to go deeper than looking at wordlists (see, Mauranen 2002). Secondly, these markers rarely constitute the criticism itself, but are simply indicators of where it is likely to follow or be implied. Criticism and negative evaluation tend to be highly specific and context-dependent for their interpretation – you criticise someone for making "a big leap", or "a pretty big extrapolation", or hearing or interpreting something "differently". Allwood (1993:27) made a similar observation in his analysis of an academic seminar: the interpretation an utterance as conflictual or cooperative depends on its relation to context. The recurrent conflictual indicators discussed here constitute scaffolding for criticism, non-critical and inconspicuous as they might appear in themselves. Metadiscourse, or discourse reflexivity, then, as one of the main types of conflictual indicator, is importantly involved in framing the expression of specific criticism. The banality and context-dependency of conflictual indicators make them indirect and implicit, while positive evaluation appears to be expressed directly and explicitly.

Of course, the strong emphasis of explicit positiveness may be a culture-specific American feature. As some social scientists put it on one of the transcripts: "the standard of politeness (in America) is such that you don't (present) direct criticism", "… anything less than enthusiasm is critical". On the other hand, the same tapescript discussed research showing that Americans were very weak at understanding indirect criticism, and appeared to take positive evaluation at its face value. There is clearly more work to be done in the handling of negative and positive evaluation.

In all, I have not seen much reason to change my earlier view that consensus is more foregrounded than conflict in academic speaking. I would like to argue, though, that they operate simultaneously but at different levels. The surface consensus appears to work much as it has been described in many standard descriptions of face-to-face conversation, whereas the undercurrents of conflict lie deeper. They are quite complex, and a good proportion of the apparent conflict in the academia is built into the institutional structures. It is important to remember that criticism is institutionally ascribed to certain roles in the university system, as a corollary to the basic ideology of scientific progress. But underlying the institutionally determined conflict lies again a fundamentally co-operative enterprise where we all participate to keep the system running, which among other things involves maintaining the tradition of criticism. Thus, the complex interplay of conflict and consensus is a product of a multilayered whole composed of different kinds of structures – some of which are more permanent and solid, such as the institutional structures and ideologies, and others faster-changing, like ongoing spoken interaction.

References

Aijmer, Karin (1996): Conversational Routines in English.Convention and Creativity. – London: Longman.
Allwood, Jens (1993): The Academic Seminar as an Arena of Conflict and Conflict Resolution. *Gothenburg Papers in Theoretical Linguistics*, No. 67.
Biber, Douglas (1988): Variation Across Speech and Writing. – Cambridge: C.U.P.
– (2001): Dimension of Variation Among University Registers: An analysis based on the T2K-SWAL Corpus. Paper given at the Third North American Symposium on Corpus Linguistics and Language Teaching, Boston, March 23–25, 2001.
Burdine, Stephanie (2001): The Lexical Phrase as Pedagogical Tool: Teaching disagreement strategies in ESL. – In: R.C Simpson, J. M. Swales (eds.): Corpus Linguistics in North America, 195–210. Ann Arbor: Michigan University Press,
Craig, Robert T./Alena L. Sanusi (2000): I'm just saying…' Discourse Markers of Standpoint Continuity. – *Argumentation* 14, 425–445.
Eggins, Suzanne/ Diane Slade (1997): Analysing Casual Conversation. – London: Cassell.
Gilbert, G./Nigel/Michael Mulkay (1984): Opening Pandora's Box: A sociological analysis of scientific discourse. – Cambridge: C.U.P.
Lindemann, Stephanie/Anna Mauranen (2001): "It's just real messy" The Occurrence and Function of *just* in a Corpus of Academic Speech. *English for Specific Purposes*, Special Issue 2001/1, 459–476.
Markkanen, Raija/Hartmut Schröder (eds.) (1997): Hedging and Discourse. Berlin: Walter de Gruyter.
Mauranen, Anna 2001. "But here's a flawed argument" Socialisation into and through metadiscourse. Paper given at the Third North American Symposium on Corpus Linguistics and Language Teaching, Boston, March 23–25, 2001.
– (2002): "A Good Question". Expressing Evaluation in Academic Speech. – In: G. Cortese, P. Riley (eds.): Domain-specific English. Textual practices across communities and classrooms, 115–140. Frankfurt: Peter Lang.
McCarthy, Michael (2001): Issues in Applied Linguistics. – Cambridge: C.U.P.

Myers, Greg (1989): The Pragmatics of Politeness in Scientific Articles. – *Applied Linguistics* 10/1, 1–35.

Poos, Deanne/Rita C. Simpson (1999): A Question of Gender? Hedging in academic spoken discourse. Paper presented at AAAL 1999, Vancouver.

Rowley-Jolivet, Elizabeth (1999): The Pivotal Role of Conference Papers in the Network of Scientific Communication. – *ASp* 23–26/ 1999, 179–196. GERAS Université Victor-Segalen Bordeaux 2.

Simpson, Rita C/ Sarah L. Briggs/Janine Ovens/ John M. Swales (1999): The Michigan Corpus of Academic Spoken English. – Ann Arbor, MI: The Regents of the University of Michigan.

Swales, John /Amy Burke (2001): "It's really fascinating work": Differences in evaluative adjectives across Academic Registers. Paper given at the Third North American Symposium on Corpus Linguistics and Language Teaching, Boston, March 23–25, 2001.

Thompson, Susan. E. (1997): Presenting Research: A Study of Interaction in Academic Monologue. Unpublished PhD dissertation. University of Liverpool.

Varttala, Teppo (1999): Remarks on the Communicative Functions of Hedging in Popular Scientific and Specialist Research Articles on Medicine. *English for Specific Purposes* 18, 2: 177–200.

Luisa Granato and Anamaría Harvey

Topic Progression in Science Interviews

1. Introduction

The widespread dissemination of scientific and technological knowledge beyond the realms of their discourse communities[1] is a characteristic of our time. Scientists and social communicators acting as reformulating agents take part in the communication process. A review of the literature shows that discursive practices in popularising scientific knowledge closely relate to the text-producing process and to the problem of "who" puts science into words and "how".

In our approach to the study of the relation between science and discourse, we start from the premise that scientific knowledge is not part of nature but rather that it is the interpretation of nature that society makes through language (Harvey 1993). Focusing on the ways discourses get written – in this particular case science interviews – forces us to acknowledge something that we sometimes overlook, namely that every written discourse is part of an interaction and that writing is a social act. As such, discourses depend on, and are generated within particular socio-historical contexts, whose parameters, participants, communicative intent, channel, genre, historical moment, determine both the form and the content of the discourse.

The object of this article is to inform about the results of a comparative study on topic presentation and development at a macro and a micro level, conducted on a sample of oral interviews and their corresponding written versions as published by the media. We are dealing with data that represents two successive and thematically linked communicative events, the first of these private and the second public. Chronologically speaking, the oral interview – a recording of the face- to- face encounter between the scientist and the journalist – comes first and takes place in the real world and in real time. The published interview, on the other hand, is actually a written simulation created by the journalist in accordance with register and genre norms and conventions, and obviously delayed in time (Granato/Harvey 2000). The written text is thus the outcome of the recontextualisation and reformulation of the oral discourse which the journalist makes to meet his/her communicative intent, bearing in mind the presumed lesser proficiency of the intended readership.

---

[1] Discourse community is understood as a socio-rhetorical grouping (Swales 1990)

The data for this case study is made up of a sample of four written interviews drawn from the total corpus of 'popular' science written interviews collected from Argentine and Chilean quality newspapers and the tape recordings of the oral interviews held with the scientists. All written texts included in this sample were taken from different issues of *La Nación*, a daily newspaper published in Buenos Aires.[2] In order to assess the changes effected to the propositional content in the passing from the oral to the written discourse, both the transcripts of the oral encounters and the written texts were scrutinised. To facilitate this task, we also set up a matrix which allowed us to differentiate between author's and writer's acts and follow the textual development of primary and secondary topics in the two discourses.

Once common themes had been identified, the rhetorical and linguistic devices utilised to present and develop the topic were analysed in each text and the features foregrounded were later compared. The results obtained from the analyses showed some similarities and also important differences in topic progression between the oral and the written interviews. The changes detected appeared to be not only conventional but also intentional and the outcome of the interplay between context and content, thus bearing upon the overall structuring of the text and the representation of the status and value of propositions.

2. The text construction process

The considerations affecting the construction of the oral and the written interviews are of a different nature and have to do with contextual features. Before and during the production of each of these physical texts, the journalist makes decisions which bear upon their construction and reconstruction. These decisions are biased by a number of factors concerning the world outside and inside the text. Among the first we have those relating to the function of the press, the editorial policy and the ideology of the corresponding mass media; among the second those influencing participants' roles and postures in the presentation, development and interpretation of the propositional content. In practical terms, the end product – the written text – is the result of a succession of steps in an ongoing process.

The communicative situation under study does not begin with the oral interview or end with the published version. On the basis of these linguistic records, however, we can reconstruct what goes on before, during and after the two successive events, and account for a number of considerations informing the decision-making process, instances in which the

---

[2] Oral recordings of Chilean face-to-face encounters were not available

social communicator is in control of the situation. Previous studies have shown the importance of these stages in the writing up of science texts addressed to non-specialists (Myers 1994; Harvey 1995; Granato/Harvey 2000). The communicative event under study has different stages which may be diagrammatically represented as follows:

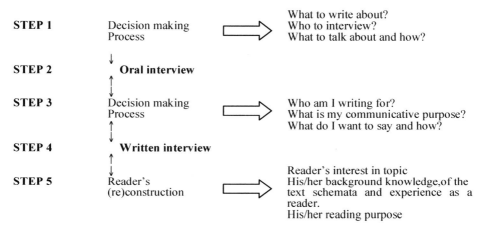

The first stage relates to the selections the journalist makes concerning what to write about and who to interview. The main considerations that condition the decisions made are: the newsworthiness assigned to the given topic and the importance of the interviewee in the field of his/her specialisation. This step begins with the gathering of information and selection of information sources and finishes with the planning of the oral interview.

The oral interview, a face-to-face encounter between journalist and scientist, represents the second step of the continuum. The data shows that the encounter, although structured as an interview, resembles more an informal conversation than institutional talk despite the fact that the purpose of the interviewer is to collect as much raw data as possible to be used as input for the writing-up phase.

The third step takes place after the oral interview and before the writing-up proper, when the journalist decides what to include, i.e. the target information, and in what way to include it, as well as what is to be discarded and omitted from the written version, in accordance with his/her communicative intent and the reader's presupposed knowledge. It also concerns the structuring of the actual text and the ordering and wording of the propositions, decisions which are mainly taken on the basis of audience considerations and writing conventions.

The final phase of the production process corresponds to the writing up of the interview and the final revision of the script which the editor in charge carries out. This is the stage (fourth step) where final alterations and adjustments are made. The end product, the published interview, initiates, in turn, the fifth and last step which represents the reconstruction of the text that a given reader finally makes, thus completing the cycle.

3. Roles and activities

The analyses of the data show that there are important differences between the two physical texts and that these differences are closely related to the roles that the same participants assume or are assigned in the two encounters, as well as to the activities that they, as interactants, perform (Granato 2000). Roles and activities bear upon the presentation and development of the topic in various ways, although it is important to remember that only the social communicator is present at the moment when both discourses are produced. In this sense, he/she is the only participant who has the possibility of making direct contributions to the written discourse. (Granato/Móccero 2000).

In the oral interviews, the journalist's responsibility is to elicit and obtain information for his/her possible reader as the ultimate addressee in this complex process, and that of the scientist to answer accordingly and provide it. In fact, they have agreed to hold a conversation whose contents will be later used to construct a public written text for the benefit of the reader. But, contrary to expectations this third party seems to fade away as the interaction progresses; in effect, the inclusion of the reader's voice in the journalist's words becomes less and less evident thus influencing topic progression to an increasingly lesser extent. As the scientist and the communicator get involved in their talk, the discourse seems to develop more for the benefit of the participants who are physically present in the interaction which in this way turns into a more symmetric encounter. Constant topic progression is observed and both participants appear to influence the direction of the conversation. In sum, the theme develops as an outcome of a co-operative behaviour throughout the series of dynamic episodes which constitute the encounter. An episode is here understood as "a bounded sequence, a discourse event with a beginning and an end surrounding a spate of talk, which is usually focused on the treatment of 'problem', 'issue' or 'topic'" (Linell 1998: 183).

In the written interview, on the other hand, it is the journalist who is in control of the flow of discourse. As stated above, the writing-up phase is mainly based on audience considerations since the knowledge the putative reader presumably possesses influences the decisions the writer makes concerning topic presentation and development. The end product is the result of the negotiations which take place between the writer and the possible reactions he/she estimates the eventual reader may have. Although the writer presents his/her text as the transcript of a real encounter, carefully signalling the difference between participants' acts through the structuring of the text and the lexico-grammatical choices, we know that in actual fact we are just in the presence of an artifact.

The dissimilarities in the discourse contexts under analysis result in substantial differences in what the participants say and do in each case. The written version reflects the manipulation of the information the journalist makes to meet his readers' needs, while in the oral interview it is both the journalist's demands for information and the scientist's recognition of these requirements that determine what they say and how they say it.

The differences referred to above in the roles and changes of posture in topic presentation and topic development may be represented as follows:

CONSTRUCTION OF THE PHYSICAL TEXTS

ORAL   WRITTEN

J ↔ S ↔ (R)   (J ↔ S) ↔ J ↔ (R)

This diagram shows that the journalist (J) and the scientist (S) interact with the future reader (R) they have in mind when they engage in the oral encounter. In the writing-up stage, on the other hand, the journalist (J), interacts, in a sort of a pendular movement, with the oral text and with the future addressee of his/her discourse, elements obviously not present in the situation.

4. Topic progression

Topic is not here considered simply as a static representation of science, but as content which brings together scientific discourse and context, and which unfolds in the course of the interaction. Although we can look at the development of content as the result of individual contributions, we believe that it is through the actions of two or more participants that topics are initiated, developed and changed in the course of a conversation. In this view, conversation has been characterised as "incrementally accomplished or achieved between persons, rather than as a meshing of two individuals' separate cognitive plans or schemas" (Arundale 1999: 125). Moreover, topic is co-constituted in the course of a conversation being another outcome of the many interactional achievements that individuals attain in the communicative processes they engage in.

In the two types of texts under analysis we can observe a dynamic process in which journalist and scientist co-operate in the development of the topic negotiating meaning, proposing changes of subject, agreeing and disagreeing as the talk progresses. They, together with the absent voices of these polyphonic encounters, provide the organising principle in the exchanges. However, this similitude is, in a way, only apparent. It is only in the oral interactions that both participants make direct contributions and co-operate in topic progression and thematic realisation through constant negotiation. The journalist produces elicitations to obtain information about a given subject and the scientist adjusts his responses to the needs expressed in the here and now of the discourse. On the other hand, the written text is fabricated by only one participant who simulates an interactive discourse but who does not co-construct the conversation in a co-operative way with his direct interlocutor. The real interaction here occurs between the text and the reader, whose world-view will be modified as the reading process advances.

Although we approached the two types of discourses as representing interactive encounters, it is clear that the written interview is not the result of a real co-construction of meaning, but a monological discourse presented as dialogue for the benefit of a third party. This being the case, the written interview was also assessed as a reformulated text and the transactional content, namely the discourse of science, considered as a result of discursive operations bearing upon the form and the content of the message.

In the written versions elicitation utterances are followed by direct answers, a strategy which permits an orderly development of the topics dealt with, typical of scientific explanations. The more spontaneous and natural production in the oral encounters, on the other hand, often produces digressions from the main expository line, which are seldom reproduced in the written.

Argumentative resources are also used in a different way. The scientist gives his/her opinion or offers new information about the topic under development and usually supports the topic with one or more arguments. In the written interviews this tends to occur within a turn without the participation of the interviewer. In the oral encounters the journalist often presents his own interpretation of facts which may lead the scientist to use refusal strategies of the type "yes, but..." to contradict the idea put forth by the journalist:

Oral: Text 3

Journalist: So, it will be possible to see a man in the moon.
Scientist: Yes, but only when we are capable to build ....

Acknowledgements, acceptances, rejections, backchannel expressions, agreements, are then frequent in face-to-face interactions, but are not usually present in the published versions which are more often than not reduced to straightforward elicitations followed by straightforward answers.

Written: Text 4
Journalist: How often are these explosions produced?
Scientist: Explosions occur ...

The alterations and changes detected at a textual level are mostly the outcome of various operations, particularly those of selection, reordering, reduction, expansion and paraphrasing. These operations, which become evident when comparing the two physical texts, are performed by the journalist in order to reformulate the content and accommodate the language to the new communicative situational context (Harvey 1997; Ciapuscio 2000; Eggins and Martin 2000).

Processes of selection are evident in the structuring of the text at a macro level, as realised especially in titles and leading sentences. Titles are short, eye-catching and predictive in nature. In fact, they are representative of the journalist's communicative intent and serve to monitor the reading process by focusing the reader's attention on what the journalists have decided to represent as primary topic. In all four cases, titles are taken from fragments of the running text of the oral interviews on account of their surprise value. They may be either direct quotations or paraphrases of the scientists' words. The four titles of the published interviews support this observation:

Text 1. "Serial fabrication of Einstein is impossible"
Text 2. "The good diagnoses"
Text 3. "We have only seen the beginning"
Text 4. "Towards the largest observatory of the world"

Moreover, a simple visual observation of the data shows striking differences in terms of length in all four pairs of texts. For instance, text 2 has 6,370 words in the oral and 1,150 in the written and text 3 a total of 5,520 in the oral and only 1,090 in the written interview. The written text is always a shorter, modified version of the oral interview, reduced not only in terms of number of words but also in quantity and quality of informational content. Selections are also evident at a micro level throughout the running texts. In this case, selection may also imply reduction or omission, when certain themes discussed in the oral interview are summarised or altogether left out from the written version. This may be due to strategic or formal reasons. In fact, the writer's evaluation of the communicative value of a given propositional content may even result in the omission of important supporting details. For example, text 1 exhibits the omission of a reference to a book which the scientist highly recommends to understand the problem of cloning. In Text 2 the examples given by the interviewee about the importance of early diagnoses in some illnesses are not mentioned. Reasons of space may also be responsible for the reduction of content.

Reordering of propositional content is found both at a macro and a micro level. The thematic progression in the written version is never the same as that of the oral encounter. Thus what appears at the beginning of the written text may be found in the middle or at the end of the oral and vice versa. The structuring of the written interview is performed by utterances with elicitation function, which do not necessarily correspond in function or wording to those of the oral one. Questions in the oral text represent a genuine request for information, whereas questions in the published interview often serve the purpose of providing the framework in order to introduce a new theme or aspect of the theme, thus fulfilling the function of topic predictors. It is also the case that the questions appearing in the written text were never uttered as such. Text 2 abounds in these occurrences: 7 out of a total of 8 elicitations are made up by the journalist. Moreover, the sequence of propositions of the oral interview is not always kept in the written texts, thus affecting the given/new or the theme and rheme organisation, as the following examples illustrate:

Text 1:
Oral: Why? Because my level of uncertainty is so small that this doesn't deserve to be studied.
Written: To prescribe a study in a case such as this is not always necessary, because the level of uncertainty is small.

Using an utterance from the running text as a quotation to contextualise and prompt the first question of the interview is also an example of reordering of the information which corresponds to the need to attract the reader's attention and awaken his/her interest, as the following example shows:

Text 3:
Written: "The history begins in 1919 with Albert Einstein's mistake", explained Goobar to *La Nación.*
Oral: Scientist: Well, in that sense Einstein was mistaken, because ...

Expansions seldom occur within the dialogue and if they do, they are limited to short additions made with the purpose of making the relationship between the propositions and the real world more evident or with the intention of appealing to the readers' emotions. In text 4, for example, there is a reference to the fact that the threatening phenomenon of the death of the universe will not affect current readers, fact which was never mentioned in the oral:

Written text 4:
"... But none of us nor our children will be able to see it".

Additional information is however added by the journalists in all four texts, prior to the interview proper, in order to contextualise the primary topic to be discussed or to introduce the interviewee and give credit to his/her authority as an expert.

Paraphrasing is the main resource utlized in popularisations other than interviews to reformulate concepts and accommodate language. The phenomenon is also present in the sample under study, although to a lesser degree. Differences and changes in modality are also frequent, and are based on communicative purpose or audience considerations, as the following occurrences illustrate:

ORAL	WRITTEN
X is	X might (could) be
It seems that ...	X believes that ...

5. Concluding remarks

The comparative analyses of the two communicative events under study show that common characteristics in topic progression are found in the formal structuring of both texts and manifested more evidently in the aspects dealt with above. The most salient differences, on the other hand, correspond to the rhetorical and linguistic devices utilised in the presentation and development of the topic. These differences originate in assumed or attributed changes in roles, attitudes and postures of the interactants or correspond to other features of the situational context.

The results obtained have supported the claim that topics contribute to rendering the discourse coherent and to creating intersubjectivity and that they should not be regarded as autonomous and fixed elements in an interactive discourse, as Linell has rightly stated.

References

Arundale, Robert. B. (1999): An Alternative Model and Ideology of Communication for an alternative politeness theory. – *Pragmatics* 9:1, 119–153. International Pragmatic Association.
Ciapuscio, Guiomar (2000): Hacia una tipología del discurso especializado. – In: H: Calsamiglia (ed.) Decir la ciencia: las prácticas divulgativas en el punto de mira. – *Revista Iberoamericana de Discurso y Sociedad.* Vol. 2 N° 2, 39–71. Barcelona: Editorial Gedisa.
Eggins, Susanne/James R. Martin (1997; 2000): Géneros y registros del discurso. – In: T. van Dijk (ed.) : El discurso como estructura y proceso, 335–379. Barcelona: Editorial Gedisa..
Granato, Luisa (2000): Los roles en entrevistas orales y escritas. – Paper presented at the Congreso de la Sociedad Argentina de Lingüística. Mar del Plata, Argentina.
Granato, Luisa/Anamaría Harvey (2000): La entrevista de divulgación científica: un estudio de casos. – *Onomazein 5*, 83–94. Chile: Instituto de Letras. Pontificia Universidad Católica de Chile
Granato, Luisa/María L. Móccero (2000): Elicitation utterances in written interviews. Paper presented at the International Association for Dialogue Analysis Conference. Bologna 2000.
Harvey, Anamaría. (1993): Interaction and Reformulation in Science Reports. Unpublished Doctoral Thesis. University of Birmingham, England.
– (1995): El fenómeno de la reformulacuión del discurso científico. – *Lengua Modernas* 22, 105–122. Chile: Universidad de Chile.

- (1997) : El fenómeno de la reformulación. – In: Proceedings of the I Coloquio Latinoamericano de Analistas del Discurso. (febrero 1995) Adriana Bolívar and Paola Bentivoglio (eds.), 163–169. Caracas: Universidad Central de Venezuela.
Linell, Per (1998) : Approaching Dialogue. Talk, interaction and contexts in dialogical perspectives. Amsterdam, Philadelphia: John Benjamins Publishing Company.
Myers, Greg (1994): Narratives of Science and Nature in Popularizing Molecular Genetics. – In: Malcolm Coulthard (ed.) Advances in Written Text Analysis, 179–190. London and New York: Routledge.
Swales, John M. (1990): Genre Analysis. English in Academic and Research Settings. Cambridge : Cambridge University Press.

Franca Poppi

Pragmatic Implications of the Use of *we* as a Receiver-including and Receiver-excluding Pronoun

1. Introduction

Textbooks play a crucial role in the learners' understanding of a subject, as they provide an epistemological map of the discipline. They tend to be organised in such a way as to make their reading quite easy for students and, as a consequence, learners are usually able to understand the principles which are being put forward.

Textbooks are therefore generally good at transmitting a canon of knowledge, but do not foster critical reading (Swales 1990) and students often find it difficult to adapt to the text types involved in more controversial materials.

Clearly, one of the main objectives of textbooks, which were included by Kuhn in the genre of popularising texts, is pedagogical, as they aim "… to communicate the vocabulary and syntax of contemporary scientific language" (Kuhn 1970: 136). Therefore, the textbook writers' decision not to put undergraduates in a position to appreciate the rhetorical manoeuvres which are all the same covertly present in textbooks (Swales 1993:226) may be attributed to their aspiration to avoid misunderstandings and to better guide students towards the acceptance of the epistemological assumptions brought about in the text (Myers1992).

Undoubtedly, the way textbooks are organised greatly depends on the presence of readers, and they may be defined as written monologues which partake of the features of a dialogue which retains clear indications of the addressee's assumed questions and comments, even if they are not explicitly mentioned.

As a consequence, banking on the assumption that "…a textbook […] is the result of a variety of dialogues in which the textbook writer engages" (Bondi 1999:38), this paper will focus on the dialogue going on between the author and the reader/learner, as exemplified in the introductory chapters of some economics textbooks. The small corpus analysed has been organised by Marina Bondi and it includes major works whose authority is established by their longevity (there have been regular revisions and numerous editions) and by their being included as set reading texts or reference texts in reading lists for university students (Bondi 1999: 39). The corpus includes ten economics textbooks (five published in the USA and five published in Great Britain), three of which have been written by single authors.[1]

In particular, this contribution will investigate the use of the first person plural pronoun *we*. The recurrence of this personal pronoun seems on the one hand to be in contrast with the slow but constant progression of depersonalisation in English scientific language noticed by Halliday (1988), and on the other hand is justified by the desire of the author to convey his message as forcefully as possible, in the attempt to elicit the reader's cooperation and to prevent misunderstandings.

Anyway, the issue at stake here is not only the meaning of the text, but persuasion as well, and the analysis will concentrate on the use of receiver-excluding and receiver-including *we*, considered as instances of a particular kind of metadiscoursal markers closely connected with the way authors represent themselves, organise their arguments and signal their attitudes to their readers. Textbook exposition, which is often described as non-argumentative, will be interpreted in terms of its argumentative techniques and of the tools adopted by the textbook writers, as the paper will try to ascertain whether there is a link between the use of receiver-including and receiver-excluding *we* and the adoption of an argumentative mode in the interaction between the author and his student-reader/s.

---

[1] Baumol, W.J./A.S. Blinder (1988): Economics. Principles and Policy, 4th Edition, – Orlando:Harcourt Brace Jovanovich.
Dolan, E.G./D.E. Linsey (1988): Economics. .5th Edition,– NY: Holt, Reinhart and Winston.
Fischer, S./R. Dornbusch (1983): Economics. – NY: McGraw-Hill.
Samuelson, P.A./W.H. Nordhaus (1992): Economics,.14th Edition. – NY: McGraw-Hill.
Wonnacot, P. / R. Wonnacot (1982), Economics 2nd Edition. – NY: McGraw-Hill.
Begg, D./S. Fischer/R. Dornbusch (1983): Economics. British Edition. – Maidenhead: McGraw-Hill.
Craven, J.(1990), Introduction to Economics. 2nd Edition. – Blackwell: Oxford.
Hardwick, P./ B. Kahn/ J. Langmead (1990), An Introduction to Modern Economics. 3rd Edition. London: Longman.
Lipsey, R. (1989), An Introduction to Positive Economics. 7th Edition. – London:Weidenfeld and Nicholson.
Stanlake, G.F. (1989), Introductory Economics. 5th Edition. – London: Longman.

2. Textbooks

2.1 Some general features of textbooks

Textbooks are a writer's attempt to construct the community's shared knowledge in the novices' minds, seeking to make propositional material explicit to them, while simultaneously socialising them to ways of speaking appropriate to the community.

All academic disciplines have conventions of rhetorical personality which influence the ways writers intrude into their texts to organise their arguments and represent themselves, their readers, their attitudes. This is largely accomplished through non-propositional material, or metadiscourse. Metadiscourse is discourse about discourse (Vande Kopple 1985) and refers to the author's linguistic manifestation in a text to "bracket the discourse organisation and the expressive implications of what is being said" (Schiffrin 1980:231). Metadiscourse is therefore a crucial rhetorical device for writers (Crismore 1989; Crismore/Farnsworth 1990).

In organising propositional information in ways that will be coherent for a particular audience and appropriate for a given purpose, writers need to resort to textual metadiscourse, while interpersonal metadiscourse is helpful to allow the authors to express a perspective towards their propositional information and their readers. Textual metadiscourse, which includes devices to assist comprehension of propositional information, such as connectives, code glosses and endophoric markers, seems to be more frequent in textbooks than in other kinds of texts, like research articles. Interpersonal metadiscourse and devices typically used to assist persuasion, such as hedges, emphatics, evidentials and person markers are less frequent in textbooks than in other kinds of texts.

Hyland (1999:12) explained this by referring to the fact that metadiscourse variations reflect the roles that different texts play in the social structures of disciplinary activity. In the context of textbook writing, the argumentative nature of science is concealed by presenting a well-established set of facts and accredited theories, as textbook writers establish facticity through their own efforts (Weintraub 1990). In fact, while we might be led to believe that a particular statement finds its way into a textbook because it is a fact, it is the reverse which actually occurs. A statement becomes a fact because it is found in a textbook (cf. Myers 1992).

Nonetheless, by presenting the propositional content in a non-argumentative tone, textbook writers argue to persuade (Klamer 1990:151), as they add factive certitude and conviction to the matters being discussed, in the attempt to prevent opposition and/or misunderstanding on the part of their student-readers.

Textbook writers see themselves as both scientists and popularisers, researchers and teachers. As scientists they will be willing to give facticity to what they talk about: as teachers they will be interacting with other educators and with students (evaluator reader and consumer reader see Swales 1995).

In this paper, for the sake of the analysis, only the latter type of audience will be taken into account.

2.2 Some features of economics textbooks

Scientific discourse is presented by Bakhtin (1981) as another form of authoritative, monologic discourse where a single voice controls the direction and meaning of the text, establishing arguments. In economics textbooks we can notice a centripetal process by means of which a heterogeneous and heterodox range of voices become integrated into a unified discursive field, by means of the process of canonisation, which was defined by Bakhtin (1981:425) as the process that "blurs heteroglossia, that is, that facilitates a naive, single-voiced entry".

Within the history of economics this notion of the process of canonisation may be used to analyse how the canon of economics texts tends to produce a single-voiced reading which is thought to speak directly to the interests and concerns of modern economic theory. In this way it presents a view of the discipline that epitomises the discipline's own sense of identity and intellectual tradition, and tends to reinforce existing paradigms (Hewings 1990, Tadros 1985).

An analysis of economics textbooks shows that they are governed to varying degrees by the requirements of order and univocity – in order to speak persuasively to practitioners of the subject (Brown 1993:81) – and dialogism, which cannot be interpreted as multivocity, but refers to the interaction between the writer and his student-readers, as he presents propositional matters, attends to their needs and, in order to make them accept his claims, deploys his rhetorical strategies.

3. The focus of the analysis

The topic of economics has generated much interest within the economics profession, as over the last decade economists have come to recognise the importance of paying attention to their own rhetoric. Undoubtedly, the most influential approach to raising rhetorical awareness has been the one adopted by McCloskey (1985), to the extent that for most economists it is probably the only approach to analysing economics discourse. His works have drawn attention to the rhetorical forms in which economics arguments are couched and his main focus of interest has been classical rhetoric, used to make the arguments more convincing and appealing. He attributes his insights into the nature of economics discourse to his discovery of literary criticism and believes that success in persuading people of the rightness of one's arguments is to be attributed to the literary ability pure and simple.

In fact in his opinion (1985:46)

" truth-pursuing is a poor theory of human motivation [...] the human scientists pursue persuasiveness, prettiness and the resolution of puzzlement, the conquest of recalcitrant details, the feeling of a job well done".

Even though McCloskey's approach can prove extremely useful, an argument that has often been raised against it, is rather that, if we ignore linguistic structures and if we do not explore the reasons why these have been adopted, there are important aspects of economists' writing that we cannot understand (Henderson,/Dudley-Evans/Backhouse 1993: 8).

This makes it natural to bring some of the techniques of applied linguistics into the debate. Approaching a text from the perspective of applied linguistics or better discourse analysis rooted in applied linguistics, implies that style is viewed in terms of specific linguistic structures and the way these structures are related to the purposes of the writing, while according to McCloskey (1991:51) style is always thought of in classical terms, involving virtues such as purity, clarity, ornament and decorum.

Since knowledge claims and language are inextricably linked, even more so in textbooks, an awareness of language matters to a discipline because claims to knowledge can only be made by using language. In order to establish the way language is working in economics texts it is necessary to analyse texts in detail, as generalisations need to be related to specific examples, the reason being that, when examples are studied in detail, surprising things may sometimes emerge.

Textbooks belong to a well-defined genre and are characterised by a set of communicative purposes (Swales 1981, 1985, 1990) identified and mutually understood by the members of the professional or academic community in which they regularly occur. Most often they are highly structured and conventionalised, with constraints on allowable contributions in terms of their intent, positioning, form and functional value. These constraints, however, are often exploited by the expert members of the discourse community to achieve private intentions within the framework of socially recognised purposes (Bhatia 1993:13).

This paper will focus on how economics textbook writers exploit the constraints associated with the particular kind of texts they are dealing with, when it comes to (author) self-representation. In particular, the analysis will investigate the use and frequency of the first person plural pronoun *we*, which was defined by Halliday/Hasan (1989: 50) as a 'personal referring to the speech roles'. In fact this personal pronoun is often non-cohesive, that is typically exophoric, and the reader does not have to seek the necessary evidence in the cotext for interpreting it, as the textbook writer uses it for the purpose of self-representation, both when he takes on an expert position and when he takes sides with his student-readers.

4. The textbook writer's self-presentation in the dialogue with the reader

Very often in ESP texts the author refers to himself by using indirect forms and 3rd person personal pronouns with noun phrases like 'the author', 'the research team,' or assigning to objects the function of expressing his own opinions through processes of personification like 'the book examines', 'the article proves'. This tendency towards depersonalisation is noticeable not only in the elimination of the subject-locutor but also in the reduction of any direct reference to the interlocutor.

However, this process of depersonalisation does not generally apply to all ESP texts. In argumentative ESP texts, for instance, the 1st person singular or plural to designate the locutor is quite frequent, because the focus is on the autonomous position of the author in the context of his own text and of his subject. The use of the 1st person pronoun clearly shows the will of the author to intervene directly in the discourse to make his attempt to convince the reader more efficiently and to better underline the argumentative structure of the discourse.

In fact, since the syntactic rules of the language allow people to express the same concept in different ways, the choice of one form rather than another is due to the pragmatic and textual factors rather than syntactic constraints. Therefore, the decision on the part of the writers of the ten economics textbooks that have been analysed never to refer to themselves by 'the author/s', 'the writer/s', or the like, preferring to resort to a person marker, is extremely meaningful.

Person markers (whose function is defined as that of explicitly referring to the author) are less frequently used in textbooks than in other kinds of texts (Hyland 1999), but their presence is nevertheless of pivotal importance and quite revealing, if closely analysed.

Writers create an impression of themselves – a discoursal self – through the discourse choices they make as they write (Ivanič 1998). Individual writers participate in the construction of their discoursal identities through selection among the subject positions they feel socially mandated, willing or daring enough to occupy.

Both writers' sense of themselves (autobiographical self) and the impression which they convey of themselves in writing (discoursal self) is normally multiple and subject to change over time. The reader-writer relationship is a crucial element in all this: the discoursal self which writers construct will depend on how they weigh their readers up and their power relationship with them. As a consequence of this, we can see how the writer/s of economics textbooks feel/s the need to shift between receiver-including and receiver-excluding *we*.

The receiver-including *we* induces the addressee to identify with the proposed collective point of view, as the distance between the writer and the addressee seems to be reduced to a minimum. The receiver-excluding *we* is frequently used when the writer is expected to stand back behind his discoveries and places himself in the tradition of earlier discoveries (Werlich 1976:139).

5. Instances from the corpus

It has often been claimed (Gotti 1991:XI) that quantitative analysis lacks interpretative insight, but at the same time it provides useful data concerning the frequency distribution of a particular element, data that need further investigation if one wants to find out the semantic and pragmatic motives that brought that element about.

Even though a distinctive frequency distribution is in itself no guarantee of stylistic relevance (Halliday 1989:116–117), there is likely to be some relevance attached to the fact that a particular feature appears to be prominent. Therefore a few figures may be quite suggestive.

The length of the ten introductory chapters that have been taken into account ranges from a maximum of 8,827 words (Fischer/Dornbusch), to a minimum of 4,266 words (Stanlake). Obviously, this process of word count is not particularly meaningful for its own sake, but may prove helpful in finding out whether the different instances of *we* occur at the beginning, at the end, or in other parts of the introductory chapter.

In the corpus, analysed by Wordsmith Tools (Scott 1996) there are 454 instances of *we*, with a frequency of 0.63%. There are 175 instances of *you*, with a frequency of 0.24%. There are seven instances of *I*, but none of them is used by the textbook writer/s to refer to himself/themselves. In fact two of the seven instances refer to a hypothetical character that can be identified with 'any human being', while the other five are to be found in direct speech citations, and refer to Humpty Dumpty (two instances), a former American Airlines flight attendant (two instances) and J.M. Keynes.

"Why, for example should **I** live modestly, just so my children may at some future date live in luxury? The future generations should be considered..."(Wonnacott and Wonnacott)

"...('What happens if **I** do this?') From these experiments, they make educated guesses as to how the real-life version will perform". (Baumol and Blinder)

"...'**I** identify more with being a third-grade teacher than **I** ever did with being a flight attendant'. So says Kendall Hagerty, a former American Airlines flight attendant, recently retired ". (Dolan and Linsey)

"**I** am sure that the power of vested interests is vastly exaggerated compared with the gradual encroachment of ideas". (Samuelson)

"The economist, it would appear, is much like Humpty Dumpty in Alice in Wonderland who said imperiously, 'When **I** use a word it means just what **I** choose it to mean -- neither more nor less.'..." (Baumol and Blinder)

The word 'author' is mentioned twice and the word 'authors' is mentioned once in the corpus. Both terms are never used by the author/s to refer to himself/themselves.

"Some literary critics discuss books by finding out the major influences on the **author** at the time of writing" (Craven)

"But when the farmer, the oil company, the **author**, the book publisher find that the prices of the goods have increased..." (Wonnacott and Wonnacott)

"When the price of books rises, **authors** feel that they are getting no more that a 'just' return for their creative efforts..."(Wonnacott and Wonnacott)

The word 'writer' appears once, while there is no mention of the word 'writers'.

"In recent years, economists have developed a reputation for being a crotchety lot who cannot agree on anything. One **writer** complained: 'If you laid all economists end to end, they still wouldn't reach a conclusion". (Samuelson)

Only three of the textbooks that have been taken into account were written by single authors (Craven, Stanlake, and Lipsey). No particularly meaningful difference has been observed between these three textbooks and the others, for what regards the writer's self-representation in the dialogue with the reader.

An analysis of the words that more frequently tend to collocate with *we* (within the range of the five closest words on the right and on the left) shows there are a few cases in which *you* is clearly juxtaposed to *we*.

"...through to check that you have understood the chapter. We suggest you always do the problems". (Begg, Fischer and Dornbusch)

"Because economics is about human behaviour, you may be surprised that we describe it as a science". (Begg, Fischer and Dornbusch)

"Instead, keep them in mind as you read. We will point them out to you as they occur by the use..." (Baumol and Blinder)

"We hope you will find that, in addition to being useful, economics is a fascinating" (Samuelson)

"We hope you will retain beyond the final exam". (Baumol and Blinder)

"We introduce three concepts which you have probably read about in the newspapers..." (Begg, Fischer and Dornbusch)

"We realise it is inevitable that you will forget..." (Baumol and Blinder)

Widening the range of our analysis we can find other examples:

"... to introduce you to economics and to provide a selective preview of what is to come, we have organised our ideas..." (Baumol and Blinder)

"To help you pick out a few of the most crucial concepts, we have selected 12 from among the many ideas contained in this book..." (Baumol and Blinder)

"... to help you get the most out of your first economics, we have devised a list of 12 important ideas..." (Baumol and Blinder)

"...important ideas that you will want to remember beyond the Final Exam. Here, we list them, very briefly..." (Baumol and Blinder)

"... so you should not expect to understand them fully after reading the first chapter. Nonetheless, "We think it useful to sketch them briefly here both to introduce you to economics..." (Baumol and Blinder)

Six of the above mentioned instances of receiver-excluding *we* are to be found in the first two pages, while five occur towards the end of the first chapter

In these cases, it is of course easy to interpret *we* as receiver-excluding as the writers, by directly addressing their student-readers by means of the pronoun *you*, claim the authority due to them because of their position of 'experts'. The textbook writers are laying the basis for establishing textual dialogue and in order to argue to convince, they distance themselves from the readers, to prevent any possible objection. No real propositional content is being expressed in these cases, but the authors seem to be intruding into the text to offer explicitly evaluative comments on their chosen course of action (aimed at favouring the student's learning process) and on the reader's cognitive process (cf. the explicit references to the students' cognitive/learning process e.g.: *to introduce you to economics, to help you get the most of your first economics, to help you pick out a few of the most crucial concepts, to understand, to keep in mind, you will forget, you will retain...*).

In addition to this, the presence of infinitive clauses of purpose utterly underlines the effort made by the authors to ease the reader's reasoning. The presence of the verb 'to help' seems to highlight the role of the writer as a teacher/mediator of knowledge.

At times the authors clearly refer to themselves as teachers,

"As college professors we realise that it is inevitable that you will forget much of what you learn in this course..." (Baumol and Blinder)

and even describe their activity as opposed to that of the economists:

"Economists maintain that this conjunction of events was no coincidence. Owing to features of our economy that we will study in parts 2 and 3, there is an agonising trade-off between inflation and unemployment, meaning that most policies that bring down inflation also cause unemployment to rise…" (Baumol and Blinder)

"We must recognise, however, that economists, like everyone else, will have their personal viewpoints on what is 'best' and we must therefore expect them to disagree on policy questions such as the desirability of Britain's membership of the common Market". (Stanlake)

Whenever we have a direct reference to the readers it is relatively simple to interpret instances of *we* as receiver-excluding. Another possible tool of analysis is the search for verbs which seem to prefer a single individual/group of individuals as the actors of the process they represent. This is for instance the case of verbs such as *describe*, *explain*, *favour*, *illustrate*, *introduce*, *list*, *mean* and *outline*.

"Because economics is about human behaviour, you may be surprised that we describe it as a science rather than a subject within the arts or humanities…" (Begg, Fischer, Dornbusch)

"…in the remainder of the chapter, we explain economic concepts like equilibrium and disequilibrium, microeconomics and macroeconomics and we outline the methodology of economic analysis…". (Hardwick, Kahn and Langmead)

"Because many of the models used in this book are depicted in diagrams, we explain the construction and use of various types of graphs in the next chapter. But sometimes economic models are expressed only in words". (Baumol and Blinder)

"In this book we favour the first two methods, because most of the conclusions reached do not require the use of mathematics". (Craven)

"In Figure 1–2 we illustrate the maximum combinations of food and film output that the economy can produce" (Begg, Fischer and Dornbusch)

'To give an idea of the building blocks of macroeconomics, we introduce three concepts which you have probably read about in the newspapers or seen discussed on television". (Begg, Fischer and Dornbusch)

"To help you get the most out of your first in economics, we have devised a list of 12 Important Ideas that you will want to remember Beyond the Final Exam. Here we list them, very briefly, indicating where each idea occurs in the book". (Baumol and Blinder)

"A recession occurs when there is a broad decline in production, causing a rise in the unemployment rate. (By broad, we mean that the decline involves a substantial fraction of the economy, and is not confined to just one or two industries, such as steel or aircraft)". (Wonnacott and Wonnacott)

"What do we mean by economic analysis? This is an approach that starts with a set of assumptions and then deduces logically certain predictions about the economic behaviour". (Samuelson)

"The unemployment rate is the percentage of the labour force without a job. By the labour force we mean those people of working age who in principle would like to work if a suitable job were available". (Begg, Fischer and Dornbusch)

Four of the above instances of *we* that have been classified as 'receiver-excluding' occur at the beginning, and four more occur towards the end of the chapter. This seems to suggest that there is a tendency for receiver-excluding *we* to occur either at the beginning, as the writer starts his dialogue with the reader and wants to assert his status of 'expert', adopting the so called 'magister mode', or at the end of the first chapter, when the writer is calling for a revision of what has already been introduced

Of course the ones that have been mentioned are just a few of the most easily recognisable instances of receiver-excluding *we*. Altogether, receiver-excluding *we* seems to be less frequently used than receiver-including *we*. This is on the one hand understandable, as textbook writers, in attending to the expectations of their readers, try to maximise their involvement in the reading process, raising the degree of intimacy. The writers share the burden of exposition with their readers, making them feel responsible for what is being said. By doing this, they are trying to sway the readers into an economist's way of reasoning.

"In drawing this figure we assume given supplies…"

"For example, suppose we begin at point C…"

"At the very core of economics is the undeniable truth that we call the law of scarcity"

"… the things we call 'value judgements…"

"In the above example we can say that in 1986 nominal GNP was…"

Receiver-including is also preferred to receiver-excluding *we* whenever a modal auxiliary verb is employed, especially with an epistemic value. This can be easily explained by considering that hypothesis making does not seem appropriate in the context of the asymmetric interaction brought about by the use of receiver-excluding *we*.

"Comparing this with the market for bicycles, we may be able to explain…"

"We may agree, for example, about what happened…"

"In such a case, we might reason as follows…"

"For example, we might find that …"

On the other hand, also the use of the modal auxiliary verb 'can' with a dynamic meaning, seems to combine well with receiver-including *we*, as the writer tries to make the reader feel more and more involved.

"… we can say that the cost of eating…"

"…in Figure 1–4 we can identify the periods when inflation has been most rapid…"

"Alternatively, we can agree that policy X will cause …"

"Going beyond the level of countries, we can think of world income…"

The textbook writer may assign the reader a variety of argumentative roles in the construction of his own argument, on the basis of an expected argumentative co-operation which will bring the reader to agreement with the writer by successive steps in the argumentative sequence. Receiver-excluding *we* is used when the writer addresses his reader as a student, in the expert/novice interaction. Receiver-including *we* is more appropriate when the reader is considered on the same level as the writer. As a consequence we are bound to find it when the reader is considered an economist-to-be, following in the footsteps of a writer who is willing to share the burden of exposition with him and goes through the various phases of the learning route, together with his reader, as he anticipates what has still to come, and remembers what has already been said.

"…in Chapters 6 and 22, we shall be dealing with the analysis of both microeconomic and …"

"…Chapter 17 to examining it in detail. And we shall also consider some suggestions …"

"…as we shall see later in the book…"

"As we shall see in Chapter 3…"

"And in Chapter 16 we will see that …"

"In Chapter 4 we will see…"

"As we will see throughout this book…"

"We have already mentioned…"

"We have already noted that the ultimate goal…"

"We have drawn the production possibility frontier…"

"… we have seen that some activities expanded…"

Otherwise, receiver-including *we* is also used whenever *we* is attributed a general meaning and is referred to 'all human beings'.

"… we and our children will have higher standards of material comfort…"

"When we are young, our minds are open to new ideas…"

"…would we be better off with a policy of laissez-faire…"

"But no sooner do we begin to understand our world than we become…"

6. Conclusions

While a classification of the instances of *we* can only approximate the complexity and fluidity of natural language use and it may give no firm evidence about author intentions or reader understanding, it is a useful means for revealing the meanings available in the text and for identifying the rhetorical strategies employed by different writers and their attitude to propositions and degrees of reader involvement.

Much of the recent literature views economists as using rhetorical persuasion to raise the plausibility of their favoured beliefs among their audiences by means of appeals to the authority. This is, for instance, what happens when the textbook writer resorts to receiver-excluding *we*. In these cases the expository structures are used with an illocutionary force that is different from the usual one. Writers do not only want to inform, but they want to argue. In fact they put forward one position in preference to others, in such a way as to prevent opposition. This is why the illocutionary force may be defined as deviant.

On the other hand, when receiver-including *we* is used, the reader's status is upgraded to economist-to-be, as he seems to share the burden of the exposition with the writer. In reality the expository mode is a sort of cover, and the reader is actually swayed into a process of appropriation of the discipline and of the writer's views and opinions. Therefore, also in this case it is possible to consider the illocutionary force as 'deviant'.

Since the evidence provided by the corpus is still too limited, the characteristics that have been discussed in this paper cannot claim to be the distinctive features of a particular genre. Yet, the ten introductory chapters are sufficiently rhetorically marked to offer instructors of economics a useful set of study materials for raising rhetorical consciousness among students, if and when that should be desired.

References

Bakhtin, Mikhail (1981): The Dialogic Imagination. – Austin: University of Texas Press.
Bhatia, Vijay K. (1993): Analysing Genre. Language Use in Professional Settings. – London: Longman.
Bondi, Marina (1999): English across Genres. – Modena: Edizioni Il Fiorino.
Brown, Vivienne (1993): Decanonizing Discourse: textual analysis and the history of economic thought. – In: Willie Henderson, Anthony Dudley-Evans, Roger Backhouse (eds.). 64–84.
Carter, Ronald /Walter Nash (1990): Seeing through Language: a guide to styles of English writing. – Oxford: Blackwell.

Crismore, Avon (1989): Talking with Readers. Metadiscourse as Rhetorical Act. – New York: Peter Lang.
Crismore, Avon and Rodney Farnsworth (1990): Metadiscourse in Popular and Professional Science Discourse. – In: R. Carter/W. Nash (eds.), 118–136.
Ghadessy, Mohsen (ed.) (1988): Registers of Written English. Situational Factors and Linguistic Features. – London: Pinter.
Gotti, Maurizio (1991): I linguaggi specialistici. Caratteristiche linguistiche e criteri pragmatici. – Firenze: La Nuova Italia.
Halliday, M.A.K. (1988): On the Language of Physical Science. – In: M. Ghadessy (ed.), 162–178.
– (1989): Spoken and Written Language. – Oxford: Oxford University Press.
Halliday, M.A.K. and Hasan, Ruqaiya (1989): Language Context and Text. Aspects of Language in a Socio-Semiotic Perspective. – Oxford: Oxford University Press.
Henderson, Willie/Dudley-Evans Anthony/Backhouse Roger (eds.) (1993): Economics and Language. – London: Routledge.
Hewings, Ann (1990): Aspects of the Language of Economics Textbooks. – In: W. Henderson, A. Dudley-Evans, R. Backhouse (eds.). 29–42.
Hyland, Ken (1999): Talking to Students: metadiscourse in introductory coursebooks. – *English for Specific Purposes* 18 , 3–26.
Ivanič, Roz (1998): Writing and Identity. The discoursal construction of identity in academic writing. – Amsterdam: Benjamins.
Klamer, Arjo (1990): The Textbook Presentation of Economic Discourse. – In: W. J. Samuels (ed.), 129–165.
Kuhn, Thomas S. (1970): The Structure of Scientific Revolutions. – Chicago: University of Chicago Press.
McCloskey, Donald (1985): The Rhetoric of Economics. – Madison, Wisconsin: University of Wisconsin Press.
– (1991): Mere Style in Economics Journals, 1920 to the Present. – *Economic Notes* 20(1), 135–158.
Myers, Greg (1992): Textbooks and the Sociology of Scientific Knowledge. – *English for Specific Purposes,* 11, 3–17.
Samuels, Warren J. (ed.) (1990): Economics as Discourse.– Boston: Kluwer Academic Publishers.
Schiffrin, Deborah (1980): Metatalk: organizational and evaluative brackets in discourse. – *Sociological Inquiry. Language and Social Interaction* 50, 199–236.
Scott, Mike (1996): Wordsmith Tools. – Oxford: Oxford University Press.
Swales, John (1981): Definitions in Science and Law: evidence for subject-specific course component. – *Fachsprache* 3(4), 106–112.
– (ed.) (1985): Episodes in ESP. – Hemel Hempstead, UK: Prentice Hall International.
– (1990): Genre Analysis. English in Academic Research Settings. – Cambridge: Cambridge University Press.
– (1993): The Paradox of Value. Six treatments in search of the reader. – In: W. Henderson, A. Dudley-Evans and R. Backhouse (eds.), 223–239.
– (1995): The Role of the Textbook in EAP Writing Research. – *English for Specific Purposes* s 28, 3–18.
Tadros, Angele (1985): Prediction in Text. – Birmingham: English Language Research Monographs.
Vande Kopple, William J. (1985): Some Exploratory Discourse on Metadiscourse. – *College Composition and Communication* 36, 82–93.
Weintraub, E. Roy (1990): Comment on "Economic as Ideology", by R.L. Heinbroner. – In: W. J. Samuels (ed.), 117–129.
Werlich, Egon (1976): A Text Grammar of English. – Heidelberg: Quelle und Meyer.

Chapter 5
Dialogue and Multilingual or Multicultural Schools

Robert Maier

Dialogues and Exclusion in Multicultural Schools

1. Introduction

In the Netherlands, as in other European countries, immigrants account for some 10% of the population. Migrants from Turkey, Suriname and Morocco form quantitatively the largest groups. At the moment, the majority of these migrant groups were born in the Netherlands, whereas their parents, or at least one of them, came to the Netherlands in the sixties or seventies in the previous century to work. The first generation of migrants were not in general very highly educated. The second or third generation migrants are currently enrolled in the Dutch education system. 50% of the migrants live in cities such as Amsterdam, Rotterdam and Utrecht, where about 25 to 33% of the schoolchildren are second and third generation immigrant children.

Extensive surveys have shown that these children have a significant educational disadvantage compared with their Dutch classmates (SCP, 1999). The last survey, published in 2001 (SCP, 2001) shows that the disadvantage is, in fact, diminishing, but not at the same rate for all migrant groups. It is also well documented that there are notable differences between the different migrant groups, and also that in some schools there is no difference at all. Turkish and Moroccan children have the most significant disadvantage, when compared with children from other migrant groups.

The general explanation for this disadvantage tends to be directed at the educational level of the parents, insufficient mastery of the Dutch language, and the specific culture of the respective groups which is, in general, preserved or recreated in the private sphere at home. These explanations are not completely wrong, but they are certainly far from satisfactory, because of their general and abstract nature. Why are second- (or third) generation girls more successful than boys? Why do significant groups of these schoolchildren who attend certain schools have almost no problems at all? How can such a general explanation account for the radical differences in success at school among children from these groups?

Several directions are currently being explored in the Netherlands in order to find more satisfactory explanations for these disadvantages, and to arrive at possible forms of intervention to solve these problems. Some researchers are studying the climate and the management of different state schools; others, such as Andriessen & Phalet (2002) relate school success to how the children adjust to the school and, more generally, to the type of adaptation strategy followed – they make a distinction, for example, between integration, separation and assimilation (at home and at school) of the families of the children involved. Another group of researchers is attempting to analyse in detail the verbal interactions in and around the classroom in order to establish links between success at school and some characteristics of these interactions.

In this paper, I will present a few examples of this last type of research. I will first outline the specific research questions and give a brief description of the schools where data were collected. I will then go on to the present, analyse and examine a passage from a discussion among teachers concerning one student in particular.

2. The research situation and research questions

The objective of the research project in which I am involved is to collect, over a period of two years, a representative sample of verbal and non-verbal interactions in the classrooms of two multicultural schools that have a high percentage of Moroccan students. In one of the schools two thirds of the students are of migrant origin, with a high percentage of Moroccan children, and in the other school one third of students are migrant origin. Video recordings were made during a number of maths lessons and also some other lessons in the same school. Extracts from these recordings were discussed with the teacher and with some students immediately after the lessons, with questions such as: 'What happened here?' This method is referred to as the 'stimulated recall' interview. Video recordings were also made of some of the discussions among teachers during 'grade-setting' meetings. During these meetings all the teachers involved with a particular class discuss the results of each student, and decide what measures, if any, need to be taken.

The recordings were made in the 'orientation'-year, which is the year between primary and secondary education, in principle at the age of twelve. This year is particularly important, because at the end of this year students go their separate ways to specific kinds of secondary schools that are considered the most suitable for the students in question.

The central question of this extensive research project was a rather modest one. By applying a variety of (micro) analysis methods, a large database of the characteristics of the various types of interaction was established. The aim was to identify specific types of interaction or specific characteristics of interaction that are connected in some way with success or failure at school.

3. Presentation of one school

In the Netherlands, state schools are obliged to publish an annual handbook (*schoolgids* in Dutch) in which each school presents itself to the outside world in a more or less standard format. The handbook is sent to all parents with children at the school and also to anyone else who might be interested in sending their children to that school in the future. A (translated) extract from one of the handbooks from a school where research data have been gathered is given below.

> *(9) Identity and general atmosphere*
>
> *We are a state school. Every pupil is welcome here irrespective of his/her philosophy of life or religion. We require all pupils and staff members to communicate with each other and to get to know each other better with respect for each other's philosophy of life, religion, origin, sexual preference and gender. All this is done in a pleasant, open and safe atmosphere; our assumption is that the encounters between many different perspectives and cultures will enrich each individual and be a suitable preparation for society at large. But also in society our pupils encounter a wide diversity of people. Knowledge of this diversity stimulates our pupils to be better prepared and mentally more richly endowed. Not only our pupils, but also our members of staff have various cultural backgrounds. We are therefore in many respects a multi-ethnic school, a reflection of the wider society. And it is a society that pupils can become familiar with with confidence.*
>
> *It is precisely because we as a school have not opted for a certain philosophy of life, that we think we can achieve this goal. We want to provide our pupils with more than just a diploma.*
>
> *Working and learning together presupposes that one agrees about a certain number of agreements so that a pleasant atmosphere is guaranteed.. Respect for each other is the most important thing. And this respect for each other's culture, convictions and property must be evident in the behaviour of all. Respect is also the key element in the interaction between adults and pupils.*

This school explicitly presents itself as a multicultural, or multi-ethnic school, and indeed when one visits the school its multicultural character is quite evident. In its handbook, this school starts by affirming some basic civil rights, and goes on to immediately affirm that these norms and values are put into practice in the day-to-day running of the school. This school presents itself as having a good and safe learning environment for students. At the same time this school also helps its students to be well-prepared to participate in the multicultural society at large.

The notion of respect is the focal point in this extract from the handbook. It is interesting to note that the term 'respect' is a word that is used very often among many migrant groups in the Netherlands. For example, they often greet each other by saying 'Hey, respect man', which is, in fact, an Anglicism that points to an element of acceptance and solidarity. I would like to point here to the astonishing association between culture, convictions and property in the last paragraph of the translated passage from the handbook.

Finally, it should be said, that all the researchers who visited the school got the impression that there does indeed seem to be a very good atmosphere at this school, as far as contacts, openness, contact between students and teachers and the involvement of the teaching staff and the management are concerned.

4. Hennia: study of a case

One particular case will be analysed in this paper. Hennia, a Moroccan girl recently came to this school with the following motivation (extract from an interview with Hennia): "I came to this school, because at my last school there was nothing but fighting every single day; here I just want to get my diploma." In other words, she presents herself as being a motivated student, whose horizons go beyond very limited lower vocational training.

Here is an extract from a general evaluation and grade-setting meeting between the teachers of the class Hennia is in. These grade-setting meetings are held three times a year, and discussions usually focus on students in the so-called "danger zone", i.e. students who risk being placed at a lower level of practical further education. This meeting took place in April 2000, three months before the end of the school year.

(Abbreviations used: En = English teacher, Ma = Maths teacher, Pr = Handicraft teacher, Du = Dutch teacher, Fr = French teacher, Bi = Biology teacher, Gy = Gymnastics teacher, Dr = Drawing teacher)

En: *I would like to discuss Hennia* (others nod in agreement)
Her comprehension is really poor; I'm afraid, really afraid that things won't work out for her; she has some low marks, and she hasn't submitted her reading list yet.
Ma: *We have to find something for her; maybe she should take an extra test, to put her in this ...*
Pr: *I'm worried more about her behaviour in the future; all it takes is for just one small thing to happen and she gets really angry; she might soon end up beating up one of the boys, Maktoub or Assad or someone else;*
Fr: *Yes, as happened a few days ago with Ionica when Maktoub made a remark about the genitals of Ionica's mother and Hennia got up to go ...!*
Ma: *I think Hennia's a really smart girl; she has some original ideas and can express them well;*
Du: *Yes, a small example on the blackboard, and she applied it immediately ...*
Fr: *She feels all too readily discriminated against; I asked her to get something from my bag, but she refused, "I can't get something from the teacher's bag because I'd be accused of stealing straight-away" ...*
Gy: *She makes fun of you; she tried something similar with me recently, looked at me and then said "Just a joke!"*
Dr: *She also sucks up to me; at the beginning of the year she said: "Miss, you are so beautiful, why don't you have your hair done in a different way?" and ... similar remarks* (the others laugh, Dr is not a beauty);
Bi: *She gets into conflict situations very quickly ...*

Dialogues and Exclusion in Multicultural Schools 249

Other fragments from or about Hennia:

-Hennia is one of six children in a single-parent Moroccan family; the father left the house years ago, but there is still some contact with him; Hennia is neither the oldest nor the youngest of the six children;
-Hennia (in an interview): "*I came to this school, because at my last school I got into a fight every day, here I just want to get my diploma... .*"
-Hennia says that she does her homework on her own, but sometimes other members of the family help her, her good friend is Patricia and also Nabila, Khadija, Hannan and Ouarda.
-Hennia (in an interview) says that she has an older girl friend, also a Moroccan, whom she calls 'sister' (but it is not a biological sister), who is very important to her;
-Ma (maths teacher) about Hennia: (in an interview on interactions in the classroom): "*They must pick up things from the lessons,, there are some who do this better than others; Hennia does it quite well, ... whereas Nouzha for example doesn't seem to learn anything from class discussions ....*"
-Ma in comments on a video taken of the maths lesson just after the lesson has ended: "... *Fabienne participates quite well, better than she does in her other work, you never hear others like Edith, Nirmala and Jeroen, how do they work? Hennia can be a nuisance at times. You can ask her sometimes what she wants, and she replies "Ooh, I forgot already", apparently there is a category of girls with their hands in the air for no apparent reason.*"

An initial, superficial reading of the teachers' discussion about Hennia shows that at least one teacher is worried about her school career prospects, that a standard solution is suggested in the form of compulsory additional teaching and that other teachers present various opinions which shed some light on this student. Reading and understanding this dialogue in this way would seem reasonable because it follows the standard procedure taken in these evaluation meetings.

However, a more detailed analysis of this discussion about Hennia among the teachers reveals a number of disturbing imbalances and tensions, particularly if the supplementary information on Hennia, provided by herself and by her maths teacher is taken into account. The maths teacher considers Hennia to be "a really smart girl; she has some original ideas and can express herself well", and the Dutch language teacher agrees and specifies: Yes, a little example from the board, and she applied it immediately. These two evaluations of Hennia clearly contrast with the rather negative assessment of Hennia by the English teacher, who started the discussion with: "... her comprehension is really poor, I'm afraid things won't work out for her ...". The question arises as to whether Hennia has some particular problems with English or with the English teacher and is therefore considered to be 'poor'. Because maths and the Dutch language are rather high status subjects, the evaluations of these two teachers should be taken seriously. The maths teacher seems to have a rather consistent perception of Hennia; see his remarks on Hennia in an interview on interaction in the classroom; see 'other fragments'. The teachers participating in this meeting do not take up this challenge, but this is, in fact, not really surprising. In fact, teachers never disagree strongly with each other during these kinds of meetings which were recorded. It seems that the procedure of these meetings precludes pointing out apparent contradictions and starting a discussion on the presuppositions of some of the participants or on the facts on which they base their assessment.

It is, therefore, not possible to arrive at a definite conclusion concerning the evaluation of Hennia from this passage; for one teacher "her comprehension is poor", whereas for other teachers she is "smart, original, able to express herself well, and she is able to apply general models to particular cases very well".

But there is more. Pr, the handicraft teacher remarks that she is more worried about Hennia's behaviour, because she all too readily "gets really angry" (is this also an implicit rejection of the English teacher's assessment?). The illustrations offered by this particular teacher and by another one show that Hennia defended herself and a girl friend against sexist jokes made by Moroccan and Dutch boys. We do not know if there are any similar examples to this, or whether Hennia's reputation is that she 'gets angry all too readily'. During the discussion in the evaluation meeting these questions were not explored at all. In other words, the real meanings of the remarks made by these two teachers were accepted at face value. As we do not have a detailed psychological profile of Hennia, we can only speculate on the meaning of her behaviour. Hennia has chosen this school because she wants to get a diploma and she wants to avoid getting into a fight all the time. In other words, she seems motivated and she has made choices, and, therefore, she can be considered to be well integrated in the school community. As these choices had to be supported by her parents, it can be assumed that her family culture is at least not characterised by a clear separation, an attitude which some migrants adopt in their private sphere (Berry/Sam 1997). Hennia told us that she does her homework on her own, but sometimes other members of her family help her, which seems to confirm the preceding conjecture. Moreover, in addition to having Moroccan friends she also has a Dutch girl friend.

In the last part of the discussion on Hennia, even more opinions with regard to Hennia are expressed. If these remarks are glossed over at a superficial level then they simply serve to provide specific information about Hennia. But, on a different level, this final part of the discussion reveals another interesting aspect of Hennia's behaviour in the school community. As is seen from these passages, Hennia is well known for joking with teachers and teasing them in various ways, without however being confrontational or aggressive.

Before saying more about this, let me underline here that during this phase, one teacher's interpretation of Hennia's behaviour is politely but definitely rejected and corrected. One teacher thinks that Hennia feels quickly discriminated against, and he gives an example. This assessment is subtly rejected by two other teachers. These two teachers are convinced that Hennia jokes and teases, and that the illustration offered by one of them can be understood in the same way. However, the question that should be asked here is whether another remark made by the mathematics teacher about Hennia should also be interpreted in this way. Indeed, this teacher (in a simulated recall interview immediately after one lesson) said that Hennia can sometimes put her hand in the air (popularly said to 'hold up one's finger') in order to get the attention of the teacher, but after some time when asked what she wants, she replies: "Oh, I've already forgotten". This expression could also be interpreted as being teasing, because sometimes students put their hand in the air for a very long time before getting any attention from the teacher.

Hennia appears to enter quite regularly into exploratory, joking interactions with several teachers, by teasing them or by admitting that it was "just a joke". This kind of behaviour on Hennia's part could be interpreted as a manifestation of her attempts to explore in detail the possibilities and constraints of norms and values governing interactions with Dutch teachers, and more generally with others in the Dutch multicultural society. This interpretation would not only be in line with the interpretation of Hennia's anger, as denoting a definite and active form of exploring 'integrative' types of interaction, but also with the opportunities explicitly offered by the school, as affirmed in the school handbook as discussed in a previous section.

I would just like to add here that, at the end of the school year, Hennia was not advised to enrol in lower vocational training. On the contrary, she was advised to enrol in higher further schooling, provided that she could continue her schooling in a class without some Moroccan and Dutch boys, because of her ongoing fights with them.

5. Final discussion

The central problem of this extensive research project was to identify possible links between characteristics of (verbal) interactions and possible forms of exclusion, either in the form of school results or as direct forms of neglect and discrimination. From the first overall conclusion it would appear that the various and rich data which were collected in two multicultural schools do not warrant the drawing of a simple conclusion regarding straightforward links between the characteristics of interaction and the effects of exclusion. No direct discriminatory attitude, behaviour or remark with immediate effects could be identified.

This initial negative result is encouraging to some extent, but it also means that one has to look for much more subtle forms of discriminatory effects construed during the various types of interactions that have been recorded and analysed. And should it be possible to identify such indirect discriminatory characteristics, it will be much more difficult to discuss with teachers these indirect forms of discrimination with the aim to eliminate them. Indeed, if teachers are not aware of these aspects of their practices, a discussion can turn into a counterproductive confrontation.

This paper presented one individual case, Hennia, and was based on the recording of a grade-setting and evaluation meeting between teachers of one particular class and on some further data concerning Hennia, provided either by herself or by the maths teacher. Hennia seemed to be in the 'danger zone', which meant that she might be advised to enrol in lower vocational training. In this discussion, the teachers seem to follow a standard format, based on the identification of a problem, some background information and a tentative solution. But this format does not really seem to fit very well in Hennia's case. First of all, two important teachers (the maths teacher and the Dutch language teacher) consider Hennia to be smart and original, she is said to have good language skills, a view that conflicts with the ideas of the English teacher. Moreover, all the other points made by the teachers, which fall under the category of 'background information', reveal that Hennia seems to be a very active student, she makes funny multicultural explorations which are not always well understood, and she defends herself and her friends against sexist remarks by Moroccan and Dutch boys. In short, this analysis reveals Hennia to be a typical Moroccan girl, who is actively attempting to find ways to function in a chosen world of multicultural interaction. She is certainly not a girl who reproduces fixed ethnic and cultural values, which would characterise an attitude of separation, according to Berry and Sam (1997). Such a path will also involve numerous conflicts, dilemmas and misunderstandings for Hennia herself, but also for the different interaction partners she encounters (Maier, 2000).

The main problem seems to be that the teachers (at least in the discussions of the meeting which has been analysed, and in the further remarks by the maths teacher) do not take into account the specific choices, actions, bids and problems Hennia is facing. Her school assessment was apparently constructed along the lines of a standard Dutch student. And it is precisely this inability or lack of openness on the part of some of the teachers that can lead to exclusion.

Indeed, Hennia appears to be an example of a girl who is exploring a transcultural path of development (Davidson, 1996). All her bids and problems are severely misconstrued and misinterpreted when one attempts to understand Hennia in the context of the standard Dutch format of intellectual and social development.

References

Andriessen, Iris/Karen Phalet (2002): Acculturation and School Success: a study among minority youth in the Netherlands. – *Intercultural Education*, 13, 1, 21–36.
Berry, John/David Sam (1977): Acculturation and Adaptation. – In: J. Berry,/M. Segall/C. Kagitcibasi (eds.). Handbook of Cross-Cultural Psychology. Vol.3. Boston: Allyn & Bacon.

Davidson, Ann (1996): Making and Molding Identity in Schools. Student Narratives on Race, Gender and Academic engagement. – Albany: State University of New York Press.
Maier, Robert (2000): Du sujet vers les dynamiques d'identités. Pour une approche théorique adaptée aux écoles multiculturelles. In: Braconnier A. (ed.) Différences ...indifférence. Actes du XVIe Congrès de l'Association des Psychologues Scolaires. – Champigneulles: CRDP Lorraine.
SCP (1999): Minderhedennota. – Den Haag: SDU.
– (2001): Rapportage Minderheden 2001. Vorderingen op school en meer werk. – Den Haag: SDU.

Silvia Gilardoni

Content and Language Integrated Learning: Interactions in Bilingual Classrooms

1. Introduction

The topic of the present paper is the analysis of classroom interaction, when a second language is used to teach non-linguistic subjects in the context of CLIL, the acronym for "Content and Language Integrated Learning". CLIL is a term recently coined in the field of applied linguistics, which in the words of Marsh and Marsland "can be thought of as a generic 'umbrella term', encompassing a wide range of initiatives in which the learning of second languages and other subjects has a joint curricular role in education" (Marsh/Marsland 1999: 9). This term is therefore helpful in indicating experiences and approaches with different names (such as bilingual education, plurilingual education, immersion programmes and so on) both in the case of new educational experiments, and regarding established methods with long traditions in European and non-European countries, as in the case of this research.

This study draws attention to the discourse strategies adopted in bilingual classrooms; it focuses in particular on the meaning of language choice and on different manifestations of language contact in discourse. The aim of this research is also to analyse the interaction between teachers and students attending a school in Milan, in which the language of teaching is above all German.

The research is based on a corpus including teacher-pupil and pupil-pupil interactions in the classroom during lessons; the data were collected at the "Swiss School" in Milan ("Scuola Svizzera di Milano"), during the school year 2000/2001.

2. The sample

The "Swiss School" in Milan, one of the sixteen Swiss schools abroad, is a meeting place for children with diverse linguistic and cultural backgrounds, in particular Swiss and Italian. It is a bilingual school where Italian and above all German are used in teaching different subjects for the whole period of studies, from kindergarten to secondary school. It is also a school in which the language used for most of the teaching, German, is not the language used in the country, the country being Italy. Furthermore for the majority of the students, as we can see also from the sample analysed, German is a second language learned through scholastic instruction and spoken almost exclusively at school.

From the point of view of the second language learning setting, the educational programme could be described as content-based instruction: the emphasis is on subject matter learning and little time is spent focussing on the formal aspects of the second language (except of course during German language lessons); the focus is on using the language, German, rather than on talking about it (Lightbown/Spada 1999: 91–92).

At the Swiss School I took part in lessons as an observer and recorded 15 class hours. The recordings included maths lessons in the middle school (grades 6–8) and the first year of the secondary school (grade 9), and some chemistry lessons in the final years of the secondary school (grades 11–13). The two teachers are Italian/German bilinguals; their bilingualism[1] can be considered as a more or less *balanced bilingualism* (or symmetrical bilingualism), that of "someone whose mastery of two languages is roughly equivalent" (Li Wei 2000: 6).

There were 70 students in the middle school and in the first year of the secondary school group (37 boys and 33 girls); another group consisted of 32 students in their final years at the secondary school (16 boys and 16 girls). The age range of the students in the first group (=group 1) is from 11 to 15 years old, and that of the second group (=group 2) is from 16 to 18. In order to determine their original language, language preferences and the measure of Italian/German bilingualism, I asked the students to fill out a questionnaire.[2]

From this questionnaire it was evident that in both groups the majority of students are of Italian nationality, followed by Swiss and then other nationalities. The Swiss students are mainly from German-speaking regions of Switzerland (Zürich, Bern, Basel, etc.). I should also mention that the majority of the students of non-Italian nationality have always lived (or were born) in Italy.

Considering the students' mother tongue (i.e. the first language learnt), most of the students in both groups had Italian as their first language. Some students, on the other hand, gave both Italian and German as their mother tongue.

---

[1] According to Lüdi, a bilingual or plurilingual person is someone who is able to express himself in two (or more) languages according to the situation and with adequate competence, independently of the acquisition modalities and of the balance between the languages (Lüdi 1997: 15).

[2] See Appendix 2.

As regards the parents' mother tongue, Italian prevails followed by Italian/German, that is, the situation that arises when one parent is German and the other Italian. With regard to the language or languages used within the family and with friends, we can observe that once again Italian prevails.

Considering the parameters referring to the language background of the students, we can group the students from the point of view of their Italian/German bilingualism into three types:

1) Students with parents of Italian mother tongue, and who live in an Italian environment: this constitutes the majority of the students in both groups. The student can be defined as *secondary bilingual*, "someone whose second language [German in our case] has been added to a first language [Italian] via instruction (Li Wei 2000: 7), or as *successive bilingual*, "someone whose second language is added at some stage after the first has begun to develop" (Li Wei 2000: 7).[3] This is valid also for the students of linguistic origins other than Italian and German, for whom German can be added as a third language.

2) Students with parents of Italian/German mother tongue (for example one German parent and one Italian) and who live in a bilingual family environment; in this case we speak about bilingualism by simultaneous acquisition. For these students Italian is however dominant in everyday life: they are generally *dominant bilinguals*, that is with greater proficiency in one of their languages and they use it significantly more than the other language, or students with a more or less *balanced bilingualism*.

3) Students with both parents of German mother tongue (this group represents the smallest part of the sample); these students have a more balanced bilingualism.

The majority of the students can also be considered as bilinguals "in the making", that is as language learners.[4]

---

[3] Generally after three years (see Lüdi 1998: 4).
[4] According to Lüdi (1998: 11) the situation of the language learners is exactly that to be "bilingues en devenir". I also asked the students for self-rating on their language proficiency in German in the four basic language abilities (listening, speaking, reading and writing) and I noticed that the two groups diverge significantly, above all in their listening ability: the self-evaluation of students in group 2 is higher than that of group 1; this depends of course on the number of years of contact with German, which is higher in group 2. Similarly, the results of the questions about the use of German during the lessons showed a divergence when I asked the students if they thought that their German knowledge was adequate for the maths or chemistry lessons: however even if the majority answered "yes" in both groups, in group 1 the number of "generally" and "not always" is higher; in reply to the question "Is German an obstacle to your understanding of the subjects?", the students answered for the most part "no", but in group 1 many more students felt that this was indeed the case.

3. Analysis of teacher-pupil interactions

According to Grosjean, bilinguals can choose between a monolingual or a bilingual language mode, or, in the words of Lüdi, between unilingual or bilingual speech (Grosjean 1995: 261–263 and Lüdi 1995: 8). In monolingual speech the language choice is rigid and one of the two competences is deactivated in the speaker, as far as this is possible. In the bilingual language mode both languages are activated and the bilingual speaker "usually chooses a base language to use with the interlocutor (that is, a main language of interaction) but can, within the same interaction, decide to switch base languages if the situation, topic, interlocutor, function of the interaction, etc. requires it" (Grosjean 1995: 263); the language choice is less definitive and the discourse is characterized by phenomena indicative of the influence of one language upon the other. This is true not only for symmetrical bilinguals, but also for bilinguals in the making. Following Lüdi, there is consequently a distinction between unilingual and bilingual interaction in addition to that between exolingual interaction (situation defined by a constitutive asymmetry between the competences of the interactants) and endolingual interaction (involving speakers with more or less symmetrical competences). The two dimensions form a bidimensional space, as shown in Figure 1, illustrating how the interlocutors are situated in the verbal interaction depending on different criteria (formality of the situation, language repertoire of the interlocutors, communicative intention, etc.) (Lüdi 1998: 11–12 and 1999: 27):

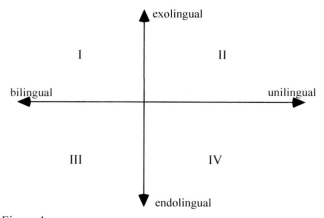

Figure 1

The exolingual or endolingual interaction is characterized by the more or less simultaneous activation in the speakers of two linguistic systems; we can mention in particular the phenomenon that Lüdi calls *marques transcodiques* which can be grouped into the following four subtypes:

– Les *interférences* sont des traces systématiques de la langue première (ou de n'importe quelle autre langue) dans la production en langue seconde, qui relèvent de l'interlangue de locuteurs non natifs [...];

– Les *emprunts* sont des éléments – le plus souvent des unités lexicales – d'une autre langue quelconque introduits dans un système linguistique afin d'en augmenter le potentiel référentiel [...];

– La *formulation transcodique* [...] consiste en un emploi potentiellement conscient, dans un énoncé en langue seconde, d'une séquence perçue par le locuteur non natif comme appartenant à une autre langue (le plus souvent la langue première du locuteur), dans le but de surmonter un obstacle communicatif; elle fait partie des stratégies compensatoires interlinguales.

– Le *code-switching* est l'insertion 'on line' de séquences – allant d'une unité lexicale minimale (on parle aussi de 'nonces', d'emprunt dynamique ou d'emprunt de parole) à des séquences des rangs les plus élevés – d'une ou plusieurs langues quelconques (= langues enchâssées) dans un texte/échange produit selon les règles d'une autre langue (= langue de base), entre bilingues, dans une situation appropriée au mode bilingue (Lüdi 1995: 150–151).

In the present study I will consider, in particular, cases of the so-called *formulation transcodique* and of code-switching.

Referring to Figure 1, which illustrates the bidimensional space of the language choice, I will try to define the type of interaction which takes place in the classrooms analyzed.

Generally speaking, the situation in the classrooms is exolingual (as is usually the case in a second language learning classroom): the communication occurs between interlocutors with asymmetrical competences, the teacher, a balanced bilingual, and the students, bilinguals in the making. From the point of view of those students who are actual balanced bilinguals or who have German as mother tongue the interaction is of course endolingual.

As regards the language mode in the teacher-pupil interaction, we can state that it is bilingual in the two classes, the maths (group 1) and the chemistry class (group 2). Nevertheless, unlike the chemistry class where the teacher himself/herself occasionally resorts to Italian during the lessons, in the maths class the choice of German is rigidly established by the teacher and also the language mode is more orientated towards the unilingual axis.

I also asked the students what languages they use with their teacher in the classroom and why. The results, actually, reflect the situation observed and just described. As shown in some answers, the use of German by the students is perceived as automatic, "obligatory", natural since this is the language which the teacher uses or because "We are at the Swiss school"; this prompts us to reflect that the choice of the language is also related to the language policy of the school. Some students declared that they also used Italian. The reasons for the choice of Italian are different in the two groups. For the students of group 1 the recourse to Italian is due to the fact that sometimes " we can't find the words". For the students of group 2 the main reason is that the teacher often uses Italian or asks the students to use it.

The situation in which a student does not know a word in German when speaking and saves the conversation by using an Italian word is an example of *formulation transcodique* (= FT). This is an exolingual-bilingual strategy; the exolingual-bilingual situation favours in fact the occurrence of the FT, which is a self-facilitating strategy adopted by the learner usually with the function of asking for help (Lüdi 1999: 28–29).

The teacher deals with FT in different ways (see Lüdi 1999: 32–34). We can say that in our data a FT is usually accepted without any problem by the teacher, so that it is seen as a resource to maintain the communication and it is also exploited to enrich the vocabulary in the target language (as is likely to happen above all in a CLIL situation which focuses in particular on meaning).

Let us analyse some classroom examples.[5] In example (1) we have an elicitation act carried out by the maths teacher: the question is about the term "leap years" (lines 1–3). In the reply student 1 uses an Italian word *bisestili* as he doesn't know the German word, *das Schaltjahr* (line 4). The teacher then questions some other students but without results (lines 5 and 10–11); he then resorts to a strategy which can be considered as bilingual and collaborative (Lüdi 1999: 33): by interpreting the previous FT as a call of help, the teacher gives the words in the target language and elicits a repetition in the pupil (line 15):[6]

(1)
1 TM: ich hatte eigentlich ein ganz anderes problem . das datum kann ich lesen\ . ich hatte das
2   problem wie ich diese tage berechne . was gibt es denn da zum beispiel mit neunzehn-
3   hundertzwei/ nur jahre von dreihundertfünfundsechzig daten/ .. oder gibt es auch andere/
4 S1: nein auch die: jahre bisestili
5 TM: wie heissen jetzt diese jahre/
6 S1: eh bisestili\
7 S2: nein
8 TM: wie [heissen die/
9 S2: [non bisestili\
10 TM: alle vier jahre wird ein tag noch angehängt und wie heisst so ein jahr/ . wie heisst es/ wie

---

[5] For the analysis of classroom interactions, see Sinclair /Coulthard 1975.
[6] In the transcriptions TM stands for the maths teacher, TC for the chemistry teacher and S for the student (S1, S2, etc. in order of appearance). The names quoted are invented. As regards the transcription conventions see Appendix 1.

```
11      heisst so ein jahr/ . wie heisst es auf deutsch/ .. normalerweise hat ein jahr
12      dreihundertfünfundsechzig tage und alle vier jahre also zum beispiel neunzehnhundertvier
13      neunzehnhundertacht neunzehnhundertzwölf\
14 S2:  zweitausend
15 TM:  zweita- zweitausend war auch ein schaltjahr\ richtig\ wie heisst das wort auf deutsch/
16 S2:  schalt-
17 TM:  schaltjahr\ schreib es bitte an die tafel/ . ein schaltjahr das heisst man schaltet noch einen
18      tag dazu\
```

In example (2) we can observe the occurrence of a FT adopted by a student in order to contribute to the conversation adding to the list of measurable sizes by mentioning the luminosity and its unit of measurement (lines 18–19); the maths teacher signals comprehension and continues without considering the lexical problem (line 20). This strategy is defined by Lüdi as clearly bilingual: the teacher points out to the pupil that the FT is a legitimate instrument to get over a lexical obstacle and that it does not require correction (Lüdi 1999: 34):

```
(2)
1  TM: was kann man noch messen/ . was kann man alles messen/
2  S1: eh . temperatur\
3  TM: temperatur kann man messen\ was noch/ .        [die zeit kann man messen\
4  S2:                                                [die zeit
5  TM: was kann man noch messen/
(…)
6  S3: kraft
7  TM: KRAFT .. du weisst du was
8  S3: <die kiloton ((in a low voice))>
9  TM: eh wie ist die einheit der kraft beigegeben/
10 S4: eh newton
11 S3: [newton
12 TM: [was/
13 S4: newton
14 TM: newton\ [ n] und früher hat man gesagt sei ein kiloton nicht/ . eh wie ist es festgelegt/ .
15      wie man messen soll/ also all diese sachen . hast du noch etwas was wir kennen/
16 S5: eh . kelvin
17 TM: eh das ist temperatur\ das ist die sogenannte absolute        [temperatur\
18 S5:                                                               [und dann lumino- eh eh die eh
19      luminosität also candela/
20 TM: ja ja . okay\ lassen wir es mal es gibt sehr viele solche dinge die man messen kann\
```

With regard to code-switching within teacher-pupil interaction, I hardly ever noticed any examples in the maths teacher's speech. As already mentioned, the language mode in the interaction in the maths classroom is orientated towards the unilingual axis, because the choice of German as base language is rigidly established by the teacher. But sometimes it is the student who is responsible for code-switching, from German into Italian of course. This is usually due to the fact, that the students use their first language, in this case Italian, spontaneously. In this example code-switching takes place between two turns, that of TM (line 1: "Who calculated the days?") and that of S4 who switches to Italian (line 5: "I did it myself"):

(3)
1 TM: wer hat die tage berechnet/
2 S1: ich ich
3 S2: ich
4 S3: ich habe alles gemacht
5 S4: io ho fatto tutto da sola

In example (4) the code-switching is within the same turn; in his initial bid act (line 1: "Excuse me") S1 starts spontaneously with Italian, but he quickly reverts to the base language of interaction:

(4)
1 S1: scusi entschuldigung/ . warum haben sie jetzt geschrieben zwei [iks] durch ein sechstel/ .
2   zwei [iks] sechstel\ und nicht/
3 TM: doch um sicher zu arbeiten damit ich ein sechstel bekomme/
4 S2: mit zwei\
5 TM: mit zwei\ .. ich wusste ja noch nicht was [iks] ist . aber wie ich das mit zwei erweitert
6   gibt's zwei [iks]\

Focussing on code-switching in the chemistry classes, I observed, instead, that the occurrences are much more frequent; this is due to the fact that in this case code-switching is used by the teacher as an added pedagogical resource, a discourse strategy which contributes to the interactional work that the teacher and the learners do (see Camilleri 1997). Code-switching occurs very frequently for example when the teacher introduces a technical term. The teacher asks for the translation from German into Italian of the term introduced; it could therefore be analysed as a 'code-switching upon request'. The translation of technical German terms is a way to clarify their meaning; clarification is also the main communicative function of code-swithcing in this case, but in addition there is the function of checking for understanding (for example when the teacher is not sure that the learners have fully understood the concept mentioned in German).[7]

In example (5) we can notice some cases of teacher requests for translation (lines 2, 13 and 23: "Translate this into Italian", "In Italian?"); the pupil replies with code-switching from German into Italian clarifying the meaning of the words "binding energy", "rich in energy" and "combustion" (lines 4–7, 15–17 and 24). The use of Italian continues in the follow-up move: in the accepting act, i.e. the repetition of the pupil's reply by the teacher (line 8), and also in the evaluation (lines 18 and 25: "right, yes"); then the teacher returns to German:

---

[7] On the clarification function of code-switching see Baker (1997: 87).

(5)
1   TC: also können wir sagen chemische en- eh energie ist mehr oder weniger gleich bedeutend
2   mit <bindungsenergie ((TC is writing on the blackboard))> ... übersetzt das auf
3   italienisch [bindungsenergie/
4   S1: [energia di legame\
5   TC: prego/
6   S1: energia [di legame
7   S2:   [energia di legame
8   TC: energia di legame\ ... (4s) da ... also eh <benzin ... metan ... glukose ((TC is writing on
9   the blackboard))>
10 S3: die kohle/
11 TC: eh . ja die kohle ist etwas kompliziert\ die kohle ist eine mischung nicht/ ich möchte da
12   nur reine stoffe\ ich würde sagen <elementare metalle ... nicht/ .. sind .. energiereiche
13   stoffe\ ((TC is writing on the blackboard))> .. energiereiche stoffe übersetzt hier das auf
14   italienisch laura/
15 S1: ricchi di energia\
16 TC: stoffe dennoch/
17 S1: sotanze ricche di energia\
18 TC: giusto sì\ ... eh .. durch einen chemischen prozess können wir da diese energie
19   herausholen/ . eben bei .. benzin metan zum beispiel durch verbrennung das ist ein
20   chemischer prozess nicht/ und meistens entsteht dann wärme\ ... (9s) also <durch einen
21   chemischen prozess (6s) kann ... diese . energie ... in wärme verwandelt werden\ ... (7s)
22   ((TC is writing on the blackboard))> also . durch einen chemischen prozess entsteht nun
23   eine verbrennung .. verbrennung auf italienisch mario/
24 S1: <combustione ((in a low voice))> .. combustione\
25 TC: sì\ ... ja gut\

In example (6), the chemistry teacher, after a demand for translation (line 2: "What does it mean in Italian?"), continues in Italian in the follow-up with an accepting act and also with a comment (line 4: "A volatile substance, not as water"):

(6)
1   TC: ein ester besteht aus molekülen/ . und ein ester ein einfacher ester ist ein flüchtiger stOff\ .
2   eine flüssigkeit eh/ .. eine flüssigkeit\ ... (6s) wie heisst es auf italienisch dario/
3   S1: mh volatile\
4   TC: volatile\ una sostanza volatile ... non come l'Acqua eh/ wie das wasser/

The following two examples are cases of code-switching upon request used by the chemistry teacher, but with corrective feedback. In example (7) we can see a so-called metalinguistic feedback, according to the model of Lyster and Ranta (Lightbown/Spada 1999: 103–106): TC points out that there is an error in translation (lines 7 and 9: "No", "Compounds are not elements"), he then gives a brief instruction (line 11: "You have to find a neutral term") trying to elicit the piece of information from the student. An explicit correction follows (line 14: "Say substance"):

(7)
1   TC: (...) also die verbindungen sind rreine stoffe die man durch einen chemischen prozess in

```
2      die elemente zerlegen kann\ .. nicht/ also <reine stoffe ... die man .. durch ... einen
3      chemischen prozess ... (7s) in die elemente zerlegen kann ... ((TC is writing on the
4      blackboard))> das ganze satz auf italienisch/ ... paolo . verstehen sie rreine stoffe die man
5      durch einen chemischen prozess in die elemente zerlegen kann\
6  S1: i composti sono elementi puri/
7  TC: no
8  S1: no
9  TC: i composti non sono        [elementi\
10 S1: [ah no .verbindungen       [composti
11 TC: [devi trovare un termine neutro\
12 S2: <materia ((in a low voice))>
13 S1: eh una materia\
14 TC: sì o una sostanza\ [di sostanza/
15 S1: [una sostanza pura .. che si può eh
16 TC: dividere
17 S1: dividere: . tramite un processo chimico .. negli elementi\
18 TC: sì
19 S1: si può dividere in elementi tramite un processo chimico\
20 TC: va bene . d'accordo . also . also stoff bitte sostanza eh/ . in deutsch sagen wir auch
21      substanz aber ich brauche . viel mehr das wort stoff\
```

In example (8) we find a particular case of elicitation: "content-based" elicitation. After a wrong translation of the term "hydrochloric acid" (lines 7–8), TC elicits the correct form saying "I'm writing the formula and then you have to know what it means" (line 9):

```
(8)
1  TC: einen solchen chemischen prozess nicht/ bei dem man . eh eine verbindung zerlegt nennen
2      wir analyse ... ich . nenne da salzsäure .. also in italienisch acido cloridrico . also . reine
3      salzsäure: wären eigentlich gasen konzentrierte salzsäure also . man macht <elektrolyse
4      ... nicht/ einer . oder . no eh von konzentrierten konzentrierten salzsäure\ ((TC is writing
5      on the blackboard))> .. konzentrierte salzsäure also auf italienisch/ .. eh salzsäure/
6  S1: eh acido
7  S2: <salino ((in a low voice))>
8  S1: salino\
9  TC: ti scrivo la formula poi tu lo devi sapere . <acca [tʃi*] elle ((TC is writing on the
10     blackboard))> . cos'è [tʃi*] elle/
11 S1: [cloro
12 S2: [cloro
13 TC: cloro\ allora è acido/
14 S1: cloridrico
15 S2: [cloridrico
16 S3: [cloridrico
17 TC: cloridrico . no/ . schreibt das bitte hier . acido cloridrico/ .. so\
```

Code-switching can also take place when the situation is less formal than usual, for example when the teacher is showing a chemical experiment, as in case (9). The teacher switches to Italian probably in order to establish a friendly relation with the learners (line 6: "You can't see anything, can you?"):

(9)
((TC is doing a chemical experiment))
1   TC: also zur elektrolyse des wassers\ ich habe schon gesagt die elektrolyse des wassers . ist
2   eine endoterme reaktion\
3   ((silence))
4   TC: so ... also ohne katalisator geht es ja schlecht\
5   ((silence))
6   TC: non si vede niente no/
7   S1: no\
8   S2: poco\
9   TC: poco o niente\
10 S3: poco o niente
11 S4: poco o niente
12 TC: aspetta eh/ .. nicht also wir haben gesehen . eh ohne katalisator . geht es eigentlich kaum
13   also wir haben das gefühl funktioniert überhaupt nichts\

In example (10), interrupting a question asked by a pupil, TC switches from German to Italian (line 4: "Wait a moment! Don't chat"); here code-switching has the function to emphasize the speaker's involvement in the message. However, the code-switching in lines 9–10 is adopted as a strategy of clarification with the purpose of explaining a chemical experiment:

(10)
1   TC: wir sollen uns das überlegen\ ... läuft mit dieser apparatur die umwandlung auch
2   umgekehrt ab/
3   S1: wenn ich (xx)
4   TC: warte ein moment/ non zabettare\
5   S1: ma chiedevo/
6   TC: also hier haben wir mechanische energie in wärme umgewandelt\ was bedeutet also
7   umgekehrt mario/
8   S2: wärme in mechanische energie umwandeln\
9   TC: ja wohl\ .. das würde also heiss . wenn wir das wasser erwärmen .. siamo noi che adesso
10   mettiamo sotto all'acqua . una fiamma .. scaldiamo l'acqua . so wird die: chinetische
11   energie der teilchen dort auch erhöht oder/ (...)

In example (11) we can find a further example of code-switching with the function of emphasis, this time in the students' speech. By switching to Italian the students underline the fact that they cannot understand the description of the experiment of Joule from the drawing on the blackboard (line 3: "Excuse me, that thread?"; line 10–14: "I can't see... What is that thing there?... Is it a hatchet?"):

(11)

1 TC: eh . dieses gefäß ist ein thermostat\ also wir denken da am besten so an einen thermos no/
2 . den gebrauchen wir eh . den kaffee warm zu halten oder ich weiss es nicht\
3 S1: senta ma quel filo/
4 TC: und da ist ein thermometer\
5 S1: aber . der faden hier/
6 TC: der faden ist dort um eh . sehr stark gewickelt\ .. an dem faden hängt das gewicht\
7 S1: ja aber eh .. und hier/
8 TC: so zeige ich das mal\
9 S2: aber da ist [die idee de- also wie ein mixer/
10 S1:   [non vedo niente/
11 S3: cos'è quella roba che c'è   [lì/
12 S4:   [ma questa cos'è un'accetta/
13 S3: cos'è quella roba/
14 S5: è una ruota con un filo\
15 TC: so bitte hörtet auf/
15 S6: entschuldigung/ ich verstehe was ist diese sache: [(xxx)
17 S7:   [wie so ein beil/
18 S6: diese so/
19 TC: es sei ein rädchen mit zwei schaukeln weisst du/
20 S6: ach so\

4. Analysis of pupil-pupil interactions

According to the questionnaire filled out by the students, the language used most by the students with their classmates is Italian. This reflects the fact that pupil-pupil interaction is a less formal situation, and the students, for whom Italian is the first language switch spontaneously to Italian. This happens also during the lessons when, for example, the students discuss an activity or an exercise, or comment on the activities, as in examples (12) and (13). In example (12), while TM is checking the homework, two students speak to each other in Italian (lines 9–12: "We calculated wrong", "I know, come on", "Look…"):

(12)

1 TM:(…) wer hat die tage noch [berechnet/
2 S1:   [ich
3 S2: ich
4 TM: ich kann . zeige sie mal
5 S1: ja aber meine:
6 S2: meine sind alle falsch
7 S1: auch [meine\
8 TM:[das mag ich jetzt nicht\
9 S2: <paolo/ . ma abbiamo calcolato sbagliato ((laughing and speaking to S1))>

```
10 S1:  Io so vieni qua\
11 S2:  <guarda . noi abbiamo fatto millenovecentonovantanove non duemila/ ((laughing and
12      speaking to S1))>
```

In example (13) some students comment in Italian on the number of elements in a chemical formula, which the teacher is writing on the blackboard (lines 6–10: "It's one", "No two…"):

```
(13)
 1 TC:  <da habe ich jetzt das (o;)\ … (6s) plus also zwei (o;) .. könnte das (ha;) zwei (o;)
 2      schreiben oder/ .. ein molekül wollen wir noch schreiben/ ich habe da keinen platz nicht
 3      mehr\ … das ist also der ester/ … (7s) also das wäre einfach schwefelsäure ester\ ((TC is
 4      writing the chemical formula of the ester on the blackboard))>
 5 ((silence))
 6 S1:  <è uno
 7 S2:  no
 8 S3:  due
 9 S2:  due o quattro
10 S4:  cinque
```

But I also noticed some interesting cases of code-switching in the pupil-pupil interaction. In the following short interaction, for example, S1 and S2 use German numbers in an Italian sentence (lines 4–5: "Look, it is two fifths", "No three…"); this is normal and it happens very frequently, as students are used to resorting to German for technical terms, numbers or letters (for example when speaking about a formula or an expression):

```
(14)
 1 TM: diktiere mir mario mal die die diese aufgabe hier/ . und dann schreiben alle gerade mal
 2      schnell her\
 3 S1:  drei fünftel . kleiner oder gleiche . fünf [iks] durch ein siebtel\
 4 S2:  mario guarda che è zwei fünftel/
 5 S1:  no drei è drei\ .. ist kleiner neun zehntel\
```

In example (15), we find a case of code-switching within a sentence, that is a mixed constituent, a lexical unit of another language embedded in the grammatical structure of the base language; this example of code-switching can also be defined as speech borrowing. While the teacher is writing the word *kürzen* (which means "reduce a fraction to its lowest term") on the blackboard, in order to help the students to remember this mathematical procedure, some students resort to the term "kürzato" and "kürzare" (lines 2 and 8–9). The word "kürzato" or "kürzare" is actually a German lexical unit, *kürzen*, plus an Italian morpheme (*-ato*, *-are*). Such phenomena are typical of a bilingual context such as the one considered; they are understandable almost only within the group of the speech community and are also a sign of belonging to it:

(15)
((T is writing the word "kürzen" on the blackboard))
1   S1: <kür- ((in a low voice))> ah/
2   S2: ah .. claudio non hai kürzato\
3   S3: ops
4   S2: auch kürzen/
5   S4: [eh brA:vo
6   TM:[no:\
7   ((laugh))
8   S1: si può kürzare/
9   S2: si DEVE kürzare\

5.   Concluding remarks

Through the analysis of the verbal teacher-pupil and pupil-pupil interaction in the context of bilingual education I have tried to show how two languages can interact and alternate in the classroom discourse. Some results of this research appear to be particularly significant:

- language alternation can be considered as a discourse strategy that can be used by the teacher with pedagogical functions (for example to establish contact with learners, to explain, to elicit a response, etc.). It can be used by the learners as a resource for their communicative aims. Code-switching and *formulation transcodique* can also become part of the learners' culture of communication and of their discoursive competence (see Lüdi 1999).

- the phenomenon of *marques transcodiques* shows that the speaker does not use a single language code in the communication process. As a matter of fact, alternation and mixing of various languages can occur in the production of a message. This then can be considered as a sign of man's freedom with respect to language, that he is free to use language to express his relationship with reality (see Rigotti 1997).

References

Baker, Colin (1997): Foundations of Bilingual Education and Bilingualism. Second Edition – Clevedon, Philadelphia, Sydney: Multilingual Matters Ltd.
Camilleri, Antoinette (1997): Codeswitching: an added pedagogical resource! – Alternance des langues et apprentissage. Situations, modèles, analyses, pratiques. 6–8 février 1997, Saint Cloud.
Grosjean, François (1995): A Psycholinguistic Approach to Code-switching: the recognition of guest words by bilinguals. – In: L. Milroy,/P. Muysken (eds.): One Speaker, Two Languages. Cross Disciplinary Perspectives on code-switching, 259–275. Cambridge: Cambridge University Press.
Li Wei (ed.) (2000): The Bilingualism Reader. – London, New York: Routledge.
Lightbown, Patsy M./Spada, Nina (1999): How Languages are Learned. Second Edition. – Oxford: Oxford University Press.
Lüdi, Georges (1995): Parler bilingue et traitements cognitifs. – *Intellectica* 20, 139–159.
– (1997): Peter Ochs: Eine mehrsprachige europäische Biographie. – Basle Electronic Working Papers in Linguistics 2, University of Basel (http://www.romsem.unibas.ch/linguistique/georges/).
– (1998): L'enfant bilingue: chance ou surcharge? – In: L. Mondada/ G. Lüdi (eds.): Dialogue entre linguistes. Recherches en linguistique à l'Institut des langues et littératures romanes de l'Université de Bâle (ARBA 8), 13–30.
– (1999): Alternance des langues et acquisition d'une langue seconde. – In: V. Castellotti/D. Moore (eds.): Alternance des langues et construction de savoirs. *Cahiers du français contemporain* 5, 25–51.
Marsh, David/Marsland, Bruce (eds.) (1999): CLIL Initiatives for the Millennium. – Jyväskyla: University of Jyväskyla Press.
Rigotti, Eddo (1997): Lezioni di linguistica generale. – Milano: Edizioni Cusl.
Sinclair, John McH./Coulthard, Malcolm (1975): Towards an Analysis of Discourse. The English Used by Teachers and Pupils. Oxford: Oxford University Press.

Appendixes

Appendix 1: Transcription conventions

[	simultaneous talk
=	latching (i.e. no interval between adjacent turns)
-	break-off/unfinished word
.	short pause
..	medium pause
…	long pause
(2s)	length of a pause in seconds
:	extended pronunciation of a vowel
nn	extended pronunciation of a consonant

/	rising intonation
\	falling intonation
AABB	segment pronounced with emphasis or a strong accent
(( )) <>	non transcribed phenomena and eventual delimitation of commented phenomena (for example: laughing)
(...)	indication of omitted part in transcription
(xxx)	unintelligible speech
[ ]	phonetic transcription

Appendix 2: Questionnaire

1. Klasse: ……..
2. Alter: ……..
3. männlich   weiblich
4. Geburtsort: ……..
5. Nationalität: ……..
6. Wenn du nicht hier in Mailand (oder in Italien) geboren bist, seit wie vielen Jahren wohnst du hier?
7. Hast du die Schweizer Schule Mailand vom Kindergarten an immer besucht?
   Ja   Nein
   Wo hast du den Kindergarten besucht? Und die Grundschule?
8. Deine Muttersprache/n (= die Sprache/n, die du als kleines Kind gelernt hast):
   Italienisch   Deutsch   Französisch   Italienisch und Deutsch
   Deutsch und Französisch   Italienisch und Französisch
   andere, und zwar ……..
9. Kannst du andere Sprachen sprechen?   Nein   Ja
   a. Welche?
   b. Aus welchem Grund kannst du andere Sprachen sprechen?
   Ich lerne sie in der Schule   Ich lerne sie mit einem Privatlehrer
   Ich lerne sie allein   Meine Eltern lehren sie mich
   Ich habe mich für eine bestimmte Zeit im Ausland aufgehalten
   anderes, und zwar …….
10. Welche ist/sind die Muttersprache/n deiner Eltern?
11. Welche Sprache/n spricht deine Mutter mit deinem Vater? Welche Sprache/n spricht dein Vater mit deiner Mutter?

12. Welche Sprache/n benutzt du, wenn <u>du</u> mit deinem Vater sprichst? – mit deiner Mutter sprichst? – mit deinen Grosseltern sprichst? – mit deinen Geschwistern sprichst? – mit deinen Freunden/innen in der Schule sprichst? – mit deinen Freunden/innen ausserhalb der Schule sprichst? – mit deinen Schulklassenkameraden/innen sprichst?
13. Welche Sprache/n benutzen die folgenden Personen, wenn sie <u>mit dir</u> sprechen? dein Vater – deine Mutter – deine Grosseltern – deine Geschwister – deine Freunde/innen in der Schule – deine Freunde/innen ausserhalb der Schule – deine Schulklassenkameraden/innen
14. Welche Sprache/n benutzt du, wenn du: im Kopf rechnest und zählst? in dein Vormerkheft (diario) schreibst?
15. Wie betrachtest du dich? Als ein Junge/Mädchen, der/das   italienisch spricht   deutsch spricht   französisch spricht   zweisprachig ist   mehrsprachig ist   anderes, und zwar ……..
16. Wie viele Leute "mischen" deiner Meinung nach die Sprachen in deiner Schule, wenn sie sprechen? wenige   einige   viele
17. Ist die deutsche Sprache deine Muttersprache?
    Ja   Nein
    a. Wie alt warst du, als du Deutsch zu lernen begonnen hast?
    b. Wie hast du Deutsch gelernt?
    in der Schule   mit einem Privatlehrer   allein   mit meinen Eltern während eines Auslandsaufenthalts (oder mehrerer)   anderes, und zwar ……..
18. Wie beurteilst du deine Deutschkenntnisse?

Hörverstehen:	sehr gut	gut	nicht sehr gut	ausreichend	nicht gut
Sprechen:	sehr gut	gut	nicht sehr gut	ausreichend	nicht gut
Lesen:	sehr gut	gut	nicht sehr gut	ausreichend	nicht gut
Schreiben:	sehr gut	gut	nicht sehr gut	ausreichend	nicht gut

19. Sind deine Deutschkenntnisse genügend, um am Chemie-/Mathematikunterricht teilzunehmen?
    ja   meistens   nicht immer   nein   ich weiss es nicht
20. Was für ein Fach ist die Chemie/Mathematik für dich?
    einfach   normal   ziemlich schwierig   schwierig
21. Ist die deutsche Sprache für dich ein Hindernis, welches das Verstehen von diesem Fach schwieriger macht?
    nein   selten   manchmal   oft   immer
    ich weiss es nicht
    Erkläre den Grund deiner Antwort.

22. Welche Sprache/n benutzt du, wenn du mit dem/der Lehrer/in in der Klasse sprichst?
    Italienisch   Deutsch   Italienisch und Deutsch   andere, und zwar ……..
    Erkläre den Grund deiner Antwort.
23. Welche Sprache/n benutzt du, wenn du mit dem/der Lehrer/in persönlich sprichst?
    Italienisch   Deutsch   Italienisch und Deutsch   andere, und zwar ……..
    Erkläre den Grund deiner Antwort.
24. Erzählst du jemandem, was du während des Chemie-/Mathematikunterrichts durchgenommen hast?   immer   oft   manchmal   selten   nie
    Welche Sprache/n benutzt du?   Italienisch   Deutsch   Italienisch und Deutsch
    andere, und zwar ……..
25. Worüber hat der/die Lehrer/in heute gesprochen? Erkläre es auf Deutsch und auf Italienisch.
26. Wie findest du die Tatsache, dass viele Fächer in deiner Schule auf Deutsch unterrichtet werden?

Chapter 6
Focus Group Discussions

Viveka Adelswärd

Virtual Participants as Communicative Resources in Discussions on Gene Technology

1. Introduction

It is often claimed that, in ordinary conversation, people "talk most of all about what others talk about – they transmit, recall, weigh and pass judgement on other people's words, opinions, assertions, information; people are upset by others' words, or agree with them, contest them, refer to them and so forth" (Bakhtin 1981:338). Thus, participants in face-to-face conversation often give the floor, or the voice, to non-present participants. Such participants, who are made present in the conversation by others quoting them or referring to their opinions, are here called *virtual participants*. This paper discusses some of the discursive functions of virtual participants.

Goffman (1974) reminds us that individuals in conversation can quote others and act out characters not their "own", but nevertheless entertain "the basic notion that in daily life the individual ordinarily speaks for himself, speaks, as it were, in his "own" character. However, when one examines speech, especially the informal variety, this traditional view proves inadequate" (Goffman 1974:512). When analysing examples of speech taken from focus-group discussions on genetically modified food (GMF) the following question is posed: Why and how are virtual participants brought into these discussions?

The data used consist of eleven focus-group discussions, audiotaped and transcribed, on genetically modified food (GMF).[1] In eight of them, the participants are "ordinary people" without any special knowledge of, or connection to, the topic of GMF. In the remaining three, the participants are executives in large companies from the food industry sector – representing production, wholesale and retailing. From these eleven focus-group discussions, sequences in which one or several of the participants brought in virtual participants (that is quoted, or voiced, others) were analysed.

The focus-group discussions referred to in this study were characterised by two things. First, the discussions not only focussed on what the participants thought about the subject, but also on what they thought others might think, and feel, about it. So, for this reason alone, virtual participants played an active role in the discussions. Another characteristic of

---

[1] For more detailed descriptions of the project generating these data see Wibeck this volume.

the discussions was the fact that the participants were in the process of discursively forming an opinion, or learning more about the topic in question, rather than arguing for a particular standpoint. All participants claimed that the question of genetically modified food was a complicated and difficult topic. The discussions seemed to provide the participants more with a means of sorting out their own thoughts than with a platform from which to persuade others to accept arguments. Thus, argumentative sequences from the discussions did not show how the participants aired an opinion, but how they were beginning to construct what an opinion could look like. Discursive work was being done in order to dramatise contradictions and make confusion visible, much in the way that Billig (1987) talks about discursive rhetoric. In a sense, focus groups could be seen as thinking cultures in miniature, displaying the thinking and arguing of groups, not only of individuals (Linell et al.in press).

In a discussion about the nature of discourse data collected from focus-group discussions, Myers (1999b) states that presenting one's own or an opposing view "allows one to qualify it, to enact tensions or contradictions, to bring out underlying motives, to acknowledge or elicit the likely responses of others. Using represented discourse in a thought experiment allows others to join in" (Myers 1999b:587).

2. What is a virtual participant and how are virtual participants made present in talk?

The notion of speaker is a problematic one, as Goffman (1981), for one, has pointed out. He suggests at least three different aspects of the notion *speaker*: *animator* (the sounding box), *author* (the agent who scripts the lines), and *principal* (the party to whose position the words attest) (Goffman 1981:226). Levinson (1988) acknowledges Goffman's view of *speaker* as a complicated and multifaceted notion, but claims that "the attributions of the roles of speakers and sources are less likely to be interactional problems than those of non-producers – speakers, after all, are usually visibly, or at least audibly locatable as current transmitters." (Levinson 1988:199.) Even if we seldom have problems locating the current speaker in conversation, it can be questioned whether this is because the speakers are "visibly locatable". Naturally, all face-to-face conversations involve speakers who are visibly present, but they also often involve speakers who are non-present. In spite of these virtual speakers' non-presence, their voices are, in general, easily located and recognised, and their status as "current transmitters" unproblematic for the other participants.

Many scholars have been interested in categorising and describing the different cues used by a speaker to signal a switch to a virtual participant. There are for instance:

- verbs signalling a quote or a thought These are not only "say", "think", but for instance "go" and "come" (cf. Romaine & Lange 1991:230; Kotsinas 1994:41; Holsánová 1998a:109)
- discourse markers such as *well, oh* (Holt 1996:236) or (in Swedish) *så här, liksom, ba', typ* (Kotsinas 1994:91ff)
- grammatical markers such as change of pronomina, tense, mode (Holt 1996:220)
- change of voice quality, prosodic features, tempo or rhythmic features such as pausing (Myers 1999a:377; Holsánová 1998b:109)
- non-verbal cues and body language (Holsánová 1998b:109)
- change of language (Kotsinas 1994:68ff)

Even when none of these cues is present the context may make it clear that such a switch takes place.

A combination of the above criteria has been used to locate the sequences in which virtual participants are "speaking" that have been analysed in this paper. It was found that virtual participants could be plural, such as "scientists" or "modern women", or singular, such as "the man on the street" or "common sense". A virtual participant can be presented as a real person, as in "Paul Drew claims..." or as someone completely hypothetical or unknown, as in "one might say...". A virtual participant can also be the speaker him/herself speaking from another perspective, time or context ("if I were young today I would say:...."). Most of the time there was no explicit mention of who the virtual participants were, but nevertheless the combined cues made it obvious who was referred to.

All participants in conversation make communicative choices. For instance, they can choose to talk or be silent. If they talk, they can either talk for themselves or for someone else – as their spokesmen or messengers. But they can also use their own turn to present someone else's words or thoughts without accepting the role as spokesman or messenger. For instance, they might make it clear that the quoted person in fact never said or thought what was uttered – but merely could have done so, or even should have done so. A spokesman for someone is often regarded as speaking in her place and uttering the words she would have uttered. However, Tannen objects to the idea that one could be a "mere" animator (Tannen 1989:108) free from all responsibility. But the speaker must not only take some responsibility for what he/she allows the virtual participant to say. The speaker must also count on the fact that listeners try to interpret his/her reason for introducing a virtual participant into the conversation.

Introducing virtual participants is a resource that can be used to solve a number of different communicative tasks. Some of these tasks may be more typical of certain genres or activity types than others. For instance, there is an interesting difference in how virtual participants seem to be used in pure narrative contexts as compared to more argumentative ones. In narratives, the virtual participants are often introduced in order to increase dramatic intensity and the feeling of immediacy. In argumentative discourse, such as academic debates, virtual participants in the form of authoritative references are more often used to reinforce chosen opinions or to present a mental opponent whose opinions are to be questioned and undermined.

3. Many different voices

The sound of a person's voice identifies her. Tannen refers to the voice of a particular speaker as her "stylistic physiognomy" (1989:99), signalling the speaker's individuality, but also the speaker's ethnic or local background, class, gender, or age. A speaker's voice might also signal what activity she is involved in – reading a sermon, managing a circus or scolding a child.

The fact that a speaker's voice signals individuality means that we hear when a speaker is voicing someone else by mimicking a dialect, sociolect or using an idiosyncratic way of speaking. A change in voice might signal a change of speaker – from a real to a virtual one, for instance. So when a speaker changes 'voice' the purpose may be to quote someone, but it could also signal the speaker's own change of attitude or emotional state. From the speaker's change to a scientific, childish or scared voice, the listener infers that the speaker suddenly wants to be regarded as a professional, remembers her childhood or is frightened, respectively.

The use of the notion *voice* suggests a basic, physiological aspect of an individual's speech. *Voice* may also refer to a collective voice, for instance that of a group of people with the same ideology, interests or sub-culture. In a recent study of environmental discourse, it was found that active environmentalists used a style and a vocabulary borrowed from the natural sciences. In other words, they spoke in the scientific voice, in order to position themselves as reliable and trustworthy, with a certain authority (Harré et al. 1999: 85). This use of *voice* comes close to how the notion is used as a theoretical concept, referring to the speaker's frame of reference or to the perspective from which the speaker approaches the topic in question. For instance, Mishler (1984) uses this notion when juxtaposing a professional and a lay perspective, for example in the discussion of how the voice of medicine and the voice of life world are heard in a doctor-patient interview. Bahktin (1981) and Wertsch (1991) are examples of other scholars who use the concept of voice not only in its sense as an individual auditory signal, but as a concept referring to the fact that all speakers' mental functioning originates in communicative processes (Wertsch 1991:13). Ideas, attitudes, feelings are being voiced, thought and felt in a dynamic interchange.

Tannen claims that "the term 'reported speech' is grossly misleading in suggesting that one can speak another's words and have them remain primarily the other's words" (Tannen 1989:101). Her main point is that "casting ideas as dialogue rather than statements is a discourse strategy for framing information in a way that communicates effectively and creates involvement" (Tannen 1989:110). In their studies of reported speech in communication between teen-agers, the Swedish scholars Eriksson (1997), Kotsinas (1994) and Nordberg (1992) have all pointed out that in this particular context the main function seems to be to create involvement and drama.

But there are many other functions of reported speech or of virtual participants. Eriksson (1997) has shown that we need virtual participants as our allies and supporters. In an analysis of discussion between teenagers, he demonstrated how virtual participants are brought onto the floor not only to create involvement, but also as an effective means for the speakers to make their listeners see things their way.

Vincent & Perrin (1999) have analysed sequences taken from French sociolinguistic interviews. They focused on the non-narrative function of reported speech and found three main functions. Virtual participants are used to underline evaluative and emotive aspects of the speaker's claim, to support the point of the utterance/story and to strengthen an argument.

Holt (1996) claims that direct speech is a useful resource because it frees the speaker from having to rephrase or sum up what was said. It also gives the listener an opportunity to experience for herself what was said and thereby access the utterance in a seemingly objective way. Direct quotations are also used to subtly show the quoted person's attitude and to generate affiliation (Holt 1999).

To put weight behind our own words, we can let the voice of someone else, an expert for instance, be heard. If this virtual participant has enough authority, he can strengthen our own position or argument. But references are not only used as direct support; virtual participants can also be cast as opponents in order to provide a more indirect – and sophisticated – form of support. If we let virtual participants voice arguments against our own position, we are then given an opportunity to refute these counterclaims.

We also need virtual participants as shields to hide behind. Some topics are sensitive – or rather constructed as sensitive – and some opinions not proper to air in all contexts. This accounts for the communicative dilemma where speakers need to distance themselves from an utterance or opinion while at the same time bringing it up as a possible conversational topic. In a study of talk on ethnic identity, Holsánová (1998a and b) has demonstrated how speakers discursively deal with sensitive topics such as complaints about immigrants or expressing negative views on people of other nationalities.

She found that quotations not only "were used to help the speaker to dramatise, to illustrate a general phenomenon in an amusing way, to play roles and create scenes, to involve the interlocutors and to characterise the others and the self" (Holsánová 1998b:256), but also as a face-preserving strategy. It was less threatening for the speakers to express evaluations of other ethnic groups by presenting such evaluations as quotations; quotations make the quoted person appear to be the speaker, and thus the party responsible for the principal utterance. So, in the context that she studied, there were people who had strong opinions, but who let virtual participants express them.

Framing one's utterances by means of humour and irony, or with the help of quotes in another language are other strategies used for distancing oneself from what is said – strategies not uncommon among young speakers. Kotsinas (1994: 68–69) found many examples of quoting in English as a form of distancing strategy in Swedish teenagers' speech.

4. Demonstrating the opinion of others and managing not to present an opinion

The first example is taken from a discussion between members of the board of a large food chain company. The participants have been discussing whether it is easier for people in general to accept gene technology when it is used for medical purposes – such as producing cheese without lactose. They are not at all certain that this is the case. In an attempt at pinpointing – and evaluating – ordinary people's opinion, one of the board members, Ingvar, tells the others that he tries to picture a breakfast scene. This takes place in an ordinary family in which a son suffers from lactose intolerance. The italicised part of the turn shows where the virtual participant (probably a parent) is heard as "speaking".

Example 1.² (turn 134)

Ingvar: But I can sort of imagine the breakfast table in front of me and there sits a, the lactose-intolerant (giggle) son and then he sits there and eats his cheese but mum and dad eat another cheese because they don't want to eat this awful stuff of his (K: no) this XXX cheese or... no no but actually it on- it turns *in a way into* (J: laughter) so to say *you can eat this, we don't want to because it is *genetically modified*, we eat this KRAV cheese*³ *instead.*

In Example 1, the speaker is portraying a scene in which he is not involved. The speaker presents what is going on, and he does not interact with the parents, the virtual participants. The virtual participant's voice seems to be used in order to demonstrate a layman's fear of GMF and to dramatise, characterise and maybe also make fun of this fear.

Example 2 is taken from a discussion between executives in a wholesale company, selling vegetables and fruit to retailers in Sweden. One of the participants, Anders, is describing the discussion going on between market economists and environmentalists, exemplified by two different camps – the multinational company Monsanto and the organisation Greenpeace.

Example 2 (turn 160)

Anders: If you take this discussion in the beginning when Monsanto and their likes focussed on the good side then comes Greenpeace and takes the other EXTREME (B:mm) and says *but what happens then? Now you have sort of made...* corn I think it was then that is resistant to... no wait... SOYBEANS are resistant to Roundup... it is Monsanto's own product so they sell two products and it is unethical in itself or (D: mm) (B: *mm*) and then but then this soybean is related to some grass sorts some weed in fact, and how difficult is it for THEM to build a new family (B: mm) and then Greenpeace gets up and says *OK you are allowed to do this under the condition that you send all personnel to pick weeds when the shit hits the fan...* and it is so teasing from both sides that it gets really difficult to GRASP doesn't it, well it isn't a... reasonable discussion sort of...

Here Greenpeace and Monsanto are portrayed as two protagonists, claiming opposite views, but they are also used as a backdrop against which the speaker can position himself. He does not interfere in the virtual discussion, he does not address himself directly to either Monsanto or Greenpeace, but he reacts to his own presentation of what he lets Greenpeace say by returning to his own voice. So, when he has decided that it was soybean and

---

² The following conventions are used in the examples
, very short pause
XXX unhearable
* * laughter in voice
CAPITALS stressed word
... short pause
( ) within parentheses feedback from other participants or comments from the author
All names are pseudonyms.

³ KRAV denotes the Swedish standard for organically produced food products.

not corn that was resistant to Roundup, he then allows the two participants to carry out their hypothetical discussion.

Both these examples show that virtual participants are used to make the discussion livelier and create involvement. But they also show that presenting virtual participants is a communicative resource with more complex functions. For instance, it allows the speakers to talk without taking a firm stand on the issue, while at the same time helping to demonstrate the nature of the debate in general.

In Examples 1 and 2, the virtual participants were called in to create involvement and clarity in a dramatic narrative that was choreographed by the speaker, who stayed outside the drama and did not interact directly with the virtual participants. In the next two examples, the virtual participants seem to have a slightly different function. They do not solely illustrate a taken position, or add dramatic qualities to a narrative. Instead they are used to illustrate the ongoing process of forming an opinion and the actual participants are more closely collaborating with the virtual ones. In Example 3, three superintendents from local food stores – Daniel, Bo and Carl – are having a discussion.

Example 3 (turns 364–366)

Daniel: but if it is, if that is the purpose so to say, you have much broader visions when it involves that, haven't you, but if sort of if you can prepare the way for gene modification of man then, or if you show that you can in fact get d- good food and perfect stuff then sort of that *look here what fine things we can do, surely we should continue along this road*, I don't know
Bo: but where
Carl: if it is like that (Daniel: possibly) then you get *no thanks*

In the first turn of example 3, Daniel brings in a virtual participant that is the typical scientist. He is heard to say that technology is good. In the third turn, Carl brings in the hypothetical *ordinary person* who says "no thanks". The example also demonstrates how Daniel and Carl are doing collaborative work to present the dialogue between the two virtual participants.

In Example 4, we hear Alice who is a member of a group of environmentalists. While presenting a virtual participant – yet another *ordinary person* – who is discussing with him/herself, she gets into an argument with the virtual participant. She thus presents the group of environmentalists to which she herself belongs as a virtual participant. In this way she can argue about whether it is reasonable to have a certain point of view. She can also let the ordinary person question this view.

Example 4 (turn 219)

Alice: But if you don't know... a whole lot about biology and chemistry but you know enough to know that OK DNA that it sort of well *it sits in a spiral* and then you think, you understand *OK you take away one part and put in another and then maybe it affects the qualities and gets bigger, better and more beautiful or redder or whatever* but... I mean actually you arrive at a way of thinking that you, that we perhaps have learned, do you see what I mean, that we who are in this room maybe find *it is **self-evident** that you have to question, it is **self-evident** that we must have thirty more years of research, it is ethically wrong and all you cannot do what you want with nature* but... but I mean imagine if you if you know what I mean, imagine if you had said that about... all new things there are always those negative to new things for everything do you see what I mean (B and C, two other participant: Mm) it it anyway be careful, and then you can be classed as, well, hostile to progress and all that (DKG: mm) they can think *but this is only to frighten us, of course it isn't dangerous, we are already interfering with the body so much* (DKG: mm) *in other ways* (BMG: (giggle)) you see what I mean

The analyses of the discussions on GMF suggest that we need a chorus of voices from virtual participants to do justice to complex topics. Many topics in modern society are complicated, and it is not always an easy task to form a clear opinion on them. Yet, we are more often than not expected to present an opinion. Our analyses of the focus-group discussions with lay persons about genetic technology in connection with food production suggest that many of the participants in the discussions felt an obligation to present a clear opinion – to be for or against (Wibeck 1998, 1999).

But instead of presenting a clear opinion, the participants used the discussions as a step towards forming an opinion, towards arriving at certainty. Virtual participants were brought in to show the complexities and contradictions and to express the ongoing, rather chaotic discussion. One way to solve the communicative dilemma of having to talk about things with which you are not familiar is to stage a chorus of hypothetical voices. In this way, the speaker can play with different possible interpretations and, by collaborating with virtual participants, present a web of different views. The virtual participants also helped the real ones to collaboratively achieve avoidance of commitment.

References

Bahktin, Mikhail (1981): The Dialogic Imagination. – Austin: University of Texas Press.
Billig, Michael (1987): Arguing and Thinking. A rhetorical approach to social psychology. – Cambridge: Cambridge University Press.
Eriksson, Mats (1997): Ungdomars berättande. (Diss.) – Uppsala: Skrifter utgivna av institutionen för nordiska språk vid Uppsala universitet 43.

Goffman, Erving (1974): Frame Analysis. An essay on the organization of experience. – Boston: Northeastern University Press.
- (1981): Forms of Talk. –Philadelphia: University of Pennsylvania Press.
Harré, Rom/Brockmeier, Jens/Mühlhäusler, Peter (1999): Greenspeak. A study of environmental discourse. – Thousand Oaks: Sage.
Holsánová, Jana (1998a): Att byta röst och rädda ansiktet. Citatanvändning i samtal om 'de andra'. – *Språk & Stil* 8, 105–133.
- (1998b): The Use of Quotations in Discourse about Ethnicities. – In: S. Cmejrková et al. (eds.). Dialogue Analysis VI. Proceedings of the 6th Conference, Prague 1996, 253–260. Tübingen: Niemeyer.
Holt, Elizabeth (1996): Reporting on Talk: The use of direct reported speech in conversation. – *Research on Language and Social Interaction* 29 (3) 219–245.
- (1999): Just Gassing: An analysis of direct reported speech in a conversation between employees of a gas supply company. – *Text* 19 (4) 505–537.
Kotsinas, Ulla-Britt (1994): Ungdomsspråk. – *Ord och stil*, 25. Uppsala: Hallgren & Fallgren.
Levinson, Stephen (1988): Putting Linguistics on a Proper Footing. – In: P. Drew/A. Wootton (eds.) Erving Goffman: Exploring the interaction order, 161–227. Oxford: Polity Press.
Linell, Per,/Wibeck, Victoria/Adelswärd, Viveka/Bakshi, Ann-Sofie. (to appear) Arguing in Conversation as a Case of Distributed Cognition: Discussing biotechnology in focus groups. – In: E. Németh (ed.) Cognition in Language Use: Selected papers from the 7th International Pragmatics Conference, Vol. 1. Amsterdam: International Pragmatics Association, 2001.
Mishler, Elliot (1984): The Discourse of Medicine: Dialectics of medical interviews. – Norwood, N.J.:Ablex.
Myers, Greg (1999a): Functions of Reported Speech in Group Discussions. – *Applied Linguistics*, 20 (3), 376–401.
- (1999b): Unspoken Speech: Hypothetical reported discourse and the rhetoric of everyday talk. – *Text* 19 (4) 571–590.
Nordberg, Bengt (1992): Onomatopoetiska uttryck och ungdomars samtalsstil. – In: S. Strömquist (ed.). *Tal och samtal*, 150–176. Lund: Studentlitteratur.
Romaine, Suzanne/Lange, Deborah (1991): The Use of *like* as a Marker of Reported Speech and Thought: A case of grammaticalization in progress. – *American Speech*, 66 (3) 227–279.
Tannen, Deborah (1989): Talking Voices. Repetition, dialogue, and imagery in conversational discourse. – Cambridge: Cambridge University Press.
Vincent, Diane/Perrin, Laurent (1999): On the Narrative vs Non-narrative Functions of Reported Speech: A socio-pragmatic study. – *Journal of Sociolinguistics* 3, (3) 291–313.
Wertsch, James (1991): Voices of the Mind. – London, Sydney, Singapore: Harvester Wheatsheaf.
Wibeck, Victoria (1998): Föreställningar om genmodifierade livsmedel. – Arbetsrapport från tema K, 1998:3.
- (1999): Pressröster om genmodifierade livsmedel. – Arbetsrapport från tema K, 1999:5.

Appendix

Examples in Swedish

Example 1.
Ingvar: men jag ser ju liksom frukostbordet framför mig, där det sitter en den laktossjuke (X: Fniss) sonen och sen så sitter han och äter sin ost men morsan och farsan äter en annan ost för dom vill inte äta det här otäcka som han drar i sig (K: *nej*) så där XXX ost eller... nej nej men alltså det ba- det blir ju på *nåt sätt så blir det ju* (J: (skratt)) så att säga *du får äta den där den vill inte vi äta för den är *genmodifierad* vi äter den här krav-osten istället*

Example 2.
Anders: om man tar den här diskussionen som är då i början när Monsanto och kompani lyfte fram det fina då kommer liksom Greenpeace och tar den andra EXTREMEN (A: Mm) och säger ja men vad händer då? Nu har ni liksom gjort ... majs tror jag det var då va som är resistent mot... nej vänta... SOJAN är ju resistent mot Roundup, det är Monsantos egen produkt så man kränger två produkter och det är oetiskt i sig då va (D: Mm) (A: *Mhm*) och sen men då är den här sojan väldigt närbesläktad till nåt åkergräs va nåt ogräs dessutom, och hur svårt är det att DOM två bildar ny släkt (A: Mm) och då ställer sig Greenpeace upp och säger okej ni får väl göra det här under förutsättning att ni skickar ut all personal och rycker upp ogräs när det är kört (.) sen då va... och det blir ju så raljant åt bägge håll så att det blir inte liksom GREPPBART det blir inte blir inte liksom en... vettig diskussion liksom

Example 3.
Daniel: men om de e de som kanske e syftet så att säga, man har betydligt större visioner när de gäller de va men på nåt sätt kan man bereda vägen för för genmodifiering i mänskan då va om man visar på att man kan alltså få fram j-- bra livsmedel å perfekta grejer då liksom *att titta här vilka fina saker vi kan göra visst ska vi väl fortsätta på den här vägen*, ja vet inte
Bo: men var
Carl: e de så då (DMM: Möjligen) blir man ju nej tack

Example 4.
Alice: men om man inte kan... så JÄTTEMYCKE om biologi å kemi och man men man kan så pass mycke att man vet att okej DNA att typ *å de sitter i en spiral* och så tänker man så fattar man okej, *man tar bort en del så stoppar man in en del å sen så kanske påverkar egenskapen så blir de större bättre å vackrare eller rödare eller va de nu blir*, men... ja menar i å för sej man kommer fram till att de e ett visst tänkandesom man som vi har kanske LÄRT OSS, förstår ni va ja menar, som vi som sitter här i rummet kanske tycker att *de e **självklart** man måste ifrågasätta, de e **självklart** man måste ha tretti år till av forskning, de de e etiskt fel å de e man inte bara göra som man vill me naturen* men... men ja menar tänk om man så förstår ni va ja menar, tänk om man så hade sagt så om... alla ny de finns ju alltid negativa förespråkare för ALLTING, förstår ni va ja menar (B + D: mm) de de i alla fall va försiktig, å då kan man bli klassad som jaa fram fram utvecklingsfientlig å så där (D: mm) dom kan tycka *men de e bara skrämselpropaganda, de e klart att de inte e farligt, vi påverkar ju redan kroppen så mycke* (D: Mm) *andra sätt* (B: (fniss)) förstår ni va ja menar

Victoria Wibeck

Exploring Focus Groups: Analysing Focus Group Data about Genetically Modified Food

1. Introduction

A group of five people have gathered in a room to discuss an issue which is urgent but, none the less, difficult to grasp, namely gene technology in connection with food production. The participants discuss vividly for about an hour; present in the room is also a moderator who introduces the topic and, at times, relevant subtopics in the form of open-ended questions. The discussion is tape-recorded, transcribed and submitted to analysis by a group of researchers. This is an example of what is called focus group methodology.[1]

Focus group discussions constitute a method for collecting data that has recently increased in popularity among social scientists. In brief, the procedure means that a small group of participants (preferably four to six) gather to discuss a given issue under the guidance of a moderator, who preferably occupies a retracted position. Focus groups have been used as a method to study what peoples' views are and which attitudes they have to, for instance, family planning (Folch-Lyon *et al* 1981), HIV/AIDS (Kitzinger 1994), drug abuse (Agar & MacDonald 1995) and chronic/severe diseases (e.g. Bülow 1998; Grace 1995; Wilkinson 1998a). Focus groups are also popular in the study of social representations (Bauer & Gaskell 1999; Gervais & Jovchelovitch 1998), and as a means of exploring the co-construction of meaning in the social context that the focus group constitutes (Wilkinson 1998a).

One of the advantages of focus group methodology often emphasised by its proponents, is the possibility for the analyst to benefit from the interaction among the group members (e.g. Stewart & Shamdasani 1990; Morgan & Krueger 1993; Krueger 1998). Focus group researcher John Knodel states that "/t/he most challenging step of virtually all research is the analysis of information collected" (1993: 42). This is not least true of focus group research, which, according to Jenny Kitzinger and Rosaline Barbour (1999: 16), can "generate large amounts of very rich and dynamic data". Nevertheless, not until recently have there appeared discourse analyses of the actual focus group dynamics and argumentation

---

[1] For an introduction to the practical use of focus group methodology, see e.g. Morgan (1988), Krueger (1994), Morgan & Krueger (1998), Wibeck (2000).

(for some examples, see Frith & C. Kitzinger 1998; J. Kitzinger 1994; Agar & MacDonald 1995; Myers 1998, 1999a, 1999b, 2000; Myers & Macnaghten 1999; Wilkinson 1998a, 1998b, 1999). Probably due to the history of focus groups as primarily a tool in market research, most studies have traditionally focused on mere content.[2] Traditionally, two approaches towards analysis have been dominant: content analysis (that may or may not be quantitative) and ethnographic analysis, which relies on, among other things, direct quotation of the group members (Morgan 1988; Wilkinson 1998c). A shortcoming of much focus group research is the absence of analytical reasoning; the reader is informed of how the study was designed and what the results were, but very little is said about the actual procedure of analysis (for a similar critique, see e.g. Wilkinson 1998c:195; Myers & Macnaghten 1999:173).

The aim of this paper is to outline a few analytical approaches that have proved fruitful in my work on a dissertation on the discourse about genetically modified food in Sweden. I draw my examples from data collected in eleven focus groups: eight among lay people and three among decision-makers at big companies related to the food industry.[3] What distinguishes this study from many other focus group studies is the role of the moderator: I have assumed a retracted role, intervening as little as possible. This proved, with some exceptions, to be fruitful insofar as the participants themselves kept the discussion going and raised issues that were of relevance to them, rather than issues determined beforehand by the researcher when designing the study.

I advocate what may be labelled a 'dialogical content analysis' (cf. Linell 2001; Linell *et al* 2001), where the dialogicity of arguments and ideas are brought into the fore. In the analytical process the dialogue of participants in developing ideas is considered, as is the dialogue of ideas and topics in the conversation. In the following I will give examples of how a thematic analysis can be made; I then pass on to discuss the analysis of some communicative devices used as resources by the participants, and finally I comment on the analysis of agents and agency (which may be considered as forming part of a thematic analysis as well).

---

[2] For a capsule history of the use of focus groups, see Morgan (1998:37–43).
[3] The first set of data collection included the following groups: Christian students, dieticians, farmers, biology students, restaurant personnel, managers of grocery stores, recent mothers, and members of the Swedish branch of the Greenpeace organisation. The second one included three groups of stake-holders, namely decision-makers from three big companies related to the Swedish food industry (production, wholesale trade and retail trade). The research project is reported in Wibeck (2002), and was made possible due to grants from K-LIV (Kunskapsplattform för livsmedelsbranschen) and the ELSA-program (Ethical, Legal, Social Aspects of gene technology). Project leader is Professor Viveka Adelswärd and project worker is Victoria Wibeck. The analytical suggestions presented here have benefited from discussions with Professor Per Linell.

2. Analysis

I will now address a few notions that should be considered a partial report of analyses made, rather than a complete analytical framework. One of the problems of focus group methodology, namely the scarcity of descriptions of the analytical process, is – paradoxically – also one of the reasons why it is so exciting working with it: as an analyst, one is rather free to find one's own entries into the data. The analytical process, thus, is an explorative process where one can allow oneself to be rather eclectic in the choice of methods. The suggestions made in this paper about possible ways of approaching focus group data should, consequently, be regarded precisely as suggestions.

2.1 Thematic analysis

After having conducted the focus groups in a series, one returns to one's desk with a huge amount of data, often difficult to sort out and overview. In my case, the eleven focus groups so far collected, generated almost 400 transcribed pages. Thus, it goes without saying that even though one is interested in pursuing analyses of communicative strategies used in the groups, or the argumentative web that forms up the discussions, an initial coding and categorisation of the material cannot be dispensed with.

Inspiration for content analysis of focus group data may be taken from Glaser and Strauss (1967) in their work on grounded theory. What they especially argue for is "grounding theory in social research itself – for generating it from the data" (p. viii), i.e. the researcher should refrain from trying to force data into categories formulated *a priori*, on the basis of existing theory. Thus, the first step of a thematic analysis of focus group data is to read through the transcripts and divide them into segments based on criteria for topic shifts (for a discussion of topic shifts, see Adelswärd 1988:55 ff.). The result of this is a list of local subtopics,[4] each of which may be assigned a label, i.e. a noun or nominal phrase summarising the content of the sequence. The ultimate goal of a thematic analysis, however, is to discover what Sandra Jovchelovitch (1995) calls "big themes", that underlie the discussions and that are recurrent in different forms on different occasions throughout the entire material. Preferably, since focus group data is often very dynamic, a content analysis should also aim at capturing the interactivity in the sense making practices.

---

[4] Given that the issue-in-focus is the main topic throughout the entire discussion, these local sequences may be labelled *sub*topics.

I will briefly account for some reasonings that were identified as an outcome of the content analysis undertaken of the focus groups consisting of lay people.[5] Earlier research, based on questionnaires and individual interviews, has shown that one important feature of consumer resistance towards genetically modified food is moral concerns (Fjaestad *et al* 1998). Thus, in planning the study I had anticipated that issues of ethics would be prevalent also in the focus groups. One of the 'big themes' was, indeed, ethical considerations often discussed in terms of boundaries (e.g. between medicine/food; animals/plants), the supremacy of nature (should we interfere with it or let it run its course?), the responsibility for the technology (researchers or politicians?) and its consequences (decreased risk for world famine or more money for multi-national companies?). However, my analyses also showed that underlying and intertwined with such ethical issues was another theme of an ethical-epistemological character. The participants posed questions like the following: "Can we trust the information that we receive?", "Who is informing?" "What is my responsibility as a consumer to keep myself informed about the new technology?" Thus, the issue of genetically modified food was not only framed as an ethical issue in its own right (is it good or bad?) but was interpreted as part of overarching questions deeply concerned with human agency (how large is our field of action?), intimately connected with everyday epistemology (how can we know what we know?) and responsibility (how much work should I do to get access to knowledge?).

To sum up: a content analysis like the above helps giving an overview of the data; patterns and tendencies in the material may be discovered and a picture of what was said in the different groups emerges. Such an analysis may of course stand alone and be presented as the outcome of the entire study (which is common e.g. in market research), but it may also be a starting point for other types of analyses: new analytical entries may be discovered and the analyst is given a hint of what would be interesting to approach in a second phase. In my case, I realised that dimensions of special interest would be the use of analogies, distinctions and quotes, as well as how the participants perceived agency.

2.2 Analysing communicative strategies

2.2.1 Analogies and distinctions

Analogies were proposed, negotiated and sometimes accepted, at other times rejected. I interpret the use of analogies as having a double purpose: first, to describe, explain, comprehend and categorise an abstract notion – what social representation theorists call "an-

---

[5] The results are discussed in Wibeck (2002).

Exploring Focus Groups

choring", i.e. a process of making the unknown seem familiar by reducing new ideas to "ordinary categories and images, to set them in a familiar context" (Moscovici 1984:29) –, and second, to argue for or evaluate a certain view on GM food.

Example 1 is an example of the categorising function of analogies, where a group of wholesalers discuss how the scientific society presents GM food :

Example 1[6]

(TEMA K: GML 2 – FG 1)

194.	D	But but friends, we were down in was it was it in Paris at this congress, and where scientists performed and... where science sort of doesn't agree on what is dangerous and what is not dangerous (B: No) and where you get different... different images and I remember one of the... one of the scientists there who appeared and talked sort of about this... the cultivation where one could use le- less pesticides and sort of (A: Yeah) how how good it was to the *environment* (B: Yeah) and then you increase the production and then you could reduce the starvation and so on... I mean, the scientists are are not clear on
195.	A	As you know we had a referendum, the nuclear- (D: Yeah exactly) There were two... there were professors with the same education (D: Yeah sure, who come to different conclusions) but it was like black and white

In this example, gene technology is contextualized in the same frame as the debate about nuclear power; it is placed within a category of technologies characterised by scientific uncertainty, disagreement among experts and difficulty to predict the consequences of an implementation. Gene technology is also regarded as one of those issues where the societal debate looks the same: depicted in black and white, and simplified in spite of it actually being very complex. One way of trying to describe and make the complicated technology more intelligible is, consequently, to fit it into categories existing beforehand, and compare it to other technologies with which one is more familiar, in this case nuclear power.

The analogy with nuclear power is also used in several groups, not only to establish an overall category to which gene technology too can be seen as belonging, but also of constituting a background for argument.

Example 2

(TEMA K: GML 1 – FG 7)

| 16. | Daniel | Then it is sort of like I think nuclear power too, nobody questions what can I |

---

[6] The extracts are given verbatim. Normal orthography has been applied. Back-channelling utterances are noted in the ongoing turn. The following conventions have been used:
Underlining signals simultaneous speech.
= signals that the turns lash immediately into each other.
Italics signals that the word is emphasised.
The analyses were performed on tape-recordings and transcripts in Swedish, but the extracts have been translated into English for the purposes of this paper.

		say the product resulting from it, cheap energy, nobody has anything against that, right? (Bo: No) But I feel sort of the same resistance like this (Bo: Yeah) it it comes from within so to speak, there is one of those *emotions* related to it... Nuclear power and stuff well we don't really know, it is it is sure- it is clean and pure and it is good but it feels a little insecure and it's the same thing with this stuff, obtaining a better product and a cheaper product, but we <u>know</u> we kind of know too little about (Bo: No exactly) and it feels a little <u>strange</u>
17.	Bo	<u>Yeah but</u> isn't it that you you it's like you say you don't know if there is going to be any damage or if you sort of will feel sick (Daniel: Yeah) or something like that (Anna+Daniel: Yeah) because of it [...]

When analogies are made with nuclear power (which was, indeed, the second most used analogy in the lay groups), they are focusing on the uncertain character of the technology. The consequences are difficult to foresee, and the technology may be abused (associations are made to the atomic bomb). By choosing to compare gene technology with nuclear power or the atomic bomb, the speaker also expresses a stand-point, namely that the former is insecure too, and easily subject to abuse. In the example given, the resistance towards the new technology is claimed to be due to emotions ("it feels a little insecure"), as well as to epistemological concerns ("we *know* we kind of know too little [...]").

As in the case of analogies, I regard distinctions as serving at least two purposes, namely as a tool in a classifying process, defining what categories *not* to place the focus issue in, and as a form of argument that often implies that "/i/f Y is acceptable (or non-acceptable), since X [=the focus issue] is different from Y, X, by contrast, should not (or should) be accepted" (Linell 2001:177). Analogies and distinctions are not always separable from each other; my analyses show that they tend to come in analogy/distinction chains. An example of this – which can be found in my data – is when one participant suggests that gene technology is a natural extension of what has been possible to do by means of traditional breeding, and another participant challenges this analogy by introducing a distinction, namely that gene technology is something qualitatively new, not to be compared to traditional breeding. When choosing either an analogy or a distinction, the participant also makes a choice which standpoint to display before the technology. It turned out that those who argued in favour of genetically modified food often made analogies between this and traditional breeding, while distinctions were more common among those who argued against it.

2.2.2 Quotes

Since discussions recorded in focus group are often very vivid and animated, at their best instances reminding of informal conversations among friends, there are certain features of talk-in-interaction that are worth analysing. One of those is reported speech. Myers

(1999a:376) notes that "reported speech is not just a literary or narrative device, but a pervasive feature of everyday talk, one speakers can use to do complex work in the ongoing, turn by turn organization of interaction". In other words, in a group there are real participants and there are 'virtual participants' (cf. Adelswärd, this volume, and Adelswärd *et al* 2002), i.e. participants whose voices are heard throughout the discussions in the form of quotes.[7] Identifying and analysing the blending of voices in focus group discussions is useful "because people develop their own opinions only in relation to, and in response to, those of others" (Myers 1999b:588). Since Viveka Adelswärd addresses the issue of the use of quotes in the present focus groups, theoretically as well as empirically, I will confine myself to presenting a few research questions that may be of relevance for a study of quotes:

Which voices are used by the participants, in the form of quotes, to support their claims and arguments?

Are there recurrent voices?

Are some voices questioned and others not?

Are the voices presented as real or as hypothetical, i.e. do the participants quote sources they believe have actually said or written something, or do they relate what could or should have been said, thought or written in the past, or what might be said, thought or written in the future? This may form part of an analysis aiming at investigating whether there are authorities or experts that the participants lean on in their argumentation, or if such voices are absent. (For a discussion about 'hypothetical speech', see Myers 1999a and 1999b.)

How does the act of quoting affect the dynamics in the group – do the participants succeed in creating involvement by using quotes? According to Tannen (1989), this is often the case, not least as quotes often appear in connection with the use of narratives (Myers 1999b).

How do the participants position themselves through quotes, i.e. by switching voices, how do they illustrate the difference in the way of speaking between themselves and others, and how do they illustrate the difference in opinions? (For a discussion about the concept of 'positioning', see Harré & van Langenhove 1991; concerning positioning through the act of quotation, see Holsánová 1998, and Myers 1999a.)

Concerning group cohesion, do the participants at all present themselves as a group with certain characteristic features as opposed to other groups, or do they rather consider themselves as individuals only gathered to display their own opinions? Furthermore, if they present themselves as a group, is there consensus about the self-presentation or is it disp

---

[7] I use the notion 'quote' rather than 'reported speech', since when another's speech is reported, it will always undergo semantic changes, even if it is correctly transmitted (Bakhtin 1981). "Reported speech" should thus not be regarded as reported but as constructed by the speaker who speaks in another speaker's voice (Tannen 1989).

2.3 Actors and agency

Related to the issue of 'virtual participants' is the following: Which actors do the participants construct as being influential versus non-influential? How are power relations discussed? How do the group members conceive of their own space of action, or, in other words, what is their sense of agency?

'Agency' is a concept describing "the relationships of action, freedom to act and power to take action" (O'Connor 1995: 432). It is also linked to moral aspects of responsibility and to reflection upon our actions. Taylor (1985: 3) states that "to be a full human agent, to be a person or a self in the ordinary meaning, is to exist in a space defined by distinctions of worth", and further that "a reflection on the kind of beings we are takes us to the centre of our existence as agents" (*ibid.*: 26). An analysis of agency may well start with an inventory of the agents mentioned by the participants and how they are presented. When I discuss agents here, I assume that they are discursively constructed by the focus group participants, and that they are contextualised within the focus group.

With the inventory of agents in mind, the data may be approached from a slightly different angle, namely in order to address the issue of agency. How do the participants conceive of the frames for their own freedom to act, and which agents do they regard as possessing the possibility of exercising influence in a given issue? For my purposes, namely to analyse how the participants in the lay focus groups conceived of consumer agency, I have used Patricia O'Connor's continuum of agency (1995: 431). In her study of criminals' autobiographical narratives, she examined how agency may be linked to a continuum of responsibility, on the one hand deflecting agency (e.g. through the phrase "we ended up getting caught"), on the other hand claiming agency (e.g. "I shot him").

Example 3 is taken from a group consisting of dieticians, and it illustrates a line of reasoning I have interpreted as deflecting consumer agency.

Example 3
(TEMA K: GML 1 – FG 3)
199.	Doris	[...] You don't know about that (Gerda: No) how much the market forces govern. 'Cause I believe that the food prices still have have great importance (Gerda: Mm) if it tastes the same
202.	Gerda	Mm... Well I think about all this about Swedish meat and and imported meat and everything about that, it has been a huge debate there and of of course it
203.	Doris	Yes who created that de<u>bate</u>
204.	Gerda	<u>Well</u> that would be the media too (Doris: Mm) of cour<u>se</u>
205.	Doris	<u>And the meat industry</u>
206.	Carina	<u>I was just going to say the</u> meat indus<u>try</u>
207.	Gerda	<u>Well</u> yeah of course but it may not only be a... bad thing, we might have sort of... partly prevented something from entering, I mean much contamination and stuff. But sure, it is sure there are always stake-holders pushing and influencing the media

Exploring Focus Groups

The example illustrates how one of the groups whose participants mainly deflected consumer agency reasoned about issues of influence and power related to genetically modified food. In turn 199, Doris claims that the market forces govern the consumers, as these are inclined to buy what is cheapest. Gerda then partly disagrees, as she mentions the debate about whether one should buy Swedish or foreign meat (I interpret this as not being in line with Doris' argument, as Swedish meat is in most cases more expensive than foreign, yet people buy it). In her next turn (201), Doris, however, links up with what she said before by asking who created the debate about the meat. Gerda's answer is the media, which Doris objects to by adding "and the meat industry". Gerda recognises this as a powerful agent, but modifies Doris' argument by stating that the food industries influence the mass medial debate. The chain of influence jointly constructed and suggested by the dieticians can thus be summarised in the following terms: The market forces control the consumers, as these are inclined to buy what is cheapest. The food industry also influences the mass medial debate, which in its turn influences consumer behaviour and opinions. The consumers' space of action is thus conceived of as restricted by several other agents.

Without going any further into the analyses of agency performed on the basis of the different discussions, I will sum them up by suggesting that it seems as if, in all the lay focus groups, agency was located in an out-group, i.e. in a group, an institution or an abstract agent of which the discussants were not part themselves. Abstract agents like nature and the market forces were perceived as influential in several of the groups, while the prevailing image of consumer agency, with a few exceptions, was that it is limited or practically non-existent. Thus, deflecting consumer agency was far more common than claiming consumer agency. In the groups of decision-makers, it seems on the contrary as though the participants conceived of the consumer as a powerful agent, setting limits for policy making related to genetically modified food.[8] Consumer fear of GM food was said to be a very strong reason why it should not be sold, even though the decision-makers claimed not to believe that the food is dangerous to human health.

---

[8] Nevertheless, some of the participants recognised a mutual sense of agency, i.e. consumers limit the companies' space of action, but the companies were also said to make consumer resistance legitimate by removing GMO-products from their assortment.

3. Conclusion

The issue of genetically modified food is an urgent issue of societal relevance. It is therefore important to analyse how people actually discuss it. Further it is a great challenge to try to develop methods for the analysis of focus group data. Along with the analytical suggestions I have briefly presented here, I have performed analyses of the interaction of different arguments and subtopics. Examples of such analyses are studies of 'topical trajectories' (i.e. when certain subtopics give rise to other subtopics following what seems to be a recurrent pattern) and chains of analogies and distinctions (how certain analogies are disputed and followed by certain distinctions following relatively standardised links).

In sum, focus groups can generate very rich and interesting data, which are often well suited for analyses that focus on the dialogue of participants as well as on the exchange of ideas and arguments.

References

Adelswärd, Viveka (1988): Styles of Success. On impression management as collaborative action in job interviews. – Linköping: Linköping Studies in Arts and Science, 23.
Adelswärd, Viveka (in this volume): Virtual Participants as Communicative Resources in Discussions on Gene Technology.
Adelswärd, Viveka/Holsánová, Jana/Wibeck, Victoria (2002): Virtual Talk as a Communicative Resource. Explorations in the field of gene technology. – *Sprachtheorie und Germanistische Linguistik* 12:3–26.
Agar, Michael/MacDonald, James (1995): Focus Groups and Ethnography. – *Human Organization* 54, 78–86.
Bakhtin, Mikhail (1981): The Dialogic Imagination. – Austin: The University of Texas Press.
Bauer, Martin/Gaskell, George (1999): Towards a Paradigm for Research on Social Representations. – *Journal for the Theory of Social Behaviour* 29, 163–186.
Bülow, Pia (1998): Utbrändhet i fokus. Hur professionella i grupp samtalar om utbrändhet. [Focusing burn-out. How professionals talk about burn-out in groups.] – Linköping: The Department of Communication Studies (= Working paper 1998:1).
Fjaestad, Björn/Olsson, Susanna/ Olofsson, Anna/ von Bergmann-Winberg, Marie-Louise (1998): Sweden. – In: J. Durant/ M. Bauer/ G. Gaskell, (eds.): Biotechnology in the Public Sphere. A European sourcebook, 130–143. London: Science Museum.
Folch-Lyon, Evelyn/de la Macorra, Luis/Schearer/ S. Bruce (1981): Focus Group and Survey Research on Family Planning in Mexico. – *Studies in Family Planning* 12:409–432.
Frith, Hannah/Kitzinger, Celia (1998): 'Emotion Work' as a Participant Resource: A feminist analysis of young women's talk-in-interaction. – *Sociology* 32:299–320.
Gervais, Marie-Claude/Jovchelovitch, Sandra (1998): The Health Beliefs of the Chinese Community in England. A qualitative research study. – London: Health Education Authority.

Glaser, Barney/ Strauss, Anselm (1967): The Discovery of Grounded Theory: Strategies for qualitative research. – New York: Aldline Publishing Company.

Grace, Victoria (1995): Problems Women Patients Experience in the Medical Encounter for Chronic Pelvic Pain: A New Zealand study. – *Health Care for Women International* 16, 509–519.

Harré, Rom/van Langenhove, Luk (1991): Varieties of Positioning. – *Journal for the Theory of Social Behaviour* 21, 393–407.

Holsánová, Jana (1998): Att byta röst och rädda ansiktet. Citatanvändning i samtal om 'de andra'. [Changing voices and saving one's face. The use of quotation in conversation about 'the others'.] – *Språk & Stil* 8, 105–133.

Jovchelovitch, Sandra (1995): Social Representations in and of the Public Sphere: Towards a theoretical articulation. – *Journal for the Theory of Social Behaviour* 25, 81–102.

Kitzinger, Jenny (1994): The Methodology of Focus Groups: the importance of interaction between research participants. – *Sociology of Health and Illness* 16, 103–121.

Kitzinger, Jenny,/Barbour, Rosaline (1998): Introduction: The challenge and promise of focus groups. – In : R. Barbour/ J. Kitzinger (eds.): Developing Focus Group Research: Politics, theory and practice, 1–20. London: Sage.

Knodel, John (1993): The Design and Analysis of Focus Group Studies. – In: D. Morgan (ed.): Successful Focus Groups. Advancing the state of the art, 35–50. Newbury Park: Sage.

Krueger, Richard (1988; [2]1994): Focus Groups. A practical guide for applied research. – Thousand Oaks: Sage.

– (1998): Analyzing & Reporting Focus Group Results. Thousand Oaks: Sage (= The Focus Group Kit 6).

Linell, Per (2001): A Dialogical Conception of Focus Groups and Social Representations. – In: U. Sätterlund Larsson (ed.): Socio-Cultural Theory and Methods: An anthology, 163–206. University of Trollhättan/Uddevalla: Department of Nursing.

Linell, Per/Wibeck, Victoria/Adelswärd, Viveka/Bakshi, Ann-Sofie (2001): Arguing in Conversation as a Case of Distributed Cognition: Discussing biotechnology in focus groups. – In: E. Németh (ed.): Cognition in Language Use: Selected papers from the 7th International Pragmatics Conference. Vol. I, 243–256. Amsterdam: International Pragmatics Association.

Morgan, David (1988): Focus Groups as Qualitative Research. – Newbury Park: Sage.

Morgan, David (1998): The Focus Group Guidebook. Thousand Oaks: Sage (= The Focus Group Kit 1).

Morgan, David/Krueger, Richard (1993): When to Use Focus Groups and Why. – In: D. Morgan (ed.): Successful Focus Groups. Advancing the state of the art, 3–19. Newbury Park: Sage.

– (1998), The Focus Group Kit 1–6. – Thousand Oaks: Sage.

Moscovici, Serge (1984): The Phenomenon of Social Representations. – In: R. Farr/S. Moscovici (eds.): Social Representations, 3–70. Cambridge: Cambridge University Press,.

Myers, Greg (1998): Displaying Opinions: Topics and disagreement in focus groups. – *Language in Society* 27, 85–111.

– (1999a): Functions of Reported Speech in Group Discussions. – *Applied Linguistics* 20:376–401.

– (1999b), Unspoken Speech: Hypothetical reported discourse and the rhetoric of everyday talk. – *Text* 19, 571–594.

– (2000), Becoming a Group: Face and sociability in moderated discussions. – In: S. Sarangi, M. Coulthard (eds.): Discourse and Social Life, 121–137. Harlow: Longman.

Myers, Greg & Macnaghten, Phil (1999): Can Focus Groups be Analysed as Talk?. In : R. Barbour, J. Kitzinger (eds.): Developing Focus Group Research: Politics, theory and practice, 173–185. London: Sage.

O'Connor, Patricia (1995): Speaking of Crime: 'I don't know what made me do it'. – *Discourse & Society* 6, 429–456.

Stewart, David, Shamdasani, Prem (1990): Focus Groups. Theory and practice. – Newbury Park: Sage.
Tannen, Deborah (1989): Talking Voices. Repetition, dialogue, and imagery in conversational discourse. – Cambridge: Cambridge University Press.
Taylor, Charles (1985): Human Agency and Language. Philosophical papers 1. – Cambridge: Cambridge University Press.
Wibeck, Victoria (2000): Fokusgrupper. Om fokuserade gruppintervjuer som undersökningsmetod. [Focus groups. On the use of focused group interviews as a research method.] – Lund: Studentlitteratur.
Wibeck, Victoria (2002): Genmat i fokus. Analyser av fokusgruppssamtal om genförändrade livsmedel. [Genetically Modified Food in Focus. Analyses of focus group discussions.] – Linköping: Linköping Studies in Arts and Science, 260.
Wilkinson, Sue (1998a): Focus Groups in Health Research: Exploring the meanings of health and illness – *Journal of Health Psychology* 3, 329–348.
– (1998b): Focus Groups in Feminist Research: Power, interaction and the co-construction of meaning. – *Women's Studies International Forum*, 21, 111–125.
– (1998c): Focus Group Methodology: A review. – *International Journal of Social Research Methodology* 1, 181–203.
– (1999): Focus Groups. A feminist method. – *Psychology of Women Quarterly* 23, 221–244.

Chapter 7
Dialogue Analysis and Corpora

Edda Weigand

Possibilities and Limitations of Corpus Linguistics

1. Introduction

At a conference on new trends in dialogue analysis, we should pay special attention to a trend which can now be considered mainstream linguistics as claimed, for instance, by Jenny Thomas, Mick Short and Jan Svartvik in their contributions in honour of Geoffrey Leech: 'Corpus linguistics has now become mainstream' (Thomas/Short 1996). The history of modern linguistics can be seen as the history of different notions of language, to mention only a few: language as a sign system, language-in-use, language as social interaction, language as dialogue, and language in a corpus or even language-as-corpus. It was indeed a striking turning point when we first problematized introspection by native speakers as a means of justifying our findings. Simulating examples became obsolete, the efforts to compile large machine-readable corpora by which to verify presumed conventions increased. Unexpectedly, however, we are again confronted with serious problems, for example, in dealing with functional concepts such as politeness or with difficult action games such as negotiations where the real purposes remain concealed. How are we to find authentic examples in a corpus for these cases? *Can we trust the text?* (Sinclair 1994) Does the text contained in the corpus tell us the whole truth? That is the question.

Looking at analyses based on corpus linguistics, we find examples such as the following from the London-Lund Corpus analysed in detail by Clark (1996: 221ff.):

(1)   Roger   now, – um do you and your husband have a j-car
            Nina   – have a car?
            Roger   yeah
            Nina   no –

Naturally, with examples like this one there is no problem. At least if you do not doubt the interlocutors' sincerity, you can trust the text. The expressions used are all verbal expressions. The meanings they carry are contained in the expressions, at least, we suppose so. Not all action games, however, are as simple as this example. The question arises: Can the corpus be our object-of-study, can we identify language-in-use, language as dialogue with the corpus? The corpus consists of empirically registrable means of communication only. Naturally, we may restrict language to empirical means of communication. We may give empirical means priority and consider other parts of linguistic behaviour as 'subliminal' (Sinclair 1994: 25). However, are we thus not again restricting ourselves to an artificial notion of language, whereas real, natural language-in-use happens elsewhere? The question therefore can be put more precisely: *Can the corpus be our object-of-study or is it only part of it?*

On the other hand, corpus linguistics has developed its own methodology: the indispensable methodology of not trusting intuition by native speakers but of *using the corpus as a tool* for checking intuition by frequency. I am going to deal with the question of what the corpus is and of what we can do with it and will thus demonstrate some of the limitations and possibilities of Corpus Linguistics.

2. The corpus as linguistic object-of-study

2.1 Can we trust the text?

According to Sinclair (1994), the text tells us all we need to know in order to understand it. Even the elusive problem of coherence is resolved in the text if we follow Sinclair and consider coherence as encapsulated in the text. Concerning this issue, I agree with Stati's position (in this volume) 'that a text can never be completely explicit', that even semantic and not only pragmatic information is often implicit, that in the end language is not the empirical means of communication or the verbal text only but dialogue.

It is, moreover, not difficult to find authentic examples which clearly contradict Sinclair's hypothesis that coherence is encapsulated in the text: in order to understand what is going on in language use, we have to participate in the action game and to analyse it *from inside*, addressing the complex directly and not reducing it to the empirical level of the text (Weigand 2002b). Western thinking is characterised by the traditional method of reduction even in pragmatics. For instance, systemic linguistics and functional grammar (e.g. Halliday 1994) reduce the complex and start from a grammar of expressions. These approaches admit to being 'in the dark' and try to overcome this feeling by '*looking outwards* from specific instances of linguistic choices to the socio-cultural factors' (Thompson 1996: 224). It is fashionable to deal with the problems that arise by categorizing the concepts as 'fuzzy' (e.g., Thompson 1996: 224, Hunston/Francis 2000: 260). Karin Aijmer (1996: 5), for instance, thus problematizes 'textual categories' as 'fuzzy' and proceeds in the same way as systemic linguists hoping that they will be better described by additional categories regarding the social situation, the setting, the topics, etc.

It is however the starting point which needs to be changed. The starting point has to be the minimal unit in which the components, among them the text and its verbal expressions, function. It is already a complex cultural unit, the unit of the action game, which is the minimal communicatively autonomous unit (Weigand 2000a). The key to opening up the complex in my opinion is to be found in the fact that human beings are purposeful beings. They have communicative, ie dialogic purposes, which they try to fulfil by communicative, not only verbal means.

I am going to give you an interesting authentic example, first, without any description of the factors around the text, ie trusting the text:

(2) H   Lassen Sie sich nicht anstecken!
     E   Sind Sie krank?
     H   Haben Sie nicht das Wasser gesehen? Jeder hat sein Hobby.
     F   Das würde ich nie machen, wo wir soviel bezahlen allein fürs Putzen.
     E   Ah, jetzt verstehe ich. Sie haben recht. Nein, da lasse ich mich nicht anstecken!

(in English translation)

     H   Don't let yourself get infected!
     E   Are you ill?
     H   Didn't you see the water? Everyone's got a hobby.
     F   I'd never do that when we pay so much just for the cleaning.
     E   Ah, now I understand. You're right. No, I won't let myself get infected!

I am quite sure that you will not understand what is going on in this action game. You may try to find some thread running through the text and arrive at an approximate partial understanding by guessing. But are we guessing in language action? On the contrary, we do not need to guess because as human beings we not only use our ability to speak but inevitably other integrative abilities, namely to perceive and to think.

Consequently, language action is not action by speaking but communicative dialogic action by the use of communicative means, ie integrated verbal, perceptual and cognitive means. In the action game we approach each other as individuals with different cognitive backgrounds and therefore cannot presuppose understanding. We negotiate meaning and understanding and have to tackle problems of understanding. In our example, the first utterance, *Don't let yourself get infected!* is not immediately understood by the interlocutor, instead he/she is the victim of a misunderstanding. Language-in-use can accept the risk of misunderstandings because they are normally immediately repaired, as in our example.

It thus becomes evident that we have to go beyond the empirical level of the text and have to add a description of the cognitive and perceptual background from which the interlocutors derive their cognitive and perceptual means of communication. Clearly, they do not trust the verbal text only but *trust cognitive means, associations and allusions* which an observer cannot understand. Thus in our example H refers to a person not present in the action game without explicitly expressing it, a person who, some days ago, had spilled water on the ground when cleaning the roof of the house entrance: *Didn't you see the water?* The action game takes place near the entrance of the house. It is therefore enough for H to raise his head and to look and move his body in the direction of the entrance hall thus alluding by perceptual means to what had happened a few days ago, and ironically commenting on it *Everyone's got a hobby*. He deliberately only uses the anonymous term *everyone* and takes it for granted that the interlocutor will understand. His wife F, too, uses a phrase whose reference is not clear: *I'd never do that* trusting that E will understand because they are supposed to share knowledge as a result of the fact that all three live in the same house. She adds a critical comment on the price they have to pay for the cleaning of the hallway. All these means together, verbal, perceptual and cognitive ones, are necessary for E to come to an understanding and to arrive via negotiation at the right meaning of *to be infected*, namely 'to be infected by a mania for cleaning'. There is no explicit disambiguation by the verbal environment.

I think the conclusions to be drawn from this example are evident: when looking for authentic examples in a corpus we address the corpus as observers and can only understand examples which are mainly based on verbal means like example (1). Language use however consists of a series of different action games, more simple ones and those which integrate different human abilities and thus transcend the verbal level. Dialogic interaction is based on this complex human ability (Weigand 2002c). Coherence is not established in the text but in the minds of the interlocutors who try to understand and to make sense of what is going on in the action game (Weigand 2000b, Givón 1993). Linguistics as a science of language only is not capable of addressing language action. Trusting the text does not lead to an understanding of the interaction. The corpus therefore constitutes *only a part of the complex object* we are trying to investigate. Against Stubbs (1996: 233) we can argue that the corpus is not a record of our behaviour because only part of the behaviour is recorded.

Let us consider other examples relevant to the question of what we can gain by analysing examples from a corpus. For instance, if we wanted to investigate politeness in directive speech acts, how should we proceed? The best way would naturally be to find authentic examples for every directive subtype in the corpus such as requests and orders. Going through the corpus as an observer it is however extremely difficult to identify directive utterances if we take into account that polite directive speech acts are often expressed in a form which has no explicit verbal indicator of the directive function. Moreover, the corpus will not tell us what the functional concept of *politeness* is about. We therefore have to find another more practicable method, for instance, by asking some native speakers how they would express a specific directive claim in a precisely described situation. We may combine both methods using authentic examples as far as we can find them, together with simulated examples, as is also proposed by Aijmer (1996: 5).

Another problematic example is dialogues of negotiation in the sense of bargaining. It is extremely difficult to identify a game of negotiation in the corpus. The texts of the corpus are not classified according to functions, and information about the setting or social roles is not enough. Let us assume that you find by chance a text which looks like negotiation. It will however be very difficult if not impossible for us as observers to uncover the cognitive strategies of the parties since the real goals of the interlocutors remain concealed. In the end, only the speaker knows what he/she had in mind. Cognition as an essential integrated part of dialogue is often not verbally expressed.

Understanding a text means bringing in many aspects beyond empirical ones. *The text alone is a deficient object.* It cannot reveal itself to us. We have to take the text as a component, the *verbal component* in the action game. It is the interlocutors, individual human beings, who are our primary reference point. Action is not an independent object. We therefore need a model which describes the complex human ability of interaction in the cultural unit of the Dialogic Action Game (Weigand 2000a). The methodology of pattern transference has to be replaced by the methodology of negotiation (Weigand/Dascal 2001). There is not only one defined way of meaning and understanding a text, not only one rule-governed pattern underlying the text which is transferred from the sender to the receiver. On the contrary, meaning and understanding are in principle different for different interlocutors and are negotiated in the action game on the basis of principles of probability. Human beings try, consciously or without being aware of it, to realize their goals effectively. Grammar and rhetoric, therefore, can no longer be separated. We have to acknowledge the necessity of changing rooted convictions by replacing a closed rule-governed model of verbal means by an open system of principles used by human beings in order to address the complex.

The assumption that human beings use verbal, perceptual and cognitive means integratively also implies a change in the notion of text. Written texts are not restricted to verbal means only as can be clearly seen, for instance, in texts of Corporate Advertising (Schnöring 2000):

(3)

Texts of this type are not based on verbal means only but integrally include the graphic means of the picture and thus create pictures in our mind. Meaning thus becomes persuasion. If you omit the picture, most of the persuasive power is lost. The written text is therefore to be defined in a broad sense as an empirical object using verbal and graphic or pictorial means but still being only a component in the action game. It is individual human beings who produce and understand these texts on the basis of specific cultural knowledge.

2.2   Can we trust the words?

Having accepted the view that the object of linguistics in the end is a complex human ability which cannot be arrived at by addressing the corpus, we will now go one step below the text level and pick out verbal parts, words, and ask whether the corpus can tell us the truth about words.

First and foremost, the corpus does not contain the analysis. Sinclair's attempt (1996) to find an algorithm for automatic translation in the text again starts from the presumption that the meaning of words is contained in the text and can be detected by a formally applicable method. For him (1991: 7) and his scholars (Hunston/Francis 2000: 255), 'there is ultimately no distinction between form and meaning'. Thus meaning becomes formally retrievable (Sinclair 1996, 1998). On the one hand, Sinclair emphasizes that item and environment ultimately cannot be separated (Sinclair 1994: 22f.), that it is the complex multi-word unit which constitutes the lexical item (1998). On the other hand, he tries to develop an algorithm which starts from single words being disambiguated by the context. It is however not the word in the context but the whole complex phrase which functions as lexical unit. *Translation is not a case of translating words by contextual disambiguation* but a case of knowing the subtle networks in which words are combined to form phrases and utterances. If we look for an algorithm we arrive at a point where we have to admit like Teubert (1996: 255): 'Something must be wrong, however' and where we necessarily come to the conclusion: 'It may well be that we will have to recognize that there are neither obvious regularities nor applicable rules.'

Even with regard to verbal means, words and phrases, we cannot trust the text, we have to find the analysis by means of hypotheses about the whole of language use in which words play their part and by using our native competence. It is the minimal functional whole, the action game, which tells us the truth about the parts. Strictly speaking, we do not do things with single words. We act by means of dialogically orientated utterances. Words have a predicating function in the utterance (Weigand 1993). Utterances however are not built up by single words inserted in syntactic structures nor by patterns whose boundaries cannot be indicated. Utterances are built up by phrases which can be syntactically defined by means of fundamental concepts such as predicate and argument (Weigand 2002a).

Let us take an example from Sinclair's corpus based multilingual analysis of a series of expressions according to the algorithm of translating the word by classifying the context (1996). In this way he arrives at the result that the pattern *know* + NP corresponds to *kennen* in German and *conoscere* in Italian whereas the pattern *know* + reported clause or *it* corresponds to *wissen* and *sapere*. This however cannot be the whole truth. Experimenting a bit with our native competence, we will easily find phrases like:

(4)   Wenn du die Einzelheiten wissen willst, mußt du Hans fragen.
      Wenn du die Wahrheit wissen willst, mußt du selbst hinfahren.

which are not equivalent to phrases with *kennen*. It even sounds strange to use *kennen* in these phrases.

Moreover, the phrase

(5.1) Du kennst keinen Maßstab.

is conventionally expressed in Italian and French by

(5.2) Non hai il senso della misura.
       Tu n'a pas le sens de la mesure.

which is not taken into account by Sinclair's algorithm. I admit that the examples (4) and (5) are simulated by native competence. They might be checked by representative corpora but, in any case, they have to be taken into consideration.

I have to emphasize that Sinclair's intention is to develop an algorithm for translation by computer. Simultaneously however he seems to be of the opinion that automatic translation can be more and more improved and will one day achieve the level of natural language use. Such a hope resembles the hope by dialogue grammarians that they will be able to arrive at authentic texts by continuously making the rules of communicative competence more precise. We have to recognize that competence which is considered to be rule-governed and performance in the action game are two different objects. Communicative competence restricted to rules is a construct. In dialogue we are acting on the basis of competence-in-performance (Weigand 2001).

Sinclair is aware of these problems and tries to resolve them by restricting the translation rules to being 'generally valid'. An algorithm however does not permit such a restriction. How should the computer deal with it? Is it supposed to learn from the errors it will inevitably make? But who should discover the errors if not the native speaker? *Generally valid* marks the crux of the approach.

Teubert (1996: 256) tries to solve the problem by introducing further features or subtypes for classifying the context. The problem however is not a problem of increasing precision, as already mentioned; it is a problem in principle as we have seen with *to be infected* in example (2). Words can cognitively be disambiguated by the interlocutors without any further verbal context. You will never arrive at natural language use via an algorithm.

Possibilities and Limitations of Corpus Linguistics 309

(3')

In some cases, translation reaches its limits because of the complex network of integrated means. Considering the German version of the advertising text (3) one might wonder whether it is a translation. It is a new creation with the same meaning but created by different verbal phrases. In contrast to the English text, metaphorical meaning comes into play. The German *dornig* is used because it finds its literal basis in the picture. In the end translation depends on the individual decision by translators who have to find their way through the complex mix of verbal means and pictures embedded in culturally different cognitive frameworks.

Not only the meaning of the utterance but also the meaning of words depends on the speaker. Words do not have a definite value. Serious misunderstandings can be caused by individual differences which are usually ignored in linguistic analyses. To give an authentic example (Weigand 2002b):

(6) Y   Come ti sei decisa?
     Z   Se non c'è più violenza, lo farò.
     Y   Cosa vuoi dire? Questo lo puoi sempre dire. Significa di no!

(in English translation)

     Y   How have you decided?
     Z   If there is no more violence, I'll do it.
     Y   What does that mean? You can always say that. That means no!

Again what is meant is not explicitly said. The dynamics of this authentic action game result from the word *violence* which for both interlocutors means something quite different. What Z calls 'violence' might be called 'rough behaviour' by Y. Meaning is not an inherent feature of words (cf. Moore/Carling 1982: 211, Coulthard 1994: 9), or as Wittgenstein puts it: 'Words have meaning only in the stream of life', and life is different for everybody.

There is another interesting problem I would like to mention. When communicating in a foreign language you may become aware that certain words have contradictory meanings, even when they occur in the same context. Speaking Italian as a foreign language, it is, for instance, sometimes very difficult to understand what *richiamo* means. *Richiamo* can mean many different things in the same verbal context, at least for a foreigner, for instance, 'to call sb back', 'to blame sb',' to tempt sb'. Other examples are *ribattere che*: when does it mean 'auf etwas bestehen', when 'etwas zurückweisen'? or *avvertire*: when does it mean 'jemanden benachrichtigen', when 'jemanden mahnen', when 'jemanden warnen'? to mention only a few examples. There is no algorithm which can tell you the meaning or help you to translate the expression. It is the subtle network of phrases embedded in a broad context and particular differences which make language use what it is.

Moreover, you have to know whole utterances and the way they are used in specific situations. For instance, you cannot translate the German

(7.1)   Wie schmeckt es dir?
        Wie schmeckt dir der Fisch?

literally but have to know the Italian conventional utterances which are not compiled in a grammar nor in a dictionary:

(7.2)   Ti piace?
        Ti piace il pesce?

(8)   Abbassa il volume!
        Mach leiser!

The conclusion to be drawn is clear: we need both: the corpus and the native speaker.

3. The corpus as a tool

To sum up, first, we cannot trust the corpus as object if we consider our object to be social interaction or natural language use. Second, the corpus will not tell us the meaning of words. You may discover regularities in the sequencing of items, you may call them patterns but what the patterns mean, their function in language use, how they are to be segmented, remains in the dark. There is no empirical evidence as such.

Let us now address the question of the corpus as a tool. The major reason why the corpus as a tool has found acceptance is the fact that introspection by the native speaker has become problematized. There are innumerable examples where you get different answers from different native speakers. That is the point where we as native speakers ask ourselves: 'Is this usage still possible?, Can we express it in this way?', where we are not sure whether a phrase is to be considered a conventional phrase, where we say: 'yes, you may say it but it sounds strange, it is not usual'. Here the corpus as a tool gives us the possibility to check varying opinions of native speakers. Possible conventions can be verified by frequency counts in a representative corpus. Example (4) or (9), respectively, is such a case:

(9.1)   Wenn du die Einzelheiten wissen willst, mußt du Hans fragen.
         Wenn du die Wahrheit wissen willst, mußt du selbst hinfahren.

(9.2)   *Wenn du die Einzelheiten kennen willst, mußt du Hans fragen.
         *Wenn du die Wahrheit kennen willst, mußt du selbst hinfahren.

(9.3)   Er kennt die Einzelheiten.   ?Er weiß die Einzelheiten.
         Er kennt die Wahrheit.   Er weiß die Wahrheit.

As a German native speaker I am not quite sure whether the examples indicated by * or question mark are conventional phrases. If we accept them, they seem to have a different meaning from the corresponding phrases. On the one hand, it becomes evident that we need a corpus to check our native speaker competence. On the other hand however it becomes evident too that the corpus linguistic analysis as used in Sinclair's project (1996) for the translation of *know* does not reflect natural language use. It is based on inadequate methodological premises such as the following:

- Words having a definite value can be translated word by word if the context is classified. Translation thus becomes a kind of contextual disambiguation.

- Recurring environmental patterns are associated with specific meanings.

I will give another example which demonstrates the uncertainty of native intuition and the need to verify it by a corpus. In my opinion, it is an interesting example insofar as it additionally shows that monolingual analysis is not yet sufficient even if it is supported by a corpus. Often pecularities of a language become evident only by language comparison. The example belongs to the area of degree adjectives (Weigand 1996). In German you can use *groß* and *tief* with certain nouns to intensify the feeling, e.g.

(10) mit großem Erstaunen, mit tiefem Erstaunen
mit großem Ernst, mit tiefem Ernst
zur großen Überraschung, *zur tiefen Überraschung

In English you have, according to native speakers,

(11) with great astonishment, *with deep astonishment
with high seriousness, with no great seriousness, ?with great seriousness, *with deep seriousness
with great surprise, *with deep surprise

If we consider multiword expressions as lexical units, *tief* corresponds to *high* and is synonymous in these phrases. Even if the Collins Cobuild Dictionary (Sinclair et al. 1987) is compiled on the basis of a representative corpus, it is of little help in dealing with these subtle but important differences which will be discovered only by language comparison.

Frequency checked by corpus linguistics is a valuable criterion in another respect, too, as Karin Aijmer (1996: 4) has emphasized. The corpus as a tool can help us to describe text types by indicating the frequency of specific verbal means in specific types, for instance, oral versus written texts (cf. Biber 1988). The issue however of what constitutes a text type has to be settled elsewhere.

Using the corpus as a tool we should be clear about the crucial question of what can be verified at all. The frequency of a phenomenon can be verified, nothing else. The conclusions to be drawn depend on the kind of phenomenon checked in this way. Hudson (1994), for instance, discovered that in corpora of written English texts of various genres 'about 37 per cent of word-tokens are nouns'. The question was directed at the frequency of nouns, and that is the answer. For Hudson the data 'cry out for an explanation' (p. 331) which however cannot be found. He has to admit (p. 337) that Biber's analysis of spoken English (1988) 'unfortunately' uses nominal categories which 'are hard to align with' his own. On the other hand: what explanation should there be? One might think of conclusions concerning the style of the text; but that is a further question to be elaborated elsewhere.

Beside formal exercises of this type, there is the important phenomenon of the pattern in the Cobuild Grammar Pattern Series (e.g. Francis/Hunston/Manning 1996, 1998). It is a characteristic feature of the pattern that it cannot be clearly separated nor defined. Insofar as in the pattern approach 'the traditional distinction between lexis and grammar is blurred', 'a description of a word and its patterns cannot be classified under the heading either of 'lexis' or of 'grammar'' (Hunston/Francis 2000: 250). Pattern therefore simply means some sort of recurring sequencing structure. In this case, checking the frequency of a pattern, in my opinion, does not add essential further insight beyond the vague hope expressed by Hunston and Francis that large amounts of data 'can inspire new theories' (also Stubbs 1996: 232).

Next there are phenomena like the algorithm for word translation in Sinclair's project (1996) which are phenomena dependent on methodology, i.e. artificial phenomena. Alleged rules of the algorithm may be checked with regard to their frequency in a corpus. The corpus in this case can verify the frequency of a methodological phenomenon not its adequacy for natural language use. There remain the disturbing cases which are simply ignored.

If however the phenomenon to be checked by frequency refers to natural language use, for instance, specific collocations, the frequency in the corpus can verify the conventionality of these phrases. How this phenomenon of multi-word units is to be described, however, is not yet clarified by frequency alone.

4. Conclusions

Let me try to summarize the essential points. When asking for our object of study we have to decide what we want to describe and explain. *If we aim at the whole*, at natural language use or social interaction, our object is the whole complex not only the corpus. We have to address the complex directly by first trying to understand the object which is not accessible by formal means only. The complex is more than can be gained from patterns. Second, an adequate methodology has to be derived from the object. The model – comprising premises about the object and the derived methodology – is to be verified by authentic examples. These examples are in general to be derived from inside the action game; only simple cases may be retrieved from a corpus by addressing the corpus as an observer.

On the other hand, *we can be content with a more simple, reduced object* belonging to the verbal level and governed by an algorithm. The description goes as far as the algorithm allows, remaining within the *limits of automatic language production and translation*.

Despite the critical points I mentioned, I do not want to close without emphasising the high value of *corpora as a tool* for linguistic analyses. We cannot do without them. Language use is far more complex than we imagined years ago and can only insufficiently be grasped by simulating examples. The only way of verifying conventions of language use is by checking frequency in a representative corpus. We can thus find out how words are actually used and can overcome contradicting views of individual native speakers. Future dictionaries have to be based on corpora. Sinclair has given us a first illuminating example with his Cobuild Collins Dictionary (Sinclair et al. 1987). We have to proceed in this way and tackle the problem of multilingual dictionaries on the basis of large corpora.

Corpora as a tool are embedded in our attempt to understand the object which for me is human dialogic interaction. We must not forget that there is no absolute truth to be discovered empirically, only human beings claiming truth for certain states of affairs. Human cognition is not to be transcended. In order to understand what is going on in the action game, we should first try to understand our complex object. There is no natural language as a separate empirical object. The methodology follows from the criteria derived from the object. Within the spectrum of different notions of language I would therefore like to make a plea not for language as contained in a corpus but for language as an integrated part of a complex human ability. Linguistics in this regard is to be considered as some sort of human linguistics describing and explaining human dialogic interaction (Weigand 2003).

References

Aijmer, Karin (1996): Conversational Routines in English. Convention and Creativity. – London, New York: Longman (= Studies in Language and Linguistics).
Biber, Douglas (1988): Variation across Speech and Writing. – Cambridge: CUP.
Clark, Herbert H. (1996): Using Language. – Cambridge: CUP.
Coulthard, Malcolm (1994): On Analysing and Evaluating Written Text. – In: M. Coulthard (ed.): Advances in Written Text Analysis, 1–11. London: Routledge.
Francis, Gill/Hunston, Susan/Manning, Elizabeth (1996): Collins COBUILD Grammar Patterns 1: Verbs. – London: Harper/Collins.
– (1998): Collins COBUILD Grammar Patterns 2: Nouns and Adjectives. – London: Harper/Collins.
Givón, Talmy (1993): Coherence in Text and in Mind. – *Pragmatics & Cognition* 1, 171–227.
Halliday, M.A.K. (1985, ^{2}1994): An Introduction to Functional Grammar. – London, New York, Sydney, Auckland: Arnold.
Hudson, Richard (1994): About 37% of word-tokens are nouns. – *Language* 70, 331–9.
Hunston, Susan/Francis, Gill (2000): Pattern Grammar. A corpus-driven approach to the lexical grammar of English. – Amsterdam, Philadelphia: Benjamins (= Studies in Corpus Linguistics 4).
Moore, Terence/Carling, Christine (1982): Understanding Language: towards a post-Chomskyan linguistics. – London etc.: Macmillan.
Schnöring, Stefanie (2000): Personalimageanzeigen. – Ms. Münster.
Sinclair, John (1991): Corpus, Concordance, Collocation. – Oxford: Oxford University Press (= Describing English Language).

- (1994): Trust the Text. – In: M. Coulthard (ed.): Advances in Written Text Analysis, 12–25. London: Routledge.
- (1996): Multilingual Databases. An international project in multilingual lexicography. – *International Journal of Lexicography* 9/3, 179–196.
- (1998): The Lexical Item. – In: E. Weigand (ed.): Contrastive Lexical Semantics, 1–24. Amsterdam, Philadelphia: Benjamins (= CILT 171).

Sinclair, John et al. (eds.) (1987): Collins Cobuild English Language Dictionary. – London, Glasgow: Collins, Stuttgart: Klett.

Stati, Sorin (in this volume): Misunderstanding – a Dialogic Problem.

Stubbs, Michael (1996): Text and Corpus Analysis. Computer-assisted studies of language and culture. – Oxford: Blackwell (= Language in Society 23).

Teubert, Wolfgang (1996): Comparable or Parallel Corpora? – *International Journal of Lexicography* 9/3, 238–264.

Thomas, Jenny/Short, Mick (eds.) (1996): Using Corpora for Language Research. – London, New York: Longman.

Thompson, Geoff (1996): Introducing Functional Grammar. – London, New York, Sydney, Auckland: Arnold.

Weigand, Edda (1993): Word Meaning and Utterance Meaning. – *Journal of Pragmatics* 20, 253–268.
- (1996): Word and their Role in Language Use. – In: E. Weigand, F. Hundsnurscher (eds.): Lexical Structures and Language Use. Vol. 1, 151–168. Tübingen: Niemeyer (= Beiträge zur Dialogforschung 9).
- (2000a): The Dialogic Action Game. – In: M. Coulthard et al. (eds.): Dialogue Analysis VII: Working with Dialogue, 1–18. Tübingen: Niemeyer (= Beiträge zur Dialogforschung 22).
- (2000b): Coherence in Discourse – a never-ending problem. – In: S. Beckmann, P. P. König, G. Wolf, (eds.): Sprachspiel und Bedeutung. Festschrift für Franz Hundsnurscher zum 65. Geburtstag, 267–274. Tübingen: Niemeyer.
- (2001): Competenza interazionale plurilingue. – In: S. Cigada, S.Gilardoni, M. Matthey (eds.): Comunicare in ambiente professionale plurilingue, 87–105. USI Lugano.
- (2002a): Lexical Units and Syntactic Structures: Words, phrases, and utterances considered from a comparative viewpoint, 129–148. – In: C. Gruaz (ed.): Quand le mot fait signe. Publications de l'Université de Rouen, Collection Dyalang.
- (2002b): The Language Myth and Linguistics Humanised. – In: R. Harris (ed.): The Language Myth in Western Culture, 55–83. Richmond/Surrey: Curzon Press.
- (2002c): Constitutive Features of Human Dialogic Interaction. Mirror neurons and what they tell us about human abilities. – In: M. Stamenov, V. Gallese (eds.): Mirror Neurons and the Evolution of Brain and Language, 229–248. Amsterdam, Philadelphia: Benjamins (= Advances in Consciousness Research).
- (2003): Dialogue Analysis 2000: Towards a human linguistics. – In: M. Bondi, S. Stati (eds.): Dialogue Analysis 2000, 15–28. Tübingen: Niemeyer (= Beiträge zur Dialogforschung).

Weigand, Edda/Dascal, Marcelo (eds.) (2001): Negotiation and Power in Dialogic Interaction. – Amsterdam, Philadelphia: Benjamins (= CILT 214).